MW00775071

ENDORSEMENTS

Thinking Orthodox is as informative as it is engaging. Part One, on Orthodox Phronema, provides more than a contextual or methodological framework; it delineates a "mindset" that is foundational for a proper understanding of Orthodox Theology, which is treated extensively in Part Two. This is followed, in Part Three, by the Application of Orthodox Theology. In her 380-page book, Dr. Eugenia Scarvelis Constantinou not only lays out the development of the theology of the Eastern Church, but provides compelling arguments along with the necessary approach for understanding it. Her perspective is, at the same time, refreshing and challenging. An indispensable resource for the trained theologian and a must read for the layperson who wishes to attain a solid grounding in the faith of the early Church.

—HIS EMINENCE METROPOLITAN GERASIMOS
of San Francisco, Greek Orthodox Archdiocese of America

Dr. Jeannie Constantinou's book is a precious and very valuable addition to the English library of must-have Orthodox books. The book explores the ethos, spirituality and unique characteristics of living the Orthodox Christian faith, mainly in the western Christian context. The book, itself a wonderful read, is something that every single home should have. It can easily serve as a valuable resource for priests and seminarians alike. Many non-Orthodox Christians would better understand Orthodox Christianity as a way of living, with its different approaches to theology, soteriology, and relationship with Christ our Lord, after being acquainted with the contents of this book. It is a tool to communicate to western Christians, and in many cases even to Orthodox Christians in America and the West, who Orthodox Christians are.

—BISHOP VAHAN HOVHANESSIAN,
Primate of the Diocese of the Armenian Orthodox Church
in France and Pontifical Legate to Western Europe

Thinking Orthodox: Understanding and Acquiring the Orthodox Christian Mind is a true rudder that offers a solid guidance in and towards Orthodoxy. The dynamic exposition, with concise chapters and subsections, flows easily and most appropriately through the Scriptures and the Tradition, anchored in the experience of faith as it must be lived in the Church at all times and in all places. Dr. Eugenia Constantinou puts forward a true formative program for the one who seeks to understand truly the Orthodox Church, through an invitation to discipline, obedience, humility and most specially to love the Truth and its pure expression, both pastoral and missionary. The book is a must read for the Orthodox faithful who are called to correctly understand the Church and Her ways, and also for those who seek to learn about and desire to embrace the Orthodox Church.

+ ANDREI HOARSTE, PhD, Bishop of Cleveland,
Romanian Orthodox Episcopate of America

Orthodox Christians, living in the West, have a need to be grounded in the phronema of Orthodoxy as we are tossed about as a minority group of Christians in a sea of religious and secular voices that can lead us away from the true faith. So much confusion and private opinion surrounds us, and we need to have a light to guide us to a safe harbor. In *Thinking Orthodox* we have such a light. It is a joy to read and a treasure to have.

—Archpriest Chad Hatfield, D.Min, D.D., President & Professor of Pastoral Theology, St. Vladimir's Seminary

Dr. Constantinou has put into words what many of us have experienced, living as Orthodox Christians in our culture. Her extensive patristic, biblical, and historical research is delightfully fleshed out with many stories and examples from her own life. At the midpoint of the book she reminds us that tradition is not a retreat from the world. Rather than disengaging from modern life, she urges Orthodox Christians to bring the Church's transforming presence to a world that desperately needs it: "Nothing is more powerful than Orthodox Christianity as an antidote to despair and loss of meaning in modern society, not as a set of beliefs, but as a way of life promoting healing, wholeness, and holiness" (page 154). May we find and live this holy and wholesome way of life.

—Mother Abbess Christophora
Orthodox Monastery of the Transfiguration, Ellwood City, Pennsylvania

Becoming Orthodox is difficult, especially for non-Orthodox, Western Christians. Many inquirers are drawn to Orthodoxy's liturgical beauty, historical continuity, and theological stability. These are relatively easy to appreciate and access. However, the challenge is in acquiring a truly Orthodox way of thinking. This is precisely where Dr. Constantinou's book is a godsend. As a convert myself, I spent years trying to shoehorn Orthodox theology into my Protestant categories. It was a futile exercise; the more I tried, the more frustrated I became. In this powerful book, Dr. Constantinou demonstrates why this was the case and why it doesn't work. More importantly, she explains exactly how anyone can acquire an Orthodox mind. The book is at once academically rigorous and yet easily accessible to anyone who desires to become fully Orthodox.

—Dn. Michael Hyatt, *New York Times* bestselling author

With brilliant historical insight, the author successfully navigates very difficult and complex issues surrounding the meaning and mindset (*phronema*) of holy Tradition. She reveals a theological method that is largely foreign to the intellectual heritage of the Christian West, without minimizing the role of reason. This is the book I have long wanted to write, but one that is far better than I could have ever done!

—Bradley Nassif, co-editor of *The Philokalia:*
A Classic Text in Orthodox Spirituality, and Professor of
Biblical and Theological Studies, North Park University

Thinking Orthodox is a compelling reminder of the double meaning of the word "Orthodoxy," "right belief" and "right worship" due God. We are thereby reminded that to be Orthodox presupposes an Orthodox way of life, referred to as *phronema*. In an age beset by conflicting arguments, each one claiming to preserve our authenticity as a Church, it is refreshing to be challenged by the approach put forth in this book. No matter how convincing one's argument may seem, it does not stand up to the awareness of what constitutes *phronema*. The spirit of Orthodoxy throughout history is recognized by its genuine openness to the world, its needs, concerns, and problems. The ability to gain this openness can only come about by living and understanding this *phronema*. *Thinking Orthodox* shows us how. I therefore highly recommend it as a valuable resource in understanding the Orthodox faith.

—DR. LEWIS J. PATSAVOS, Professor of Canon Law, Emeritus
Holy Cross Greek Orthodox School of Theology

Presvytera Eugenia's book continually renews the remembrance of the noble origins of Christian character, of the harmony between the manner of thought and moral action, a noble origin that has nothing to do with any "manic" achievement of perfection but functions "in a relaxed mode." She follows the Apostle Paul to bring the meaning of true phronema closer to the operation of the nous and for this reason the book functions as a "medical manual." It operates as a common denominator to assist a physician of bodies in the same way as it helps a spiritual guide in directing Christians in the journey toward God, or even assisting those cultivating civilization in every form, especially in interpretation of texts, or arts or theatrical representations. Presvytera Eugenia proposes that we embody this timeless message of the "medical pedagogy" of Orthodoxy in our intellectual and spiritual approach to be initiated into Orthodox phronema.

—ARCHIMANDRITE NEOPHYTOS ENKLEISTRIOTIS, Councilor
Holy Stavropegic Monastery of St. Neophytos, Paphos, Cyprus

Written in an exceptionally readable style, *Thinking Orthodox* offers a traditional Orthodox view of how to think (theologize) about God. Although seemingly written for a general readership of Orthodox and non-Orthodox Christians alike, Constantinou does not shy away from challenging herself and her fellow Orthodox theologians to think with an Orthodox *phronema*. Echoing the warnings of many of the Fathers of the Church, Constantinou encourages Orthodox theologians to pursue their all-important task of bringing the message of salvation through Jesus Christ to all people with humility and self-reflection. *Thinking Orthodox* is not simply an exercise in intellectual and academic theology; rather it challenges the reader to consider how one thinks about God in relation to how one lives one's life, both in prayer and action. Orthodoxy is a Way of life and thus to think in an Orthodox manner, as Constantinou perspicuously illustrates, is to live in an Orthodox manner. The book is an intellectual foray in the "mind of the Fathers," a dialogue with contemporary academic scholarship, an assessment of non-Orthodox theology and thinking, a warning to those untrained in theology, and a call to integrate theology with praxis. How one lives one's life cannot be divorced from the correct way of thinking about God. Thank you for writing this book!

—JAMES SKEDROS, ThD, Michael G. and Anastasia Cantonis Professor of Byzantine Studies and Professor of Early Christianity, Holy Cross Greek Orthodox School of Theology

It is my pleasure to write an endorsement for the book Dr. Eugenia Scarvelis Constantinou, PhD has written, *Thinking Orthodox, Understanding and Acquiring the Orthodox Christian Mind*. From the moment I saw and then read the book I knew I needed to ask Dr. Constantinou to be on our program. I have found the book fascinating, so much so that I asked Eugenia to join me on our *Let's Talk Live* program over the past few months to share and teach what it means to think in an Orthodox Christian way. Living in the post-truth era it is extremely important that people have faith in what they listen to and read. Dr. Constantinou's book should become a part of every Orthodox Christian's home library, read at all Orthodox Christian seminaries and studied by all who seek to know the true faith of Orthodox Christianity. We have now shared it on our programs, heard and seen in over 190 countries. May her efforts be blessed.

—REV. DR. CHRISTOPHER T. METROPULOS, Executive Director, Orthodox Christian Network (OCN)

Thinking
ORTHODOX

*Understanding and Acquiring
the Orthodox Christian Mind*

EUGENIA SCARVELIS CONSTANTINOU, PH.D.

ANCIENT FAITH PUBLISHING   CHESTERTON, INDIANA

Published by:
    Ancient Faith Publishing
    A Division of Ancient Faith Ministries
    P.O. Box 748
    Chesterton, IN 46304

Scripture quotations are taken from the Revised Standard Version (RSV) unless otherwise identified.

ISBN: 978-1-944967-70-3

Library of Congress Control Number: 2020947147

30 29 28 27 26 25 24 23 22   19 18 17 16 15 14 13 12 11 10 9 8 7 6 5 4

This book is dedicated to
Holy Wisdom: The Father, Son, and Holy Spirit
and
to our only-begotten and beloved son, Christopher,
who I pray will always have an Orthodox phronema.

Contents

Contents

Foreword

D R. CONSTANTINOU HAS WRITTEN A marvellously timely book that is an education in itself as well as being a delight to read. Her long professional background as an eminent professor, and her years as a speaker on Ancient Faith Radio, have given her the gift of being able to communicate deep truths with great clarity and force. Her lifetime of pastoral and spiritual immersion in the Orthodox Church also makes her a teacher whose touch is light and unfailingly gracious.

The work sets out to do something quite complex and difficult, but the reader would hardly know this from the fluent lucidity with which she writes. The book sets out to present the whole ethos of the Orthodox Church, through the lens of what it means to be a theologian. An ethos is a very difficult thing to pin down. Many people in the world today, where every other person seems to have a keyboard and an internet uploader ready to hand, try to speak for the Orthodox experience. Many of them come across as rigid, antiquarian, closed off and, basically, unpleasantly narrow. This is disheartening because the true experience of the Eastern Orthodox ethos is one of liberating spirituality and mystical joy—the experience, at root, of finding the grace of the Risen Christ. That some voices present the Church as a joyless cell comprised of forbidding rules and patriarchal grandiosity, serves to draw a false Icon of the Christ whom Orthodoxy knows. I once knew of a monastery where a young novice asked a blessing to paint an icon of Christ. When he finished it he brought it to his abbot. The figure of the Lord looked rather pained and constrained: the whole icon was hunched and severe. The abbot looked at it for a while and said to the young monk: "You have a lot you must still understand about the love of the Lord. Don't paint anymore for a long time."

Dr. Constantinou has certainly understood the pathways of the life of the Orthodox Church, and truly entered into its spirit and culture. Having encountered many narrowly bigoted guides on modern media, who claim to be speaking for the whole church, she makes a fine response—like the abbot I mentioned. Beginning with the witness of St. Gregory the Theologian who, in his *First Theological Discourse* (Oration 27), warned against those who rashly undertake the task of speaking about theology, and set out the kinds of characteristics that invariably accompany the genuine theologian, Dr. Constantinou begins a patient and thorough account of what it is to inhabit the spiritual, theological, and sacramental world of Eastern Orthodoxy.

By the time she ends her study she has taken us on a "Grand Tour" through patristics and spirituality, through the Orthodox Church's customs and feasts: and above all that "inner mind" that grows on one, and in one, as a person accommodates him or herself to the growing culture of Orthodoxy which being in the Church nurtures and fosters within a person. This is what St. Paul called "that mindset which was in Christ Jesus," the *phronema Christou* (Phil. 2.5). How this grows in us, and what it entails for those who wish to develop it, is the key subject of this book.

The book opens with an extended study of what an Orthodox mindset is, and how it often is at such an angle of diffraction to the presumptions of Western forms of Christianity (Roman Catholic and Protestant alike) that people are usually unaware that they are foisting onto Orthodoxy their own presumptions and thinking they have it sewn up when all along they have very little knowledge or empathy for a Church that is often more hidden than revealed. It places the experience of paradox at the heart of Orthodoxy's confession: at once ambivalent and sure; perfectly eloquent while being mysteriously quiet and open-ended; yet proven as true in the remarkable consonance it demonstrates across the centuries and across living generations of men and women who have adopted it into their hearts and souls, and thus demonstrate the self-same signs of the possession of the grace of the Risen Lord in their day-to-day lives.

I would like to imagine that anyone who considers opening up an internet blog-site purporting to speak for Orthodoxy, would "have to" study this book as a prerequisite, and pass a basic comprehension exam on its basis. That is a forlorn hope: but I can dream what I dream. But with a more realistic hope, I would also like to see this placed into the hands of every seminarian (of any church) who was going on towards possible ordination and the office of teaching other Christians. It contains all the most important material that rarely gets mentioned in a graduate theology course: the kind of things that ought to be the preliminary foundation. Priests would find here much to share. I loved the little aside that a rambling priest with nothing to say in a sermon fools nobody: least of all himself. Even when the sting lands home, it is all done with kindly graciousness. Illustrating her thesis, all the way through the book, with patristic and historical examples, the study becomes a veritable little library of patristics: deep and useful, and always engaging the interest.

I wholeheartedly recommend this book as essential reading and I hope and pray it will have a wide dissemination, for it pulls our public Orthodox discourse back onto true and solid ground. In that, it is like the vesperal bell sounding over the fields as evening falls, reminding us of the Joyful Light we have because of the glory that God has given us as Orthodox: but also that duty we may well not have thought about enough, as yet; which is to communicate the grace of the Lord as best we can by offering to others those shining treasures we have in our most beautiful Church.

Archpriest John A. McGuckin, PhD., D.D., DLitt.
Professor of Early Christian Thought, Theology Faculty, Oxford University
Fellow of the British Royal Historical Society

Abbreviations

ANF   Ante-Nicene Fathers of the Church
FOTC   Fathers of the Church Series
LXX   The Septuagint
NIV   New International Version
NKJV   New King James Version
NPNF-1   Nicene and Post-Nicene Fathers of the Church, First Series
NPNF-2   Nicene and Post-Nicene Fathers of the Church, Second Series
OSB   Orthodox Study Bible
RSV   Revised Standard Version
TDNT   Theological Dictionary of the New Testament

Scripture citations are taken from the Revised Standard Version unless otherwise stated.

Some patristic quotations from the Ante-Nicene Fathers and the Nicene and Post-Nicene Fathers of the Church have been slightly modified to reflect contemporary English usage.

I think it is dangerous either to accept the responsibility for other souls or to take up theology.

—St. Gregory the Theologian

Introduction

HOW DOES ONE DISCUSS THE process of thought? Each of us inhabits a private inner world, a unique landscape created by various influences. It is extraordinarily difficult to explain a thought process and worldview, but it is essential at least to make an attempt to explain the uniquely Orthodox mind, our *phronema* (FROH-nee-mah). This differs significantly not only from the mindset of the world at large but from that of other expressions of Christianity.

Orthodoxy today is not insulated from the world at large. It finds itself confronted with different ways of thinking—cultural, political, social, and religious. The gospel itself demands that the Church present itself and interact with the entire world as the authentic and living continuation of the ancient Church.

East and West

ORTHODOX TEACHING DOES NOT MERELY differ from Western Christianity in *content,* but the reason for the difference is equally important. After reading this book, Western Christians still may not understand our mentality, but perhaps they will begin to realize that the difference between Orthodoxy and Western Christianity is significant and more far-reaching than a few doctrines, ancient rituals, and a refusal to submit to the pope. The variance is deeper than appears on the surface, extending to how theology is conceived, conceptualized, taught, and approached. To complicate matters, often the same terminology is used in East and West, but basic terms or

1

concepts do not have the same meaning at all. What is sin? What is salvation? What is forgiveness?

To Protestants, Orthodoxy may seem quite "Catholic," but actually the Protestant mind is very similar to the Catholic mind, and both are extremely different from an Orthodox mind and theological framework. While some of their beliefs differ tremendously, Catholics and Protestants assume many of the same theological presumptions and employ the same style of theological analysis, argumentation, and discussion, based on medieval models that developed in Western Europe. It is easier for Protestants and Catholics to understand each other, even if they fundamentally disagree on their conclusions, than for Orthodox and Catholics to understand each other, even though they share many similar outward characteristics—liturgy, priesthood, hierarchy, sacraments, and so forth.

Not only the content but the approach to theology differs. The Orthodox Church has almost no "official" teachings or statements, and it purposely avoids making them. So how do we explain ourselves to Western Christians, who are accustomed to exact definitions and official statements?

Recently, one of my graduate students who was once a Lutheran and is now Catholic was quite astonished to hear me say that Orthodox theology does not employ logic and philosophy as a means to arrive at truth. "How can you do theology without logic?" he asked. As we discussed concepts such as the Immaculate Conception, sin, and Anselm's theory of substitutionary atonement, he made every point with great confidence and precision.

Everything he said relied on logic, lists, definitions, and deductive reasoning. Of course, he could not comprehend how one could theologize in any other way. But none of his lists, definitions, or logical explanations was persuasive to me. Not only were they unconvincing, they were—from an Orthodox perspective—entirely irrelevant to the issues. For my dear student, the definitions were handy, reliable, logical, precise, and specific. In a sense this was comforting to him, because he had neat answers for almost every question. Orthodoxy does not function that way, and we do not even expect such things.

To say that Orthodoxy is "Eastern" and that Catholic and Protestant Christianity are "Western" is not a poetic description or a mere matter of geography. The terms have long been employed to indicate real differences in historical experiences and thought—not simply the final conclusions but the *process* by which we arrive at those conclusions. My student's explanations and definitions were irrelevant to me, regardless of how "logical" he considered them, because we Orthodox do not accept the same premises. They are foreign to our basic understanding of sin and salvation. The early Church never heard of the categories and definitions that form many of the most common assumptions in Western Christianity today, not to mention all the consequences those distinctions create.

Catholic Christians believe they understand us, perhaps because we have common roots in the early Church and we use the same terminology, but quite often they do not. They believe that many points of theological disagreement are simply a matter of finding the right language to convince us that we are both saying the same thing with different expressions. But our view is not the same, and the difference is keenly felt by Orthodox Christians who theologize in the West, because it is not simply the conclusion that differs but the *process* by which we arrive at our conclusions. And the thought process matters, because that is how Orthodox Christianity maintains orthodoxy and unity of the faith. The thought process—the Orthodox phronema—is the reason all the logical definitions and explanations so valued in the West are irrelevant to Orthodox Christian theology.

This difference in the way Orthodox Christians think is nearly impossible to convey to Western Christians and extremely difficult for Orthodox Christians even to articulate. Nonetheless, this book attempts to explain how Orthodox Christians think and how an Orthodox Christian theologian theologizes (what the West calls "doing theology"). The book is intended for Orthodox and non-Orthodox alike and is based on over forty years of experience in reading, studying, speaking, learning, and teaching theology and biblical studies, as a professor and as a guest speaker in Catholic, Protestant, and Orthodox settings, as well as in giving presentations to secular groups and teaching at public institutions.

Western Christians are increasingly embracing Orthodox Christianity, but they find it challenging to learn how to "think Orthodox." They are not alone. Many "cradle" Orthodox have been raised in the West and have appropriated characteristics of Western Christian thought. Occasionally my colleagues and students might ask me about Orthodox teaching on a particular issue. But when I respond, the information is invariably received and placed in a Western theological framework, which often distorts it. The Orthodox teaching is often misunderstood, not intentionally, but because it is interpreted through a different conceptual lens, an entirely different phronema.

For the past twelve years, through my podcast *Search the Scriptures* on Ancient Faith Radio,[1] I have spoken about the importance of acquiring an Orthodox phronema—meaning an Orthodox mindset, mentality, or stance. I have witnessed torturous mental gymnastics as converts to the Orthodox faith struggle to resolve theological questions they find troubling but which simply don't exist in Orthodoxy. Others engage in extensive debates over issues Orthodox Christians would ordinarily never consider debating: Which is greater, man's free will or God's sovereignty? How did the dinosaurs die if death came into the world with Adam and Eve? Why does communion still look and taste like bread and wine even though we say that it has become the Body and Blood of Christ? How do I convince X about Y? How do I prove Z?

This is not a criticism of converts, nor is this book directed primarily at converts. It is not a criticism of those who are not theologians or priests. At times, even Orthodox Christians who are born into the faith, including Orthodox priests and theologians, can lack a correct Orthodox phronema. Each of us is a product of our background. Countless factors shape our thought processes and the way we view the world: our general rearing and education, religious training, culture, life experiences, gender, age, race. This reality is inescapable, and it is not a negative. Our distinct perspectives and experiences join our unique talents and insights to enrich the Church and theological dialogue.

However, Orthodoxy is characterized by *unity* of the faith and *preserving* that faith unchanged across generations, languages, cultures, and believers. This oneness of mind continues to be manifested to a remarkable degree in the Orthodox Church. Unity of the faith is possible only because of the Orthodox phronema: a specific approach to theologizing. This book begins with a discussion about phronema in general, what Orthodox phronema is, and how to acquire it. The

---

1   Dr. Jeannie Constantinou, *Search the Scriptures,* podcast, www.ancientfaith.com
     /podcasts/searchthescriptures. A second podcast consisting of a live, call-in program,
     Search the Scriptures LIVE!, airs on Mondays at 8:00 PM (EST) at www.ancientfaith
     .com/radio/live.

second and third parts of the book concern the nature of theology, what makes for a true Orthodox theologian, and the dangers of theologizing. These sections are not simply for people who are professional theologians but for all Christians, because all of us at some time or another talk about God. We theologize.

Many Orthodox Christians, both cradle and converts to the faith, have heard the term *phronema* and may even understand that it refers to an Orthodox mind or attitude. But they may have no idea how to achieve it. The primary purpose of this book is to articulate what it means to *think* Orthodox, to explain how our phronema makes the Orthodox Christian mind and attitude distinctive, and to help the reader understand why it is important to acquire, cherish, and preserve this phronema.

Wide varieties of opinion exist among Roman Catholics and even more so within the Protestant camp. I am well aware that my comments are broad generalities, but I hope that I have avoided stereotypes and caricatures. It is a stereotype to describe Western Christianity as "rigid and legalistic" and Eastern Christianity as "experiential and mystical." The West has its share of mystics, and the East certainly has many legalists. Resorting to simplifications does not tell the entire story, but generalities point to some truths that might provide a starting point for mutual understanding.

Whatever distinctions I draw between Orthodoxy and the West are not intended to be disrespectful or a distortion. Just as Catholics and Protestants cannot understand what it is to think Orthodox, I cannot think Catholic or Protestant. This book is not intended to provide a nuanced understanding of the Catholic or Protestant mentality. I have sketched broad outlines of Western theological thought and methodology to explain how Orthodox thought and theology differ and the roots of the difference. Any errors I have made in my presentation of either Western or Orthodox Christianity are entirely my own, and I ask your forgiveness.

Repetition, Ambiguity, Uncertainty, and Paradox

PHRONEMA—BASICALLY, ONE'S MENTALITY—IS A VERY difficult subject. Orthodox phronema both affects and reflects theological beliefs, overall religious culture and practices, and the way one views God and the world.

Everything is interconnected in Orthodoxy. We cannot discuss Scripture without talking about Tradition and the Fathers. We cannot discuss theology without including spirituality and lifestyle. We do not separately discuss or define anything, because to do so distorts Orthodoxy and creates a false presentation. It may be that I repeat some concepts frequently in the chapters of this book. But as the Greek proverb goes, "Repetition is the mother of learning," and since the subject is impossible to explain clearly, my hope is that perhaps through repetition of the same concepts from different angles, the reader will eventually grasp what it means to *think* as an Orthodox Christian.

Repetition of the basic Orthodox mental framework is necessary because Orthodoxy tends to resist and avoid definitions. While Western Christianity strives for precise definitions and statements, it is difficult to find anything in Orthodoxy that is clear, defined, and accepted by all, except for conciliar statements. Some would argue that even canons and the Nicene Creed are not actually "definitions" but simply "language" or formulations that express certain theological limitations.

In addition to repeating myself, at times it may appear that I am contradicting myself. This is inevitable because Orthodoxy involves charting a middle course between extremes. Often the truth is neither one alternative nor the other but both. Being Orthodox in mind requires that one accept ambiguity, uncertainty, mystery, and paradox. Perhaps this encourages humility before God. We cannot rely on clever explanations or beloved definitions, and we must accept that we cannot completely explain or fully understand our faith. Therefore, we must rely solely on the grace and mercy of God. Perhaps this allows us to focus less on the mind and more on the heart, which is where we encounter God.

Perhaps Orthodox resistance to definitions and guarantees is due to the fact that the Bible offers neither. The New Testament itself presents no formulas or guarantees in answer to the question, "What must I do to be saved?" In fact, the Scriptures would seem to offer contradictory advice on this question. One must love God and love his neighbor as himself. One must keep the commandments. One must accept the Lord Jesus. One must be baptized. One must feed the hungry and give drink to the thirsty. One must believe in the Son whom the Father has sent. Other responses could also be given.

All these instructions are given in the Bible as key to salvation. But which is the "right" answer? (To even ask that question is to think like a Westerner!) The answer is all of them—or maybe none of them. How do we rationally explain the repentant thief on the cross who was the first to enter paradise (Luke 23:43), having done *none* of those things, except to recognize Jesus for who He was? How do we explain the parable of the laborers in the vineyard (Matt. 20:1–16), all of whom received exactly the same reward (the same wages), even though some worked all day and others for only one hour?

All these different answers to a basic question—what must I do to be saved?—are found in the New Testament. Why? Perhaps so that we will not be certain of our individual salvation, not become proud, not rely on ourselves, not become complacent, and not believe we are already saved with nothing at all needed on our part. Perhaps the uncertainty encourages us to evaluate ourselves constantly, remain humble, not judge our brothers and sisters, and continually seek the Lord.

Accepting ambiguity, uncertainty, and paradox is part of Orthodox phronema. We can either accept and think with an Eastern mind—that there is no single answer and we can never be certain of our individual salvation—or we can assume that there *must* be clear, rational answers, then choose one or more of those answers and create a theology that supports that view. But that was not the approach of the early Church, which held the phronema we still maintain. Because of this, Orthodox Christians are accustomed to the lack of definitions and the absence of certainty. Instead of definitions and formulas, we have broad guidelines and concepts, and we operate within those boundaries, which we do not violate.

My Experience with Phronema

I FIRST BEGAN TO PONDER the question of phronema a long time ago, before I even knew the word or concept. I was a college student majoring in religious studies at the University of San Diego, a Catholic institution. I did not start college expecting to become a religion major, but the bachelor's degree required three courses in religion. I discovered that I enjoyed my theology classes more than any other subject, so I chose the field as my major.

Yet in spite of my overall positive experience studying theology at USD, I often experienced an unsettled feeling, a disconnect, a religious cognitive dissonance. The information given in class occasionally seemed "off" somehow, and this puzzled me. Most of our lectures and assigned readings were fine, especially when lessons focused on early church history or biblical history. But in matters of theology, the statements made, expressions used, and rationale given for theological positions felt askew.

I could neither clarify in my own mind nor articulate specifically what seemed awry about the way my professors approached a theological problem, explained a doctrine, or described spiritual practices. The unsettled feeling compelled me to do my own research and write my term papers on the Orthodox view of whatever the subject matter of that course was: marriage, sacraments, spirituality, Christology, prophecy, or what have you.

At that time, the mid-1970s, learning about Orthodoxy wasn't easy. There was no internet, and far fewer books were available in English on Orthodox Christianity. Our college library had five such books, and four of them were written by Catholics to refute the Orthodox faith. I complained about this to one of my professors, who must have alerted the library to this deficiency. In short order we acquired several more books on Orthodox Christianity, these actually authored by Orthodox Christians.

Slowly, my own reading in Orthodoxy resolved my questions for each theology course, and the experience forced me to learn about and to articulate my Orthodox faith. My professors were mostly Catholics, but one beloved professor was a Lutheran priest, and another wonderful professor was Episcopalian. All my professors knew I was Orthodox, and they not only respected my tradition, but they also encouraged and supported me. I am a better professor today because of their example. I am eternally grateful to them for their many kindnesses in word and in deed. But I knew they could not help me resolve my problem. I never discussed it, since I was unable to articulate to anyone the unsettled feeling I had in class or to understand why I continued to experience it.

For years I puzzled over this. What intrigued me was *how* I knew that what I was hearing in theology class was not exactly correct. I was still a teenager when I began studying theology in college. How did I *know* that something was wrong, that what I was hearing was not entirely Orthodox? *Why* didn't

I accept everything my professors said? Other students did. I sometimes watched them quickly taking notes while I sat, *not* writing, but thinking to myself, "That's not right!" I instinctively knew what the professor said was not correct, but I could not explain *how* I knew or exactly *what* was not correct. The only possible explanation is that I had already formed an Orthodox phronema.

How did this happen? I had never met an Orthodox theologian. The only priest I knew was our parish priest. I was not raised in a very religious home. My mother had read us Bible stories, and sometimes we talked about Christ, but no one ever discussed theology. Everyone in my family was involved in some aspect of real estate, so at every family gathering our kitchen-table talk was about construction, mortgages, escrows, financing, and deeds. Theology was not even in the periphery of the conversation. I grew up in Southern California, where we had no Orthodox schools, bookstores, or libraries. We were isolated, far from the centers of Greek Orthodoxy in America: New York, Chicago, Boston. Almost all the priests I had ever met had come from those far-away places, if not from Greece itself.

We were not a particularly devout family. My father was not a strong believer and rarely attended church if he was not serving on the parish council. My mother was personally devout but not a fanatic. We attended church regularly but not absolutely every Sunday. We were exposed to the cycle of major feasts and fasts, although there was not a great deal of fasting in our home. We simply participated in the life of the community, with various members of the family involved in different types of activities and groups, and we went to the divine services of the church, even when everything was mostly in Greek and we did not always understand the services. In short, our family was nothing exceptional. We were just *there*. At church. *But* we *were there,* part of the worshipping community. I believe this made all the difference in my acquisition of an Orthodox phronema.

I returned to USD several years after graduation and enrolled as a graduate student in theology. At about thirty years of age, I was the youngest member of our New Testament class. My classmates, who numbered about twenty, were mostly Roman Catholics, very involved in their parishes in a variety of roles: catechetical instructors, a Catholic activist author, a social worker, a parochial school principal, youth workers, a couple of deacons, and others with significant involvement in a variety of ministries. These were certainly not average Catholics. They were more engaged, more knowledgeable, and very committed to ministry.

At that time, an Episcopalian bishop had been openly stating that he did not believe in the physical Resurrection of Christ. He denounced many traditional Christian doctrines, and yet he remained an Episcopalian bishop. This led to a discussion in our New Testament class. Our professor asked a hypothetical question: "If the bones of Jesus were discovered, and if there were some way to absolutely confirm that they were the bones of Jesus, would you still be a Christian?"

Every other member of the class confirmed that he or she would remain a Christian, making statements such as "I would not lose my faith," or "Jesus was a great teacher and philosopher."

I was dumbfounded and utterly dismayed. How was it possible that such intelligent, committed, and educated Catholics could give such responses? Did they not realize the fundamental importance of the Resurrection of Christ? If not, *why* not? My response was, "If the bones of Jesus were discovered, I would be outta here! I would no longer be a Christian!" I explained that the Resurrection is an absolute necessity to the Christian faith. The class listened politely, but no one seemed at all impressed or influenced by my answer.[2]

It so happened that this discussion took place during Holy Week. On Sunday, the Greek Orthodox parish of St. Spyridon would be holding its annual Easter picnic, a local tradition that our fine Southern California weather allows. Sunshine, Greek dancing, and barbequed lamb. After the rigors of Holy Week, what could be better?

But I decided to ask people at the picnic whether it made any difference that Jesus rose from the dead. I began with my eighteen-year-old niece and my seventy-year-old mother. Neither had any theological education. I questioned each independently: "Does the Resurrection of Jesus make any difference?"

---

2   To be fair, this episode was a snapshot of that group at that time and probably not representative of most Catholics. I recently asked the same question of my own students at the Franciscan School of Theology, and all of them immediately affirmed the importance of the Resurrection.

"Yes," they both answered immediately.

"Why?" I asked. I remained silent as each of them struggled to articulate a response. But eventually they both arrived at the same correct answer. My niece said that the Resurrection of Christ restored the relationship between us and God, and my mother said that it opened up heaven to us. I was impressed. Every Orthodox Christian of whom I have asked this question has also given me a similar response.

This only fueled my curiosity: Why did these ordinary Orthodox Christians know the theological significance of the Resurrection of Christ—and believe it *mattered*—when my graduate school theology classmates seemingly did not? It could not be a matter of formal education. It could only have been learned in some other way. The Orthodox people I talked to had acquired an Orthodox phronema.

Since that time, I have pondered phronema and its mysterious nature. The present book is the fruit of forty years of theological study, teaching, and lecturing, as well as numerous experiences inside and outside the classroom. I pray that the book is useful to the reader and that both the reader and the Lord may forgive my mistakes and deficiencies.

I have had very positive experiences over the years with my Catholic and Protestant colleagues, students, and friends. They have been generous with their time and insight. When I was a student at non-Orthodox institutions, my professors were always supportive. I am deeply grateful that they treated me and my Orthodox faith with respect and with a generosity of spirit that is too often lacking among Orthodox Christians.

I have been blessed with many delightful students who are deeply pious, committed to Christ and to their respective churches: Catholics, Protestants, and Orthodox. I have the highest regard for them, and I thank them for their kindness and encouragement. I also wish to thank all my students over the years for enriching me and enlightening me through our many discussions. I pray that nothing in the book is offensive, since my only intent was honestly and respectfully to articulate that which can be very difficult to define and express.

I offer special thanks and gratitude to my husband, Costas, for his extraordinary patience and encouragement as I worked on this book. I hope it serves to promote greater understanding between Eastern and Western Christians. For Orthodox Christians, to whom the book is primarily addressed, I pray that the book helps to deepen your understanding of our precious Orthodox faith and helps you to acquire and maintain an Orthodox phronema.

PART I

The Orthodox Phronema

CHAPTER 1

The Distinctiveness of Orthodox Christianity

WHAT TRULY MAKES ORTHODOX CHRISTIANITY different? Is it simply that we do not have a pope? That we preserve ancient liturgical forms and rituals? That married men can be priests?

The question does not lend itself to a simple answer because the reality is complex. In fact, the essence of Orthodox uniqueness lies far beyond these fundamentals. The root of the variance between Orthodoxy and virtually every form of Western Christianity is challenging to articulate since it is innate in the Orthodox mind. It is hidden, subtle, deeper than the outward forms, customs, or specific theological beliefs that manifest the divergence. The Orthodox phronema ("mentality," "stance," or "approach") is the foundation of Orthodox Christianity. It is usually unexpressed and unexamined, and rarely discussed, but it affects not simply what we believe and why but—above all else—how we think.

Those who grow up outside of Orthodoxy and embrace it later in life inevitably face a challenge. As they slowly enculturate themselves into church life and thought, they must learn not only what to do but how to think as Orthodox Christians. This is much more difficult. Learning when to fast, how to fast, and why to fast, for example, is much easier than acquiring a correct attitude or understanding about fasting. It is not uncommon for a new convert to learn the norms of fasting and then apply them with the rigidity and zeal of an evangelical preacher at a revival who insists on the exact formula of what one "must do" to "be saved." But equally important to the practice of physical fasting is the mental attitude—the phronema—which ought to accompany it.

A fasting phronema is ambiguous and vague, much harder to grasp than simply learning rules. This is why it is difficult to describe the Orthodox phronema. One cannot quickly learn to think as an Orthodox Christian. It requires effort, but an Orthodox phronema will develop over time for those who are conscientious, faithful, and aware that they must acquire and keep their phronema. The wonderful result is peace, a peace that neither our minds nor the world's intellectual constructs can give.

Orthodox Christians with a correct phronema do not feel obligated to be perfect, obsessing over details such as applying exact rules of fasting, dotting every "i" or crossing every "t." A severe and inflexible approach to such matters is not Orthodox but pharisaical. We never feel compelled to explain theological mystery, nor do we fixate on defining each facet of Orthodox belief. The Orthodox phronema allows us to accept who we are (our limitations) and who God is (the Unlimited) so that we may simply exist in the presence of God, worshipping the All-Holy Trinity without struggling to intellectually resolve the unresolvable.

We take the Church, our spiritual lives, and our doctrine extremely seriously, and yet the Orthodox phronema is essentially *relaxed*. It is not rigid, not demanding, not stressed, but calm. Anxiety and obsessiveness are qualities of the world, but our relationship with Christ results in freedom and inner peace. This is reflected in our phronema.

Phronema Matters

THE ORTHODOX PHRONEMA IS A consistent attitude that has been known and experienced in the Church from the beginning and is unconcerned with conforming to the expectations of this world. Our phronema is the reason for the stability of Orthodoxy. It is why we are calm, confident, and comfortable with the assurance that we—as a Church and as individuals—know who we are, what we believe, and where we stand. The Orthodox Church of one hundred years ago and one thousand years ago is the Orthodox Church of today.

We know that it will also look, feel, and be the same Church one hundred years from now and up until Christ returns.

Other articles and books have discussed the Orthodox theological method. These writings focus primarily on what distinguishes Orthodox theology from other academic pursuits or from other Christian theological methods. Such works have typically emphasized adherence to Tradition, reliance on the Fathers of the Church, and the importance of the spiritual life of those who theologize. These topics will also be discussed in this book.

However, two important components are frequently absent or neglected in the discussion: the dangers inherent in theologizing and the need for actual theological education or training. We must not ignore the absolute necessity of laying a proper foundation prior to attempting the sacred task, nor should we fail to mention the risks that attend one who goes "unarmed and defenseless" and yet nonetheless chooses to "plunge into the fray."[1]

Internet "Experts"

GENERATIONS PAST WERE MORE MODEST in their self-assessment concerning their ability to theologize. While the typical Orthodox believer does not attempt to discuss the procession of the Holy Spirit or how the Theotokos remained a virgin while giving birth, some Orthodox Christians today treat such matters as ordinary subjects for discussion and debate, particularly on internet sites. This book hopes to correct that situation. It is a plea for caution and an attempt to sound an alert to the dangers of theologizing, which are not widely understood, especially by untrained theologians. Even if one is not involved in theological debates or discussions, it is important to

---

1   John Chrysostom, *Homilies on John*, Homily 66. Chrysostom wanted his congregation to confront heretics and defend orthodoxy, but he cautioned them against it because they were without real knowledge ("unarmed and defenseless"), particularly about the Bible and how to respond to heretical use of Scripture passages. He lamented their inability to meet the challenge and feared they would be overcome by the arguments of the heretics if they chose to "plunge into the fray." John Chrysostom, *Commentary on St. John the Apostle and Evangelist,* Fathers of the Church (hereinafter FOTC), vols. 33 and 41, trans. Sr. Thomas Aquinas Goggin (Washington, DC: Catholic University of America Press, 1957 and 1959), 2:224.

recognize the boundaries of propriety for theological discourse, piety, and practices.

Recently, even some trained priests and theologians have lost an Orthodox phronema and reflect a more scholastic form of theology that is influenced by Western Christian thought and Western culture. These theologians do not even realize that their phronema has gone awry when they attempt to present reasonable explanations for our theology, morality, and biblical interpretation that will satisfy contemporary sensibilities, or when they present rational, worldly explanations for why the Church's position should change.

We have forgotten who we are if we believe that we must present Orthodoxy to modern society in a manner that will make it palatable to the world, if by doing so we apologize for, dilute, or hesitate to express Orthodox faith and morality. The temptation faced by Orthodox Christian theologians is to compromise or hesitate because we do not wish to be perceived as rigid, backward, unforgiving, or lacking in love on contemporary issues such as abortion, homosexuality, and women's roles.

The Proliferation of Amateur Theologians

THE INTELLECTUALIZATION OF WESTERN CULTURE has also contributed to the development of many amateur theologians who approach the Orthodox Faith as an object for study. Their enthusiasm is wonderful and they are well intentioned, but in general they lack an Orthodox phronema. They do not realize that even if their statements are mostly correct, they create spiritual problems for themselves and others, because knowledge of the faith is more than simply book learning. Four primary factors have contributed to the loss of phronema among clergy and theologians, the rise of amateur theologians, and the distorted presentation of Orthodoxy.

First, we live in the information age. A tremendous amount of information is readily available within seconds, often free and on demand. Books, once rare and precious, are now inexpensive. Almost any book can be located, ordered, and delivered to one's home in days. The library at Qumran, a first-century Jewish religious community on the shores of the Dead Sea, consisted of approximately a thousand scrolls (known as the "Dead Sea Scrolls") and was considered a very large library at that time. By contrast, I easily have more than a thousand books in my home alone, not to mention those I can borrow from my university's library, with even more available through inter-library loan, public libraries, and borrowing from colleagues and friends.

In addition to physical books, the amount of information available through the internet boggles the mind. Today we have instant access to information with no more effort than the tap of a finger on a cell-phone screen. But we also often fail to recognize that information gleaned from the internet is not neces-sarily reliable or accurate.

Paradoxically, the vast amount of easily accessible information has led to intellectual laziness and a "mirage of knowledge."[2] Deep thought is rarely encouraged or expected. Instead, shallowness of thought prevails, along with impatience when we must wait an extra ten seconds for information to load onto the computer. Likewise, theology is too often perceived as something that someone can dabble in, just as one might casually participate in a hobby such as painting. Having done some reading, we think it is enough to have learned the basics, and then we feel free to share with great self-confidence what we think we know. We consider ourselves qualified to answer theo-logical questions and direct others in their spiritual lives and theological investigations.

Not long ago, it was recognized that a little knowledge is a dangerous thing, because a little knowledge leads us to overestimate our true abilities and com-prehension of an issue. But that maxim has long been forgotten. Today we delude ourselves and readily believe that we know more than we actually do about almost every subject.

A clear trend of "hostility toward established knowledge" has also been observed, not only in theological circles but in virtually every profession. Peo-ple are no longer "merely uninformed" but rather are "aggressively wrong," writes Tom Nichols, who has studied this phenomenon. People become hostile and combative when those with actual knowledge and real expertise

---

2   This modern phenomenon of "hostility" toward established knowledge and toward peo-ple with real expertise is discussed by Tom Nichols in *Death of Expertise: The Campaign against Established Knowledge and Why It Matters* (Oxford: Oxford University Press, 2017).

challenge the amateur dabblers. Furthermore, the amateurs are "unwilling to learn" when they are corrected by experts, and they "reject professional know-how" with anger.[3]

The easy availability of information via the internet leads people to be overly confident in their knowledge, and many behave as pseudo-experts because they have researched a topic for a few hours on the web. Because they have learned something, they are confident that they understand it. They have no appreciation for the complexity of the subject, which they actually know almost nothing about. Others have devoted their lives to studying a specific subject deeply, but this means little to the amateur who is overconfident in his competency.

The dabblers also lack the ability to evaluate the information they do stumble upon. The internet is full of misinformation as well good information. Without real training and education, those who rely on the internet for information are unable to critically evaluate what they read. They have no basis for discerning truth or falsehood, no means to evaluate the qualifications of the person who posted the information, and no ability to recognize a bias. Even the fact that internet users endlessly post and repost a great deal of misinformation is often disregarded.

The internet is a "mirage of knowledge" with an inexhaustible supply of "facts" to confirm any bias. It "encourages not only the illusion that we are all equally competent" but also the illusion "that we are all peers."[4] Since our society is based on the principle that we are all equal, we are encouraged to believe that everyone's opinion is equally valid, regardless of whether it is based on actual knowledge. Reporters routinely ask ordinary people for their opinions, and "talking heads" on news programs spend hours speculating and pontificating on matters of which they have no direct knowledge, their comments based on presumptions with no attempt even to hide their biases. Any idea of maintaining a clear line between fact and opinion seems to have disappeared.

---

3   Lydialyle Gibson, "The Mirage of Knowledge," *Harvard Magazine,* March–April 2018, 32–35, 33, discussing the book *The Death of Expertise* by Tom Nichols.

4   Gibson, 33.

Other Factors

A SECOND FACTOR CONTRIBUTING TO the increase in amateur theologians is the accessibility of education. People are generally more educated overall than previous generations. My grandmothers read at a third- or fourth-grade level. My mother was proud to be a high school graduate, an accomplishment unattainable for many during the Great Depression. I doubt that these women knew what a Ph.D. was or could ever imagine the educational level or professional opportunities available to me.

Although more people are more educated today than in the past, common sense is often lacking, and we have not necessarily become more intelligent. Yet we *believe* ourselves to be more intelligent, and we convince ourselves that we have expertise in areas that require years of intense study because we are confident in our education and because technology allows us to access a superficial answer to most questions in seconds.

The third factor contributing to the proliferation of armchair theologians is a lack of piety. I am more educated than my ancestors, but I am certain that my mother and grandmothers far surpassed me in piety, devotion, faith, and wisdom. Our culture is coarse. The fear of God is absent from public discourse. As Proverbs reminds us, "The fear of the LORD is the beginning of wisdom" (Prov. 9:10). Perhaps it is the lack of fear of God that has contributed to the deficiency of wisdom and understanding. Instead, sin and perversion are not only rampant but celebrated.

The general dearth of piety in society contributes to amateurs dabbling in theology because the absence of a strong spiritual foundation has diminished our humility and reverence toward God. We are less aware of our incompetence in such matters. Overly confident in our own intellect, we are convinced that we can theologize, even without any basis for such confidence. The damaging effect of this is compounded when we lack reverence for God.

Faith is declining while pseudo-knowledge and egoism are increasing. Internet discussion sites encourage conversation about matters that are either entirely inappropriate for discussion or inappropriate for such a forum. Previous generations embraced societal norms that demanded, or at least expected, a certain code of civility. Profane and immoral subjects were not openly discussed, nor was discourse on divine topics treated casually. Today everything is open for discussion. People publicly reveal the most intimate details of their lives. Is it any wonder that people do not hesitate to discuss the deepest of divine mysteries? We lack reverence and a fear of God.

Finally, the overintellectualization of religion has contributed to the belief that anyone can theologize. Our Western culture, which itself is a by-product of the Renaissance, Reformation, and so-called Age of Enlightenment, influences us to focus on the intellectual aspect of Orthodoxy. For many, faith is reduced to a set of logical precepts that they have concluded are rationally supportable and therefore acceptable.

Western society and culture emphasize reason and science as the foundation of all that can truly be known. This promotes the belief that one can comprehend or explain anything if one simply devotes one's mind to the task and is able to find the correct words to define the subject at hand.

Self-Delusion and Pride

ON AN INDIVIDUAL BASIS, ORTHODOX Christians today are more educated and have more information about the Orthodox faith available to them than in any previous era, but they are not necessarily more devout. We can easily fall victim to an inflated self-perception, oblivious to our actual inability to theologize. Saint Paul's assessment of the ancient Corinthians, that they were "puffed up" with knowledge, comes to mind (1 Cor. 4:6). Lack of piety and humility combined with an overinflated sense of self-importance has resulted in a spiritual epidemic of our age: self-delusion.

"Know thyself" is one of the greatest ancient Greek maxims. But today, almost no thought or effort is applied to genuine, deep self-knowledge. Rather, we are self-absorbed and often seek affirmation from the world to feed our pride. The emphasis in our culture is on feeling important or presenting an appealing image of oneself. Social media encourage us to present an enhanced image of ourselves in order to be admired, to gain social acceptance, to make our lives appear more interesting and ourselves more accomplished, more intelligent, more beautiful, and more exciting. In extreme cases, the consequences are emotional exhaustion, emptiness, or, even worse, depression, because we believe the illusions put forth by others while knowing that our own lives are not at all as we present them to be. This is particularly the case for youth, who tend to be very involved with social media platforms.[5]

In the theological discussions on the internet, precious time can be lavished on pointless debates, and not enough time is spent engaged in what is useful for salvation and the spiritual life. Pastoral considerations and sensitivity to the mental and spiritual state of those who participate in these discussions is also often lacking, since amateur theologians are not priests, have no pastoral concern for anyone, and are oblivious to the inherent dangers of theologizing. The amateur theologian may even be smug and insensitive to the feelings and issues faced by those who are reaching out for answers online.

The task of theology presents many unrecognized perils. In the experience of the author, too many Orthodox Christians comfortably and confidently function as armchair theologians, whom the Fathers called "dabblers," with no awareness of the consequences to themselves or to others. Those who are not trained in theology or pastoral care should avoid answering theological questions and giving spiritual advice on the internet. Often the answers and advice provided show the absence of basic Orthodox theological education and phronema. The hubris and lack of discernment can even be alarming and the naïveté dangerous.

---

5   An excellent presentation of the dramatic psychological effect of social media on youth is the award-winning 2018 documentary film *Social Animals* by Jonathan Green, who also happens to be an Orthodox Christian.

CHAPTER 2

What Is Phronema?

P HRONEMA[1] COMES FROM THE GREEK root *phren*. Although its etymo-
logical origins are somewhat uncertain, in Homeric Greek *phren* referred
to the diaphragm, which was considered the locus of one's intellectual and
spiritual activity. During the classical period, Greek philosophers developed
the idea of a certain mode of thinking and limited the word *phren* to its physical meaning. The philosophers used instead a derivative word, *phronesis*, to
refer to inner thoughts connected to activity.

Because phronesis links thought and action, it differs from wisdom
(*sophia*), which is a purely intellectual pursuit. For Plato, phronesis was the
"right state of the intellect from which all moral qualities derive." Phronesis is
a gift of God, and "what is divine and *phronimon* should rule men." For Aristotle, phronesis was "moral insight and priceless knowledge . . . which offers
counsel for a good and moral life."[2]

Phronesis is a "virtue . . . exercised in the practical domain."[3] In Latin
the term was rendered *prudentia*, or "prudence" in English. Among the

---

1   For additional details regarding the scholarly analysis of the origin and use of the word
    phronema, see *The Theological Dictionary of the New Testament*, ed. Gerhard Friedrich
    and Geoffrey W. Bromiley, trans. Geoffrey W. Bromiley (Grand Rapids, MI: William B.
    Eerdmans, 1971, 1988), 9:220, hereinafter *TDNT*.
2   *TDNT* 9:222.
3   Barbara Cassin, ed., and Steven Rendall et al., trans., *Dictionary of Untranslatables: A
    Philosophical Lexicon* (Princeton, NJ: Princeton University Press, 2014), 778.

philosophers, it was traditionally included in the four cardinal virtues along with courage, justice, and temperance (moderation), but of those virtues, only phronesis was considered intellectual. Aristotle thought of it as an intellectual virtue, and the Stoic philosophers classified it as science. It was viewed as a kind of practical knowledge because it involves behavior in both public and private matters.

Phronema in the Bible

IN THE OLD TESTAMENT SEPTUAGINT usage, phronesis is considered a characteristic of God and is often translated into English as "understanding": "The LORD by wisdom founded the earth; / by understanding [*phronesei*] he established the heavens" (Prov. 3:19 LXX). God's understanding is beyond human comprehension: "His understanding is unsearchable" (Is. 40:28). Just as the Greeks of the classical era did not separate intellectual phronesis from ethical and moral behavior, the same connection is reflected in the Septuagint use of the word: God's wisdom, understanding, and goodness are connected qualities.[4]

In the New Testament we see the verb *phroneo* and the noun used in the New Testament and today, *phronema*. Peter insisted that Jesus not go to Jerusalem after He predicted His Passion. Both Matthew and Mark report the

---

4   *TDNT* 9:225–26. The frequent use of *phronesis* in the early chapters of Proverbs, 1—9, emphasizes the ethical quality as opposed to a purely intellectual understanding. It is translated into English as "understanding," "prudence," "discernment," "insight," and occasionally "wisdom." English translations derived from the Masoretic text also reflect this variety. See Prov. 1:2, "words of insight" (RSV, NIV); 3:7, "Be not wise in your own eyes" (RSV) or "Do not rely on your own discernment" (OSB); 3:13, blessed is "the man *who* gains understanding" (NKJV), "a mortal who sees discernment" (OSB); 7:4/5 LXX, "Call insight your intimate friend" (RSV), "Gain discernment as a friend" (OSB); 8:1, "Does not . . . understanding lift up her voice" (NKJV), "that discernment may obey you" (OSB); 8:5, "understand astuteness" (OSB), "learn prudence" (RSV), "understand wisdom" (KJV); 8:14, "I have insight" (RSV), "I *am* understanding" (NKJV), "Discernment is mine" (OSB); 9:6, "Walk in the way of insight" (RSV), "Go in the way of understanding" (KJV), "Seek discernment" (OSB). The antonym is also expressed in Greek words with *phren* as the root of the negation: *aphronon*, "senseless," "without sense" in Prov. 7:7 (RSV), "undiscerning" (OSB); *aphron* also in 9:4, *aphrosenen* in 9:6, and *aphronestatos*, "*very* lacking in discernment" (OSB 9:19).

Lord's rebuke of Peter using the verb *phroneo*: "Get behind me, Satan, for you are not thinking [*ou phroneis*] the things of God but of men" (Matt. 16:23; Mark 8:33, translation mine). Thus, *phronema* can also be used to refer to an intellectual or spiritual attitude that is *not* correct. A virtuous person shows good phronema, since a proper intellectual or spiritual attitude is reflected in one's behavior. In modern usage, Greek parents sometimes admonish their children by saying "*Katse phronema!*"—literally, "Sit mindfully!" or, in other words, "Behave yourself!" Saint Paul often exhorted Christians to acquire the correct phronema, especially in his famous and influential Epistle to the Romans. He uses the verb *phroneo* once and the noun *phronema* three times in Romans 8:5–7 alone:

> For those who are according to the flesh have their minds on [*phronousin*] the things of the flesh, but those who are according to the Spirit, on the things of the Spirit. For the mindset [*phronema*] of the flesh is death, but the mindset [*phronema*] of the Spirit is life and peace. For the mindset [*phronema*] of the flesh is hostile to God, for it does not submit itself to God's law, for it cannot.[5]

The Mind of Christ

IN ROMANS 15:5, PAUL USES *phronema* again to promote unity of thought: "May the God of patience and consolation grant you [to have] the same mindset [*phronein*] among one another according to Christ Jesus."[6] In Romans 12:3, again St. Paul emphasizes a correct manner of thinking:

> For I say, through the grace given to me, to all who are among you, that each one not be high-minded [*hyperphronein*] concerning himself, more than he ought to think [*phronein*], but to think [*phronein*] in the right-minded manner [*sophronein*], according to the measure of faith as God has apportioned to each.[7]

In his short epistle to the Philippians, St. Paul uses *phronema* in various

---

5   Translation mine.
6   Translation mine.
7   Translation mine.

forms nine times, emphasizing proper attitude leading to correct behavior. Perhaps most notably, he uses it in the early verses of chapter 2 as he prepares to quote the famous "Philippian hymn" to describe Christ's humility, which the Philippians ought to imitate: "complete my joy by being of the same mind [*phronete*], having the same love, being in full accord and of one mind [*phronountes*]" (Phil. 2:2). And again, "Have this mind [*phroneite*] among yourselves, which is yours in Christ Jesus, who, though he was in the form of God, did not consider equality with God a thing to be grasped" (Phil. 2:5–6).

Phronema clearly involves the mind, but while it can be described as "mentality" or "mindset," it is neither formed nor tested by rationalism, nor is it proven by empirical methods. The most significant link is between mind and behavior.

Phronema is almost synonymous with the well-known term "mind of Christ" (1 Cor. 2:16), although the word Paul uses there is *nous*. Saint Paul explains that spiritual things can be understood only by spiritual people, not by the "natural" man, the unspiritual person. Spiritual things are understood by those who are spiritual because "we have the mind of Christ." Since the Church is the Body of Christ, to have the mind of Christ, one must belong to His Body.

Clearly, from the very beginning of the Church, Christians were encouraged to acquire and maintain a specific Christian attitude, manner of thought, and way of behaving. It was not left to individual Christians to decide for themselves what to think or believe or how to behave. Notice that in each case we have cited, Paul is emphasizing the need for correct phronema, which he links to appropriate Christian behavior. This is further seen in Romans 14:6, where Paul uses *phronema* to express the proper attitude toward eating food or abstaining from it: "The one who regards [*phronōn*] the day, regards it [*phronei*] for the Lord. He also who eats, eats for the Lord, for he gives thanks to God, and the one who does not eat, does not eat for the Lord and gives thanks to God."[8]

Saint John Chrysostom commented on St. Paul's distinction between the spiritual man and the natural man and what it means to have the mind of

---

8   Translation mine.

Christ. His preference for spiritual insight over the application of human reasoning is completely consistent with the patristic (and thus, Orthodox) view of the use of human wisdom and philosophy in theology.

> "The natural man does not receive the things of the Spirit." For he is "a natural man," who attributes everything to reasonings of the mind and considers not that he needs help from above; which is a mark of sheer folly. For God bestowed it that it might learn and receive help from Him, not that it should consider itself sufficient unto itself. . . . For the mind which we have about these things we have of Christ; that is, the knowledge which we have concerning the things of the faith is spiritual; so that with reason we are "judged of no man." For it is not possible that a natural man should know divine things. . . . For reason was absolutely made of no effect by our inability to apprehend through Gentile wisdom the things above us. You may observe, too, that it was more advantageous to learn in this way from the Spirit. For that is the easiest and clearest of all teaching. . . . "But we have the mind of Christ" (1 Cor. 2:16), that is, spiritual, divine, that which has nothing human. For it is not of Plato, nor of Pythagoras, but it is Christ Himself, putting His own things into our mind.[9]

Phronema in the Fathers

THE GREEK FATHERS OF THE Church also use the words *phronema* and *phronesis* in a similar manner to reflect thought, purpose, will, faith, doctrine, and opinion.[10] Ethical behavior is not equivalent to phronema, since one can be a very moral or ethical person and yet entirely lack a Christian phronema. Although a moral lifestyle does not prove phronema, the correct Orthodox phronema is shown in and confirmed by a moral life because phronema

---

9   Chrysostom commenting on 1 Cor. 2:14. *Homily on Paul's Epistles to the Corinthians,* 7.9, 12–13. Philip Schaff, ed., and J. Walker, J. Sheppard, H. Brown, trans., *St. Chrysostom Homilies on the Epistles of Paul to the Corinthians.* Nicene and Post-Nicene Fathers of the Church (hereinafter NPNF-1), vol. 12 (Grand Rapids, MI: William B. Eerdmans, 1956), 38–39.

10   G.H.W. Lampe, ed., *A Patristic Greek Lexicon* (Oxford: Clarendon, 1991), 1490–91.

requires the harmony of thought and action. Conversely, incorrect phronema is demonstrated by immoral people and heretics. The demons fell from heaven because of the wrong phronesis.[11]

Saint Gregory Palamas discusses proper attitude and its effect on behavior:

> As long as we are faithful to the ways of salvation, our mind is at one with itself and with God, the first and highest Mind. Whenever we open the door to the passions, immediately it is dispersed, wandering continually among fleshly and earthly things, all kinds of pleasures and passionate thoughts about them. The wealth of the mind is prudence [*phronesis*] which stays with it, discerning between what is better and what is worse, for as long as the mind itself stays obedient to the commandments and counsels of the heavenly Father. Once the mind rebels, prudence is dispersed in fornication and foolishness, shared out between both evils.[12]

Phronema for Orthodox Christians: Life and Mentality

PHRONEMA IS TRANSLATED WITH A variety of English words, such as "mind," "mentality," "thought," "attitude," "approach," and "stance." Orthodox Christians sometimes describe it as a worldview, an orientation, "a particular spirit, theological sentiment or frame of mind."[13] It is difficult to define because phronema involves not just mental attitude but one's entire way of life. It is "a scriptural, traditional, doctrinal, historical spirit" that "is reflected and existentialized in the liturgical life of the individual."[14] Father George Nicozisin described how the elements of early Christian life combined to form a specific phronema, which is the phronema preserved today in the Orthodox Church.

---

11 Athanasius the Great, *Life of Antony* 22, Robert Gregg, trans., *Athanasius: Life of Antony and Letter to Marcellinus* (New York: Paulist, 1980), 39.

12 Gregory Palamas, Homily 3, "On the Parable of the Prodigal," 14. Christopher Veniamin, trans. and ed., *St. Gregory Palamas: The Homilies* (Waymart, PA: Mount Thabor, 2009), 19.

13 Fr. George Nicozisin, *The Road to Orthodox Phronema* (Brookline, MA: Holy Cross Orthodox Press, 1977), xiii.

14 Nicozisin, xiii.

It was the way the early Christians expressed their theology long before doctrines, creeds and canons were promulgated and decreed through official councils. The words of the Lord Jesus Christ were first lived as a tradition and then put into sentences and chapters that formed the written source of knowledge we know as scripture. As tradition and scripture surfaced, they did so through the annals of history. As each of these four dimensions—scripture, tradition, doctrine and history—converged and blended, they became the pillar and foundation comprising the *phronema*, and whose mode of expression became liturgical life for both the Church and the believers.[15]

He eloquently expressed how phronema guided the lives of Orthodox Christians in the New World:

When Orthodox people came to the shores of the American continent, they did not come fortified with books of theology, nor even Bibles, for the most part. What they brought with them was something intangible. They brought with them the Orthodox Christian *phronema*, the *parakatathiki* ("deposit"), the heritage and legacy of scripture, tradition, doctrine and history which they received as a deposit, from one generation to another.[16]

Nicozisin's book, written decades ago, is a warning that Orthodox Christian religious education in the New World is failing because Orthodox Christians in America are using Protestant and Catholic models of religious education, rather than instilling the Orthodox phronema in our children in the home. He stressed that Bible stories, church traditions, history, and liturgics cannot be merely taught as though they were something detached from everyday life. The lifestyle and devotion to their faith of those immigrants who brought Orthodox Christianity to other lands was never based on book learning, knowledge of Scripture, or theology, just as phronema was never based on those things for the very first Christians. Those immigrants were Orthodox because of their

---

15 Nicozisin, xiii.
16 Nicozisin, xiii.

phronema, and their Orthodoxy was completely integrated into their daily lives.

> They prayed and called upon the Name of the Lord, *Panaghia,* the Angels and Saints in their everyday life, as though it were *second nature.* They kept strict fasts; observed Feast days and name days; censed their homes each Saturday night and eve of holy days; journeyed through the Lenten seasons for the Dormition of the Holy Theotokos, Christmas, and Easter as spiritual pilgrims; looked upon *Ta Phota* (Epiphany) and Pentecost as days of rededication; and they unconsciously made arrangements for Memorials, *Artoklasia* (Blessing of Five Loaves), *Parakleses* (Prayers of Supplication), Ephchelia (Unction), and a host of other Orthodox Christian religious practices which were a part of their life from as far back as they could remember.[17]

Acquiring an Orthodox phronema is not primarily an intellectual task. Phronema is formed consistently, habitually, regularly through behaviors. But phronema is not merely moral values that people profess. It is a way of life based on complete faith and confidence in the Church. In that respect, phronema is "the completely *self-sacrificial* trust and faith in religious and ethical truths which derive not from human *experience* and *wisdom,* but from the voice of God through revelation which is self-evident and does not undergo censure or doubt."[18]

Orthodox phronema rests on a fundamental belief shared by Orthodox Christians that the Church has preserved apostolic Tradition and will continue to faithfully preserve it. We know this from experience and believe that as the Church has been faithful in the past, it is faithful to the apostolic truth in the present day, even as it faces various issues, crises, and struggles in this world. Because we are confident in the Church, we do not replace its teachings and guidance with our own individual opinions. That itself is part of the phronema.

---

17 Nicozisin, xii–xiv.
18 Stylianos Harkianakis, "The Theologian in Modern Society: Phronema and Behavior," *Voice of Orthodoxy* 19, no. 11 (1998): 121–124, 121. Emphasis in the original.

The Indefinable Nature of Phronema

THE FAITHFUL ARE BOTH CHARACTERIZED and upheld by phronema, which can never be reduced to an ideology. This is why true Orthodoxy is never rigid or legalistic. Faith and phronema intersect and reflect each other.

Phronema, along with virtually everything else in Orthodoxy, cannot be perfectly defined or explained. Explaining Orthodoxy to non-Orthodox has always been a challenge for Orthodox theologians. The lack of definitions in Orthodox Christianity, simply accepted as reality by the Orthodox, can result in consternation and confusion among Western Christians. John Meyendorff articulated the same issue when it was faced by Orthodox theologians during twentieth-century ecumenical dialogues. Western theologians asked the Orthodox theologians to explain what functions as a "permanent criterion for truth" in Orthodox theology. Meyendorff commented on the dilemma faced by the Orthodox representatives:

> Their embarrassment before the challenge makes them look like subjectivists or liberals. But on the other hand, their basic concern for truth and their unwillingness to surrender anything to fashionable doctrinal relativism associates them with extreme conservatism. They themselves, however, refuse to be identified with either.[19]

Alexander Schmemann also commented on the difficulties experienced by Orthodox Christians at ecumenical dialogues because of the radically different phronema.

> For while it is true that the Orthodox Church is hierarchical, sacramental, traditional, horizontal, dogmatical, Catholic, and so forth, neither the affirmation and defense of these characteristics by the Roman Catholics nor their

---

19   John Meyendorff, "Doing Theology in an Eastern Orthodox Perspective," *Eastern Orthodox Theology: A Contemporary Reader,* ed. Daniel Clendenin, 2nd ed. (Grand Rapids, MI: Baker Academic, 2003), 86–87.

negation and criticism by the Protestants coincide with the Eastern approach. Orthodoxy cannot be simply reduced to the Orthodox doctrine of apostolic succession, seven sacraments, three degrees of hierarchy, and it is even doubtful whether such doctrines exist in a clearly defined form. Many of these terms themselves have been borrowed directly from Western manuals and are to be still evaluated in the light of the total and genuine Orthodox tradition. Yet it was precisely as a "position" on this or that question that Orthodoxy was always presented and represented in the ecumenical conversation, but virtually never as a totality, as a living spiritual reality which alone gives life and meaning to its external forms. And then this position itself was usually identified with an existing Western category which only enforced the accepted theological framework.[20]

Schmemann explains that the Orthodox representatives were continually forced to attach "separate Orthodox statements" to the "reports of virtually all major ecumenical conferences." This illustrated the "often helpless" feeling they experienced "of being in a false position, which was almost always the feeling of the Orthodox delegates."[21] Non-Orthodox delegates at ecumenical dialogues never understood the Orthodox position, and the Orthodox could never clearly articulate their position because the foundational presuppositions and premises of Orthodoxy were never recognized. Instead, everything was framed in terms of the Catholic-Protestant dichotomy.

Theological conversations were often odd, uncomfortable, and unnatural for the Orthodox. The effort was destined to fail, but not for any reasons that the Western delegates could ever understand. The basic phronema of Orthodoxy was utterly unrecognized by the Western Christians, and the Orthodox delegates could not even begin to express Orthodox theology within the artificial parameters and categories created by the West.

---

20   Alexander Schmemann, "Moment of Truth for Orthodoxy," in *Eastern Orthodox Theology: A Contemporary Reader,* Daniel Clendenin, ed., 2nd ed. (Grand Rapids, MI: Baker Academic, 2003), 208–209.

21   Schmemann, 209.

This meant not only that she [Orthodoxy] was somehow forced to identify herself with one of the two opposing Western positions, but also that she had to make her own all the derived dichotomies—word and sacrament, vertical and horizontal, authority and freedom, and so on—typical of the Western theological situation, but fundamentally alien to the real Orthodox tradition. [At the World Council of Churches] in the absence of Rome, she was assigned the role of the ecumenically acceptable Catholicism at the extreme right wing of the whole spectrum of Protestant denominations.[22]

The Western phronema expects, even requires, definition, guidelines, and explanations. This is a product of developments in the West during the Middle Ages.

Tradition, phronema, and so many aspects of Orthodoxy are inexplicable and indefinable. Perhaps this is why Orthodox Christians rarely attempt to articulate the nature of phronema. And yet it is our *experience* of Orthodoxy, impossible to explain or describe, that continually confirms our truth and compels us to adhere to it firmly and with great confidence. We know this reality from actual experience.

The *phronema* of the faithful in general, and the theologian in particular, is an unshakeable certainty about the truth of Faith. Even when this cannot be contained in linguistic or other formulations, it remains undiminished and vibrant throughout life, a continually verified daily experience.[23]

We begin to truly appreciate the wisdom, love, and sacrifice of our parents only when we reach adulthood. Likewise, our confidence in Orthodox phronema grows as we mature in Orthodoxy. With the passage of time we come to realize, through our own personal lived experience, the truth and wisdom of the Church as expressed in the divine services and through the writings of the Fathers and the lives of the saints. Practices we once performed merely because we were "supposed to" are eventually embraced as genuinely

22 Schmemann, 208.
23 Harkianakis, "Theologian in Modern Society," 122.

useful, necessary, and organic expressions of inner devotion. Beliefs we simply accepted because Orthodoxy "has always taught this" are recognized as pointing to profound realities beyond words or comprehension. It is our *experience* through our life in the Church that confirms us in its truth. This is why we adhere so faithfully and so firmly to Tradition. Perhaps it is for this reason that a monastic friend told me simply that "phronema is Tradition."

CHAPTER 3

Phronema in the Western Christian Tradition

E VERYONE HAS A PHRONEMA, A particular attitude or approach, not only to theology but to life in general. The Greek linguistic roots of *phronema*, which link thought and conduct, reveal that a true Orthodox phronema leads to correct Orthodox behavior. This is not unlike the word *orthodox* itself, which means both "correct belief or opinion" and "correct glory or worship." If we have the proper attitude, this will be reflected in the way we live. Returning to the fasting example, if we insist on rigidity and a pharisaical approach in our fasting practices, we are not displaying an Orthodox phronema. On the other hand, ignoring, minimizing, or marginalizing fasting equally indicates a lack of Orthodox phronema.

This type of balance in theology and in practice, deviating neither to the right nor to the left, is also seen in the teachings and spiritual advice of the Fathers of the Church.[1] A correct Orthodox phronema is particularly essential for the Orthodox theologian, since it determines not only personal behavior but what a theologian will say, do, and write in his or her capacity as a theologian. Before we discuss the Orthodox phronema in greater depth, let us take a broad view of the basic foundations of Western Christian phronema.

---

1   Especially St. Gregory the Theologian. Emphasis on balance in the Fathers was based on biblical injunctions such as "Turn aside neither to the right nor to the left" (Prov. 4:27) and "Strive therefore diligently to keep and do all things that are written in the book of the Law of Moses, that you not turn aside to the right or to the left" (Josh. 23:6).

The Protestant Phronema: Sola Scriptura

AS WE HAVE SEEN, ST. Paul emphasized a unity of thought and will, oneness of mind within the Church, formed by a common orientation toward the gospel and life in Christ. All Christians read and recognize the New Testament as authoritative. Christians also sincerely wish to be united with Christ and each other. Why is it then that all Christians do not share the same phronema? Saint Paul's words instructing us to conform to a Christian phronema have not created Christian unity, even for those who attempt to follow his scriptural directives. Unity of faith and mind is not found among different types of Christians, even though we all share the same Scriptures and regard them as authoritative. This is because that which shapes one's theological perspective is not the Scriptures themselves but the mindset through which one reads and applies those Scriptures. This is especially true in the Protestant tradition.

Protestant adherence to Martin Luther's dictum *sola scriptura* ("the Scriptures alone") renders a unified phronema impossible. Luther was less extreme than his followers and maintained many traditional Catholic views. But sola scriptura became the dominant Protestant mantra and the most prominent characteristic of the Protestant phronema. But it is not only the Scriptures *alone*, but the Scriptures *apart*—apart from the Church, from any church authority or the authority of traditional interpretation. Sola scriptura is the most fundamental and foundational principle of the Protestant mindset: one can determine for oneself what the Scriptures mean. The claim, therefore, is in effect not just "the Scriptures alone" but "myself alone."

This is not the meaning of sola scriptura, but that is its effect, since Protestants recognize no other authority that might create guidelines for understanding Scripture. The Scriptures themselves are held to be the sole authority, but Scripture is not self-interpretive. It obviously cannot be, since even Protestants do not agree on its meaning. If the Scriptures were self-interpretive, everyone would arrive at the same conclusions and interpretations. Therefore, the unmistakable consequence of sola scriptura is the belief that everyone interprets the Scriptures for himself and presumes his interpretation is valid. The result is an astonishing variety of Protestant denominations and independent congregations.

The Protestant Reformation revolved around the rejection of Catholic traditions that were denounced by the Reformers as errors and deviations from early Church belief and practice. The Reformers championed "the Scriptures alone," and the Catholic Church responded with "Scripture and Tradition." Because the Catholics insisted on the authority of Tradition, the concept of Tradition as the basis for anything in the Church came to be rejected in the Protestant world. Now "the very antitraditionalism of the Reformation has itself become a tradition."[2]

PROTESTANT LEGALISM

A SUBTLE SPIRIT OF LEGALISM prevails in many Protestant circles in terms of expected behaviors and beliefs. Protestants themselves have specific actions they consider necessary for one to be saved, such as being sorry for one's sins, accepting Jesus Christ as one's personal Savior, inviting Him into your heart, saying the sinner's prayer, and so on. For some, one must say with his mouth that Jesus is Lord and believe in his heart that God raised Jesus from the dead (Rom. 10:9). These specific steps or others, such as laying on of hands or baptism, must be followed in order for a person to be recognized as "saved" or "born again." A certain rigidity applies even though the requirements for each group differ.

The Protestant emphasis on the word *justification* also has legalistic overtones. The Greek word that is typically translated into English as "justification" is *dikaiosyne*, "righteousness," which actually hints at virtue and right conduct, including practices of piety. Translating the word as "justification" promotes and strengthens a legalistic view of our relationship with God and a transactional concept of salvation.

Christ's sacrifice on the cross as atonement for sins is the sole explanation of salvation for many Protestants. Christ paid the price for our sins, and we are justified by the blood of Jesus; there is nothing for us to contribute. This explanation is appealing in its simplicity and possibly because it demands

---

2   Jaroslav Pelikan, *The Vindication of Tradition* (New Haven, CT: Yale University Press, 1984), 11.

nothing from the believer other than assent. Apart from the artificial and legalistic framework this understanding of sin creates to explain our relationship to God and salvation, it minimizes or ignores the ongoing effects or consequences of sin.

Many Protestants find themselves still struggling with their personal sins. They can only attempt to ignore the problem, say it does not matter since Jesus has justified them, or remain perplexed as to why they are trapped, repeating the same patterns and unable to overcome their personal weaknesses. No theological construct exists for them to recognize the difference between Christ's redemptive death for all of us for all time and the need for each of us to respond to that gift with our own efforts and mold ourselves to "put on Christ" (Gal. 3:27). Without the fullness of the grace of God through the sacraments to assist and comfort them, how do they actualize—make real—the redemptive victory of Christ on a personal and individual basis? What they really hunger for is deep spiritual transformation, but what is available to them is often reduced to a mere emotional response to Christ, which can be rather shallow and unfulfilling, or a pumped-up gospel of positive thinking and prosperity, which does not reflect the reality of daily life or the truth of our human condition.

In actuality, there is no single Protestant phronema, since a plethora of scriptural interpretations has resulted from sola scriptura, leading to divergent doctrines, spiritualities, and moral opinions, and infinite varieties of phronema. When one disagrees with the pastor's opinion, it is easy enough to change to another denomination or to create one's own congregation. The Protestant phronema of the "Scriptures alone" and each individual as the arbiter of the Scriptures unavoidably leads to disunity and fragmentation.[3]

---

3   A Gallup poll conducted in 2016 reported that the percentage of US adults who identified with any particular Protestant denomination dropped to 30 percent, a dramatic decline from 50 percent in 2000. People who identify as any *specific type* of Protestant decreased overall from 57 percent to 47 percent during that period of time, with many switching to identify simply as "Christian." The hundreds of Protestant denominations in the US today allow Protestants "to easily switch between denominations, with the result that many Protestants are not as fixed in their religious identity as would be the case for Catholics, Jews or those from other religious traditions." Frank Newport, "More US Protestants Have No Specific Denominational Identity," *Gallup*, July 18, 2017,

The Roman Catholic Phronema

THE PHRONEMA OF THE ROMAN Catholic Church is quite interesting. A wide variety of opinions exists among Catholic theologians in matters of theology, morality, spirituality, and methodology.[4] Because Roman Catholic views are always evolving and because they range from extremely liberal to very conservative, it is difficult to grasp and articulate Catholic thought in a conclusive manner. For this reason I am relying here primarily on statements found in official Vatican documents, Catholic canons, and the official Catholic Catechism. I will focus on only four aspects of the Catholic phronema: Roman centrality, faith and reason, the development of doctrine, and legalism.

THE FIRST ASPECT: ROMAN CENTRALITY

FOR CATHOLICS, UNITY OF FAITH is demonstrated by and through union with Rome. The pope is the visible symbol of union, "the vicar of Christ" on earth.[5] Conformity to official Catholic teaching and papal decrees and decisions is often considered the mark of a devout Catholic and is literally demanded in some Vatican documents. The Catholic Church also maintains a process by which Catholic books are approved for publication via the *Imprimatur,* an official license to publish Catholic books. Until recently, all Catholic publishers were required to receive the Imprimatur. On the back of a book's title page were found the words *nihil obstat* ("nothing hinders"), indicating that the book contained nothing contrary to Catholic teaching or morals.[6]

---

https://news.gallup.com/poll/214208/protestants-no-specific-denominational-iden-tity.aspx?g_source=link.

4   A brief but very interesting overview of this development during the late twentieth century is described by Thomas Rauch in *Reconciling Faith and Reason: Apologists, Evangelists, and Theologians in a Divided Church* (Collegeville, MN: Liturgical Press, 2000).

5   "Code of Canon Law," 331. http://www.vatican.va/archive/ENG1104/__PC.HTM.

6   According to the Catholic Church's Code of Canon Law, certain books still require Church approval, including Bible translations, prayer books, liturgical books, catechisms, catechetical publications, all theological textbooks, and any book sold, displayed, or distributed in churches. It is recommended that other books on faith and morals be submitted and approved, but it is no longer *required* that all books read by the Catholic faithful receive the Imprimatur. "Code of Canon Law," Canons 824–830, http://www.vatican.va/archive/ENG1104/__P2Q.HTM.

In practice and in private opinion, many Catholics deviate from official Catholic teaching and doctrine, yet they generally recognize the supreme authority of the Roman pontiff and the magisterium.[7] The pope's supremacy and the mandate that Catholic faithful submit to his absolute authority are explicit, strong, and unequivocal, although many Catholics seem uncomfortable with this and tend to minimize it. *Lumen Gentium,* a document from the Second Vatican Council (the most recent council Catholics recognize as an ecumenical council), states:

> and the faithful, for their part, are *obliged to submit* to their bishops' decision, made in the name of Christ, in matters of faith and morals, and *to adhere to it* with a ready and respectful allegiance of mind. *This loyal submission of the will and intellect must be given* in a *special way* to the authentic teaching authority of the Roman Pontiff, *even when* he does not speak ex cathedra, in such wise, indeed, that *his supreme teaching authority be acknowledged* with respect, and sincere assent be given to decisions made by him, conformably with his manifest mind and intention.[8]

Many faithful who strongly dissent from traditional teachings nonetheless self-identify as Catholic. This is true for dissenting theologians as well, most of whom remain dedicated to their Church with a hope and expectation that they can influence it, change it, and reform it. The Catholic Church has actual rules and definitions of dissent, including when one is "in dissent," what one can dissent from, under what circumstances one may dissent, and the specific state of mind required for one to be permitted to be "in dissent."[9]

---

7   The body recognized as holding teaching authority in the Catholic Church, specifically the pope and the college of bishops.

8   *Lumen Gentium,* 25. Emphasis added. This council, known as "Vatican II," was held from 1962 to 1965. *Vatican Council II,* Austin Flannery, ed. (Collegeville, MN: Liturgical Press, 1975), 379. The strong language of "submission" is softened on the Vatican website, where the more recent English translation reads, "the faithful are to accept their teaching and adhere to it with a religious assent. This religious submission of mind and will must be shown in a special way to the authentic magisterium of the Roman Pontiff." http://www.vatican.va/archive/hist_councils/ii_vatican_council/documents/vat-ii_const_19641121_lumen-gentium_en.html.

9   See *Donum Veritatis, Instruction on the Ecclesial Vocation of the Theologian* (May

Roman centrality and adoption of Roman thought and practice has been strongly promoted at least since the time of Gregory the Great (d. 604). Catholic theologians focus on Rome and its statements when they seek to define, affirm, or conversely to reform or dispute Catholic teaching. The Catholic Church produces an official catechism.[10] Specific doctrinal beliefs and practices are also articulated, expounded, and expanded through countless documents issued by various Vatican departments.

Vatican documents are cited and discussed frequently by Catholic scholars and faithful in the same manner in which Orthodox Christians cite the Fathers of the Church. This has been demonstrated in my personal experience on countless occasions over decades of interaction with Roman Catholics. Typically, when Catholic students wish to research and report Catholic teaching on a particular issue, they turn to "the documents." Also among faculty in discussions on Catholic teaching, I hear comments that begin, "There is a document..."

Catholic Christians also believe that the Scriptures and the Fathers are important authorities. However, these sources are quoted in brief statements or excerpts to support what is written in Vatican documents, church canons, or the official catechism. This is not to say that Catholics do not read the Scriptures or the Fathers, but the authority of the ancient sources is presented through Vatican documents, which synthesize and interpret the Scriptures and the Fathers. The Roman documents then become the lens through which the ancient sources are understood and applied, or, conversely, the means by which a position is rejected if the Catholic theologian is contravening Catholic teaching.

24, 1990), a document by the Congregation for the Doctrine of the Faith, http://www.vatican.va/ roman_curia/congregations/ cfaith/documents/rc_con_cfaith_doc_19900524_theologian-vocation_en.html. See especially paragraphs 32–39, which deal with the question of dissent. The Congregation for the Doctrine of the Faith is one of the most important and powerful departments of the Vatican and is responsible for promoting and defending the Catholic faith. Cardinal Joseph Ratzinger headed this department for many years until he was elected to the papacy and became Pope Benedict XVI.

10 This is available in print and online at http://www.vatican.va/archive/ENG0015/_INDEX.HTM. The Orthodox Church has no "official" catechism.

Although Catholics consider the Roman Church to be founded on St. Peter, "the Rock," an unshakable, constant, and reliable bastion of truth, in fact the Catholic Church has undergone momentous change over the centuries, continuing to this day. Why does the Roman Catholic Church experience dramatic changes, tremendous disunity, and a plethora of theological opinions? Because of the second aspect of Catholic phronema: faith and reason.

THE SECOND ASPECT: FAITH AND REASON

IF SOLA SCRIPTURA IS THE bedrock of Protestant Christianity, "faith and reason" is the mantra and driving principle of Catholic theology. The foundation for this was laid by St. Augustine (d. 430), whose writings so dominated the Latin Church that they fundamentally changed Western thought. Augustine was trained and educated as a philosopher and rhetorician. Later, as a bishop of the Church, he tried to resolve theological questions by the application of reason and logical deduction. Lacking a formal theological education, Augustine relied on his philosophical training. He believed that truth could not conflict with reason because God is the source of both. Therefore, he concluded that deductive reasoning can be utilized in the service of theology.

His writings often demonstrated this approach, as he would pose a question which he then carefully analyzed and answered, point by point and possibility by possibility. After he eventually arrived at a rational conclusion, he would proceed to the next question, and so forth. Augustine employed the Scriptures and Church Tradition for his responses; however, he also relied on logical deduction for many conclusions. A theological style based almost exclusively on deductive reasoning had not been used in the East.

Augustine initiated the trajectory that ultimately resulted in the schism between East and West. He sowed the seeds of a different phronema, which over ensuing centuries gradually grew in the West due to his immense influence. Relying on his training in philosophy, he arrived at his own divergent conclusions to some theological questions, many of which had already been resolved by important church councils and notable Greek Fathers.

Augustine attempted to follow apostolic Tradition and often succeeded, but he also applied human logic to theological questions. He introduced certain theological innovations that became widespread in the West and contribute to this day to the separation between the Catholic and Orthodox Churches. Even though his deviations may have seemed philosophically logical, linguistically minor, or justified in their rationale or purpose, they had serious and lasting consequences.

Owing to his enormous literary output in Latin, Augustine became the theological authority par excellence in the West. His prolific writing and sustained influence were unequaled there. As a result, Augustine himself became the standard of orthodoxy for the Latins, resulting in a new, Latin Tradition. Subsequent Latin Christians relied heavily on Augustine, especially after the decline of the Western Roman Empire. The numerous Greek Fathers had not deviated from apostolic Tradition, but they were read far less frequently, if at all, in the West. With the change in orientation from apostolic Tradition as the source of theology to a strong reliance on the application of reason, the phronema of the West began to diverge from that of the East.

During the Middle Ages, another important Latin theologian, Anselm of Canterbury (d. 1109), described the task of theology as "faith seeking understanding." Anselm's writings and methodology reinforced the Latin emphasis on the use of logic and deductive reasoning in theology.

The Catholic Church's use of reason should not be misunderstood. The Church does not believe in the use of reason *alone*. Extremes such as rationalism, biblicism, fideism, and radical traditionalism are expressly rejected.[11] Yet Catholics find it impossible to theologize without deductive reasoning—a characteristic shared by virtually all Western Christians. Protestants inherited and subconsciously accept the reliance on deductive reasoning in theology, since that phronema had developed and permeated Western Christianity long before the Reformation.

The Catholic Church continues to emphasize and value deductive reasoning in discovering theological truth, and it affirms that one can know God

---

11 *Fides et Ratio 52, Encyclical Letter Fides et Ratio of the Supreme Pontiff John Paul II to the Bishops of the Catholic Church on the Relationship between Faith and Reason* (Washington, DC: Unites States Catholic Conference, 1998), Publication 5-302, 79. The First Vatican Council (1869–70), an ecumenical council for the Catholic Church, dogmatically pronounced the relationship between faith and reason in its document *Dei Filius*.

through the application of the mind. Catholics do not believe that all mysteries can be understood through reason, and they do believe everything begins
with God's revelation to humanity. However, the pervasive emphasis is on the
capacity of human reason to arrive at knowledge of God. The *Catechism of the
Catholic Church* states:

> Our holy mother, the Church, holds and teaches that God, the first principle
> and last end of all things, can be known with certainty from the created world
> by the natural light of human reason.[12]

Orthodox Christians would agree that creation reveals the existence of
God. That is a biblical concept and can be seen in countless verses, such as
"The heavens declare the glory of God" (Ps. 19:1 [NKJV]). Saint Paul stated
that through human observation of the created world one can realize that God
exists (Rom. 1:20). The revelation of God's existence began with His action
and initiative and is innate in all human beings. But the Catholic phronema
goes much further: it confidently affirms that truths about God or actual
knowledge of God can be attained through the application of human deductive reasoning. Therefore, since reason is the means by which one can know
God, if one does not believe in God or if one has incorrect belief, what stands
in need of correction is not the soul but one's faculty of reason. If one applies
the correct reasoning, one will arrive at the correct theological beliefs. For
example, the Catholic Code of Canon Law states:

> The law of God entrusted to the Church is taught to the faithful as the way
> of life and truth. The faithful therefore have the right to be instructed in the
> divine saving precepts that *purify judgment* and, with grace, *heal wounded
> human reason.*[13]

---

12   Catechism of the Catholic Church I.1.III.36, citing Vatican Council I, *Dei Filius* 2: DS
      3004 cf. 3026; Vatican Council II, *Dei Verbum* 6. http://www.vatican.va/archive
      /ENG0015/_INDEX.HTM.
13   Emphasis added. Citing *Codex Iuris Canonici*, Canon 213. "CIC" is the Latin rite's *Code
      of Canon Law.* The Catholic Church has a separate Code of Canon Law for Eastern Rite
      Catholics, known as *Corpus Canonum Ecclesiarum Orientalium.*

The theological methodology initiated by Augustine and strengthened by Anselm was confirmed and cemented permanently in Western Christianity by Thomas Aquinas (d. 1274). Aquinas valued the Scriptures and apostolic Tradition and often referred to them. But by his time, the use of deductive reasoning in theology was firmly established in the Latin Church. Aquinas relied on Aristotelian philosophy and deductive reasoning, and he especially labored to prove that reason did not contradict his theology.

In stark contrast, St. Gregory Palamas, Archbishop of Thessalonika (1347–1359), who flourished not long after Aquinas, considered pagan philosophy to be "overly centered on the activity of the rational aspect of the mind (based principally on discursive thinking, syllogism and so forth)."[14] The foundational use of philosophy requires theological claims to have a nontheological justification. "This view makes theology dependent on philosophy and regards human reason as the ultimate universal arbiter."[15] Theology in the East is based not on discursive thought but on "knowledge that stems from the vision of God."[16] The Western approach is fundamentally intellectual; the Eastern is fundamentally spiritual.

By the Middle Ages a clear divide in phronema was evident. Yoking reason to theology, developing logical syllogisms, and addressing theological matters through a progressive series of questions and answers[17] characterized Catholic theology of the Middle Ages.

The result was a massive and permanent imprint on the Catholic phronema and theological method. Today Catholic seminarians receive years of training in philosophy. The importance of philosophy as an indispensable foundation for theological study was emphasized by Pope John Paul II in his encyclical *Faith and Reason*.[18] Confidence in the harmony between faith and

---

14   *St. Gregory: The Homilies*, 622–23, note 860. Comments by Christopher Veniamin.

15   Christoph Schneider, "Introduction: The Quest for a Christian Philosophy," *Theology and Philosophy in Eastern Orthodoxy*, Christoph Schneider, ed. (Eugene, OR: Pickwick Publications, 2019), 8.

16   *St. Gregory: The Homilies*, 622–23, note 860.

17   This is a rhetorical device known as *hypophora*. From an Eastern Christian perspective, this method in fact "proves" nothing, since the truth of the conclusion is highly dependent on the validity of the underlying premises.

18   In *Fides et Ratio* (*Faith and Reason*) John Paul II wrote: "I wish to repeat clearly that the

reason has led to the third aspect of Catholic phronema: the development of doctrine.

THE THIRD ASPECT: DEVELOPMENT OF DOCTRINE

ROME'S ESTEEM FOR THE USE of reason contributes to the Catholic impetus to delineate, define, and explain almost everything theological. In fact, this is encouraged because, although divine truth "was declared once and for all in the mystery of Jesus," it was "immersed therefore in time and history."[19] The Catholic Church teaches that with the passage of time, theological truth can be better understood and expressed. Catholic doctrine continually developed over different periods of history because "as the centuries succeed one another, the Church constantly progresses towards the fullness of divine truth."[20]

This is quite different from the Orthodox view, which is that the fullness of divine revelation was given to the Church *once*, at Pentecost.[21] The Orthodox Church accepts that we can grow in understanding or that the Church has found ways to articulate the truth with specific language over time. However, Orthodoxy maintains that the Church *already* possesses the *fullness* of the truth, not that it is progressively growing toward greater understanding of the truth. For this reason, Orthodoxy rejects the development of new doctrines or the idea that the Church can receive new or greater revelation.

---

study of philosophy is fundamental and indispensable to the structure of theological studies and to the formation of candidates for the priesthood. . . . [This is] rooted in the experience which matured through the Middle Ages, when the importance of a constructive harmony of philosophical and theological learning emerged." *Fides et Ratio* 62, U.S.C.C. S-302, 93.

19 *Fides et Ratio* 11, U.S.C.C. S-302, 17.

20 *Fides et Ratio* 11, U.S.C.C. S-302, 18–19, quoting the Vatican II document *Dei Verbum*.

21 This is the ancient belief of the Church and the patristic view. It is based on the patristic understanding of John 16:13, when Christ declares to the disciples that He will send them the Spirit, who "will lead" them to the truth. The Greek future tense of the verb "will lead" is known as the "future of one moment"; therefore, the Spirit completely revealed all truth at Pentecost. To imply continuous revelation, the verb would have been expressed by the continuous future form of the verb: the Holy Spirit "will be leading you" to the truth.

From the Middle Ages until the mid-twentieth century, Catholic theological manuals and textbooks presented arguments in a systematic and methodical manner. Proofs were presented from the Bible, the Fathers, church documents, and logical deduction. Deductive reasoning as proof that a doctrine was true became popular in the Middle Ages. The basic rationale was the following: "God (or Christ) *could* do something; it was *fitting* that he should; therefore, he *did it. Potuit, decuit, fecit.*"[22]

The most obvious examples of a doctrinal innovation in the Catholic Church that directly resulted from this rationale (He *could*, therefore He *should*, therefore He *did*) are certain doctrines about Mary.[23] Because Catholicism appropriated Augustine's view of original sin as inherited guilt and a taint on the soul, its theologians reasoned that Mary should not have been born with original sin because she was to be the mother of Christ, the incarnate Son of God. God *could* protect her from original sin. He *should* do it. Therefore, they concluded, He *did* it. This idea was promoted and accepted over time until eventually the Immaculate Conception—the teaching that Mary was conceived without original sin and preserved without sin—was declared a dogma.[24] Catholic hierarchs and theologians searched for patristic statements (which they misinterpreted or took out of context) to justify this new dogma.

The dogma of the Immaculate Conception developed gradually, and it evolved entirely because of rational deduction, not because the Fathers imagined it, taught it, or believed it. The doctrine was promoted long before it was officially declared as dogma.[25] Dogmatic declaration of the Immaculate

---

22 Richard P. McBrien, *Catholicism*, 2 vols. (Minneapolis: Winston Press, 1980), 2:874.

23 Papal infallibility is another obvious and historically traceable example of the creeping progression and expansion of a theological idea until its pronouncement as a dogma that is unrecognizable from anything that was taught or believed in the early Church.

24 "The most Blessed Virgin Mary was, from the first moment of her conception, by a singular grace and privilege of almighty God and by virtue of the merits of Jesus Christ, Saviour of the human race, preserved immune from all stain of original sin." Pope Pius IX, *Ineffabilis Deus*, 1854, DS 2803. This was the formal proclamation of the dogma, but it was the result of developments in doctrine about Mary since the Middle Ages, based largely on *potuit, decuit, fecit*.

25 The idea was promoted for hundreds of years, and this is precisely what allowed it to eventually be proclaimed as an actual dogma. It was assumed that this teaching had

Conception was followed by the next logical assertion: If she did not have *any* sin, even original sin, Mary must not have died, since death is the consequence of sin. Many Catholics, including leading theologians, insist that Mary never died.[26]

In the twentieth century, Pope Pius XII declared the Bodily Assumption of Mary as dogma, although he refrained from explicitly stating whether or not she had actually died. The pope specifically noted, however, that the push to officially declare the Assumption of the Virgin Mary as a dogma was a theological progression resulting directly from the proclamation of the Immaculate Conception.[27]

The development of doctrine was famously championed by Cardinal John Newman in the nineteenth century.[28] He claimed the apostles left seeds of doctrine that would naturally grow and develop over time. Newman describes the work of the Fathers of the Church almost entirely as a process of thought: "fixing their minds" on a question, "grasping" the concepts, "viewing" various sides, "weighing" possibilities. The Fathers might even be "left in ignorance" to be followed by another generation of "teachers" to complete their work as "the anxious process of thought went on."[29] Newman's emphasis was on the operation of the mind to arrive at theological truths. Rarely did he mention the necessity of prayer or a profound relationship with God as contributing to theological insight.

Significant development of doctrine has occurred in the Catholic Church since the time of the apostles primarily due to an impetus to apply human reason to theology to the fullest extent possible. This methodology was expressed by Pope John Paul II, who wrote:

---

been part of the apostolic Tradition because it had been discussed by Catholics since the Middle Ages, and it seemed suitably "rational."

26 They also take this position because Mary's death is described as her "falling asleep" or Dormition. But this is the term used for death by Christ Himself and the apostles. (See John 11:11; 1 Thess. 4:13; 1 Cor. 15:6.)

27 Pope Pius XII, Apostolic Constitution *Munificentissimus Deus* ("Most Bountiful God"), 1950. Pius XII proclaimed the dogma of the Assumption because he was *encouraged* by the clergy and faithful to *continue* to develop doctrine about Mary.

28 Cardinal John Henry Newman, *The Development of Christian Doctrine* (Westminster, MD: Christian Classics, 1968, repr.).

29 Newman, 367.

Revelation therefore introduces into our history a universal and ultimate truth which stirs the human mind to ceaseless effort; indeed, it impels reason continually to extend the range of its knowledge until it senses that it has done all in its power, leaving no stone unturned.[30]

THE FOURTH ASPECT: LEGALISM

THE CATHOLIC CHURCH OPERATES IN a highly structured fashion and expresses itself with the language of law. Saints are canonized after a lengthy and technical legal process. Catholic pronouncements routinely emphasize regulation, conformity to law, and submission to official positions in a way that is quite startling to an Orthodox Christian.

A juridical mentality is foreign to the Orthodox phronema. The Orthodox refer to their canons as the "Holy Canons," rather than "The Code of Canon Law," and Orthodox canons are not codified, systematized, organized, or even updated. The canons also do not function as law in the manner in which Catholics apply and interpret their canon law.

Sin as Debt

Legalism in Catholic theology is reflected in the Roman Catholic view of sin and its removal. This also has its roots in the thought of St. Augustine, who concluded that all human beings "not only inherit mortality and the inclination to sin" from Adam, "but they are guilty and legally liable before God for Adam's sin. This doctrine profoundly affects the perspective of *how* one is saved and *from what* he is saved."[31]

Augustine made a distinction between the inclination to sin after the Fall (the Eastern view) and an inherited legal liability of "guilt" before God for Adam's sin.[32] Because Protestantism emerged from the Catholic Church, Protestants share the Catholic conception of sin. Since Western Christianity emphasizes that Christ paid the "debt" owed to the Father, it is hardly

---

30   John Paul II, *Fides et Ratio* 14, U.S.C.C. 5-302, 23.
31   Sergius Bowyer, *Acquiring the Mind of Christ* (Waymart, PA: St. Tikhon's Monastery Press, 2015), 27. Emphasis in the original.
32   Bowyer, 27–28.

surprising that many Protestants reject any need for the Church or a sacramental life. "Atonement theology effectively makes the Roman Catholic Church the means of legal justification which pronounces 'not guilty' through the sacraments, rather than a process which restores the innate goodness of man."[33]

From the Reformation on, Protestants and Catholics shared not only a common phronema but a common set of questions. Both "Roman and Reformed were content to argue about the same problems—neither side questioned the agenda. Both shared the assumptions of Western theology."[34] The East, on the other hand, never experienced "the question and answer" of the Reformation and Counter-Reformation, the "tension of rival authorities" and "conflicting theologies of grace and sacraments."[35] The problem of guilt was central and an ingrained starting point in the West, whereas for the East, the focal point was not human sin but human destiny: to become godlike.[36]

The difference may also be the result of approaching the question of salvation from either a negative or a positive perspective. When approached negatively, salvation has been called "redemption and justification," but the "positive dimension is that of sanctification or deification."[37] The Orthodox think of sin not as an offense against God that demands punishment or restitution, but primarily as an illness that needs healing. Recent Catholic theology has attempted to recover this view, and today Catholics sometimes describe sin as "illness," but Catholic theology and piety strongly preserve and perpetuate a more legalistic understanding of sin.

The doctrine of purgatory is a combination of Roman Catholic legalism and the development of doctrine. The Vatican continues periodically to

---

33 Bowyer, 27–28.
34 Joseph C. McLelland, "Sailing to Byzantium," *The New Man: An Orthodox and Reformed Dialogue,* John Meyendorff and Joseph McLelland, eds. (New Brunswick, NJ: Agora Books, 1973), 14.
35 McLelland, 14.
36 McLelland, 15.
37 Maximos Aghiorgoussis, *In the Image of God* (Brookline, MA: Holy Cross Orthodox Press, 1999), 115.

offer indulgences,[38] a practice that is made possible by the Roman Catholic concepts of sin and purgatory. According to Catholic teaching, the guilt of the sin may be forgiven but not the punishment that sin requires. This view is clearly affirmed in a Vatican document, the "Apostolic Constitution" *Indulgentiarum Doctrina*:

> It is a divinely revealed truth that sins bring punishments inflicted by God's sanctity and justice. These must be expiated either on this earth through the sorrows, miseries and calamities of this life and above all through death, or else in the life beyond through fire and torments or "purifying" punishments.... These punishments are imposed by the just and merciful judgment of God for the purification of souls, the defense of the sanctity of the moral order and the restoration of the glory of God to its full majesty.... That punishment or the vestiges of sin may remain to be expiated or cleansed and that they in fact frequently do even after the remission of guilt is clearly demonstrated by the doctrine on purgatory.... For all men who walk this earth daily commit at least venial sins; thus all need the mercy of God to be set free from the penal consequences of sin.[39]

Catholic teaching is clear: sin disrupts "the sanctity of the moral order" and requires "the restoration of the glory of God to its full majesty." Therefore, one must pay the consequential penalty so that the order and majesty of God might be restored. The guilt of the sin may be forgiven; however, the penalty (the "penal consequence") remains. Further purification is also required after death by means of purgatory.

---

38   For example, various indulgences were proclaimed in September 2015 for the Extraordinary Jubilee of Mercy (http://w2.vatican.va/content/francesco/en/letters/2015 /documents/papa-francesco_20150901_lettera-indulgenza-giubileo-misericordia . html), and a plenary indulgence was proclaimed in July 2013 by Pope Francis for the 28th World Youth Day (http://www.vatican.va/roman_curia/tribunals/apost_penit /documents/rc_trib_appen_doc_20130709_decreto-indulgenze-gmg_en.html). Specific actions must be taken in order to receive the benefits of the indulgences. Catholicism teaches that indulgences diminish the "time" spent in purgatory suffering for one's minor or "venial" sins.

39   Pope Paul VI, *Indulgentiarum Doctrina* I.2-3, https://w2.vatican.va/content/paul-vi/en /apost_constitutions/documents/hf_p-vi_apc_01011967_indulgentiarum-doctrina .html.

This is a tremendous departure from the understanding of sin in the early Church, and to this day in Orthodox Christianity, which holds that sin distorts the relationship between the human person and God and between human beings. It is impossible for us to imagine that any human action, no matter how heinous, could detract from or diminish the glory or majesty of God. Furthermore, sacramental forgiveness in the Orthodox Church is always complete and immediate. The relationship with God is completely restored with no penalty remaining to be paid.

Thus, it is evident that the gulf between the Orthodox and Western Christianity in the critical matter of sin and forgiveness is enormous.

Merit

Another corollary of legalism reflected in Catholic spirituality is the concept of *merit* and receiving benefit from the merits—the good deeds, if you will—of the saints, of Mary, or of Christ. The merits of Christ and the saints contribute to satisfy the debt (punishment) required from the sinner.[40] Basically, Christ and the saints have a reward owed to them by God, and we can tap into their accomplishments to receive a benefit.

This mentality is totally absent from the Orthodox, who consider the saints exemplars and intercessors only. The term *merit* is never used, and Orthodoxy has no concept of a treasury of stored benefits accumulated by one person that can be shared with another. Each person will be judged, and each will stand or fall, on the basis of his or her life alone. We receive grace from God, but grace is not merit, a term that implies a highly legalistic and transactional view of

---

40 Catholic Canon 992 states: "An indulgence is the *remission* before God of temporal *punishment for sins* whose *guilt is already forgiven,* which a properly disposed member of the Christian faithful gains under certain and defined conditions by the assistance of the Church which as minister of redemption *dispenses* and applies authoritatively the *treasury of the satisfactions* of Christ and the saints." Canon 993 explains: "An indulgence is partial or plenary insofar as it partially or totally frees from the temporal punishment due to sins." Canon 994 provides that one may "gain partial or plenary indulgences for oneself *or apply them to the dead* by way of suffrage." Emphasis added in each. http:// www.vatican.va/archive/ENG1104/_P3I.HTM. The 2015 indulgence proclaimed by Pope Francis specifically stated that "the Jubilee Indulgence can also be obtained for the deceased." http://www.vatican.va/content/francesco/en/letters/2015/documents /papa-francesco_20150901_lettera-indulgenza-giubileo-misericordia.html.

the relationship between God and humans, between sin and salvation.

I was fifteen years old when my family moved to San Diego in the 1970s. My parents enrolled me at a Catholic high school. I had never spent any time around Catholics, and the whole experience brought something new and puzzling almost every day. In many ways it was a typical high school, but in other ways, it was a different world. I had never met a nun, never been to Mass, and was often surprised by ordinary statements and behaviors, inside and outside of class.

Once I borrowed a magazine from the school library. The magazine cover was barely attached, being held on by only one staple in the center of the spine. While in my possession, it further loosened, and the cover became completely detached from the magazine itself. The school librarian was an older nun who still wore the full black habit. When I returned the magazine, I showed her that the cover was still with the magazine but no longer attached to it. "I'm sorry, Sister," I said. "The cover fell off."

The librarian nun replied, "Say ten Hail Marys and one Our Father." I walked away bewildered. I had no idea what she was talking about. I knew what the "Hail Mary" and "Our Father" were, but what did that have to do with the magazine? The idea behind her reaction was so foreign to me that several days passed before I realized she was giving me a "penance."

Many concepts that are basic, fundamental, and foundational in the Catholic mind are entirely absent from Orthodoxy. The terms *satisfaction, merit,* and *atonement* fit into a view of salvation that is highly juridical. In the Catholic Church today these ideas often seem too legalistic even to Catholics. But this concept of sin has a thousand-year history in Western Christianity. It is deeply ingrained in Protestant Christianity as well, as seen in the emphasis on Christ "paying the price" for sin, believers being "washed by the blood" of Christ, the idea that sin creates a penalty that must be paid, and so forth.

Of course, Orthodox Christians believe that Jesus Christ died for our sins, that His death was redemptive. But this is not the only way the Scriptures explain the death of Christ, and it is not what the early Church emphasized about it. Christ came for the life of the world (John 3:16), not to pay a price demanded by the Father, not because somehow the majesty of God was violated, and certainly not because an imbalance occurred in the universe that could be corrected only by payment in blood through the death of the Son. Those are distortions and exaggerations rooted in medieval thought. Christ sacrificed Himself out of love, not out of necessity. If anything is understood in Orthodoxy by the "blood," it is the union of the believer with Christ, sharing His life through the Body and Blood.

The early Church repeatedly emphasized the Incarnation of the Son as far more consequential than the Crucifixion. The Incarnation was the union of the human and the divine in Christ. Through this union within His Person, Jesus Christ sanctified human nature and made it possible for us once again to be united to God. After the cross came the Resurrection, and the gates of paradise were opened again for us. The cross is never separated from the Resurrection.

The Western Christian conception of sin as an offense against God that diminishes Him in some manner, or as a violation that must be paid for through the blood of Christ, through the merits of Christ and the saints, or through suffering during this life or after death in purgatory is totally foreign to the Orthodox Church and its phronema.

CHAPTER 4

The Orthodox Phronema

C HRISTIANITY EXISTS IN THOUSANDS OF varieties in the world, but it is the Orthodox who have preserved the ancient faith, practices, teachings, and traditions of the early Church deliberately and continually from the time of the apostles. Other Christians have elements of the early Church. Many have tried to incorporate what they perceive as early Christian faith and practice. But the Orthodox Church is historically and demonstrably the closest to the early Church in faith and practice because of our direct historical continuity with the ancient Church and our uncompromising adherence to its beliefs and way of life. This purposeful commitment to preserve Tradition, neither adding to it nor taking away from it, is what creates the unity of faith present in Orthodox Christianity.

The Timeless Quality of Orthodox Christianity

EXPLAINING HOW ORTHODOX CHRISTIANS THINK about the past, one scholar remarked that

> the past constantly flows towards the future and, in so doing, lives in the present. The past is not tidily compartmentalised and detached, as an object for disinterested study. This is not to deny the possibility of Orthodox Christians engaging professionally and seriously in historical study, even in the historical

study of Orthodoxy. Rather, it is to make a claim about the process of continuously appropriating the past that animates Orthodox theology.[1]

Two features make Orthodox unity of faith possible, both of which are related to our dedication to Tradition: (1) we possess the uniquely Orthodox phronema, and (2) we recognize the presence—or lack—of that phronema in others. Those who have an Orthodox phronema reject the behavior, writings, statements, and ideas of laity, clergy, and theologians who manifestly lack an Orthodox mind or spirit—even if such persons bear the name "Orthodox." Without an Orthodox phronema, one cannot truly express Orthodox Christianity. A strong and unified Orthodox theological mind actively practicing the faith protects, promotes, and supports the unity of the faith. It is not automatic. It happens neither by itself, nor because one is a member of the Orthodox Church, nor because one intellectually agrees with the tenets of Orthodox Christianity.

Looking at the outward form of the Orthodox Church, the West might be surprised at the claim of unity. The West often refers to the Orthodox Churches, rather than the Orthodox Church, but we are One Church. In terms of governance, Orthodoxy includes many jurisdictions. The Church consists of a number of self-governing (autocephalous) churches throughout the world, and at times these squabble among themselves. But in terms of the faith, there is only one Church, and the unity of the faith among the Orthodox is quite strong. Protestant Christians have no unity; Catholics have organizational unity through allegiance to Rome. But the Orthodox are united by a common faith, practice, and phronema rather than by a centralized authority.

Acquiring an Orthodox phronema is a tremendous challenge for converts. Those who are born into the faith and are steeped in Orthodoxy from the beginning of their lives ordinarily do not face the challenge of unlearning Western theological paradigms, explanations, thought patterns, and assumptions. However, attitudes among Orthodox Christians living in the West are

---

1   Augustine Casiday, "Church Fathers and the Shaping of Orthodox Theology," *The Cambridge Companion to Orthodox Christian Theology,* Mary B. Cunningham and Elizabeth Theokritoff, eds. (Cambridge: Cambridge University Press, 2008), 167.

increasingly influenced and shaped by our culture and secular education to such an extent that many cradle Orthodox clergy, faithful, and theologians today are influenced by Western phronema, often without realizing it. Their comments, concerns, and conclusions easily reveal the lack of an Orthodox phronema.

It is not surprising that Orthodox Christians would take on aspects of the phronema of Western culture, and this is not necessarily negative. We can have the phronema of an inquisitive Australian, a patriotic American, or an adventurous Canadian. But we must always carefully assess and evaluate whether we have adopted values that conflict with our Orthodox faith.

Lack of Centrality, Definitions, and Documents

EXPLAINING ORTHODOXY IS CHALLENGING DUE to its decentralized organization and lack of official documents and theological statements. The Western Christian mind is often uncomfortable with Orthodox phronema since it craves clarity, certainty, rationality, and definitions. The Orthodox approach appears imprecise and impossible to grasp.

Orthodox theologians do not have a body of official statements—similar to Vatican documents or Protestant confessional statements—that define the Orthodox Faith. We have no official (or even *unofficial*) catechism. No theological source or filter exists for interpreting the Fathers or the Scriptures other than one's phronema. There is no papacy or magisterium to make authoritative pronouncements. No ecclesiastical structures or external restraints direct the Orthodox theologian toward acceptable Orthodox theological conclusions. Nothing like an imprimatur exists to approve one's writings or officially recognize that a book presents acceptable Orthodox teaching. The Orthodox Church issues no documents or canons which demand that one submit in will and intellect to church teachings or to bishops.

The Orthodox Unity of the Faith

IT WOULD SEEM THAT WITHOUT such processes in place, the Orthodox would not be theologically unified. But in fact, Orthodox Christians have a much stronger theological unity than Catholics. To Catholic Christians, Orthodox unity is incomprehensible and appears impossible.[2] They assume that Orthodoxy is chaotic. How can the Orthodox maintain a visible jurisdictional disunity and yet insist that they are one Faith and one Church? Without direct authority from one source and one head making final decisions, how do the Orthodox know what to believe? Who is in charge? How are decisions made? How is discipline maintained? But all of this is achieved and understood innately by Orthodox Christians through our phronema, which is something that Catholics do not comprehend because they have never experienced it.

Avoiding Definitions

THE STRUGGLE IN THE WEST to understand Orthodoxy, and the compulsion to create Western categories to explain Orthodoxy, is seen in the recurring tendency among some Western Christians to point to so-called "symbolic books" of the Eastern Church, in particular Metropolitan of Kiev Peter Mogila's *Orthodox Confession,* as well as the statements of Patriarch Dosethios and the Decrees of the Council of Jerusalem in 1672. These statements appeal to Western Christians because they employ Western categories and are highly influenced by Western Christian thought.

As they search for something recognizable to explain Orthodoxy, it is difficult for non-Orthodox to believe that these "confessions" carry virtually no authority in Orthodox Christianity. Most Orthodox Christians have never heard of them; Orthodox theologians ignore them and never cite them as authority.[3] These statements are almost oddities and aberrations in Orthodox history. They are not authoritative in Orthodoxy, and their presentation of the Orthodox faith is unnatural, not only in terms of how they express concepts

---

2   This is particularly true when disputes arise between various Orthodox bishops over disciplinary or jurisdictional issues. This is when Catholics are most confident in their system and structure.

3   See Paul Ladouceur's discussion of various Orthodox theological statements and "confessions" made during encounters with the West in *Modern Orthodox Theology* (London: T & T Clark, 2019), 7–30.

but in terms of what they fail to state. Orthodox Christianity can never communicate itself to the West by using Western concepts, categories, and presumptions. And yet the West cannot understand Orthodoxy without placing Orthodox beliefs within those parameters.

A Western Christian may believe he or she understands the content of Orthodox doctrine, but without our phronema one cannot truly understand Orthodoxy. As shown in the previous chapter, even basic concepts such as sin and salvation are understood differently in Orthodoxy than in the West. Comparing statements of belief or even reading Orthodox theological books yields little deep insight into Orthodox Christianity.

Occasionally a question is posed to me that begins, "What is the official teaching of the Orthodox Church about . . . ?" Unless the answer can be given from the ecumenical councils or the Nicene Creed, a reply is nearly impossible, because the question itself presumes a Western ecclesiastical structure and mode of thought. A question about "official" Orthodoxy does not reflect our phronema—neither the way we think, theologize, nor operate as a Church.

The Nicene Creed is definitely an official statement of faith. But the Orthodox Church has almost no official theological statements other than the Nicene Creed,[4] the canons (which are ancient and sometimes contradictory), and the decisions of the seven ecumenical councils. Even when contemporary councils of bishops release statements or make decisions, these do not operate as official declarations as the term is understood or applied in the West, since they are not a mandate and they do not apply to the entire Orthodox Church. Conversely, and to further complicate matters, the fact that a teaching or practice is not formally expressed in canons or conciliar decisions does not mean that it is *not* universally acknowledged and accepted among Orthodox Christians.[5]

---

4 The Creed is not actually a "definition." In Greek it is called the "symbol" of the faith. It points to what God is but does not define God. Furthermore, formal doctrinal pronouncements such as the Creed and conciliar statements were concerned only with essentials. Meyendorff, 90. Meyendorff explains that "doctrinal definitions have a primarily negative role—that of preventing the spread of error—and that, in any case, their aim is not to exhaust the truth or freeze the teachings of the church into verbal formulae or systems but only to indicate the 'boundaries' of truth." Meyendorff, "Doing Theology," 89.

5 One example of this is the bodily assumption of the Virgin Mary. This is an extremely ancient tradition, well established and universally accepted among Orthodox

Consistent Use of Ancient Sources

To ANALYZE OR DISCUSS A theological question, an Orthodox theologian will turn first to the authority of ancient sources: scriptural, patristic, and canonical. Orthodox Christian scholars consistently cite ancient writings.[6] The difference in phronema between Orthodoxy and Western Christianity is quite obvious in this area. Catholics are oriented toward Vatican documents, but the Orthodox have no contemporary documents or statements that function in the same manner as Vatican documents do for Catholics. Nor do the Orthodox limit themselves, as Protestants do, to the Bible alone and how it has been interpreted through the lens of the Reformation or according to private opinion.

The Orthodox Church does not offer exact definitions and explanations for theological mysteries. The Orthodox Church has always preferred apophatic theology, that is, expressing what God is *not,* since God is beyond description.[7] Orthodox theologians know what they can speak of or write about and what they must not. They consistently cite the Holy Scriptures, the writings of the Church Fathers, the holy canons,[8] and the decisions of the ecumenical

---

Christians. However, it is not a dogma, and the Orthodox would not "define" it as an "official" teaching, if there even is such a thing in Orthodoxy.

6   They may also cite respected contemporary Orthodox theologians, if and because those theologians are faithful to the Tradition and reflect an Orthodox *phronema* in their life and work.

7   For example, God cannot be seen. He is *in*visible. He cannot be comprehended, so He is *in*comprehensible. God is not only beyond human words, He is beyond all human understanding. And yet, as a concession to our humanity, God condescends to our weakness by allowing Himself to be discussed and "described" using human language. Since God is beyond all human understanding, we prefer the language of negation.

8   The holy canons, which are sometimes referred to as "canon law," are not actually "law" for the Orthodox and do not function in the same way they do for the Catholic Church. They are not codified, organized, or systematized. Canons that have been superseded by a later council remain in the canonical collection. Dogmatic canons stand alongside disciplinary ones. An understanding of the function and application of the holy canons is difficult and requires an Orthodox education, phronema, and spiritual discernment. Dr. Lewis Patsavos, a professor and expert in the holy canons, observes that this is also an issue that inhibits Catholic understanding of the Orthodox canonical tradition. "This is precisely what the West finds hard to deal with in our canonical tradition, because they can't put their finger on it." "Salvation and the Free Life of the Spirit in the Orthodox Canonical Tradition," *Road to Emmaus* 14, no. 4 (2013): 3–35, 20.

councils. All of these are important aspects of Tradition and as such carry authority. This, in itself, creates our phronema. Since Orthodoxy does not routinely generate official and contemporary authoritative definitions and statements, Orthodox theologians turn again and again to the ancient sources.

Jaroslav Pelikan noted the surprising contrast between the attitude of Greeks toward their ordinary, even risky activities and their approach to theology. "Boldness to the point of rashness" was the attitude that "the Byzantines manifested as sailors and warriors when they ventured forth into the unknown." And yet, they showed tremendous restraint in matters of theology, revealing an "attitude of caution to the point of timidity about crossing the boundary lines of ancient religious tradition, whether liturgical or dogmatic."[9]

The timelessness of Tradition contributes to Orthodox theological unity because the sources are the same for all Orthodox theologians throughout the world, of every generation, time and again, now and in the past. Regardless of our era or culture, what we read, discuss, cite, and ponder is the same as what previous generations of Orthodox read, discussed, cited, and pondered.

Even when more recent luminaries are recognized as Fathers, such as St. John of Kronstadt (d. 1909), they are read, cited, and acknowledged as Fathers because they faithfully reflected the thought of earlier Fathers and did not deviate from the Tradition. When the writings of modern Orthodox theologians are read and quoted, it is not because they are offering something entirely new, innovative, or novel. Rather, it is because their comments accurately express Orthodox Tradition in a way that speaks to the present generation. Therefore, the Orthodox phronema is continually strengthened and reestablished, and that phronema is ancient, Eastern, and apostolic.

The Catholic Church creates new documents and periodically updates its Official Catechism and Code of Canon Law. New Protestant theologies and denominations are constantly emerging. But the Orthodox practice of turning primarily to Scripture and the Fathers automatically gives the Orthodox theologian a consistent orientation toward the early Church. This perspective is not mediated through a lens that changes with time or culture, by

---

9   Jaroslav Pelikan, *Credo* (New Haven: Yale University Press, 2003), 398.

someone's application of his personal logic, by attempts to conform to modernity, through devotion to a specific place (e.g., Rome), or through allegiance to a specific person or personality (e.g., the pope, John Calvin, Martin Luther, Ignatius of Loyola, John Wesley, Francis of Assisi, et al.). Constantly reading the same Scriptures and the same Fathers, praying the same way, and participating in the same Liturgy, sacraments, and feasts, over hundreds and hundreds of years, shapes the Orthodox phronema and creates a consistent mindset, orientation, and approach.

Holiness of Mind Rather Than Deductive Reasoning

ORTHODOX CHRISTIANITY DOES NOT USE deductive reasoning to defend or explain the faith, nor does it attempt to resolve conflicts between faith and reason. It does not modify the faith to conform to human thought or opinions. This should not be misunderstood: Orthodoxy does not reject the contribution of the human intellect, nor does it reject science or education. The Fathers of the Church were also rational in their arguments against heresy, but they did not rely on deductive reasoning to resolve theological questions. They discussed the importance of the human intellect in the comprehension of God. In fact, it is the intellect, or *nous*,[10] that is enlightened and can articulate theological truths, but not through deductive reasoning and scholarly study. Rather it is through prayer and one's relationship with God that the intellect achieves true enlightenment.

Holiness of mind is not contrary to the application of reason, which itself is God-given. Reason is part of the image of God within us; it is that which distinguishes the human person from animals. Indeed, the Orthodox Church often refers to the human person as "reason-endowed" because God gave us the capacity to reason. Reason can "help put words on the spiritual experience of proximity with the divine. In that sense, 'reason' and 'holiness' of mind are not opposite realities when reason is the ability to put words on the spiritual experience."[11]

---

10 The *nous* is that aspect of the human mind that has the capacity to contemplate God. This will be discussed further in chapter 5.

11 From personal correspondence. I am indebted to Fr. Neophytos Enkleistriotis for this

The human capacity for reason is to be distinguished from the application of deductive reasoning as a theological method. Human reasoning is part of the created order, which can never apprehend the uncreated nature of God, for He is radically dissimilar and is not part of the created order.

Because dialectical thought requires initial premises followed by the application of deductive human reasoning, the results achieved and the theological conclusions reached will vary, depending on the initial premise. The direct consequence of this method in the West is a much wider variety of theological views, whereas the avoidance of deductive reasoning has contributed to Orthodox theological unity. Although it is no longer applied in an extremely formal manner, nonetheless deductive reasoning remains operative in Western Christian theology, and arguments based on this methodology are quite striking and foreign to an Eastern Christian mind.

Philosophy is foundational and irreplaceable in Catholic theology, but Orthodox seminarians are not expected to know philosophy as a requirement for theological studies. Although the Greek Fathers were educated in philosophy and used philosophical terminology to articulate church doctrine, unlike Augustine they never felt compelled to use logic or deductive reasoning to defend or prove theological truths. They achieved a good balance by adapting philosophy for their use, neither rejecting philosophy entirely nor valuing it too highly.[12]

Over time, the preaching of the apostles was articulated and defined as dogma by the Fathers of the Church, but when they expressed the apostolic message, the Fathers themselves "theologized in the manner of the fishermen, not of Aristotle," wrote Gregory the Theologian.[13] They did not systematically ask questions and then methodically answer them with rational deduction to arrive at a theological opinion or conclusion. Saint Paul noted that the gospel does not comport with human reasoning when he reminded the Corinthians that he preached a crucified Messiah (1 Cor. 1:23–24). His

---

beautiful expression of the intersection of human reason and holiness of mind.

12 See Rico Vitz, "Orthodoxy, Philosophy and Ethics," *Theology and Philosophy in Eastern Orthodoxy*, Christoph Schneider, ed. (Eugene, OR: Pickwick Publications, 2019), 146.

13 *Or.* 23.12. *St. Gregory Nazianzus: Festal Orations*, Nonna Verna Harrison, trans., Popular Patristics Series, vol. 36 (Crestwood, NY: St. Vladimir's Seminary Press, 2008), 182.

extensive discussion on the weakness of human wisdom and the inherent conflict between human reasoning and the gospel continues to be embraced by the Orthodox phronema.

Ascent of Mind

ORTHODOX THEOLOGY IS INTELLECTUALLY CHALLENGING and satisfying, not in complexities of thought and categories nor in sophistication of expression, but because of the depth of the mystery to be plumbed. The study of Orthodox theology is a deeply spiritual experience as much as it is an intellectual one. Orthodox theology is patristic, and in spite of their advanced education, the Fathers of the Church rejected any hint of "epistemological elitism."[14]

The words used by the Fathers for increased knowledge of God are always words of ascent, *anabasis*, an upward movement of gradual understanding based on spiritual maturity. Theological insight results primarily from one's relationship with God, which, contrary to book learning, is open to all— clergy and laity, monastics and those living in the world, men and women, the highly educated and the uneducated. This does not mean, however, that Orthodox theology is anti-intellectual, only that the typical methodologies used by the sciences or social sciences, which have been adopted by many modern Christian theologians, cannot yield objective insight or truth about God. God can be known through His creation, but He cannot be understood or analyzed as though He were part of the created order, because He is uncreated and beyond human comprehension.

Christos Yannaras observes that the analytical methodology of the West is based on "man's claim by intellectual effort to secure mastery over the whole realm of accessible truth, and his tendency to define and distinguish the boundaries between man's capacities and the transcendent reality of God."[15]

---

14   K. M. George Kondothra, "Orthodox Theological Education: Some Historical Perspectives" (academic paper), Aug. 14–20, 1994, Fifth International Consultation of Orthodox Theological Schools, Halki, Turkey, 1–7, 5.

15   Christos Yannaras, "Orthodoxy and the West," *Orthodoxy: Life and Freedom*, A. J. Philippou, ed. (Oxford: Studion, 1973), 131.

Therefore, Western Christian theological methodology is fundamentally anthropocentric, "the disposition of man to master what truth is accessible to him and to master it as an individual." A boundary is set between the divine and human nature. The consequence of this is to neglect "the possibility of personal *participation* in, and not merely logical 'clarification' of, the divine truth concerning God." The difference is enormous.

Yannaras continues that in the Western scholastic tradition the human person "does not participate *personally* in the truth of the cosmos" or seek to "bring out the meaning, the *logos* of things, the disclosure of the personal activity of God."[16] God remains at a distance, but as St. Maximos the Confessor observed in a profound statement about the divergence between human thought and the nature of God, God is neither a "subject" nor an "object" to be "studied."

> Every concept involves those who think and what is thought, subject and object. But God is neither of those who think nor of what is thought for he is beyond them. Otherwise, he would be limited if as a thinker he stood in need of the relationship to what was thought or as an object of thought he would naturally lapse to the level of the subject thinking through a relationship. Thus there remains only the rejoinder that God can neither conceive nor be conceived but is beyond conception and being conceived. To conceive and to be conceived pertain by nature to those things which are secondary to him.[17]

Metropolitan Hierotheos Vlachos also noted the difference in process and perspective between Latin scholasticism and the patristic approach. He concluded that the emphasis on human reasoning led to the collapse of Western Christian theology.

> The scholastics first acknowledged God and then by rational arguments and logical categories they attempted to prove God's existence. In the Orthodox Church, as it has been expressed by the holy Fathers, we say that faith is God's

---

16 Yannaras, 131.
17 *Chapters on Knowledge* 2.2. *Maximos the Confessor: Selected Writings*, George C. Berthold, trans., Classics in Western Spirituality series (New York: Paulist, 1985), 148.

revelation to man. We accept the faith of the saints as we hear it, not so as to understand it afterwards, but in order that our hearts may be purified and we may arrive at the faith that comes from *theoria* and experience the revelation. Scholastic theology, however, accepted something first, then struggled to understand it through logical arguments. . . . Scholasticism linked theology with philosophy and especially with metaphysics. This resulted, on the one hand, in a distortion of the faith, and on the other hand in scholasticism falling into complete disrepute, when the world image of metaphysics which prevailed in the West collapsed.[18]

Human Reasoning and Theological Dialogue with the West

WESTERN CHRISTIANS HAVE NEVER UNDERSTOOD the Orthodox phronema, especially Orthodox insistence on preserving Tradition rather than depending on deductive human reasoning. This has resulted in significant frustration for Western Christians in theological discussions with the East. A thirteenth-century Catholic theologian, Humbert of Romans, said about the Greeks:

> They do not understand what is said to them with reasons, but always adhere to some councils or other, and to what has been handed down on to them by their predecessors, like some individual heretics, for whom reason is of no avail.[19]

Two centuries later, fundamental differences in phronema would again be an obstacle to union between the West and the East at the Council of Florence in 1439. Catholics presented rational arguments for their positions, and the Orthodox responded by citing apostolic Tradition. It was "the constant conviction of the Latins that they always won the disputation, and of the Greeks

---

18   Hierotheos Vlachos, *The Mind of the Orthodox Church* (*Ekklesia kai Ekklesiastiko Phronema*), Esther Williams, trans. (Levadia, Greece: Birth of the Theotokos Monastery, 1998 [2nd rev. trans., 3rd ed. of the Greek original, 2017]), 207. *Theoria* is spiritual insight granted by God by prayer and contemplation.
19   George Every, *Misunderstandings between East and West* (Richmond, VA: John Knox Press, 1966), 42, note 2, citing the second part of *Opus Tripartitum* by Humbert of Romans, in Peter Crabbe, *Concilia*, ii, 2nd ed. (Cologne, 1551), 993.

that no Latin argument ever touched the heart of the problem."[20] Even today, when Orthodox Christians reject Western Christian beliefs, it is because they violate apostolic Tradition, not because those teachings are irrational by some Orthodox standard of reason. But since Western Christianity considers its own theology unassailably rational, and presumes that faith must conform to human reason, often the only explanation they can imagine for Orthodox rejection of Western Christian doctrines is that the Orthodox are simply stubborn and obstinate.

Preservation of the Faith, Not Development of Doctrine

THE IDEA THAT A THEOLOGIAN can arrive at deeper truths or new truths is soundly rejected in Orthodoxy. From an Orthodox perspective, development of doctrine is a complete abandonment of apostolic Tradition because it suggests that what is believed, taught, and transmitted today differs from what was previously taught and believed. Orthodoxy holds that the fullness of the Faith was revealed to the Church at Pentecost, once and for all. The Greek Fathers utilized their education in the service of the Church to explain doctrine, not to find new truths, since the fullness of the truth was received at Pentecost.

The apostles had full knowledge of all truths and doctrines. These doctrines were known to the Church from the beginning. A certain amount of time was needed to find correct terminology and to specifically articulate difficult concepts, such as the Trinity. Explanations, definitions, and doctrinal articulations would not be considered a development. Theological definitions were declared only reluctantly by the Church, only if absolutely necessary, and only to the extent necessary to oppose specific heresies. The Orthodox object to the promulgation of entirely new doctrines about which the Fathers were silent, such as purgatory, the Immaculate Conception, and papal infallibility on the Catholic side, and sola scriptura, the rapture, and "once saved, always saved" on the Protestant side.

The very essence of Tradition is to preserve what the apostles taught.

---

20   Every, *Misunderstandings*, 42–43.

Dogmas of the Church are not to be expanded, regardless of how rational or obvious a concept may seem according to an individual's human reasoning. Human reasoning cannot be employed to arrive at theological truth since it is inconsistent, unreliable, and differs from person to person. Furthermore, the mind is limited and fallible. The writings of the Fathers of the Church are not simply revered guideposts or reference points; they intimately shape our thought, establish our methodology, confirm our personal limitations and sinfulness, and remind us of the extent to which we can actually discuss God.

Western theologians who disagree with aspects of their church's teaching or practice mostly remain dedicated to their particular church with a hope and expectation that they can influence it, change it, or reform it. By contrast, the true Orthodox theologian does not try to change, develop, or improve the Orthodox Church but seeks to conform his own mind to the mind of Christ and the Church, to achieve a deeper understanding of what has already been received.

Orthodoxy manifests a unique cultural expression in different countries, but the faith is the same. The Orthodox theologian reflects on the Tradition, presents it in a manner that speaks to the culture, and adopts appropriate elements of the culture, but keeps, protects, and preserves the apostolic Tradition.

Authority and Tradition in Orthodoxy

AUTHORITY IN ORTHODOX CHRISTIANITY IS often said to reside in Scripture and Tradition. Scripture is actually the written deposit and expression of Tradition. Protestants reject Tradition because they associate it with Catholicism. They rarely recognize that they have created, enshrined, and virtually dogmatized their own traditions, beliefs, and phronema, which are not necessarily ancient or apostolic. Catholics are confident that they have apostolic Tradition because Rome possesses it. But Tradition is neither possessed by any single see nor guaranteed by any one see or person.

A Catholic seminarian recently said to me, "The Orthodox follow Tradition for the sake of Tradition." Another remarked, "The Orthodox are devoted to beauty, but Rome is devoted to truth." Such comments reflect a Western misconception that we love ritual for ritual's sake or Tradition for Tradition's sake, that preserving Tradition is the goal in itself rather than being the means by which we preserve the truth that guides us to salvation.

These misperceptions are not entirely surprising, since Western Christians do not understand how Tradition functions for the Orthodox. For Catholics, truth is guaranteed by union with Rome. For Protestants, truth is guaranteed by nothing more than their own interpretation of the Bible. But from an Orthodox perspective, Tradition itself functions as the authority. It is the locus, depository, standard, and guarantor of truth because it is the preservation of apostolic teaching unchanged. It does not depend on any particular era, council, or episcopal see, or any one person's insight or interpretation of the Bible. Tradition includes many elements—Scripture, canons, Fathers, councils, and an entire way of life. We are confident in Tradition because of our unwavering devotion to preserving apostolic teaching unchanged.

Sin, Salvation, and Legalism

A SPIRIT OF LEGALISM IS foreign to the Orthodox phronema, especially with respect to sin and our relationship to God. For the Orthodox, sin indicates spiritual illness. The imagery used of salvation is medical. A common title for Christ in Orthodox prayers is "the One who loves mankind" (*Philanthropos*). He is also often described as the "Physician of our souls and bodies." His Incarnation restored our relationship with God by restoring fallen humanity to physical, mental, and spiritual health and wholeness.

Nothing could be further from Anselm of Canterbury's explanation of why God became man. Anselm's landmark work, *Cur Deus Homo* (*Why God Became Man*, c. 1094), became the primary model for understanding sin and salvation in Western Christianity, and it remains so today after nearly a thousand years.

Anselm began with the presumption that God is just and sin is an offense against God that demands punishment. Humans commit the sins, so a human must pay the penalty. However, no human is able to pay such a huge penalty. Only God could possibly pay such a high price. Therefore, God had to become man. God was incarnate in the person of Jesus Christ in order to die on the cross and satisfy divine justice. This view, commonly known as "substitutionary atonement," has deep roots and is accepted in some form by most Western Christians.

The broad acceptance of Anselm's logic speaks to the extreme legalism and the radical departure from apostolic Tradition that had developed in the medieval West. It is ironic that Anselm's conclusion was so readily accepted in the West. The Catholic Church affirms the development of doctrine and holds that medieval and scholastic theologians understood the faith and expressed its concepts in a manner superior to that of the Fathers. And yet Anselm's theology is crude, faulty, shallow, simplistic, and manifestly inferior to the understanding of salvation among the Church Fathers. It can hardly be considered superior to or an improvement on their work.

Saint Gregory (Nazianzen) the Theologian addressed such impoverished reasoning centuries before Anselm's time and easily destroyed it with his analysis:

> To whom was the blood poured out for us, and why was it poured out, that great and renowned blood of God, who is both high priest and victim? For we were held in bondage by the Evil One, sold under sin, and received pleasure in exchange for evil. But if the ransom is not given to anyone except the one holding us in bondage, I ask to whom this was paid and for what cause? If to the Evil One, what an outrage! For the robber would receive not only a ransom from God, but God himself as a ransom. . . . But if it was given to the Father, in the first place, how? For we were not conquered by him. And secondly, on what principle would the blood of the Only-Begotten delight the Father, who would not receive Isaac, when he was offered by his father but switched the sacrifice, giving a ram in place of the reason-endowed victim? It is clear that the Father accepts him, though he neither asked for this nor needed it, because of the divine plan and because the human being must be sanctified by the humanity of God, that God himself might set us free and conquer the tyrant by force.[21]

Metropolitan Vlachos accurately assesses the fundamental theological flaw in Anselm's theory when he points out that this view in fact makes God "subject

---

21 *Or.* 45.22. *St. Gregory Nazianzus: Festal Orations*, 182.

to the laws of necessity." God therefore *"requires* the satisfaction and propitiation . . . thus, the purpose of the incarnation of the Word and His sacrifice on the Cross was the propitiation of divine justice, which was offended by man's sin."[22] He continues to remark that not only is this *invalid* from an Orthodox perspective, but it can even be considered *heretical*, a point of view that would certainly surprise Western Christians, since this theory is so widely accepted.[23]

This view of sin and salvation is rejected by Orthodox Christianity because, among other things, it suggests that *God* is the problem, not humanity. God by nature is free of any necessity or self-interest. Without question, the death of Christ on the cross was a sacrifice and redemption for the human race. But that is only one model by which we understand the entire Divine Economy (plan of salvation). The imagery has limitations and must not be overemphasized or distorted to the extent that it perverts our understanding of God, the purpose of the Incarnation, and the meaning of the cross. The death of Christ on the cross was not transactional, nor demanded by the Father, nor necessary to satisfy divine justice.

Furthermore, such language is unworthy of God and even blasphemous because it lowers God to the level of sinful humanity. Scriptural language is still human language, which is always inadequate to describe God. Terms such as *redemption* and *propitiation* must be understood according to apostolic Tradition and early Church phronema, not from the perspective of medieval legalism. Metropolitan Vlachos explains why this portrayal of God is so disturbing from an Orthodox perspective:

> It is sinful to ascribe to God the characteristic features of fallen man by alleging, for example, that God is angry and vengeful, and therefore He must be propitiated and appeased. Such an attitude wants to make it appear that it is *God* Who needs curing, and not man. But this is sacrilegious. The sinful man, who is characterized by egoism and arrogance, is offended. We cannot say that God is offended. . . . Consequently, sin is not an insult to *God*, Who must be cured, but our own illness, and therefore *we* need to be cured.[24]

---

22 Vlachos, *Mind of the Orthodox Church*, 173–74. Emphasis added.
23 Vlachos, 174.
24 Vlachos, 174. Emphasis added.

Humans Cannot Affect God

According to Catholic doctrine, sin offends God, disrupts the moral order, and deprives God of His glory and majesty. Punishment for the sin restores order and the glory of God.[25] Many Protestants have a similar view of sin as primarily an offense against God which requires some payment or punishment.

But Vlachos notes that according to the Holy Fathers, no one can harm God, nor make Him shine more brightly, nor affect His "majesty," to use Catholic terminology. He does not require anything because of our sin. The Incarnation, Crucifixion, and Resurrection reconcile man to God, not God to man.

The difference in outlook is immense. God never departs from us. It is we who depart from Him. It is we who become spiritually ill through sin. It is we who need to be cured and restored. The Orthodox view is that "by his sacrifice on the Cross Christ did not propitiate his Father, but he cured the ailing nature of man."[26]

Anselm's view distorts the entire Trinity and the plan of salvation. The inadequacy of this theology was brilliantly deconstructed by Vladimir Lossky, whose analysis reveals why this opinion results in other problems that manifest themselves in Western Christian theology:

> Christian horizons are limited by the drama played between God, who is infinitely offended by sin, and man, who is unable to satisfy the impossible demands of vindictive justice. The drama finds its resolution in the death of Christ, the Son of God who has become man in order to substitute Himself for us and pay our debt to divine justice. What becomes of the dispensation of the Holy Spirit here? His part is reduced to that of an auxiliary, an assistant in redemption, causing us to receive Christ's expiated merit. . . . The price of our redemption having been paid in the death of Christ, the resurrection and the ascension are only a glorious happy end of his work, a kind of apotheosis

---

25 Pope Paul VI, *Indulgentiarum Doctrina* 1.2.5. "These punishments are imposed by the just and merciful judgment of God for the purification of souls, the defense of the sanctity of the moral order and the restoration of the glory of God to its full majesty."

26 Vlachos, *Mind of the Orthodox Church*, 176.

without direct relationship to our human destiny. This redemptionist theology, placing all the emphasis on the passion, seems to take no interest in the triumph of Christ over death. The very work of the Christ-Redeemer, to which this theology is confined, seems to be truncated, impoverished, reduced to a change of the divine attitude toward fallen men, unrelated to the nature of humanity.[27]

The Orthodox view of sin and salvation, fundamentally different from that of Western Christianity, is the result of an entirely different phronema. Occasionally, Western Christians visiting an Orthodox Church are put off by the constant repetition of the phrase "Lord, have mercy." It reminds them of the Western Christian notion of a fearsome, judgmental God who demands satisfaction for the offense of sin, to which our response is to cower in fear and plead for mercy. But in Orthodoxy, the request for mercy is medical; it follows the biblical example of people who encountered Christ during His earthly ministry and asked for healing.[28] Sin is consistently understood as illness of the soul. This is reflected in the doxology that is sung prior to every Divine Liturgy: "I said, Lord, have mercy on me. *Heal* my soul, for I have sinned against you."

The West gradually changed its phronema to adopt a legalistic framework for salvation. Orthodox Christianity's fidelity to Tradition maintained the original biblical and patristic understanding of both sin and salvation, in which the emphasis is not on a transaction—Christ paying for our sins by His blood or us restoring the appropriate majesty to God—but on the healing and sanctifying effects of His Incarnation, Crucifixion, and Resurrection.

---

27 Vladimir Lossky, *In the Image and Likeness of God*, John Erickson and Thomas Bird, eds. (Crestwood, NY: St. Vladimir's Seminary Press, 1974), 99.

28 "Have mercy on us, Son of David!" was the cry of two blind men (Matt. 9:27). The Canaanite woman cried out on behalf of her daughter, "Have mercy on me, Lord" (Matt. 15:22), and a father said, "Lord, have mercy on my son" (Matt. 17:15). See also Matt. 20:30–31, Mark 10:47–48, Luke 17:13; 18:38–39. There are other examples as well.

CHAPTER 5

Acquiring an Orthodox Phronema

The Nous and Knowledge of God

But I, brethren, could not address you as spiritual men, but as men of the flesh, as babes in Christ. I fed you with milk, not solid food; for you were not ready for it; and even yet you are not ready, for you are still of the flesh. (1 Cor. 3:1–3)

S AINT PAUL WANTED TO DISCUSS advanced spiritual matters with the Corinthians, but he was able to address them only on an elementary level, since they lacked the proper phronema. They did *not* lack the intellectual capacity or the ability to *reason*. Rather, their low level of spirituality inhibited their comprehension of divine truths. They lacked the necessary phronema, since they were not spiritual but "of the flesh."

How does one acquire an Orthodox phronema, and what does it mean to have it? It is to have "the mind of Christ," which is also the mind of the Church, since the Church is the Body of Christ. This means that one is essentially living a spiritual life. The opposite of a spiritual life is a life of the flesh, of the world, a secular life, in which one adopts the manner of life and manner of thought of "the world."[1] Saint Paul encouraged Christians to have

---

1   "The world" in this sense simply denotes that which is opposed to Christ, the realm of sin and darkness. God made the world, and all of creation and humanity are essentially good. However, the terms "world" and "flesh" are commonly used to signify that which is opposed to God and the spiritual life, since Christ Himself used "world" in that manner. For example, see John 8:23, 15:18–19, 16:33, 17:16.

"the mind of Christ" (1 Cor. 2:16), for which he used the Greek word *nous*.

The term *nous* (rhymes with "juice") is important in Orthodox spirituality and the Fathers. *Nous* originally referred simply to the intellect, the means by which one could apprehend truth. In the New Testament, St. Paul often used *nous* in its ordinary Greek cultural sense of "mind." The Fathers of the Church also used the word *nous* and other terms from Greek culture and philosophy; however, through their use in the Church, these terms acquired a specific Christian meaning. Among the Fathers, *nous* became a theological "term of art"—in other words, it has a specific and specialized meaning.

Nous has been defined and described in various ways. In Orthodox theology, nous refers not to the rational operation of the mind but to that part of the soul that allows the human person to know God, "the purest part of the soul, the eye of the soul."[2] "Man has two centers of knowing: the *nous*, which is the appropriate organ for receiving the revelation of God that is later put into words through the reason, and the reason which knows the sensible world around us."[3]

The Fathers frequently referred to the nous, and it has a very specific role in theology according to their experience and understanding. The Fathers rejected the idea that one could acquire knowledge of God by discursive reasoning (*dianoia*). True knowledge of God is gained through purification of the intellect (nous), and this comes about only with prayer. A famous statement known to all Orthodox theologians is, "The true theologian is one who prays." A purified intellect grows in its knowledge of God through spiritual experience, not through dialectical reasoning, application of philosophical techniques, or the acquisition of mental skills. "The knowledge of reason is consequently of lower order than spiritual knowledge, apprehension or perception [of divine truth], which is the function of the intellect [nous] and is beyond the scope of reason."[4]

---

2   Vlachos, *Mind of the Orthodox Church*, 247.

3   Hierotheos Vlachos, *The Person in Orthodox Tradition*, trans. Effie Mavromichali (Levadia, Greece: Monastery of the Birth of the Theotokos, 1994), 24.

4   *Philokalia: The Complete Text* (3 vols.), trans. and ed. G.E.H. Palmer, Philip Sherrard and Kallistos Ware, Bishop of Diocleia (London: Faber and Faber, 1979), 1:363.

The Nous, the Holy Spirit, and Illumination

A FULL DISCUSSION OF THE concept of *nous* is outside the scope of this book. In brief, the nous is not a "thing" that exists within you but the capacity to know God, to have a relationship with God. All human beings possess the capacity to know God as part of our human nature, since we were created for that purpose. As a result of the Fall, however, the nous was darkened. Through illumination of the nous we can know God and achieve *theosis*, or union with God.

From the earliest years of the Church, and still today in the Orthodox Tradition, Holy Baptism is called "Holy Illumination." It marks the beginning of the process to restore our ability to know God and our relationship with God. At baptism and chrismation we receive the Holy Spirit. As the Spirit lives and works within us, we grow in our capacity to know God. We do not acquire true knowledge of God intellectually or through mental concepts but by direct experience, which occurs through participation in divine grace. By using the term *nous* to describe this capacity of the mind, the Fathers *specifically distinguished* it from the process of rational thought, which is what we typically consider to be the function of the mind.

As mentioned in the discussion of phronema in chapter 2, St. Paul uses *phronema* in Romans 8:5 to explain that "those who live according to the flesh set their minds on the things of the flesh, but those who live according to the Spirit set their minds on the things of the Spirit." Therefore, to have the mind of Christ and the mind of the Church is to live a life directed by the Spirit. Before Christ ascended, He did not give us Scriptures, canons, doctrines, rules, or definitions. He bestowed the Holy Spirit on the Eleven in the Upper Room (John 20:22) and later sent the Holy Spirit to the entire Church at Pentecost (Acts 2). The Holy Spirit illuminates, sanctifies, and actualizes the life in Christ. As we participate fully in the life of the Church, we acquire an Orthodox phronema, a mind shaped not by the world but by the Spirit.

[Phronema] in the biblical and patristic tradition means the whole way of thinking which prevails in someone from the way in which he lives, and from the relationship which he has with God. And literally, if the *nous* is darkened, then the whole mind is carnal. But if the *nous* is illuminated, which means that it has the Holy Spirit within it, then the whole mind is a mind of spirit and, of course, a mind of the Church.[5]

Baptism does not guarantee illumination of the *nous*. One can receive the Holy Spirit in baptism and chrismation and still live a carnal life, even if one has virtues. "Carnality, according to the teaching of the Apostle Paul, does not refer to a category of 'bodily' sins, but the whole life of the human being who is not inspired by the Holy Spirit."[6] Having an Orthodox phronema, the mind of the Church, is inextricably bound to participation in the life of the Church in its *totality*. Since one's phronema reflects the totality of one's life, one cannot intellectually learn or be taught how to *think* Orthodox or how to *be* Orthodox. It is an attitude, mentality, perspective, a desire, an orientation that governs one's entire way of life. This can only be acquired organically and gradually over time by active and full engagement in the life of the Church.

Effort Required for Growth in Phronema

AN ORTHODOX PHRONEMA FORMS AS one is illuminated and guided by the Holy Spirit. This also requires a conscious and sustained effort on the part of the individual. Acquiring phronema is not simply a matter of studying theology, standing in Church, or saying one's prayers in a mechanical manner. We may initially begin to perform these actions in a routine manner, but they must eventually become united with the soul and truly an organic part of our general orientation toward life, toward others and the world—just as prayer also begins with the lips but must enter into the heart to truly become noetic ["of the nous"] prayer, the "prayer of the heart."

Consider what was necessary for each of us to mature from a newborn infant into a fully functional adult. As newborns we knew and understood nothing. But gradually over the course of time, we came to understand the world around us, through experimentation and observation (touching,

---

5   Vlachos, *Mind of the Orthodox Church*, 126.
6   Vlachos, 125.

tasting, smelling, dropping, observing), through effort (turning over, crawling, walking, riding a bike), through education (phonetic sounds, the alphabet, learning to count), through socialization (siblings, cousins, neighborhood children, the classroom, groups of friends, dating, etc.). Slowly we all learned to function and navigate in our family, our society, and the world at large. We learned what worked and what did not work. We learned the rules, spoken and unspoken. We learned what is expected of us, what is acceptable, and when we had crossed the line.

This is not dissimilar to what is needed to acquire an Orthodox phronema. Our understanding will improve, deepen, and continually grow. As mature adults we never stop learning, and we still make missteps. Likewise, our understanding of Orthodoxy will perpetually deepen and increase as long as we continue to pray, study, and practice our Orthodox faith with humility. But we must *all* begin as infants in the faith, whether or not we were Orthodox in our physical infancy.

Many cradle Orthodox Christians unfortunately do not realize that they have remained infants in the faith in spite of spending a lifetime as Orthodox Christians. They have no greater understanding or experience of God nor any deeper faith than they had as children, because for them Orthodoxy has been reduced to a series of practices or obligations rather than embraced as a complete life in Christ animated by the Holy Spirit.

Our relationship with God must be an ongoing, never-ending process of growth. Therefore, we must never think that we have arrived—finally—at an Orthodox phronema to the extent that we no longer need to examine ourselves, our behavior, and our attitudes. We live in this world, and we are constantly assaulted by the values, images, and ideas of this world, which can easily creep into our minds and affect our phronema. This is a danger not only for ordinary laypeople but also for theologians, priests, bishops, and monastics, who can also become corrupted. A previously illuminated nous can become darkened again.[7]

---

7   St. Symeon the New Theologian had experienced the Uncreated Light (a direct experience of God) at a very young age, even before he had become a monk. But as he continued his life in the world, he became lax and insensitive to God. He experienced the Uncreated Light again later in his life after he had become a monk. (See chapter 6.)

Therefore, we must remain vigilant in our spiritual lives and regularly ask ourselves whether our thoughts and actions reflect the mind of the Church and of Christ or whether they reflect the mind of the world. Acquiring an Orthodox phronema is not a passive process, just as salvation requires active engagement and struggle. Great effort is required, and we must fight to attain it. "To him who conquers I will grant to eat of the tree of life, which is in the paradise of God" (Rev. 2:7).

Spiritual Warfare

WE ARE LARGELY UNAWARE OF the impact that marketing and advertising techniques have on our consumer behavior: labels, graphics, colors, product placement, commercial tunes, product sponsorships, and other factors influence us. We easily recall songs, commercial jingles, and slogans from decades ago, as well as catch phrases from old television programs and favorite lines from movies. Constant exposure to the general culture shapes us. There is no doubt: we *have* acquired the *world's* phronema. Music, movies, television, social media, education, workplace, friends, activities, and a thousand other influences are continually at work on us. Today many people cannot allow a half hour to elapse without checking their cell phones for messages, news, and social media postings. Is this not affecting our minds and our values? How different would our phronema be if we said a prayer every few minutes rather than checking emails or our phones? How can we possibly acquire the mind of Christ, an Orthodox phronema, in the midst of this overwhelming assault by the world?

The power and influence of the world and the extreme depth of its reach are far worse today than ever before. Radio, television, and the internet have brought the world's phronema into our very homes twenty-four hours a day. Previously, exposure to the values of the world was limited to certain activities and a certain number of hours per day, such as television viewing in the evening. But cell phones and other personal devices have virtually taken us prisoners, or, more accurately, we have willingly surrendered ourselves to these devices. They besiege us and capture our attention countless times daily.

We must not passively accept this as "the way things are" but mount a resistance and counterassault. We must engage in spiritual warfare. An invasion is taking place, more serious than any invasion of migrants streaming across borders. An infiltration of the mind and soul is occurring, more dangerous than any political ideology or religious extremism. It is a rapidly spreading contagion far more consequential than any germ, microbe, or virus. All worldly threats recede in the face of the greatest risk of all: the death of the soul and the loss of eternal salvation. By succumbing to the world and its enticements, we are turning away from Christ. But we can emerge victorious by fighting back, by aligning ourselves with Christ and the saints, by refusing to retreat or surrender to the world, through a determined and resolute effort to conform ourselves to Christ, who assured us, "Be of good cheer, I have overcome the world" (John 16:33).

Practical Advice

WE CAN SUCCESSFULLY FIGHT THE influence of the world and attain an Orthodox phronema by immersing ourselves in the totality of the life of the Church.

> The life of the Church is assimilated and known only through life—not in the abstract, not in a rational way. If one must nevertheless apply concepts of the life of the Church, the most appropriate concepts would be not juridical and archeological ones but biological and aesthetic ones.... The Orthodox taste, the Orthodox temper is *felt* but is not subject to arithmetical calculation. Orthodoxy is *shown*, not proved. This is why there is only one way to understand Orthodoxy: through direct Orthodox experience.... To become Orthodox it is necessary to immerse oneself all at once in the very element of Orthodoxy, to begin living in an Orthodox way. There is no other way.[8]

Many elements of Orthodox life shape our phronema, including church attendance, receiving the Holy Mysteries, prayer and spiritual direction,

---

8   Pavel Florensky, *The Pillar and Ground of the Truth: An Essay in Orthodox Theodicy and Twelve Letters*, Boris Jakim, trans. (Princeton: Princeton University Press, 1997), 8–9.

reading Scripture and spiritual books, observing the feasts and fasts of the Church, practicing virtue, and observance of many seemingly inconsequential little things.

THE LITURGICAL LIFE AND THE HOLY MYSTERIES

THE LITURGICAL LIFE IS CRUCIAL in shaping an Orthodox mind, not simply by attendance but by active participation, through chanting, singing, following the divine services closely, and praying the prayers. One should attend not only the Sunday Divine Liturgy, but also liturgies for feast days of the Lord, the Theotokos, and the saints, Matins and Vespers services, as well as other services such as the Salutations (Akathist) or the Paraklesis (Consolation) as much as possible. An active and deeply engaged liturgical life is especially important for anyone who is seeking to truly become Orthodox in mind and heart.

Initial acceptance into the Church through Baptism or Holy Chrismation only commences the process to acquire the mind of Christ and the Church. As we pray the prayers and hymns of the Church, our minds are shaped and formed to conform to an Orthodox way of thinking. The hymns and prayers express Orthodox theology and spirituality. As we learn them, sing them, and recite them, they become part of who we are. The prayers heal our souls, reorient our minds, and illuminate the nous. By participating in liturgical prayer, we attract the grace of the Holy Spirit and sanctify ourselves in ways that we do not even realize. Just as we are oblivious to the influence of the culture around us and yet we unconsciously absorb it, the same effect occurs in church. When we participate in liturgical worship, we also join the communion of the saints and the angels in the Kingdom of heaven.

How does church attendance create an Orthodox mind? We become what we think, hear, and see. Billions of dollars are spent on advertising and marketing for this reason. A myriad of influences assaults us and shapes us subconsciously from the moment we are born in order to form a particular worldview. However, we can counteract this influence considerably by a conscious effort to acquire an Orthodox phronema. The more frequently we engage in liturgical prayer, the sooner and more deeply we illuminate our minds and conform them to the mind of Christ. The same hymns and prayers have been sung and recited for hundreds of years, and "the fixed character of our liturgical texts means that they are spiritually and theologically dependable. . . . We are not singing anyone's new opinion or idea. We're singing words that have been tried and tested as true."[9]

The Holy Mysteries (sacraments) of the Church also shape us, especially those of Communion and Confession. All the sacraments assist our efforts toward sanctification; however, nothing greater exists than to unite ourselves physically to the Body and Blood of Christ. If we wish to acquire the mind of Christ, we should certainly recognize the benefit of being united to Christ physically, spiritually, and sacramentally through the Mystery of Holy Communion.

We must be careful, of course, to prepare ourselves by fasting, by arriving at the Liturgy on time, by active participation in the service, by forgiving others, by avoiding impure and hateful thoughts, and by attending to the many other factors that influence how the sacrament affects us. We must not receive Holy Communion at all times or in every condition since, as the communion prayers teach us, we can receive the sacrament to our judgment or condemnation if we receive unworthily or without preparation.

Holy Confession not only benefits us in the obvious way, by granting forgiveness of sins, but it is of the greatest usefulness in shaping an Orthodox phronema. Those who have never confessed or rarely confess their sins to a priest cannot acquire an Orthodox phronema. To reject Holy Confession reveals an attitude of pride, ignorance, and the unwillingness to humble oneself before God. To reject confession is to reject the experience of the saints and the two-thousand-year-old teaching of the Church. How can one acquire the mind of Christ when one rejects this important sacrament? To believe that confession is unnecessary reveals an attitude of arrogance entirely incompatible with an Orthodox phronema.

---

9   Peter Bouteneff, *Sweeter Than Honey: Orthodox Thinking on Dogma and Truth* (Crestwood, NY: St. Vladimir's Seminary Press, 2006), 163.

Various excuses are raised by those who reject confession. They may believe that they have done nothing requiring confession; that it is enough to confess to God privately before the icons; that the priest will think less of them when he hears their confession; or that the priest will reveal the content of their confession to others. In every case the excuse reveals a worldly phronema and a nous that fails to recognize those excuses as temptations and tricks of the evil one to keep us away from the grace of Holy Confession and to deprive us of salvation.

Confession is also extremely useful because it prompts us regularly to make an honest self-assessment and to humble ourselves before another human being, even though the priest reminds us that we are not confessing to *him* but to *Christ*. Confession leads us to be more careful and conscious of our words, actions, choices, and relationships. It motivates us to remedy our faults and shortcomings. It helps us to avoid sin and harmful situations by acting as a deterrent when we realize, as we contemplate committing a sin, that we will have to confess that sin later. We receive important guidance from the priest, who gives us an unbiased and spiritual perspective on our life. If there is no salvation without humility and repentance, there is certainly no Orthodox phronema without those qualities and without confession.

SCRIPTURE AND SPIRITUAL READING

READING THE HOLY SCRIPTURES, THE lives of the saints, and books on subjects such as virtue or prayer is very important for shaping our Orthodox phronema. Reading the lives of the saints is especially effective because the stories are inspirational, easy to understand, and easy to remember, and they teach us by example how to orient our minds toward Christ. Works of the Fathers on prayer and the spiritual life are very useful. Theological treatises are probably less useful, especially at the beginning of one's journey toward an Orthodox phronema.

Bible reading also aids our salvation. Orthodoxy has always encouraged Scripture reading for all Christians. When the Faith was brought to a new country, translating the Divine Liturgy and the Scriptures into the language of the people was always a priority. Saint John Chrysostom in particular repeatedly encouraged his fourth-century congregation to read the Scriptures, frequently comparing the Bible to a gold mine containing great treasure or a medicine chest that could cure any ailment.[10]

We should not be intimidated by the Bible. The Old Testament can be difficult to understand, but it is not necessary to read the entire Bible if one finds that too daunting. It is perfectly acceptable to read only the New Testament and the Psalms and to skip difficult books such as Revelation or Leviticus. We should not worry if we do not understand everything we read, because we will understand most of it, and we will derive much benefit from it.

Saint John Chrysostom said that Scripture reading attracts the grace of the Spirit. It certainly shapes our phronema. Some Orthodox Christians are already very familiar with the Bible. For those who were raised as Protestants, understanding the Bible as an Orthodox Christian will require some adjustment and patience. Books and podcasts can help us acquire an Orthodox phronema of the Bible. An Orthodox understanding will gradually replace a previous Western approach.

The Fathers often advocated singing of psalms. Chrysostom challenged his congregation because most of them could not recite even a single psalm, and yet they knew countless worldly songs, including immoral ones.[11] His congregation claimed they did not have time to read the Scriptures, but he replied that they made time for other pursuits.[12] Books were extremely expensive in Chrysostom's time, yet he did not accept the high cost of books as an excuse for not purchasing a Gospel and reading the Scriptures daily.[13] How can we excuse ourselves today, when Bibles are inexpensive, free online, and available on our cell phones and through podcasts? Let us attract the grace of the Spirit[14] by reading the Scriptures and singing psalms.

---

10   As a treasure (*Homilies on Genesis* 3.1, 5.1, 8.3), a gold mine (*Homilies on Genesis* 21.2), and as a medicine chest (*Homilies on Colossians* 9). These are only three examples of many metaphors used by St. John Chrysostom to describe the benefits of Scripture reading.
11   Chrysostom, *Homilies on Colossians,* Homily 9.
12   Chrysostom, *Homilies on John,* Homily 58.
13   Chrysostom, *Homilies on John,* Homily 11.
14   Chrysostom, *Homilies on John,* Homily 32.

THE FEASTS

OUR ORTHODOX PHRONEMA IS ALSO strongly shaped by observing the feasts and fasts of the Church. By orienting ourselves to the liturgical cycle, we acquire the mind of the Church. We look forward to certain feast days. The hymns of the Church announce that a feast is coming, and sometimes we prepare with a fast prior to its arrival. After the feast has passed, the hymns remind us of what took place. On the day of the feast and during a festal period, the hymns explain the theological and spiritual meaning of the event. This is why attendance at church for the feast days is so important: participation in feast days forms us by continually teaching and shaping us.

The life of the Church is not a dead remembrance of past events. Again and again in our prayers and hymns we use the word "today." "*Today* the Virgin goes to the cave to give birth . . . ," "*Today* the Jordan is turned back . . . ," "*Today* is hung upon the Cross . . . ," and so forth. We never say "Christ has risen" or "Christ was born," but "Christ *is* risen!" "Christ *is* born!" These are never past events; they happen *today* for each of us because we experience them in the present as a living reality, and through them we participate in eternity.

In the course of the ecclesiastical year, we relive the lives of Christ, the Theotokos, and the saints. The same liturgical and festal cycle is repeated year after year after year, as it has been for hundreds of years. As we participate fully in the life of the Church through the feasts, slowly our minds and hearts are shaped. We orient our minds to the mind of the Church and our lives to the life of the Church as one festal period ends and another is anticipated. Over the course of time this creates an Orthodox phronema.

The outside world has its calendar, celebrations, and schedule. We live our lives mostly in the secular world, which has its own routine for job, school, family responsibilities, social and civic expectations, and a myriad of other worldly distractions. But the Church's festal cycle is like a parallel universe that exists alongside life in this world. When we periodically step into it, we join eternity and the kingdom of heaven. Through the festal cycle of the church year, we both participate in and anticipate the life to come. The more frequently we do this, the more we shape our phronema.

THE FASTS AND ASKESIS

ALONG WITH THE FEASTS COME the fasts. Fasting has always been part of the Christian life, and those who practice it know its usefulness, not as an exercise in itself but as a part of *askesis*. Our English word *ascetic* comes from the Greek word *askesis* (AH-skee-cease), which literally means "struggle." In practical terms, ascetic exercises are activities of self-control designed to master the body and bring it under the control or subjection of the soul.

How can *askesis* possibly aid the pursuit of theology and an Orthodox phronema? Both theology and phronema are ultimately knowledge of God gained through spiritual experience, not through the exercise of the mind. Fasting and ascetic exercises help heal the soul and illuminate the nous. It is not sufficient only to think about or intellectually learn about the faith. Orthodox theology and life are distorted, ineffectual, and impoverished if they are divorced from the ascetic efforts that heal the soul. Everything in the Church, whether icons, theology, music, sacraments, or liturgics, has as its purpose the upward ascent toward stages of spiritual purification, illumination, and deification.

Although it is important to learn about Orthodoxy, we must take care not to focus merely on intellectually understanding our faith and practices while ignoring the spiritual healing the Church offers. Thinking about, rationalizing, reasoning about God are mental activities divorced from the ascetic life, which is designed to heal the soul. "It's not that we suspend our rational minds—not at all. . . . But the way that truth is sought and engaged with is not through detachment but through a living relationship of faith and love with the object we seek."[15] The Church is a hospital for souls, a very common image among the Fathers, who recognized that everything in the Church is designed to heal the soul and lead it to purification, illumination, and finally deification. Without the recognition that spiritual healing is the goal of everything we do, we derive no profit, no benefit. It is not enough to revive the liturgical life without the ascetic life. Orthodox life without askesis is secular, because it is divorced from spiritual struggle and improvement.

---

15   Bouteneff, *Sweeter Than Honey*, 36.

PRAYER

PRAYER IS ESSENTIAL TO OUR relationship with God and should be part of our daily routine. All Orthodox Christians should know the basic set of Trisagion prayers[16] as well as morning, evening, and mealtime prayers. They are easy to memorize if we pray them regularly. Many Orthodox prayer books are available that contain these and other prayers, such as prayers to the Theotokos, your guardian angel, and your patron saint, and prayers for specific situations or circumstances. Every Orthodox Christian should have a prayer book and his or her own personal rule of prayer. The Jesus Prayer is the cornerstone of Orthodox spirituality and should be incorporated into our daily life. Exactly what your rule of prayer consists of should be determined by your spiritual father or parish priest, because he knows your circumstances and can guide you appropriately.

SPIRITUAL DIRECTION

DEVELOPING AN ORTHODOX PHRONEMA ALSO requires spiritual direction. Orthodox Christians should have a spiritual father or father confessor. This can be, and ideally should be, your parish priest, but it can also be another Orthodox priest, preferably in your area. A spiritual father is like a doctor for your soul. He is the one who cares for your spiritual health and provides advice and guidance for your spiritual life. We also discuss personal problems with our spiritual fathers, since every aspect of life in this world can affect our spiritual life and our salvation.

If you do not have a specific spiritual father, this does not mean that you should not go to confession. Most Orthodox priests will hear confessions, and anyone can usually confess to any Orthodox priest. They have different styles, and all priests are not equally effective as spiritual guides, but this should not be an excuse to reject confession. The grace we receive from confession does not depend on the interpersonal skills or the personal holiness of the priest. The Lord always forgives our sins through the Mystery of Holy Confession if we are truly repentant and have not concealed any sin.

---

16   "Holy God, Holy Mighty, Holy Immortal . . . , All Holy Trinity . . . , Our Father . . ."

The choice of a spiritual father is a very personal one and a serious decision. When we place ourselves under the direction of a spiritual father, we submit to that priest and are to be obedient to him. This is the Orthodox tradition. This seems very strange to worldly people, but obedience is an important virtue and essential for acquiring humility.

Generally speaking, the relationship between a spiritual father and spiritual child is close and very precious. A spiritual father is more experienced in the spiritual life, and he offers knowledge and a perspective you do not have. He knows your life circumstances, what you are able to do, what you are ready to hear, what you are ready to receive, and what you "cannot bear" at the moment (John 16:12). You may be requesting meat, but he will know if you are capable only of digesting milk, as St. Paul told the Corinthians (1 Cor. 3:1–2). The spiritual father can assess your life and your spiritual situation objectively. What may seem like a good idea or a decision you are convinced is the will of God for your life may in fact be quite harmful to you.

The evil one employs thousands of treacherous and deceptive techniques. He often uses our good intentions and our godly motives against us, tempting us by what seems to be good and manipulating us to take actions that ultimately harm ourselves and others. It is axiomatic in Orthodoxy that we are never to rely on ourselves. Avoiding the evil one's traps requires experience, discernment, and especially a trustworthy spiritual guide.

On the other hand, obedience is not stupidity. In rare cases, spiritual directors have abused their positions of authority to ask for money or to seek a sexual relationship. One should *never* submit to such things as a matter of "obedience." This is a serious warning sign, and one should flee from such a priest at the slightest hint of anything inappropriate.

Another misuse of the role of a spiritual father is to encourage or demand a cult-like obedience. This is also *not* Orthodox. Unfortunately, cultish Orthodoxy occurs among those who misunderstand the virtue of obedience and the true role of a spiritual father. In cult-like parishes, parishioners are expected to conform to a specific lifestyle and even to obtain approval from the parish priest for ordinary life decisions. "A spiritual father must never see himself as one who issues edicts, but as one who leads the layperson given to his care by

God; he leads by word and deed."[17] Occasionally, guidance in everyday matters might be needed, but ordinarily a parish priest or spiritual father directs our *spiritual* life. It is *not* Orthodox for a parish priest to dictate or direct every detail of one's daily life. A parish priest or spiritual father who expects to control every detail of your life is falling into error, even if he is a devoted pastor and well intentioned. That level of involvement is appropriate for spiritual fathers providing spiritual direction to *monks,* but not for a parish priest giving spiritual direction to people in the world.

FALSE PIETY AND FEIGNED HUMILITY

EXTREME PRACTICES AND BEHAVIORS CAN easily develop among those who are enthusiastic for the Orthodox Faith. Exaggerations and distortions develop out of piety and a sincere desire to fully embrace Orthodoxy. The desire is well intentioned but misinformed. Piety and virtue should be manifested as a natural expression of spiritual growth from within—or better yet, they should be hidden altogether. But instead, some Orthodox Christians adopt certain external characteristics to imitate the way they perceive a true Orthodox Christian should look or behave. For example, a man might grow a beard, or a woman might wear only ankle-length skirts. This author has even known Orthodox Christians who advocate specific mannerisms, such as always looking down because downcast eyes are a sign of humility. This is actually quite *un*-Orthodox and unhealthy because it is a pretense and false humility, which is a sin. If one avoided eye contact because one possessed *actual* humility, this would *not* be inappropriate. But *imitating* that behavior artificially in order to feign virtue is exactly the type of behavior the Lord condemned as hypocrisy among the Pharisees (Matt. 23:5). Likewise, adopting a certain manner of dress out of modesty is quite different from adopting it because one is trying to look Orthodox. It is better to lack a virtue and work to acquire it than to pretend to possess it, especially when the purpose is to be admired or accepted by others through a false display. True Orthodox

---

17 Alexey Young, "Obedience and the Layman," *Obedience* (Brookline, MA: Holy Cross Orthodox Press, 1984), 44.

spirituality encourages us to hide our virtues. This is Orthodox, and this is biblical (Matt. 6:1–6).

APPROPRIATE LIFESTYLE

MISCONCEPTIONS OF A TRUE ORTHODOX lifestyle usually develop when well-intentioned Orthodox Christians read spiritual books and attempt to apply Orthodox practices in the wrong way or in the wrong circumstances. Many classic Orthodox spiritual books, such as *The Ladder of Divine Ascent*,[18] were written by and for monastics. Orthodox Christian spirituality is essentially monastic because it is essentially ascetic. Orthodox spirituality is the same for everyone in the Church, but the *degree* to which we engage in certain spiritual practices *differs* depending on our spiritual level and whether we are monastics or live in the world.

The Orthodox Church has no monastic orders or different styles of spirituality. Orthodoxy has one form of monasticism and one spirituality. Monastics have committed their entire lives to prayer and the monastic lifestyle. The rest of us practice the same spirituality but to a lesser degree. We have many daily responsibilities and commitments in the world. It is improper and even harmful for those of us in the world to attempt to apply the lifestyle and spiritual practices intended for monks.

Virtually every aspect of a monastic's life is controlled by the monastery's way of life: the schedule, the diet, the work and daily tasks, and so on. Monasteries are governed by community rules and rules of prayer. Monastics receive direction from the abbot or spiritual father on a daily basis. But that is the *monastic* way of life, and it is not appropriate for those living in the world. We have spouses, children, jobs, homes, parents, errands, property, possessions, contracts, business trips, mortgages, and other obligations monastics do not have. It is entirely inappropriate for a married person in the world to try to live like a monk, just as it would be inappropriate for a monk to adopt the lifestyle of a person in the world. In both cases, adopting

---

18 This classic of Orthodox spirituality, written by St. John Climacus, describes stages of spiritual perfection.

a lifestyle unsuitable to their vocation is unnatural and harmful, not helpful.

Monastic spirituality is the ideal spirituality of the Orthodox Church, but it is modified and adjusted for those of us living in the world. The extent to which we adopt certain spiritual practices is highly dependent on our specific life circumstances and our spiritual abilities. This is why the guidance of a spiritual father is important. There are no rules that apply to everyone, no "one size fits all" in Orthodoxy.

Sometimes people assume that the best spiritual father is a monk. But this is not necessarily true, because a monk does not live in the world and may have little experience with the challenges faced by people in the world. Your own parish priest can be just as effective and is more easily consulted for guidance than a monk in a distant location. Sometimes, out of embarrassment, people want to go to a monastery and confess to a hieromonk (a priest-monk) whom they have never met. But would they seek out a doctor whom they had never met and knew nothing about, consult him only once, and never intend to return for any follow-up? It is best to find a priest in your area with whom you can have an ongoing relationship. Confession is not simply stating our sins but receiving spiritual guidance for our improvement over the course of our lives.

THE DANGER OF EXTREMISM

INSTRUCTIONS INTENDED FOR MONKS CAN be inappropriate advice for people in the world, as noted above. Failure to recognize our limitations—in our lives, our roles, our spiritual abilities—is a distortion of Orthodoxy and can result in serious spiritual problems. It can actually lead to the loss of our salvation or that of others.

On the other hand, we must not fall into the opposite temptation and ignore the tools the Church gives us for our salvation, excusing ourselves on the basis that we are not monks. "I do not need to go to confession." "I do not need to read the Bible." "I do not need to go to church every Sunday." "I do not need to fast." "None of this applies to me, because I am not a monk." This thinking is also to be rejected. Orthodox Christians in the world attend the same services and engage in the same spiritual practices as monastics but to a lesser degree. We actually need these tools *more* than monks do, but we should neither attempt to live like monks, nor should we use our life in the world as an excuse not to pray, fast, go to church, read the Bible, or receive spiritual direction.

GOOD DEEDS AND VIRTUE

THE PRACTICE OF VIRTUE IS a cornerstone of the Christian life, not because we earn our salvation through good deeds but because virtue is connected to our union with Christ. The Lord often spoke of the importance of virtues such as meekness, purity of heart, forgiveness, mercy, love, and humility. Atheists can also have these characteristics, but the behavior has a different meaning and a different context than when that same virtue is manifest in a Christian. Without Christ, it is not a spiritual virtue, and since it does not come from a nous illuminated by God, it does not have the same effect.

Just as we do not teach an abstract theology attained by knowledge or reason, true virtue likewise cannot be divorced from its source: Christ. Saint Gregory the Theologian said that if you wish to become a theologian, you must keep the commandments.[19] Virtue is manifest when one thinks and acts in a particular way because one is united to Christ.[20]

Virtue requires effort and struggle. If we have certain virtues as part of our natural disposition (for example, if we are naturally patient), that is not admirable, nor does it result in any reward from God. Saint John Chrysostom explains that virtues which come naturally to a person are not truly virtues because they did not require any effort to acquire.[21] Virtue is the fruit of askesis, spiritual struggle.

After a particularly difficult bout fighting against many demons, St. Anthony complained to the Lord. He had felt abandoned, and after the struggle was over he asked Christ, "Where were You?" The Lord replied, "I was

---

19 *Or.* 20.12.
20 Vlachos, *Mind of the Orthodox Church*, 132. As Met. Hierotheos astutely observes: "In the Church we do not believe in abstract values and ideas, but in virtues which are fruits of the Holy Spirit and an experience of the uncreated energy of God because love, peace, righteousness, and so on are natural or essential energies of God."
21 Chrysostom, *Homilies on John*, Homily 36.2.

here, Anthony, but I wanted to watch your struggle."[22] We acquire virtues through struggle to overcome temptations. This is what is praiseworthy and helps us become Godlike.

LITTLE THINGS

ATTENDANCE AT WEEKDAY DIVINE LITURGIES and other services has diminished significantly in many parishes. Church attendance is not a priority for most Orthodox Christians today in the same way that it was for our Orthodox ancestors. Churches were once packed for services such as the Friday night Lenten Akathist hymn, the Presanctified Divine Liturgy, or the parish feast day. It was understood and expected that nearly everyone would travel to a neighboring parish to celebrate that parish's feast day. Parishioners frequently asked for prayers to be said over them while they knelt under the priest's stole. They requested house blessings or asked the priest to meet them at the cemetery to say prayers over a grave or to come to their home for a service of Holy Unction.

Why are these actions much less common today when they were so common among the cradle Orthodox of the past? Are we busier than they were? Do we know more than they did? Or is it that we no longer sense a need for God and do not understand the importance of these practices? It is certainly the latter. These actions, devotions, and gestures were so entrenched in the lives of our Orthodox ancestors that they did not have to think about how to be Orthodox or what they should do. They never felt the need to read a book like this one. Their Orthodoxy was deeply embedded in their identity, manifested daily in their habits and lifestyle. We must not underestimate the extent to which little customs shaped previous generations' phronema. Some actions were performed daily and others only on special occasions during the year. But they were meaningful, reliable, consistent, a predictable part of life.

In countless little ways, Orthodox Christians still create and maintain an Orthodox phronema on a daily basis. They keep holy water in their houses and

---

22   Athanasius the Great, *Life of Antony,* 10. *Athanasius. Life of Antony and Letter to Marcellinus,* Robert Gregg, trans. (New York: Paulist Press, 1980), 39.

drink it when they need a blessing. They ask the priest to bless their homes, cars, farms, and businesses. They remember those who have fallen asleep, pray for them, make boiled wheat (*kolyva*), and regularly have memorial services for the departed. They make the sign of the cross as they leave home in the morning and as they pass by a church. They make and bring offering bread (*prosforon*) to the church with a list of names for the priest to commemorate, as well as sweet bread (*artoklasia*) for the five-loaves service to celebrate the name day of a family member. They remember feast days and name days and call their friends to wish them many years on their feast day. They pray daily before the icons in their home and before meals.

They keep their home free of immoral books, programs, and foul language. Their house is indeed a little church in which the entire family is on the journey of salvation together. They encourage each other, help each other, and remind each other about the life in Christ. They embrace the life in Christ all day, every day, not as a list of chores or deeds to be accomplished but as a natural part of daily life. In traditional Orthodox countries, the general culture supports, or at least is not hostile toward, Orthodox phronema. But in other countries, Orthodox Christians are usually a tiny minority in a sea of other religious traditions. Acquiring and maintaining our Orthodox phronema in a very pluralistic society is much more difficult and requires real effort and dedication.

Orthodoxy in Life, Not Theological Knowledge

ORTHODOXY WAS PART OF THE daily routine for those who came before us in the faith. It was not confined to Sunday liturgy and having icons in their homes. Most of our Orthodox ancestors never read a book on theology nor any writings of the Fathers. They did not have the vocabulary to explain the theology of the Church, but they knew it in the depths of their being because they *lived* it. Every village in Orthodox countries has a patron saint. Familiar stories of countless miracles great and small are told and retold. Accounts of local martyrs, healings, blessings, appearances of angels and saints are commonplace and accepted as an ordinary part of life, not as strange events only read about in books. Saints and angels are not relegated to the past or to the old country. Those of us in the New World also have many such experiences as the faithful still regularly call upon the Theotokos, angels, and the saints, who respond to their prayer requests.

Orthodoxy is a living reality deeply embedded in Orthodox countries. Some Orthodox people perform certain actions out of superstition. But superstition is a sin, and Orthodox practices should never be observed out of superstition or treated as if they were magic. On the other hand, some practices of cradle Orthodox may seem more like folklore traditions or superstitions to those of us in the West, but if carried out with an Orthodox phronema, these small actions hold great meaning that is unappreciated by those who approach everything intellectually.

The piety and faith of ordinary people is often quite extraordinary. They are spiritually impressive, while outwardly they seem quite normal and unimpressive, like treasures in earthen vessels. I have encountered many examples of this in my lifetime: ordinary Orthodox Christians who have humbled and amazed me with their extraordinary faith, piety, and spiritual depth. Sometimes they have achieved what the rest of us would deem impossible. They faced starvation, massacre, religious persecution, war, deprivations, and hardships unimaginable to most of us. They survived and thrived often against unbelievable odds, even building churches, shrines, and monasteries that we, with our knowledge and expertise, would have never attempted because we lacked the faith and conviction that God would make the impossible a reality. They experience many miracles, have encounters with angels, and enjoy real relationships with saints.

Not all cradle Orthodox are pious, but I would caution Orthodox converts not to be dismissive of cradle Orthodox who seem simple or intellectually uneducated in their faith. They have much to teach us all. Faith and phronema are not a matter of book learning but of *living*. I have often been impressed by people who could barely read and yet had a depth of faith, piety, and an Orthodox phronema that I—with all my education—can only hope to attain.

AVOIDING SELF-RIGHTEOUSNESS AND HYPOCRISY

ORTHODOX CHRISTIANS CAN EASILY DEVELOP an attitude of self-righteousness by carefully observing an Orthodox lifestyle, creating a false sense of security or accomplishment. Now they have found the True Faith and believe they know exactly what to do. But Orthodox Christianity requires a willingness to accept mystery, paradox, and uncertainty, and to relinquish any sense of control. Instead, we must accept that we cannot understand mystery. Everything is paradox, and we throw ourselves upon the mercy of God.

We must recognize that we are undeserving of anything at all, even of salvation itself. The Scriptures contain many promises of salvation. These promises are our hope but not our certainty. They motivate us, but no formula or observance of rules can guarantee our personal salvation. Orthodox Christians know and affirm that God is in control of everything in the universe, where not even a hair on our heads remains uncounted. Christ saved all humankind once and forever. We know that God desires all people "to be saved and to come to knowledge of the truth" (1 Tim. 2:4). But we can claim nothing for ourselves, and we should anticipate only the struggle for sanctification for our entire lives. This life is the life of the arena, where we contend with the principalities and powers of darkness (Eph. 6:12). Our task is to rely on God and to seek Him continually. Like the repentant thief on the cross, in a moment we can be saved (Luke 23:42), but in a moment we can also lose our salvation.

Orthodox Christians are vulnerable to the danger of hypocrisy and self-righteousness because we emphasize the importance of fasting, prostrations, the rule of prayer, and various behaviors or actions. We can delude ourselves into thinking we have arrived because we manifest all the outward signs and have done all the right things, while in fact we are far from God. The Lord warned us: "On that day many will say to me, 'Lord, Lord, did we not prophesy in your name, and cast out demons in your name, and do many mighty works in your name?' And then will I declare to them, 'I never knew you; depart from me, you evildoers'" (Matt. 7:22–23). Orthodox Christians should always remember the icon of the Ladder of Divine Ascent, which is placed before us on the Fourth Sunday of Great Lent and serves as a sober warning. As high as we might ascend spiritually, we can instantly fall from the highest rungs of the ladder, not only through our deeds but more likely through the wrong attitude, a wrong phronema.

In some cases, a type of Ortho-fundamentalism develops in which the purpose of spiritual or ascetic practices is entirely forgotten. We can become self-satisfied, like the Pharisee in the parable (Luke 18:9–14), because we believe we are doing everything we should do: "I accept the correct doctrines, I receive Holy Communion weekly, I go to confession, I wear a beard/cover my head, I keep all the fasts perfectly, my parish is genuinely Orthodox since my priest wears a cassock everywhere," and so forth. With such an attitude, Christ is forgotten. If we focus on completing behaviors without the proper inner disposition, we can fall into pride, condemnation of others, and self-righteousness. We cannot hope to have a healthy relationship with God nor even hope to be saved without humility.

AVOIDING LEGALISM

CONVERTS TO ORTHODOXY ARE PARTICULARLY vulnerable to the need to create a sense of control, safety, and certainty. A tendency to define, delineate, and create specific structures and rules is inherent in the Western mentality. This goes hand in hand with the desire to rationally explain and understand. But that attitude distorts the Orthodox phronema. Some Orthodox Christians enthusiastically embrace actions they believe are "required," but the observance of these practices can be inherently un-Orthodox if it is devoid of an Orthodox phronema. It is not uncommon for new Orthodox Christians simply to replace a Protestant or Catholic set of requirements or expectations with a new, but Orthodox, set of rules. The West employs formulas, lists, and definitions for beliefs, procedures, and even for salvation itself. Observing Orthodox practices is no more a guarantee of salvation than abiding by all the decisions of the pope and the magisterium, or speaking in tongues, or saying the "sinner's prayer" and acknowledging Jesus Christ as your personal Lord and Savior.

Adhering to Orthodox practices to the letter is legalism, and legalism distorts the entire spiritual life. True Orthodoxy is devoid of a spirit of legalism. As St. Paul wrote, "The letter kills but the spirit gives life" (2 Cor. 3:6 [NKJV]). Some Orthodox Christians mistakenly equate Orthodoxy with being conservative, unyielding, and rigid. Their legalism, which they perceive as a badge of honor, is actually pride. In their minds, they (and their group) alone are *truly*

Orthodox. They are models of Orthodoxy, superior to others in their scrupulosity. But to think like this is to become like the Pharisees, who believed themselves to be superior to others based on their exact adherence to the Law of Moses. The Lord condemned them for self-righteousness, for hypocrisy, and for "straining out a gnat and swallowing a camel" (Matt. 23:24)—observing external regulations exactly while overlooking much more important matters. This should be a sobering reminder that Orthodoxy is not rigidity. It is not "conservative" but *traditional*.

> Conservatism retains the ossified forms of the past, estranged from life, while tradition, having life and experiencing it, conveys it in forms of the present. Thus it is by nature impossible to connect and identify the Orthodox Church with legalism, which does not presuppose the existence and experience of true life. . . . Law is the will of God and legalism is living by the letter of the law, estranged from the spirit of the law.[23]

The practices of Orthodox life—icons, prayers, feasts, fasts, services—are tools intended to shape a correct phronema, not idols or ideals to be achieved as ends in themselves. Once we have become proud of our fasting, our prostrations, or our phronema itself, we have lost whatever we had hoped to gain. These practices are not virtues but exercises designed to assist our spiritual healing. If we observe them in a fundamentalist manner—as an obligation, a goal, as proof of one's Orthodoxy—whatever spiritual value they may have offered is lost.

Our goal is union with God, which comes through sanctification. The first step toward that goal is the denial of the self. This is not a false humility, pretentious posturing, or a playing-the-martyr mentality, but an honest recognition that we are far from God, that we are spiritually sick and require healing. The paradox is that the closer we come to God, the farther away He seems, as we become more acutely aware of our own sinfulness. And yet God is not far from us but within us, intimately connected to us, our very breath and our very life.

---

23   Vlachos, *Mind of the Orthodox Church*, 169–70.

Freedom and Obedience

ORTHODOX CHRISTIANITY IS FUNDAMENTALLY ABOUT freedom in Christ. The Orthodox understanding of freedom is difficult to discuss or describe, since it does not conform to what the world usually means by the term *freedom*. It does not mean to be governed by one's own will or opinion. True freedom is only found in a relationship with God.

Converts to Orthodox Christianity at times find themselves falling into a rule-oriented mentality or becoming compulsive about doing things in a specific way. They sincerely wish to be Orthodox and acquire an Orthodox phronema. This is wonderful and admirable, but they must remind themselves that obsession with rules is *not* Orthodox. We should have devotion but not obsession. The fruits of the Holy Spirit are peace and joy, not anxiety and stress. The heart of Orthodoxy is freedom, not slavery to laws and rules.

Freedom does not mean that we do as we please or that there is no effort involved. Freedom means that we are not slaves. Demands are not made of us, and the same expectations do not apply to everyone. This is why, for example, we do not apply the holy canons as laws, imposing the same expectations on everyone. This is why people in the world are not expected to behave like monastics.

I attended an all-girl Catholic high school. As morning announcements were being made over the intercom, we sometimes heard the stern voice of our religion teacher, Sister Fay, booming through the classrooms and hallways: "Girls, tomorrow is a *holy day of obligation*." I had never heard such a term before attending Catholic school, but I realized that it meant Catholics were required to attend Mass. The Orthodox do not use that type of language, nor do we have such a concept in Orthodoxy. Nothing is described as an "obligation." You are *invited* to attend the Liturgy, you *ought* to attend the Liturgy, but consent and obedience are never *demanded* or *obligated*.

Obedience is very important in Orthodox Christianity. The difference between obligation and obedience is more than mere semantics. An *obligation* is imposed on us, but *obedience*, as the Church uses and understands that term, is self-chosen. In the world, one can coerce or compel obedience, but that is sinful. The Greek word for "obedience" is *hypakoe*. It comes from the root word *akouo* ("to hear"). The relationship between hearing and obedience is clear in the Scriptures: one obeys when one hears the word of God and does it. This is different from *hypotassomai*, "to submit." The root of this word is *tasso*, which means "to order" or "to appoint." The Greek prefix *hypo-* means "under." Thus *hypotasso* ("I submit") was used to convey subordination to parents, to authorities, of slaves to masters; it generally suggests "giving precedence to others." Christ does not ask us to submit to Him, but to hear Him and to do or to keep His words.

Orthodoxy never equates obedience with compulsion. An Orthodox Christian freely chooses to be obedient to the Tradition, to observe its way of life. The Orthodox Christian freely chooses to be obedient to a spiritual father, to place himself or herself under his direction. The spiritual father applies the appropriate remedies for spiritual healing for that particular individual, just as a doctor would consider the individual health of each patient. Our relationship to God, the Church, and our spiritual father is based on free will.

John McGuckin expressed how the Orthodox firmly adhere to Tradition and yet maintain a strong sense of freedom.

> It is at once a wonderful thing and yet a historical burden, to have such a profoundly ancient heritage to sustain. Outside observers, noting this aspect of the Orthodox Church, have often found it difficult to assess, or understand. It is more clear to the Orthodox themselves: how at one and the same moment they know themselves to be bound to numerous standards, and canons, and authorities and yet at the same time completely free.[24]

The spirit of Orthodoxy is essentially relaxed because we are free. If we experience stress in attempting to live our lives in the Church, something is wrong. At an Ancient Faith Women's Retreat, Molly Sabourin eloquently

---

24   John McGuckin, *The Orthodox Church* (West Sussex, UK: Wiley-Blackwell, 2011), 248. The faithful experience a similar sense of freedom in the relationship between the laity and their hierarchs. "This is a spirit which has given to the Orthodox a general freedom from subservience (even to the highest leaders of the churches) while at the same time having a profound sense of respect for the leaders and teachers of the faith." McGuckin's observation is correct. The Orthodox do not experience ecclesiastical authority as a heavy weight imposed upon them from the top.

described her struggle to find balance in her life as a young wife, mother, blogger, and author, attempting to accomplish her checklist of spiritual activities along with her other duties. She put time and effort into prayer, fasting, Bible reading, and so on. When she accomplished what she had set out to do, it fed her pride, which is opposite to the goal of our spiritual efforts. On other occasions she was not able to do what she knew she ought to do, and then she felt guilty. The stress she imposed on herself because she had not been able to accomplish her spiritual rule for that day led to anxiety, which is also not the purpose of our spiritual disciplines. Molly explained that she vacillated "between guilt and pride" until she realized that the activities our Church prescribes are not an obligation but a "gift to lead you to [spiritual] health."[25]

Spiritual practices and disciplines such as fasting, our rule of prayer, or attending the divine services are useful, but if we allow them to become stressful, we must examine our attitude. God desires our effort and our love. He wishes to see us struggle and strive. He wants us to come to Him with a "broken spirit, a broken and contrite heart" (Ps. 50/51:17). But God does not demand perfection, nor does He demand obedience. Saint John Chrysostom's analysis of the sacrifice of Cain is very instructive on this point: Cain's offering was rejected by God because he did not offer his sacrifice out of love but out of obligation.[26]

Slipping Up and Backsliding

ALL OF US WILL FAIL. All of us will fall. Repeatedly. The greatest threat to our salvation is not falling but a lack of humility. After recognizing that we have spoken, thought, or behaved in an unchristian manner, we must repent of this, contemplate how we erred, and then correct and reorient ourselves toward the truth. The more frequently we assess and reorient ourselves, the more strongly we reinforce our Orthodox phronema. Initially, this will require consistent, strong, and conscious effort. The fact that we are Orthodox, attend

25 Molly Sabourin, "Filled with Less" (oral presentation), November 15, 2019, Ancient Faith Women's Retreat, Antiochian Village, Ligonier, PA, https://www.ancientfaith.com/specials/the_ancient_faith_womens_retreat_2019/filled_with_less.
26 John Chrysostom, *Homilies on Genesis*, Homily 18.17–22, FOTC 82:13–17.

church, receive the Mysteries, and so forth, does not mean that we are firmly and safely Orthodox in both mind and heart.

Father John Whiteford offered a useful analogy when he explained the difficulty of abandoning residual patterns and habits even after we have willingly adopted Orthodox Christianity. He compared it to changing from one style of martial arts to another, from Tae Kwon Do to Kung Fu:

> The problem was that many of the stances and forms, as well as punches and kicks were very similar—but just different enough to make it very difficult to learn to do it the Kung Fu way. But when it came time to put these techniques into practice—when we sparred—this problem became even more apparent. With time, many of these converts learned to do the stances and forms correctly (though the Tae Kwon Do influence could still be seen at times) but when they would spar—many of them would spar as if they had never studied Kung Fu at all. . . . The reason these people reverted back to Tae Kwon Do while sparring is simple—when you're sparring, you've got to think and act fast, and Tae Kwon Do was *what came natural to them*—in fact it was preventing them from arriving at the point at which Kung Fu would become natural, and so until they could come to the point at which they would lay aside their Tae Kwon Do techniques—little progress in Kung Fu could possibly be made.[27]

This is an excellent analogy, because it demonstrates with a physical comparison what happens to us mentally when we have become accustomed to thinking one way and then decide to change. A pianist rarely makes an effort to memorize a piece of music. The memory comes by itself after hours of practice. The pianist does not consciously think about what notes to play. The fingers automatically go to where they have been trained by practice. Likewise, the Western mind has been trained by years of instruction, reading, and practice to think in one way. But Orthodoxy is fundamentally different from Western Christian thought and the thought of the world. We must be retrained, and we must accept, with humility, that we may revert at times to what is not

---

27   Fr. John Whiteford, "The Orthodox Mind" (oral presentation), July 1995, Southwest
      Missions Conference, Dallas, TX, http://www.orthodox.net/articles/orthodox-mind
      .html. Emphasis added.

Orthodox but is familiar and habitual. We must continually check and reevaluate ourselves.

Not only converts but all of us are susceptible to reversion because we are socialized, educated, and live in a Western cultural framework. We can also revert back to the wrong phronema in a more serious and unconscious manner as we become more experienced and educated about Orthodoxy, because we can fall into pride. We have been Orthodox for years. We are pleased with our accomplishments. We believe that we know better than others, including the priest, bishops, and theologians, and we believe that we are surpassing others with our progress. We do not even realize that when such a thought comes to our mind, it painfully reveals that we are not Orthodox at all.

We revert when we subconsciously believe, or we behave as though, we are earning our salvation. We revert when we are performing actions outwardly—such as observing the fasts, going to church, and so forth—but inwardly our mind does not have the right disposition, or these practices have not changed us at all. We observe an Orthodox lifestyle as an obligation, or our devotion has become lukewarm indifference. We have reverted if we convince ourselves that simply by applying our minds we can find logical, rational, or scientific explanations to biblical conundrums that will satisfy modern sensibilities. We have reverted if we approach salvation as an intellectual matter rather than as a healing of the soul, of inner transformation. We have reverted when we forget that we are called to "be transformed by the renewal of your mind" (Rom. 12:2).

PART II

Orthodox Theology and the Shaping of Phronema

CHAPTER 6

Theology and the Theologian

What Is Theology?

THE WORD THEOLOGY (THEOLOGIA) LITERALLY means "talking or teaching about God." It also denotes a "mystical knowledge" of God.[1] The same word functions as a verb in Greek: "I theologize" (*theologeo*),[2] meaning, "I pronounce words about God" or "I speak about God." When a person teaches about God, speaks about God, speaks *to* God in prayer, or in general speaks about or discusses divine truths, he or she is "theologizing." The Incarnation— the union of the two natures, divine and human, in the one person of Jesus Christ—makes possible our union as limited, mortal, fleshy human beings with the incomprehensible, immortal, eternal, spiritual Divine. Thus, "the source of true Christian theology is the confession of the Incarnation of the Son of God."[3]

The Holy Fathers used the term "theologian" (*theologos*) to refer to those who spoke about God, the Fathers who had preceded them,[4] and a variety of other figures who preached or taught about God, including David, the prophets,

---

1 Lampe, *Patristic Greek Lexicon*, 627. Pronounced "theh-oh-loh-GHEE-ah."
2 Lampe, 626–27. Pronounced "theh-oh-loh-GHEH-oh."
3 Vladimir Lossky, *Orthodox Theology: An Introduction* (Crestwood, NY: St. Vladimir's Seminary Press, 1978), 34.
4 For example, Gregory Palamas referred to St. John Chrysostom as "theologian" when he quoted Chrysostom's explanation of the word *transfigured*: "What do the words 'and was transfigured' mean? Chrysostom the theologian said that . . ." Homily 34.10, "On the Transfiguration," *Gregory Palamas: The Homilies*, 270.

107

Moses, and the four Evangelists, especially John.[5] The Fathers also used the term "theologian" for one who practices mystical prayer. Theology can only be from above, since it is words about God. Theology is offered to the glory of God, not ourselves. Since it is divine, it can never be based on human reasoning, ideas, speculation, or clever argumentation. Orthodox theology can never be disconnected from the spiritual life of the theologian or from the life of the Church. Authentic Orthodox theology is "liturgical, doxological and mystical."[6]

What Is a Theologian?

THE CLASSIC ORTHODOX DEFINITION OF a theologian is well known and frequently repeated in Orthodox circles: "A true theologian is one who prays," or "One who prays is a true theologian."[7] This legendary saying reflects the Orthodox phronema and stands in stark contrast to the Western Christian phronema, which strongly emphasizes use of the mind for comprehension of theological truths and rational deduction as a theological method.

Perhaps the well-known proverb, "One who prays is a true theologian," resonates among Orthodox Christians because it perfectly encapsulates the acute awareness that one cannot truly *know* God through book learning or the application of the intellect. Human reason fails because growth in knowledge of God is possible only through growth in holiness, and one does not acquire holiness through study but through prayer. Academic learning and study are important and beneficial in the pursuit of theological truth, but they never substitute for the spiritual life.

Humility versus Self-Reliance

GENUINE AND SINCERE ORTHODOX THEOLOGIANS are always mindful that the true theologian is the one who *prays*. This precept is taken seriously,

---

5   Lampe, *Patristic Greek Lexicon,* 628.
6   Kallistos Ware, "Theological Education in Scripture and the Fathers" (academic paper), August 14–20, 1994, Fifth International Consultation of Orthodox Theological Schools, Halki School of Theology, Turkey, 2.
7   Attributed originally to Evagrios of Pontus (d. 399).

and, furthermore, it supplies an important restraint. Rather than enthusiastically forging ahead, enamored with his own thoughts, a truly Orthodox theologian will pause before making theological statements or arriving at conclusions to ask himself: Am I overstepping my bounds? Am I being faithful to apostolic Tradition? Are the Fathers in agreement with this view? Is this opinion consistent with the mind of the Fathers, even if they have never spoken on this subject specifically? Should I defer to another's opinion? Should I pray about this? Should I speak to my spiritual father about this? Should I decline to speak about this topic entirely?

> We divide people into theologians and non-theologians. We consider that theologians are those who possess some intellectual knowledge about God, and we think that theology is a specialty of some people who make a systematic study of the history of the Church. Without excluding this as a way of distinguishing students or teachers, we must say that theology is chiefly *life and experience*, and that theologians, according to the teaching of the Church, are essentially those who see God.[8]

The proverb is never far from the mind of a genuine Orthodox theologian, and it acts as a check against two great enemies of authentic theology: pride and innovation. Recollection that the true theologian is one who prays undermines confidence in oneself and reliance on one's own thoughts and conclusions. In the eyes of the world, self-confidence is commendable and valued. Intellectual rigor has an important place in Orthodoxy as well, and we celebrate our God-given ability to reason and comprehend. But Western theology *encourages* the theologian to ponder with the mind and to have confidence in his or her conclusions after a thorough intellectual examination and rational analysis of the subject being studied. The emphasis is on "faith and reason" or "faith seeking understanding." Emphasis on the intellect and reason is what gives Western Christian theology a more secular and scholastic character. But not all truth conforms to human reason or is verifiable by historical proof or scientific analysis. This applies especially to divine truths, since God is beyond

---

8   Vlachos, *Mind of the Orthodox Church*, 156. Emphasis added.

human comprehension and "not an object to be studied," as St. Maximos the Confessor reminds us. "I would even venture to affirm that every thought capable of forming an impression in the intellect is nothing other than an elementary outline, pointing to realities that are beyond it."[9]

Orthodox theology is essentially a spiritual pursuit. Reliance on the self in spiritual matters is the beginning of one's fall. Orthodox Christianity's understanding of theology as a spiritual activity does not mean that it is devoid of an intellectual component, that we entirely reject reason or do not endeavor to accurately express our views. It only means that theologizing cannot exist apart from the spiritual life.

> Remember that the intellect is the servant of the heart, which is our life; if it leads the heart to truth, peace, joy and life, then it fulfills its purpose, it is true; but if it leads the heart to doubt, disturbance, torment, despondency, darkness, then it does not fulfil its purpose, and is absolutely false—*knowledge, falsely so called*.[10]

It goes without saying that an Orthodox theologian must have an Orthodox phronema. Furthermore, a theologian must be well educated in all aspects of the Tradition, rather than being a specialist in only one area.

The Title "Theologian"

THREE IMPORTANT SAINTS HAVE BEEN given the term "theologian" as a title to indicate their unique contribution to the theology of the Church: St. John the Theologian (the Evangelist), St. Gregory the Theologian (of Nazianzus), and St. Symeon the New Theologian.

---

9   Maximos the Confessor, Ambiguum 21, *On Difficulties in the Church Fathers: The Ambigua* (2 vols.), Nicholas Constas, ed. and trans., Dumbarton Oaks Medieval Library, vols. 28 and 29 (Cambridge, MA: Harvard University Press, 2014), 1:425.
10 John of Kronstadt, *The Spiritual Counsels of Father John of Kronstadt: Select Passages from My Life in Christ,* W. Jardine Grisbrooke, ed. (Cambridge: James Clarke, 1967; Crestwood, NY: St. Vladimir's Seminary Press, 1981), 210. Citations refer to the SVS edition. Emphasis in the original.

SAINT JOHN THE THEOLOGIAN

SAINT JOHN THE THEOLOGIAN WAS one of the Twelve, the closest disciples of Christ who formed an inner circle of leaders among the large number of Christ's followers during His earthly ministry. Raised in Galilee as the son of a fisherman named Zebedee, John and his older brother James left everything to follow Jesus. John was the youngest among the Twelve, probably still a teenager at that time. Because they were enthusiastic and possibly even boisterous by nature, the Lord gave the two brothers a nickname: the "sons of thunder" (Mark 3:17).

John and James, along with St. Peter, formed an even smaller group of three within the Twelve as the very closest disciples of the Lord. We see this many times in the Gospels when the Lord took those three with Him at special moments, such as the Transfiguration (Matt. 17:1–8; Mark 9:2–8; Luke 9:28–35).[11] John was the only one among the Twelve to witness the Lord's Crucifixion and death (John 19:26–27). He was also the first male disciple to see the empty tomb following the Resurrection (John 20:4).

John's closeness to the Lord is expressed by another epithet for him found in the Fourth Gospel: "the Beloved Disciple" or "the disciple whom Jesus loved" (John 13:23; 19:26; 20:2; 21:7, 20). This is not to say that the Lord did not love all His disciples, but the description speaks to a unique friendship and the deep love Christ had for John and John for Christ. When the Lord was dying on the cross, He showed His confidence in and respect for John by giving His own mother over to John's care. From that very hour, the Gospel tells us, John took her to his own home (John 19:27).

Perhaps the Lord's great love for John was due to the purity of his soul. He lived to extreme old age and never married, devoting himself to the care of the Lord's mother and the preaching of the gospel. Saint Gregory Palamas explained St. John's extraordinary holiness in this way:

> He alone, not only of the apostles but of all eminent men before and after him, was called "virgin" by everyone, for it seems that he alone kept both soul and

---

11   Other examples are the raising of Jairus's daughter and when the Lord prayed in the Garden of Gethsemane prior to His arrest.

body, mind and senses, virginal throughout his life. Few people practice bodily virginity, but nearly everyone knows what it is, whereas perfect virginity of the soul means keeping the mind free from all association with evil. So this name bears witness to the fact that John was almost sinless, and that is why he came to be beloved of Christ, who alone was sinless by nature, and he alone was characterized as the disciple whom Jesus loved.[12]

After Pentecost, John went to Asia Minor, preaching the gospel, establishing churches there, and finally settling in Ephesus. He suffered for Christ many times and in many ways through hardships, beatings, and imprisonments. When persecution began under the Roman emperor Domitian (who reigned AD 81–96), the Christians of Asia Minor faced torture, imprisonment, and martyrdom. Saint John himself was put into a large vat full of boiling oil, but he survived. The Romans resorted to exiling John to the island of Patmos, where he wrote the Book of Revelation, in which he encouraged the seven churches of Asia to remain faithful to Christ even if it meant martyrdom. After the death of Domitian, John's exile ended, and he returned to Ephesus.[13] John lived to extreme old age and died during the reign of Trajan.[14] Saint John the Theologian's feast day is September 26, or October 9 on the old calendar.[15]

Saint John as Theologian

Why did the Church give St. John the title "the Theologian"? Saint John Chrysostom said of him that "it is plain that no part of the teaching of this

---

12   Gregory Palamas, Homily 44.3, *Palamas: The Homilies*, 347.

13   Eusebius of Caesarea, *Ecclesiastical History* 3.20.11. *Eusebius Pamphilius: Church History, Life of Constantine, Oration in Praise of Constantine*, NPNF-2, vol. 1, Philip Schaff and Henry Wace, eds., Arthur Cushman McGiffert, trans. (Grand Rapids, MI: William B. Eerdmans, 1890), 171.

14   Trajan reigned 98–117. Saint Irenaeus reports in his work *Against Heresies* 3.3.4 that John died during Trajan's reign. This is also reported by Eusebius in *Ecclesiastical History*, 3.23.3–4.

15   This date commemorates his falling asleep. A second feast day commemorating St. John is May 8 (or May 21), on which the Church remembers a unique event that took place every year at his tomb in Ephesus. A delicate but fragrant dust accumulated on the tomb on that date. The faithful would gather it and use it to heal the sick.

man is human, but divine and heavenly are the instructions which have come to us through this divine soul."[16] All four evangelists understood and demonstrated that the Lord is both human and divine. All of them conveyed His life and teachings with eloquence and special insight. All four Gospel writers give us a unique, inspired, and important depiction of the Lord's character and His earthly ministry. But of the four, John's Gospel expressed the deepest and most profound truths regarding the divine nature of the Son of God, His eternal existence, and the relationship between the Father, the Son, and the Holy Spirit.

The Theologian's Gospel provided the sword of the Spirit that enabled the Church to slay heresy. The Holy Fathers were able to refute the heresies that denied the full divinity of the Son of God and of the Holy Spirit by citing verses from the Gospel of John. The language of the Fourth Gospel is embedded and enshrined in the Nicene Creed.[17] John the Theologian distinctly and unequivocally articulated that the Son of God always existed; that He is God equal to the Father, begotten of the Father, not created; that the Son took on human flesh and became man; that the Holy Spirit proceeds from God the Father; and other sublime truths. Such mystical concepts, incomprehensible to the human mind, were rendered into human words by St. John the Theologian, whose mind had been illuminated by divine grace.

SAINT GREGORY THE THEOLOGIAN

Early Life

Saint Gregory the Theologian was born in 330 at his family's home at Arianzum, a small city near Nazianzus in Cappadocia (now in central Turkey). His father, also named Gregory, was a bishop. His mother, Nonna, was a woman of deep piety who exerted a strong religious influence on the family. Young Gregory received an exemplary education, first in Nazianzus, then in Caesarea, the largest and most important city in the province of Cappadocia. From there he

---

16 John Chrysostom, *Commentary on St. John,* Homily 2. FOTC, 33:20.
17 Important language about the Son and the Holy Spirit that was in the Fourth Gospel and incorporated into the Nicene Creed is that Jesus Christ is the "only begotten" Son of God (John 1:18) and that the Holy Spirit "proceeds from the Father" (John 15:26).

went to Caesarea in Palestine, then to Alexandria, Egypt, finally completing his studies in Athens.

Gregory and St. Basil the Great met and became the closest of friends when they were students together in Athens. After finishing their education, the two young men lived for a time in the wilderness of Pontus near the Black Sea, engaged in prayer and fasting as well as reading and studying the Bible, patristic writings, and spiritual books. But neither would be allowed to remain too long in prayer, study, and solitude.

Called upon by the Church for greater things, eventually Basil and Gregory were each elevated to the priesthood and then to the episcopacy. It was impossible that such remarkable minds and exemplary characters would not be engaged in the great theological controversies of the day, especially since the very survival of the apostolic faith was at stake. Basil and Gregory had matured during the era of the Arian heresy. The Arians, who denied the divinity of the Son of God and the Holy Spirit, had overwhelmed the Church and vigorously promoted their falsehoods. The First Ecumenical Council at Nicaea had condemned Arianism in 325. But during the decades following the Nicene Council, the heresy had actually grown in strength and in number of adherents, due in part to the support it received from Arian emperors during the mid-fourth century.

Gregory and Basil had both hoped for quiet lives of prayer and seclusion. When Basil left his quiet life for a brief visit to his family in Caesarea, Cappadocia, the archbishop of the city implored him to remain and assist him with the fight against the Arian heresy. Basil acquiesced. But Gregory, quiet and introspective by nature, preferred to live far away from cities, strife, and controversy. He loved learning and had given priority to his studies, including his secular education, which he was convinced could be useful in the service of the Church.

Although Gregory yearned only for silence, prayer, and study, his father desperately needed him to assist him in his own diocese with the theological upheaval and controversies of the time, just as Basil had agreed to help the Archbishop of Caesarea. Thus, the elder Gregory ordained his son as a presbyter in 361 against the younger's desires. Gregory dutifully assisted his father with various ecclesiastical responsibilities in Nazianzus for ten years as a presbyter, praying all the while that he would not be called to an even higher office. But, once again, he was unwillingly pressed into service, this time by his friend Basil, who by then had become Archbishop of Caesarea.

Saint Gregory Is Ordained a Bishop

Caesarea was the capital city of Cappadocia, which was a very large province. As archbishop, Basil was responsible for the ecclesiastical administration of the province. The emperor Valens, an Arian who opposed orthodox Christianity, ruled the Roman Empire at that time. He opposed the decision of the Council at Nicaea and opposed Basil, since Basil was a popular bishop and a vocal supporter of Nicaea. Valens sought to undermine Basil's authority and influence by dividing the sizable province of Cappadocia into two provinces. This created a position for a rival bishop and a haven for Arians who did not wish to be under Basil's authority. To reinforce his position and bolster orthodox Christianity, Basil wanted to ordain bishops who supported him and the decision at Nicaea, and he naturally wanted his friend Gregory to become one of his bishops.

Gregory's father, already a bishop himself, had also been aware of his son's extraordinary abilities and had pushed Gregory to accept the episcopacy. Basil ordained a reluctant Gregory as bishop of Sasima in 372. But Gregory did not want to be a bishop and spent little time in Sasima, which has been described as not even a village but a mere crossroads. It would not be the last time Gregory was pressed into service for the Church, contrary to his personal desire for quiet and solitude, prayer and study.

The Arian heresy infected the entire empire, including "New Rome," Constantinople, which was the eastern capital. Basil died in 379, but before departing this life he urged his fellow orthodox bishops to enlist the help of Gregory to fight the Arian heresy. They did exactly that. Pressured once more to enter the theological battlefield, Gregory set off for Constantinople, where not even a single church remained under orthodox control. Gregory transformed his residence into a small church, where he preached his famous Five Theological Orations (Orations 27–31) on the Persons of the Holy Trinity. As he continued to preach and teach, he slowly transformed the city, leading it back to Nicene orthodoxy. Gregory was chosen to become Archbishop of Constantinople.

Through his deep theological insight and oratorical skills, Gregory accurately and persuasively expressed the relationship between the Father, Son, and Holy Spirit. It was not easy. His Arian opponents claimed that Gregory was inciting violence and disturbing the peace with his preaching. They slandered him, claiming that he was teaching that there are three gods. Gregory was attacked by thugs who even attempted to murder him. Stones were hurled at him, and at times violent mobs even descended on the small church and threatened his life.

But Gregory persisted, and he gradually changed hearts and minds. As archbishop of Constantinople, he presided over the Second Ecumenical Council in 381. The council completed the Creed, most of which had been written at Nicaea. The final section was composed at Constantinople, including the line that clearly proclaimed the divinity of the Holy Spirit.[18]

Gregory employed his oratorical skills, excellent education, brilliant mind, holiness, and deep life of prayer to defeat Arianism and other heresies that also threatened the apostolic faith. Acknowledging his unique contribution, the Church gratefully bestowed upon Gregory the title by which he would forever be known: "the Theologian."

Saint Gregory and the "Middle Way"

Saint Gregory rejected theological extremes and often promoted the "middle way," neither too far to the right nor to the left, in both theology and behavior.[19] One heretical sect, the Eunomians, maintained that God could be comprehended through the operation of the rational mind alone. A different heretical sect, the Apollinarians, taught that the human mind was so hopelessly sinful that it could not know God at all. Both sides took extreme positions, and neither was correct. Against the Eunomians, Gregory refuted the idea that one can achieve actual knowledge of God simply through the mind and the use of human reason. But he also opposed the Apollinarians, who rejected actual knowledge of God, because we were created to know God, since the entire

---

18   "And I believe in the Holy Spirit, the Lord, the Creator of life, who proceeds from the Father, who together with the Father and Son is worshipped and glorified, who spoke through the prophets."

19   Gregory, *Or.* 2.34. NPNF-2, 7:212.

human person, including the human mind, was made in the image and likeness of God.

Gregory explained that knowledge of God is achieved gradually, and most people never attain it. He also rejected idle curiosity and theological sophistry, strongly opposing "futile and blasphemous argumentation." He warned against theologizing prematurely and without due preparation.[20] Although Gregory used philosophical terms, he opposed theological discussions based on clever argumentation, preferring "the philosophy of the fishermen" to that of Aristotle.[21]

Gregory affirmed and articulated the divinity of the Son and the Holy Spirit, and he explained the relationships between the Persons of the Trinity. But his extraordinary and invaluable explanations about the *work* of theology itself are important additional contributions to the theological tradition. Perhaps more than any other Father of the Church, Gregory openly discussed the difficulties, errors, and pitfalls in theologizing. He tried to articulate a framework for the practice of theology, albeit one that is rooted above all in prayer and silence. He advocated restraint in theologizing and sometimes even refused to theologize (to speak of God) to his own bishops. Although one must *think* of God constantly, he said, one must not *speak* of God quickly or readily.[22] One acquires knowledge of God through the mind, but only with the aid of prayer and ascetic discipline. Gregory taught that theology is not for all people or for all occasions. Knowledge of theological matters is not necessary for salvation; only simple faith is needed. Speaking of God is a great task, but spiritual purification is far more important.[23] His thoughtful comments on the sacred task of theology are invaluable guidelines for theologians today.[24]

---

20 Gregory, *Or.* 27. NPNF-2, 7:285–288.
21 Gregory, *Or.* 23.12. FOTC, 107:140.
22 Gregory, *Or.* 27.5. NPNF-2, 7:286.
23 Gregory, *Or.* 20.11. FOTC, 107:115.
24 For more information on the life and thought of St. Gregory the Theologian, see John McGuckin, *St. Gregory of Nazianzus: An Intellectual Biography* (Crestwood, NY: St. Vladimir's Seminary Press, 2011); Christopher Beeley, *Gregory of Nazianzus on the Trinity and the Knowledge of God* (Oxford: Oxford University Press, 2008); and Brian Daley, *Gregory of Nazianzus* (New York: Routledge, 2006). Georges Florovsky has a concise

SAINT SYMEON THE NEW THEOLOGIAN

Early Life

Saint Symeon the New Theologian was born in Galatia, in Asia Minor, in 949 to upper-middle-class parents whose relatives had connections in the court of the Byzantine emperor.[25] An uncle recognized Symeon's unique qualities, brought him to Constantinople, advanced his education, and encouraged his ascent in Byzantine society. Symeon worked at a variety of jobs, including manager of an aristocrat's household. Eventually he assumed various responsibilities as a minor imperial official, possibly even serving as a diplomat for the emperor.

All the while, however, his deepest desire was to become a monk. At the age of fourteen the young Symeon had met St. Symeon the Studite at the famous monastery in Constantinople known as the Studion. Saint Symeon became the young Symeon's spiritual father, but he forbade the younger Symeon to enter the monastic life before the age of twenty-seven. In the intervening years, young Symeon worked during the day at his occupation in the world while he spent his evenings immersed in intense prayer and reading spiritual writings as directed by his spiritual father. At this early point in his life, even before he had been tonsured a monk, he saw the Uncreated Light, a direct experience of God.[26]

---

summary of the theology of the important Eastern Fathers, including Gregory, in *The Collected Works of Georges Florovsky* (14 vols.), Richard Haugh, ed., Catherine Edmunds, trans., vol. 7, *The Eastern Fathers of the Fourth Century* (Vaduz: Büchervertriebsanstalt, 1987).

25   For more on the life and teachings of St. Symeon the New Theologian, see *St. Symeon the New Theologian: On the Mystical Life* (3 vols.), Alexander Golitzin, trans. (Crestwood, NY: St. Vladimir's Seminary Press, 1995); and *St. Symeon the New Theologian: The Discourses*, C. J. deCatanzaro, trans., Classics of Western Spirituality, introduction by George Maloney (New York: Paulist Press, 1980).

26   Discourse 22. Symeon the New Theologian, *Discourses*, 243–246. Orthodox teaching is that we can experience God directly through His "energies," which are distinct from the essence of God that can never be known or directly experienced. This distinction goes back to the Cappadocian Fathers (fourth century) and is essential to the Orthodox understanding of "deification" or union with God. Many saints have seen the Uncreated Light, especially through extensive practice of the Jesus Prayer. Saint Gregory Palamas defended Orthodox theology of deification and the practice of the Jesus Prayer by appealing to the Fathers, the Tradition of the Church, and the genuine experience of the Uncreated Light by saints of the Church in his famous work *In Defense of the Holy Hesychasts*, composed around 1340.

At age twenty-seven Symeon entered the Monastery of St. Mammas at Constantinople, and by the age of thirty-one he had already been ordained a priest and elected the abbot of the monastery. The spiritual health of the monks there was poor, and Symeon began a vigorous campaign to restore true Orthodox spirituality and the monastic lifestyle.

The Byzantine Empire was flourishing, and a secular spirit prevailed. Many monks had become quite worldly, especially those living in large cities such as Constantinople. Monasteries were wealthy, and the monastic lifestyle was no longer marked by poverty and detachment from material possessions. Furthermore, the divine services had become rigid and formal, with emphasis on the observance of ritualized forms rather than on achieving communion with God.

Symeon encouraged monastic reform, calling for a return to traditional monasticism with its ascetic practices and deep prayer life. Yet his desire for spiritual improvement was not limited to monasteries. Symeon enthusiastically insisted that all Christians can and should experience the Holy Spirit's activity within them. Knowledge that they possessed the Spirit by virtue of their baptism and chrismation was not sufficient. Symeon insisted that it is not enough to have knowledge *about* God; every Christian ought to have a genuine experience *of* God, which is possible through fasting, repentance, and prayer. He knew this to be true since he himself had experienced the Uncreated Light while still a layman living in the world.

Saint Symeon and Spiritual Renewal

Just as the liturgical life of the Church suffered at that time from rigidity and formalism, those characteristics had also influenced the way theology itself was being taught, discussed, and practiced. A type of Western, almost scholastic quality was creeping into Orthodox theology at that time—an abstract, technical, and philosophically based style and methodology. It was secular because it was divorced from the spiritual life. But it was also rigid, conservative, and therefore considered "Orthodox" by many. The content may have been traditional, but the spirit and manner of theologizing at that time were foreign to the Orthodox phronema.

Symeon's critics were among the most powerful, highly educated, elite men in Byzantine society. They considered themselves to be the guardians of Orthodox theology and tradition. But their theology had begun to imitate Western Christianity's highly stylized and overly intellectual approach, displacing the Orthodox stress on spirituality and true knowledge of God through a life of prayer. Symeon advocated a *true* theology: knowledge of God through a robust life of the Spirit rather than a theology of dead formalism. His message was not well received.

As Symeon pushed the monks of his monastery toward higher levels of holiness and contemplation, most of them failed to appreciate his efforts and reforms. Quite a few rebelled against him, and on one occasion some monks even attempted to attack him violently. Other critics opposed him outside the monastery. Symeon had enemies in very high places. The chief theologian advising the emperor was Archbishop Stephen, who fought against Symeon's ideas, believing they threatened and undermined ecclesiastical authority in favor of individualistic charismatic experiences.

Symeon also attacked corruption among the priests and bishops at that time, which further alienated Church authorities. Symeon was undermining neither Holy Tradition nor Church authority but was passionately promoting the primary goal of the Christian life, which was being neglected: personal transformation and intimate communion with God.

Saint Symeon spoke openly about his own mystical experiences—a shocking thing, especially for a monk, but he did so because he believed that the Holy Spirit compelled him to. This, no doubt, also undermined his credibility with powerful men in the Church, since it suggested a lack of humility. Eventually, Symeon was exiled from Constantinople in 1009. He crossed the Bosporus and lived in a small town on the seashore, where he established a humble monastery at the Church of St. Marina. His exile was later lifted, and he was invited to return to Constantinople, but St. Symeon chose to remain at St. Marina, living a quiet life, writing and offering spiritual direction until his death in 1022.

A "New" Theologian

It is quite likely that the appellation "the New Theologian" was not intended as a compliment. Orthodox Christianity rejects innovation in favor of maintaining sacred Tradition unchanged. Symeon's zeal and enthusiasm were surprising, and some of his statements could easily be misunderstood. Saint Symeon actually said nothing new or innovative. He advocated a return to *true* theology: the theologian as the one who *prays*.

His description as "the New Theologian," probably initially intended to be derogatory and critical, survived and was actually embraced by the Church after his death, indicating that rather than deviating *from* Tradition, the saint had effected a return *to* it. If indeed his teachings had been entirely new, he would not have been regarded as a theologian at all. His enthusiastic insistence on the inner mystical life was not a departure from the Holy Fathers but a restoration and a reminder to the faithful that the heart and essence of Orthodox theology is the spiritual life and intimate communion with God.

Saint Symeon's most unique contribution remains his candid descriptions of his personal encounters with the living Christ and his participation in the life of the Holy Trinity. The experiences themselves were not unique to Symeon. The delightful sweetness of Christ and the indescribable joy of encountering God are mentioned by many Fathers and saints, but only in brief hints. Orthodox Christians, particularly monastics, are taught not to speak of their personal spiritual life and experiences. But Symeon described his own personal experiences to the greatest extent possible with words. Never has any Orthodox saint so deliberately or purposefully attempted to communicate such deep and inexpressible spiritual delights.

Saint Symeon's unique content and style led to criticism, suspicion, and the initially sarcastic label "the *New* Theologian." He endured sharp criticism, hardship, and even exile for his writings and sermons, but he was driven by the Holy Spirit, not by his own ego. He longed to motivate the monks under his direction to pursue such experiences, assuring them of the potential for a deeply spiritual life. His life and work endure as a reminder of the profound spiritual transformation possible for all Christians.

THE SAINTS AS THE TRUE THEOLOGIANS

THEOLOGY IS NOTHING OTHER THAN contemplation, *theoria*, or vision of God. In other words, it is communion with God. This inextricably ties theology to worship, prayer, ascetic practice, and the spiritual life, since that is how one comes to know and encounter God. Metropolitan Kallistos Ware asks whether anyone can dare to call himself or herself a theologian, considering what this truly means. But he notes that, in fact, the term is used routinely to describe those who serve the Church as teachers of theology. He points to the distinction made by St. Gregory Palamas, who referred to the saints as the true theologians, but said that those who *trust* the experience of the saints can also be called theologians and may even become good theologians, but on a "secondary" level. Others, who do not have experience of God nor trust the saints, are bad theologians or actually not theologians at all.[27]

Ultimately, theology is not a set of definitions or theories. Theology is mystery since it transcends the rational mind and attempts to express the inexpressible. In schools of theology and seminaries, theology is indeed an academic subject and, as such, it requires accuracy and embraces a certain "intellectual rigour," as Met. Kallistos remarks. This does not conflict with Orthodoxy, since "we do not serve the Kingdom of God through vagueness, muddle and lazy thinking."[28] But he also notes that in other sciences or areas of investigation, the personal sanctity of the scientist or inquirer is irrelevant. This is not the case with theology, which requires *metanoia* (repentance), *catharsis* (purification), and *askesis* (spiritual struggle).

The theologian recognizes that theology is ultimately inexplicable mystery, and any illumination received by the theologian is *charisma*, a free gift of God's grace.[29] Since human language is entirely incapable of expressing divine mystery, the theologian cannot entirely conceptualize, understand, or explain these mysteries but seeks to convey, as best he or she can, the experience of God as well as His activity in the Church and in the world, for the glory of God and for the benefit of the Church.

27 Ware, "Theological Education," 8.
28 Ware, 6.
29 Ware, 3.

CHAPTER 7

Orthodox Theology and the Shaping of Phronema: Tradition

The Foundation: Tradition, Scripture, and the Fathers

THE WORD *TRADITION* IS USED in a variety of ways among Christians, to mean teaching in general, doctrine, an understanding of doctrine that developed over time, a source of information, the Bible, or everything that has been handed down from the beginning. But to articulate and grasp what is meant by Tradition in the Orthodox Church and how it functions in the Orthodox mind and theology is a significant challenge.

As we have seen, in Orthodox Christianity theology, "talking about God" is fundamentally spiritual. True knowledge of God is dependent on one's *spiritual* life. Theology is not simply an activity of the intellect but of the entire person and his or her way of life. While we may speak of a unique Orthodox methodology in terms of a basic approach, Orthodox theology cannot be pursued methodically or systematically. For this reason, the study of dogma or doctrine in Orthodoxy is called "dogmatic theology," not "systematic theology," as it is typically referred to in the West.

Theologizing in an Orthodox context is truly holistic, organic, and interconnected to everything else in the Orthodox Church. "All theology in the Orthodox Church is rooted in the experience of the Incarnation, not simply as a past historic event, but as a continuing reality which is believed, celebrated, taught and lived by God's people."[1]

Nonetheless, good, true, and accurate theology requires study, effort, and education, and it is undeniable that to some extent theology is also an academic and intellectual pursuit. We shall discuss three primary components of Orthodox theology and theological methodology, which are also rooted in acquired intellectual knowledge: Tradition, Scripture, and the Fathers. Other aspects of Orthodox life are certainly important factors and sources of theological insight. These include the holy canons, ecumenical councils, hymnology, iconography, personal prayer, virtue, the sacramental life, and the liturgical life. All of these shape and inform the nous, the phronema, and all contribute to theological understanding and expression. However, the focus in these chapters will be on the most basic and foundational elements of Orthodox theology: Tradition, Scripture, and the Fathers. The latter two especially require an education.

These chapters are not intended to be a comprehensive discussion of these elements, but merely a brief introduction. Any attempt to define and isolate specific aspects of Orthodox theology or phronema is artificial and contrary to the holistic nature of Orthodox thought. Each aspect can be different, but "like labeling the limbs and organs of a body" there is nonetheless an "organic relationship between all the elements thus labeled."[2] Nonetheless, the following chapters offer a brief overview of how Tradition, Scripture, and the Fathers function in Orthodox Christianity and contribute to Orthodox theological content and phronema.

The Origins of Christian Tradition

AS IS THE CASE WITH almost every aspect of Orthodox life and faith, the Orthodox theological method defies neat explanations or definitions. If Orthodox theology were to be reduced to only one word, however, that word

---

1   Lewis Patsavos, "The Methodology of Theology" (academic paper), January 12–18, 1982, Second Consultation of Orthodox Theological Schools, New York, 1–4, 1.
2   Andrew Louth, *Introducing Eastern Orthodox Theology* (Downer's Grove, IL: IVP Academic, 2013), 6.

would be "Tradition." Holy Scripture and the Fathers of the Church, also central in Orthodox thought and theology, will be discussed in the two chapters that follow. But it can fairly be said that Scripture and the Fathers are elements of, completely integrated into, and reflective of Tradition itself. Therefore, let us begin with Tradition.

THE BEGINNING

WHEN ST. PAUL AND OTHER apostles brought the gospel to the world, they brought it as an oral message. The epistles of Paul (written between AD 51 and 65) most likely predate the canonical Gospels, which probably took final form after the apostles began to die off, especially after the first Roman persecution of Christians under the emperor Nero around the year 65. A few decades passed from the time of Christ until the oral apostolic message (the gospel preaching, *kerygma*) appeared in writing as books which today we call "the Gospels."

For us who live in modern times, the idea of a purely oral presentation of the gospel message is quite strange. We rely heavily on the written word and cannot imagine conveying news or information without writing. But in antiquity books were rare and expensive, and fewer people could read. Oral teaching was the norm, and it was actually *preferred* because you knew your teacher, who his teacher had been, and most likely the teacher who had instructed him. The expertise of the instructor was verifiable in that manner, and students relied on this chain of knowledge—the reputation and expertise of the teacher. Books were considered less reliable than oral teaching, since all books were hand-copied. Their contents could easily be changed by a copyist and sometimes were. All education, including Christian catechism, was primarily oral. Therefore, the oral witness of the apostles—those who actually knew Christ and who had personally experienced His life, ministry, and Resurrection—was considered more reliable than anything in writing.

This preference for the oral transmission of apostolic teaching, even over the written Gospels, continued long after the death of the apostles. Preference for oral teaching is seen in the words of Papias (c. 70–140), the early-second–century bishop of Hierapolis, who wrote:

If, then, anyone came, who had been a follower of the elders, I questioned him in regard to the words of the elders—what Andrew or what Peter said, or what was said by Philip, or by Thomas, or by James, or by John, or by Matthew, or by any other of the disciples of the Lord, and what things Aristion and the presbyter John, the disciples of the Lord, say. For I did not think that what was to be gotten from the books would profit me as much as what came from the living and abiding voice.[3]

Everything about Christ and the Church—the teachings of Christ, stories about Christ, basics of the Christian lifestyle, and foundational apostolic teaching—were all transmitted primarily orally, not only in the initial decades of the Church but for many generations thereafter. Oral transmission about the Lord's life and teachings continued at least into the mid-third century.[4] Saint John's first epistle confirms that the message was an oral proclamation by the apostles based on their personal experience with Jesus Christ: "that which we have seen and heard we proclaim also to you" (1 John 1:3).

THE ORAL CHARACTER OF THE NEW TESTAMENT

COUNTLESS INDICATIONS OF THE ORAL character of apostolic teaching can be seen in the New Testament. Paul occasionally wrote letters to the communities he established when he was apart from them and the need arose for additional instruction. However, we can see that his letters generally do not convey the core gospel message, since Paul's letters focused on disciplinary, moral, and lifestyle issues faced at that moment by that particular congregation. Paul had already preached the gospel itself to them orally when he established those communities.

When writing to them later, he often reminded his congregations of what he had taught them orally, that they had accepted the teaching, and on the basis of that teaching had become Christians. When reminding the

---

3   Eusebius, *Ecclesiastical History* 3.39.4. NPNF-2, 1:171.

4   For example, Origen (c. 185–254) quotes from oral teachings of Christ. See s.v. "agrapha," *International Standard Bible Encyclopedia* (4 vols.), Geoffrey Bromily, ed. (Grand Rapids, MI: William B. Eerdmans, 1979).

Corinthians about the meaning of Holy Communion and appropriate behavior during worship services, he began: "For *I received* from the Lord *what I also delivered* to you" (1 Cor. 11:23). Later in the same epistle, he recalled what he had been taught orally about the Lord's Resurrection when he himself was catechized, which he had in turn taught the Corinthians: "*I delivered to you* as of first importance *what I also received,* that Christ died for our sins," and so forth (1 Cor. 15:3).

In both cases St. Paul spoke of "delivering" to the Corinthians what he himself had "received." We see the same concept elsewhere when St. Paul insists that the church of Thessalonika preserve the oral traditions he had taught them: "Now we command you, brethren, in the name of our Lord Jesus Christ, that you keep away from any brother who is living in idleness and not in accord with *the tradition that you received from us*" (2 Thess. 3:6). "So then, brethren, *stand firm and hold to the traditions which you were taught by us, either by word of mouth or by letter*" (2 Thess. 2:15). Saint Paul also praises the church of Corinth for preserving the traditions he had taught them orally: "I commend you because you remember me in everything and *maintain the traditions even as I have delivered them to you*" (1 Cor. 11:2). (All emphasis mine.)

In some English translations, the Greek word for "tradition" (*paradosis*) has been mistranslated as "teachings" or "doctrines." Although the term "tradition" is used negatively when the Lord condemns some practices of the Pharisees as "traditions of men," this should not be misunderstood as a rejection of holy, apostolic Tradition. Teachings and traditions of the apostles did not originate with them. The apostles received these teachings and traditions from the Lord Himself. Thus, early Christian traditions are not "traditions *of men*" but traditions "*of the Lord.*"

Before His Crucifixion, Christ gave final instructions to the disciples at the Last Supper, saying, "I have yet many things to say to you, but you cannot bear them now" (John 16:12). After the Resurrection, He continued to instruct them, as early as the day of the Resurrection itself when he explained the Scriptures to Cleopas and another disciple on the road to Emmaus (Luke 24:27). When the Lord sent the apostles out into the world, He commanded them to "make disciples of all nations, baptizing them . . . *teaching them to observe all that I have commanded* you" (Matt. 28:18–20, emphasis mine).

127

When the Lord ascended into heaven, He did not leave a manual or even Scriptures behind. Instead, He left a set of oral teachings, which He entrusted to the apostles, and a phronema, a mindset and lifestyle, which the apostles observed during the years when they lived with the Lord. The role of Tradition is to "bear witness to experience—to what has been seen and heard" by the apostles.[5] What they received and observed from the Lord is what they taught to the first Christians. This is the basis of Tradition.

THE WORLD OF THE EARLY CHURCH

THE FIRST FOLLOWERS OF JESUS never heard of the word "Christian." Initially they were simply Jews who accepted Jesus as the Messiah and Lord. They called their movement "the Way" (Acts 9:2) and were considered a Jewish sect until they were formally cursed and expelled from Judaism around the year 85. It is easy to forget how dramatically different early Christian beliefs and lifestyle were from the culture that surrounded them. The Christian way of life was unique. On the one hand, it was free of the thousands of rules concerning ritual purity that dominated Jewish life. But on the other hand, Christians were conspicuous in their rejection of the idolatry and hedonism of the Roman lifestyle as well. The early Christians made up only a tiny minority in the Roman Empire during the first century.

The Way was much more than a set of intellectual beliefs about Jesus; it was an entire way of life. Greco-Roman beliefs about the world, the gods, the daily pagan lifestyle, and morality contrasted greatly with Christian beliefs and lifestyle. Pagan gods were not holy and virtuous. The gods did not create the world, and they had little concern for humanity. To suggest that a god would actually become a human being and submit to death on the cross was so ridiculous as to be laughable. Christians were ridiculed for their belief in the Incarnation and Resurrection of Christ.

Moral laxity was accepted among pagans, but in contrast, the lifestyle and social interactions of first-century Jews were very restricted. Righteousness

---

5   Lazarus Moore, *Sacred Tradition in the Orthodox Church* (Minneapolis: Light and Life, 1984), 8.

was largely based on observance of ritual purity as determined by thousands of regulations of the Law of Moses. Jews rejected the idolatry and immorality of the pagan world around them and espoused a God who is holy, eternal, and the Creator of the world. However, Jews also rejected the idea that God even had a Son, let alone one who became a human being and died on the cross. For Jews that notion was utter blasphemy. It was in this environment, where both pagans and Jews were hostile to Christian beliefs and ideas, that the faith was planted.

Followers of the Way learned a phronema, a way of life. They had no books to guide them. The apostles traveled and established Christian communities, living among new believers for a time and then moving on to the next town. After the apostle who had evangelized an area departed, the new believers maintained their faith and lifestyle. When they accepted the gospel message they learned not only what to *believe* as a Christian but how to *behave* as a Christian. They learned this by listening, praying, worshipping, observing, and working and living alongside the apostle who had brought them the gospel.

For this reason, St. Paul instructed the Philippian community, *"What you have learned and received and heard and seen in me, do,* and the God of peace will be with you" (Phil. 4:9). When the Corinthians were struggling with many significant problems, he instructed them twice to imitate him: "I urge you, then, be *imitators* of me" (1 Cor. 4:16), and "Be *imitators* of me, as I am of Christ" (1 Cor. 11:1). What the apostles taught was not only intellectual information about Jesus, His words, His life, theology, or Scripture interpretation. They conveyed an entire way of life, including piety, liturgy, prayers, fasting, morality, ethics, good deeds, virtues, and so on. The apostles consistently shaped a unique Christian phronema they had received from the Lord in every city they evangelized, resulting in consistent beliefs and practices among widely separated communities.

Paul was not trying to create a cult of his personality when he said, "imitate me." He was encouraging the new Christians to maintain the same phronema the apostles had learned from the Lord, which Paul had conveyed to them. When St. Paul reminded the Corinthians of the apostolic preaching concerning the Lord's Resurrection, he ended by emphasizing that the testimony and teaching among all of the apostles was the same: "Whether then it was I or they, so we preach and so you believed" (1 Cor. 15:11). The Corinthian community had deviated from the teachings of the Church, and St. Paul wrote the letter we know today as 1 Corinthians to correct them. He sent the letter with Timothy, who would recatechize them, repeating orally the lessons Paul had previously taught them orally himself. "Therefore I sent to you Timothy, my beloved and faithful child in the Lord, to remind you of my ways in Christ, as I teach them everywhere in every church" (1 Cor. 4:17).

Notice two important details in Paul's comment. First, Timothy would remind the Corinthians of Paul's "ways" in Christ, meaning a lifestyle, a Christian attitude, a phronema. This is clear from the content of the epistle and the many behavioral problems Paul corrects. The Corinthian Christians had not forgotten information about Christ. They had not ceased to believe in Christ. Their attitude and way of life, their *phronema*, was the problem. Second, Paul mentioned that what he had taught to the Corinthians was not unique to them, even though the epistle itself is unique due to the particular situation in the congregation. The content of the faith did not differ from place to place or from apostle to apostle. Rather, it was the same "everywhere in every church."

TRADITION AND PHRONEMA

"Phronema is Tradition," my monastic friend said. By that he meant that Tradition is not only *what* we receive but *how* we receive it and how we live our lives. Phronema is Tradition because it is not merely the content of apostolic teaching, a deposit of teachings and customs, but how that faith is appropriated and expressed as an entire way of life.

Understood properly, then, Tradition is not the mindless repetition of the past or the preservation of antiquated customs, but sharing the beliefs and experiencing the life in Christ just as our Orthodox ancestors did. Tradition is the most "fundamental and essential characteristic of the Orthodox Church."[6] Our unwavering adherence to Holy Tradition has led some to call

---

6   Panagiotis Bratsiotis, "The Fundamental Principles and Main Characteristics of the Orthodox Church," in *The Orthodox Ethos,* A. J. Philippou, ed. (Oxford: Holywell Press, 1964), 24.

Orthodoxy "the Church of tradition, and this is its highest honour."[7]

Although the Orthodox have been criticized for it, "adherence to Tradition has been a fundamental principle and an essential characteristic of the Church of Christ ever since it was founded."[8] Tradition for the first Christians was more than simply stories, sayings, or facts about Jesus passed along orally or reduced to a few letters or written gospels. Tradition was an entire way of life: that which the apostles had learned, observed, and knew from their daily interactions with the Lord over a long period of time. This was emphasized by St. Athanasius:

> Let us look at the very tradition, teaching, and faith of the catholic Church from the beginning, which the Lord gave, the Apostles preached, and the Fathers kept. Upon this the Church is founded, and he who should fall away from it would not be a Christian, and should no longer be so called.[9]

As we can see, a Christian phronema existed from the time of the early Church. These first Christians were not handed a Bible and taught beliefs about Jesus but were introduced to a way of life, which they were expected to follow if they were to be considered Christians at all. That phronema is preserved and expressed today in Tradition: the lifestyle, teaching, practices, and beliefs of the first Christians as they had been taught by the apostles, which the apostles themselves had received from the Lord. This is phronema. This is what Orthodox Christianity has preserved.

Saint Irenaeus (d. c. 200) wrote about the phronema present in the early Church, the consistency of thought and action, its continuation of apostolic teaching and practice, and that this was observed among Christians in all parts of the Roman world.[10]

---

7 Bratsiotis, 24. But while the Orthodox pride themselves on preserving apostolic Tradition, Bratsiotis also observes that this has led many non-Orthodox theologians to call Orthodoxy a "petrified mummy."

8 Bratsiotis, 25.

9 Athanasius the Great, *First Letter to Serapion* 28. *The Letters of St. Athanasius to Bishop Serapion Concerning the Holy Spirit*, C. R. B. Shapland, trans. (London: Epworth Press, 1951), 48.

10 The universally held character of early Christian belief and lifestyle is rejected by many contemporary theologians. The term "early Christianity" has routinely been replaced

As I have already observed, the Church, having received this preaching and this faith, although scattered throughout the whole world, yet, as if occupying but one house, carefully preserves it. She also believes these points [of doctrine] just as if she had but one soul, and one and the same heart, and she proclaims them, and teaches them, and hands them down, with perfect harmony, as if she possessed only one mouth. For, although the languages of the world are dissimilar, yet the import of the tradition is one and the same. For the Churches which have been planted in Germany do not believe or hand down anything different, nor do those in Spain, nor those in Gaul, nor those in the East, nor those in Egypt, nor those in Libya, nor those which have been established in the central regions of the world. But as the sun, that creature of God, is one and the same throughout the whole world, so also the preaching of the truth shines everywhere, and enlightens all men that are willing to come to a knowledge of the truth. Nor will any one of the rulers in the Churches, however highly gifted he may be in point of eloquence, teach doctrines different from these (for no one is greater than the Master); nor, on the other hand, will he who is deficient in power of expression inflict injury on the tradition. For the faith being ever one and the same, neither does one who is able at great length to discourse regarding it, make any addition to it, nor does one, who can say but little diminish it.[11]

DEMANDS FOR WRITTEN PROOF

ORTHODOX CHRISTIANS ARE OFTEN CHALLENGED to produce proof that some teaching or practice, such as infant baptism or the importance of the Virgin Mary, was apostolic or part of early Christianity, because that

---

with "early Christianities" in academic circles because scholars claim that there were many "forms" of early Christianity. There were certainly many heresies, but not multiple legitimate "Christianities." The Church itself recognized only two realities: orthodoxy and heresy. This is the testimony of Irenaeus, who insists that the faith and phronema of early Christians was the same everywhere in the world, regardless of language or location.

11   Irenaeus of Lyons, *Against Heresies* 1.10.2. *The Apostolic Fathers: Justin Martyr, Irenaeus*, Alexander Roberts and James Donaldson, eds., Ante-Nicene Fathers of the Church (hereinafter ANF), vol 1. (Grand Rapids, MI: William B. Eerdmans, 1885), 331.

element of the faith is not specifically mentioned in the Bible. Sometimes I receive emails asking, "What is the earliest written reference to . . . ?" But the early Church did not commit even *most* of its beliefs and practices to writing. Supplying written proof of these early beliefs and practices is impossible, and Orthodox Christians should not entertain any demands to defend Tradition on the basis of written documents. Such demands reveal a complete miscomprehension of the life and practice of the early Church. That is the hallmark of a Western phronema.

Orthodox Christians do not obsess over finding proof. To do so is to lack an Orthodox phronema. Orthodoxy considers it unnecessary to prove any early Church practice or belief by producing written documents to defend or justify it.

The Gospels themselves are very short. It would be quite obvious that not everything Jesus said and did was recorded in them, even if the Scriptures did not explicitly say so (John 20:30). To assume that everything important in the early Church would have been memorialized in a written document is illogical, anachronistic, and unhistorical. Furthermore, imposing our cultural norms and expectations—which demand scientific proof and historical documentation in writing—on people living in an entirely different time, place, and culture is unfair, unrealistic, and ethnocentric.

Written documents could not possibly have contained all the important teachings and practices of the early Church, for a variety of reasons. One of the earliest Christian writers, St. Irenaeus, who was bishop of Lyons around the year AD 178, comments on the fact that the gospel had already been spread to many nations, including some who had no written language. "Many nations of those barbarians[12] who believe in Christ do assent, having salvation written in their hearts by the Spirit, without paper or ink, and, carefully preserving the ancient tradition." As St. Irenaeus continues, he lists the common beliefs the "barbarian" Christians had also accepted: the existence of one God; Jesus Christ being the Son of God, born of a virgin, crucified under Pontius Pilate; the Second Coming; and so forth. These Christians, without any education or

---

12 "Barbarians" was not a pejorative term but the word used by Greeks for non-Greek speakers, meaning those who were uneducated in the Greek language and culture.

written language, were deeply devoted to preserving apostolic Tradition, Irenaeus explained. He affirmed that these uneducated Christians had accepted apostolic Tradition and rejected any deviation from it, even if the false teachings were presented in their own language.

> Those who, in the absence of written documents, have believed this faith, are barbarians, so far as regards our language; but as regards doctrine, manner, and tenor of life, they are, because of faith, very wise indeed; and they do please God, ordering their conversation in all righteousness, chastity, and wisdom. If any one were to preach to these men the inventions of the heretics, speaking to them in their own language, they would at once stop their ears, and flee as far off as possible, not enduring even to listen to the blasphemous address. Thus, by means of that ancient tradition of the apostles, they do not suffer their mind to conceive anything of the [doctrines suggested by the] portentous language of these teachers, among whom neither Church nor doctrine has ever been established.[13]

As we have seen, apostolic teaching was oral in character, considered more reliable than written documents because the apostles were eyewitnesses of the teachings, miracles, and Resurrection of the Lord. Writings were considered less reliable, since one could not be confident that the contents of a book had not been altered by a previous copyist, either by mistake or intentionally.

For this reason, it would have been absolutely impossible for the early Church to have functioned by sola scriptura. Not only does all historical evidence contradict that notion, but it would have been impossible since even the Jews did not agree on what books were considered "Scripture" at the time the Church began and for a long time afterward.[14] As hard as this is for us to imagine, the Scriptures were not the basis of the Jewish faith nor even the most important aspect of it. The Jewish Scriptures were important because they contained the Law, which shaped their way of life. But the Jews agreed only on the Torah, which consists of just the first five books of

---

13   Irenaeus, *Against Heresies* 3.4.2, ANF, 1:417.
14   The Jews did not decide which books they would accept as "Scripture" until about AD 200, long after the Church was already in existence.

the Bible. Many other Jewish books were read, and many Jews considered the writings of the Prophets and Psalms to be Scripture, but no consensus existed.

What mattered for first-century Jews was their *lifestyle*. That was the basis of whether one was considered righteous or not. That was what made you a member of the Jewish community or not. It was in this historical and cultural context that the Church was born: the way you lived your life determined who you were, not which books you recognized as Scripture. This is a far cry from the situation imagined by the Reformers who championed the notion of "the Scriptures alone." The early Church had no Scripture of its own, and the Jews had no defined canon of Scripture; therefore, sola scriptura as the foundation for what Christians believed was absolutely impossible.

Other reasons can be cited for early Christian reliance on oral apostolic Tradition. From a practical standpoint, as noted earlier, most people did not own a single book, even if they could read. Apostolic writings did not even exist at first, and after they were composed, they were not immediately considered Scripture. People expected instruction of all types to be oral, and extensive memorization of long lessons was the norm. One other factor must be considered that seems unimaginable in the information age: oral apostolic teaching was unwritten because Christian doctrines were secret. Only baptized members of the Church were allowed to witness the most holy, sublime Mysteries or to hear profound statements of faith such as the Creed. This secrecy continued after Christianity was legalized in 313 and even after it became the official religion of the empire in 380.

After Christianity was legalized and churches were constructed, Christian worship became public—but only to a limited extent. The uninitiated (unbaptized) were permitted to be present for the first part of the Divine Liturgy. They could hear prayers and petitions, Scripture readings and a sermon, but they were required to leave the church after the sermon. Great reverence was shown to unwritten traditions, which often contained the most precious mysteries of the faith, not shared with outsiders.[15] When Cyril of Jerusalem

---

15   As a matter of fact, because Christian beliefs and practices were secret, wild rumors about Christian worship abounded in the Roman Empire, including accusations of cannibalism and incest.

was teaching newly baptized Christians the Creed, he told them not to write it down or let others overhear them practice reciting it.[16]

Orthodox Christianity cannot satisfy the expectations of Western Christians or others who accept as proof only that which is written and documented. Such demands are unreasonable, unhistorical, and do not consider the mystical, sacred, and secret aspects of the Faith so treasured and carefully preserved by those early believers. They refused to discuss these mysteries with outsiders, and many beliefs and practices, including the most important, were not committed to writing lest they fall into the wrong hands. In the late fourth century, long after Christianity had been legalized, St. Basil considered it perfectly reasonable that some teachings of the Church were proclaimed publicly and in writing, while others were reserved for the believers and transmitted secretly as oral tradition. Both sources, the public and the secret, were equally important and equally valid. He wrote:

> Both sources have equal force in true religion. No one would deny either source—no one, at any rate, who is even slightly familiar with the ordinances of the Church. If we attacked unwritten customs, claiming them to be of little importance, we would fatally mutilate the Gospel, no matter what our intentions—or rather, we would reduce the Gospel teachings to bare words.[17]

As St. Basil continued his remarks, he provided examples of unwritten traditions such as facing east to pray. But he also cited examples of a more mystical character, such as baptizing by triple immersion, and the exact words used by the priest to invoke the Holy Spirit to change bread and wine at the Divine Liturgy or to bless the water prior to baptism.

Perhaps today some may wish that the early Church had committed more

---

16 "This summary I wish you both to commit to memory when I recite it and to rehearse it with all diligence among yourselves, not writing it out on paper, but engraving it by the memory on your heart, taking care while you rehearse it that no Catechumen chance to overhear the things which I have delivered to you." Cyril of Jerusalem, *Catechetical Lecture* 5.12, NPNF-2, 7:32.

17 Basil the Great, *On the Holy Spirit* 66. *St. Basil the Great: On the Holy Spirit,* David Anderson, trans., Popular Patristics, vol. 42 (Crestwood, NY: St. Vladimir's Seminary Press, 1980), 98–99.

of its traditions to writing to provide proof to those who challenge Orthodox insistence on Tradition. But, in reality, observing Tradition rather than relying on documents is what has created the Orthodox phronema. Preserving traditions, small and great, has preserved the faith when writings were not available or when people could not read. Observing Tradition has instilled Orthodox phronema deep within us in a way that reliance on mere writings could never accomplish.

Exactly What Is Tradition?

EXACTLY WHAT IS TRADITION? How does Tradition relate to Scripture, the Fathers, and the life of the Church? Is it a body of teachings that stand alongside Scripture as an authority or source? Lossky wrote that Tradition "is one of those terms which, through being too rich in meanings, runs the risk of finally having none."[18] Generally speaking, when we refer to Tradition with a capital "T," we are referring to Holy Tradition—teachings, practices, lifestyle, and phronema which were taught by Christ to the apostles and have been passed down to us. Tradition conveys the essential teachings and life of the Church, a long unbroken thread reaching back in time.[19]

Holy Tradition is also not limited to the original apostolic teaching. As a matter of fact, it has been said that the apostolic experience is *not* Tradition because the apostles were taught by Christ Himself, who is God. Their situation and position were unique in the life of the Church because they were eyewitnesses who were taught directly by God. Apostolic experience and teaching are the foundation of the ongoing Tradition. On this basis, Tradition has

---

18 Lossky, *Image and Likeness*, 141.

19 A favorite description of Holy Tradition, one that has often been repeated, was given by St. Vincent of Lerin: "What has been believed everywhere, always and by all." Unfortunately, that definition is not useful, and Georges Florovsky had the courage to question this famous definition of Tradition. The sentiment is appealing and poetic; however, Florovsky correctly observed that "it is not clear whether this is an empirical criterion or not. If this be so, then the 'Vincentian Canon' proves to be inapplicable and quite false, because in fact Holy Tradition has not always been taught and believed everywhere and by all people." Georges Florovsky, *Bible, Church and Tradition: An Eastern Orthodox View*, in *Collected Works*, vol. 1, 51.

been called "the continuous interpretation and expression of the Apostolic teaching in the life of the Church."[20]

After the apostolic era, issues arose, certain disciplines and practices were created, doctrinal expressions took shape, and procedures were developed in the Church. As the Church responded to the needs of the faithful at each time and in each place, its response was rooted in Tradition, which meant that Tradition has a living quality. "Holy Tradition is not something static, to be safeguarded by dogmatic formulas; it is the dynamic movement of God in history in which man shares as part of the perfect humanity of Christ. It is in this sense that we dare to speak of the tradition as *Holy*."[21] Tradition has also been called the "general conscience"[22] of the Church, that which guides the Church to know what is correct or incorrect. It is a profound reality that "only in the general conscience of the Church can the essence of the faith be dynamically reinterpreted for the situation in which we are called to live."[23] Human traditions "perpetuate things that are transient," but Holy Tradition is "the river of life that goes on forever and keeps fresh by running."[24] Tradition in the Church "is not merely the continuity of human memory, or the permanence of rites and habits. Ultimately, 'tradition' is the continuity of divine assistance, the abiding presence of the Holy Spirit."[25] Theologically speaking, Tradition can be described as "how the Spirit is experienced within the Church of Christ as the charism of truth."[26]

Tradition cannot be defined or explained. No clear delineation of its boundaries is possible. It can only be understood and more fully appreciated gradually over time through participation in the total life of the Church. Tradition is a paradox.

20 Gerasimos Papadopoulos, "The Revelatory Character of the New Testament," *Greek Orthodox Theological Review* 2, no. 1 (1956): 41–55, 54.
21 Nikos Nissiotis, "The Importance of the Doctrine of the Trinity for Church Life and Theology," *The Orthodox Ethos*, A. J. Philippou, ed. (Oxford: Holywell Press, 1964), 101. Emphasis in the original.
22 Papadopoulos, "Revelatory Character," 45.
23 Nissiotis, "Importance of the Doctrine of the Trinity," 101.
24 Moore, *Sacred Tradition*, 24.
25 Georges Florovsky, "Patristic Theology and the Ethos of the Orthodox Church," in *Aspects of Church History*, vol. 4 of Collected Works, 15–16.
26 McGuckin, *Orthodox Church*, 90.

It can be conceptualized, but it is more than any collection of concepts. It can be written down, but it is more than any book. It is distinguished from Scripture, which it interprets, but is itself rooted in Scripture. It was expressed in the life of the Church in the past, but is a present living reality. It is found in Christian history, but opens Christianity to the future. It is "handed down" and "lived up to" in the Christian life. It is the "rule of faith," the "apostolic preaching," the "ecclesial mind-set," the on-going and developing yet consistent and paradoxically coherent "life in the Spirit." [27]

THE DYNAMIC NATURE OF TRADITION

TRADITION IS NOT AN EXTERNAL authority. It is not mere repetition of formulas or patristic quotes. It is not blindly following ancient customs. Tradition is possible and operative through the activity of the Holy Spirit within the life of the Church. It is the Holy Spirit that gives the Tradition flexibility to adapt to new cultures and new situations when the previous formulas and expressions might be inadequate. The Holy Spirit allows Tradition to be both dynamic and constant, creative and timeless. For this reason, rigidity in the form of an Orthodox "fundamentalism" is not Orthodox at all. Tradition is "not so much a protective and preservative principle as a principle of growth and regeneration," not simply a deposit but "a dynamic and inexhaustible source of life, power and inspiration, capable of infinite renewal and development." [28]

Tradition is the life of the Spirit in the Church. Its purpose is not to preserve practices from the past but to embrace the life in Christ and His Church now. Since Tradition is the life of the Holy Spirit in the Church and the Holy Spirit is constantly renewing the world, we must recognize that Tradition includes the element of renewal. It is not mindless repetition of custom, but becoming what our forefathers and foremothers in the faith were, experiencing God as they experienced Him.

---

27 Stanley Harakas, "Tradition in Eastern Orthodox Thought," *Christian Scholar's Review* 22, no. 2 (December 1992): 144–165, 164–65.
28 Moore, *Sacred Tradition*, 16.

TRADITION AS LIVING COMMUNION AND COMMUNITY

THE WORD TRADITION (LATIN TRADITIO; Greek *paradosis*) means literally "to hand over." Tradition presumes two important components. First, that a teaching or a practice exists. In other words, Tradition must include actual *content* (that which is being passed on). Second, that content is *transmitted* because of a *relationship* between the one conveying the content and the one receiving it. A tradition is preserved and passed on because it is important, because it is special, because it is meaningful. This is the case not only with sacred Tradition but with ordinary human traditions in families, cultures, and societies.

Tradition is not something confined to the past, nor is it a static deposit of information. It is creative, living, dynamic, and interpersonal. We see this in the epistles of Paul and his relationship with the Corinthian and the Thessalonian communities. Paul's teachings can only be understood within the context of the community. The apostles brought their message to living human beings who created the first Christian communities.

The apostles experienced Jesus, the Incarnate Word of God, and they conveyed that experience to the first Christian believers. The Bible is not merely a historical record but a statement of faith. Saint Paul reminded the Corinthians of what they had believed, as of "first importance," unless they "believed in vain" (1 Cor. 15:2). Apostolic teaching was life itself because the apostles offered the key to eternal life: Jesus Christ. Becoming part of the faith community, the *koinotita*, they experienced communion, *koinonia*, with Christ, the Holy Spirit, and each other. In that light, Tradition is not merely content but the life in Christ through the Holy Spirit, which makes Tradition known, understood, and lived. In this dynamic experience, we know as we are known (see 1 Cor. 13:12). Not only do we *receive* Tradition, but we *are* received *into* the Tradition.

Tradition is community and communion, "not so much a thing we receive as the context within which we are received into the divine life . . . the life of the spirit in the Church."[29] Tradition is "the communal experience of salvation

---

29   Marcus Plested, "Tradition and Traditionalism" (academic paper), August

itself, the living and continuous presence of the Holy Spirit in the Church's ongoing life."[30]

> What we call Tradition in the Orthodox Church—in a sense which is utterly misunderstood and misrepresented by non-Orthodox theologians—is nothing else but the life experience of the Holy Scriptures by the Church within its age-long history. Since tradition is life, namely the act of receiving and handing down the treasure of faith, it is not in any way a static and emaciated affair but has the essential features of a living organism: movement, progress, assimilation of the environment, its transformation and, finally, elimination or rejection of particular elements which have lost their organic relation to the living body of Christ.[31]

TRADITION IS NOT ANTIQUITY

TRADITION IS NOT SIMPLY ANTIQUITY. Custom, tradition, and antiquity do not equate to truth. The Orthodox respect antiquity, but it is not synonymous with Tradition. The Church was established on truth, not on tradition or antiquity. Antiquity alone does not protect us against error and is not a measure of truth.

Initially, the gospel message was a novelty. Saint Paul expressed the Christian movement as the old passing away and everything being made new (2 Cor. 5:17). One reason the ancient Romans persecuted the Christians was that the Faith was new, while Romans revered antiquity and their centuries-old traditions. They called the Christian faith a new *superstitio* (superstition). Pagans and heretics often appealed to antiquity for their views. In their own defense, Christians cited the importance of truth over custom. Saint Cyprian famously

---

25–September 2, 2001, the Syndesmos Festival, Saint-Maurin, France, 1–5, 3.

30   Theodore Stylianopoulos, "Scripture and Tradition in the Church," *The Cambridge Companion to Orthodox Christian Theology*, Mary B. Cunningham and Elizabeth Theokritoff, eds. (Cambridge: Cambridge University Press, 2008), 29.

31   Ioannis Karavidopoulos, "The Interpretation of the New Testament in the Orthodox Church," *Jesus Christus als die Mitte der Schrift: Studien zur Hermeneutik des Evangeliums* (Berlin: Walter de Gruyter, 1997), 249–262, 250–51.

stated, "Custom without truth is the antiquity of error."[32] Firmilian, Bishop of Caesarea in Cappadocia (d. 269), wrote:

> But with respect to the refutation of custom which they seem to oppose to the truth, who is so foolish as to prefer custom to truth, or when he sees the light, not to forsake the darkness? . . . When you knew the truth you forsook the error of custom. But we join custom to truth, and to the Romans' custom we oppose custom, but the custom of truth; holding from the beginning that which was delivered by Christ and the apostles.[33]

TRADITION IS NOT CONSENSUS

TRUTH IS NOT ESTABLISHED BY consensus, nor does consensus equate to Tradition. Consensus is important and helpful but, like antiquity, it is not sufficient by itself. On some occasions in the life of the Church, the majority of Christians accepted erroneous doctrines, and occasionally even decisions by church councils were incorrect. Famous examples in which one figure stood nearly alone against heresies or councils that had achieved widespread acceptance include St. Athanasius's fight against Arianism, St. Maximos the Confessor fighting Monothelitism, and St. Mark of Ephesus fighting against the false union of the Council of Florence in 1439.

The Church does not operate by democratic principles or majority rule, since it is possible for the majority to be in error. For this reason, a council was not considered "ecumenical" until its decisions were ratified by a subsequent ecumenical council.[34]

---

32 Cyprian of Carthage, Letter 73.9, "To Pompey against the Epistle of Stephen about the Baptism of Heretics." *Fathers of the Third Century: Hippolytus, Cyprian, Caius, Novatian,* ANF 5, Alexander Roberts and James Donaldson, eds. (Grand Rapids, MI: William B. Eerdmans, 1985), 389.

33 Firmilian, Bishop of Cæsarea in Cappadocia, to Cyprian, "Against the Letter of Stephen." Cyprian, *Letters*, Letter 74.19, ANF 5:395.

34 Seven church meetings or councils are recognized in the Orthodox Church as "ecumenical," meaning that all the bishops of the Church were invited to participate. "Ecumenical" in this context does not mean that it included representatives from various religions. In the Greek language, the Roman Empire was referred to as the *Ecumeni.* Councils attended by bishops from throughout the empire are referred to as

Universality, antiquity and consensus belong together. Neither was an adequate criterion by itself. "Antiquity" as such was not a sufficient warrant of truth, unless a comprehensive *consensus* of the "ancients" could be satisfactorily demonstrated. And *consensio* as such was not conclusive unless it could be traced back continuously to Apostolic origin.[35]

TRADITION IS BOTH CONTENT AND METHOD

TRADITION IS NOT ONLY A way of life, an attitude or mentality. It must necessarily include content as well. What is the content of Holy Tradition? Tradition has been described as all the dogmas implied by the Scriptures or even absent from the Scriptures; as a body of oral teachings that stand alongside Scripture; or as a source of information or authority. Orthodox Christians have often cited "Scripture and Tradition" as the twin sources of our beliefs. But while this explanation is easy to understand, it is actually a Western concept from the Catholic Church and is misleading from an Orthodox perspective.

Tradition is not merely a body of teachings, because it consists of both content and method. It is both the true teaching of the Church and the basis on which the bishops made their decisions and confirmed that teaching. While there is some truth to the idea that Tradition includes truths or content not found in the Scriptures, describing the Church's sources of information as "Scripture and Tradition" contains a basic flaw: Scripture itself *is* Tradition, especially the New Testament. The New Testament consists of apostolic teachings that were written down; therefore, Scripture is not truly something separate or different from apostolic Tradition. Scripture also does

---

"ecumenical." Most church councils are local and only involve bishops from a particular region, and for that reason decisions of a local council are not considered to be binding on the entire Church. Ecumenical councils involved the *entire* Church, and their decisions express the conscience of the Church. Ecumenical councils are considered to possess the highest authority in Orthodox Christianity, not because they stand above the Church, just as the Scriptures are not in a position above the Church, but because the ecumenical councils and the Scriptures reflect Holy Tradition, which has always been known, experienced, and taught in and by the Church.

35   Florovsky, *Bible, Church and Tradition*, 74.

not contain the totality of the apostolic witness. There were many things the apostles did not write down, including teachings and stories about Christ, some of which were extremely well known in their time but were never committed to writing.

While it is impossible entirely to define or delineate the content or extent of Tradition, Scripture is fixed, determined, settled, and defined. There can be no argument about what the New Testament contains. It is easier to deal with, to grasp, to discuss, and to cite than other aspects of Tradition. Tradition will always feel nebulous, indefinable, and inscrutable, and yet we differentiate between truth and falsehood, right and wrong, Orthodox and not Orthodox based on whether the idea comports with Tradition. Thus, Tradition is both *content*, because what we believe is consistent with the unbroken teaching of the Church, and also *method*, because the decisions regarding who we are and what we believe are based on the experience and total life of the Church, which is itself Tradition.

TRADITION IS BOTH FIXED AND FLUID

TRADITION HAS ANOTHER PARADOXICAL QUALITY: it is both fixed and fluid. It is fixed in the sense that it contains unchanging teachings. In a manner of speaking, it is a "deposit," something that has been received and preserved. At ecumenical councils, bishops represented different local churches from different places, and yet they reached a consensus based on the consistent and universal Tradition of the Church. Tradition must have been fixed or clearly understood, since the bishops were able confidently to recognize and delineate the difference between orthodoxy and heresy. The decisions of the ecumenical councils act as records of Holy Tradition and as foundation for the dogmatic teaching of the Church.

But Tradition is also fluid in the sense that it is impossible to define it or express its limits. On the one hand, it is fixed and unchangeable with respect to teachings, especially dogmatic definitions. On the other hand, it is flexible and adaptable with respect to the manner in which those truths are expressed and lived by Orthodox Christians in a particular time and culture. Tradition always hovers "between its charismatic and intangible quality and its concrete exemplification."[36]

This same quality is also evident in the holy canons. The canonical tradition contains both dogmatic canons—specific, unchanging beliefs of the Church—and also practical or disciplinary canons, which address Christian behavior. Practical canons are cultural expressions and reflect cultural situations, but the Spirit that inspired them is the same Spirit that inspired the dogmatic canons. The practical canons also express Orthodox phronema and timeless Holy Tradition. For this reason, outdated disciplinary canons are never removed from the collection of the Holy Canons because the Tradition, the underlying truth those canons express, remains as valid as it ever was. This is also the reason the canons do not operate as laws in Orthodoxy and require spiritual experience, prayer, and discernment for their proper understanding and application.

TRADITION IS BOTH TRUTH AND
A MEASURE OF THE TRUTH

WHAT IS THE MEASURE OF truth? How can we know what is true? The Scriptures are of supreme importance in the Orthodox Church, but the Church does not accept sola scriptura, since the Scriptures can be interpreted in various ways. We have also seen that we cannot rely on consensus, antiquity, or custom to guarantee truth. Tradition is not simply old customs or habit. Tradition must be *true*. It is a living and dynamic force, not simply the continuation of rites and customs but the continuing presence of the Holy Spirit in the life of the Church.

Our salvation depends on receiving the truth. If neither antiquity, nor the majority opinion of believers, nor church councils, nor even the Scriptures alone can guarantee truth, how is truth maintained? By Holy Tradition. Without it, there is no criterion for knowing truth or method for preserving truth.

---

36   McGuckin, *Orthodox Church*, 92.

We don't believe dogmas because they are dogmas but because they are *true*. How do we *know* they are true, and that Orthodoxy has preserved the fullness of the truth? Because of our absolute devotion to preserving the faith and phronema handed down to us by the apostles and confirmed by the experience of Orthodox believers through the centuries. The truth that we affirm is not "the traditions of men," because Holy Tradition came from Christ Himself, the Son of God. It does not depend on human reasoning, innovation, or intellect. Tradition is both content and method; it is both the content of truth and the means by which the Church preserves that truth today.

Tradition, then, is the means by which we measure truth. The first heresy to seriously threaten the Church was gnosticism, a movement that emerged in the second century. Among other things, gnostics taught that Jesus Christ was never incarnate as a human being who was crucified and rose from the dead. He was simply one of many *aeons,* divine beings. Jesus brought secret knowledge about the spirit world to the earth, and when a person died, the soul would be questioned about the spirit world. Souls of those who knew the "secrets" could ascend upward.

Gnostics tried to use the true Gospels to promote their falsified portrayal of Jesus. Later they wrote *apocrypha*, false apostolic writings, to promote their heretical ideas. Saint Irenaeus of Lyons vigorously combatted gnosticism by appealing to apostolic teaching and the continuous Tradition of the Church, which he called the "rule of truth" and the "rule of faith." By simply comparing gnostic claims against the consistent teaching of the Church from the time of the apostles, he proved that gnosticism was an obvious heresy. It was incompatible with what the apostles themselves had experienced, believed, and taught, and it was incompatible with what the Church had continued to experience, believe, and teach since the time of the apostles.

Tradition was both the content and the method by which Irenaeus expressed truth and exposed the heresy. He compared the continuous teaching of the Church to the false gnostic claims that Jesus Christ was not the incarnate Son of God. Irenaeus affirmed that the humanity of Christ had always been the teaching of the Christian Church. "This teaching has come down to us having been preserved without the use of any forged writings, by being handed down in its complete fullness, neither receiving addition nor suffering curtailment, and reading without falsification and honest and steady exposition of the Scriptures without either danger or blasphemy."[37]

Irenaeus's description displays a remarkable likeness to the typical response among ordinary Orthodox Christians when they are asked to explain Orthodox Christianity. They usually say that it is the original Church that has preserved the apostolic faith exactly as it was received, neither adding anything to it nor subtracting anything from it. This simple explanation shows the Church to be both ancient and patristic.

The role and concept of Tradition in Orthodoxy is difficult for the West to understand, since it defies definition and resists clear parameters. Catholic Christians also respect and follow early Christian tradition to some degree, but their respect for Tradition pales in comparison to the Orthodox believers' absolute devotion to it.

Catholics look to the pope and the magisterium as a guarantee of truth and for the assurance that they stand within the stream of Tradition. They are taught that the Roman hierarchy preserves Tradition and that the role of the faithful is one of pious obedience to Vatican directives.[38] Protestants cite sola scriptura, ignoring the fact that the Scriptures could not even exist without Tradition since they are based on Tradition, and the Church did not rely on Scriptures for its knowledge of apostolic teaching.

The Orthodox alone insist on Tradition as the primary safeguard and guarantee of truth. Moreover, even ordinary Orthodox Christians maintain a strong sense of responsibility for preserving Tradition, which they consider a sacred duty shared by all the faithful. Truth is not guaranteed by the Scriptures alone, which each person interprets as he or she will; nor is truth guaranteed by allegiance to one bishop or to a magisterium. Rather, Orthodox Christians each individually consider themselves responsible to protect the truth by preserving Tradition unchanged and handing it off to the next generation.

---

37 Irenaeus, *Against Heresies* 4.33.8. ANF 1:508.
38 This is what is conveyed in Vatican teaching; however, the Catholic laity are not passive. Many believe that it is their obligation to question and actively challenge their church and its hierarchs.

Holy Tradition and Human Traditions

AT TIMES, HOLY TRADITION HAS been distinguished from local or cultural traditions by referring to Tradition with a capital "T" versus tradition with a small "t." This is simplistic and imperfect, but it can be a useful distinction. When someone asks why we do certain things in the Church, the answer often given is, "It is Tradition" or "It is a tradition." The living faith and life of the Church is Holy Tradition, but it is expressed in various ways in the lives of Orthodox Christians. Small "t" traditions are also sometimes referred to as "customs." Holy Tradition is salvific, but customs are not. Customs are expressions of Tradition in a specific era and culture. They should not be enshrined or elevated to the status of Holy Tradition or the holy canons.

We must take care not to confuse Holy Tradition, the consistent and unchanging foundation of the Church, with minor human traditions. Nonetheless, even the small "t" traditions or customs can be important. They teach us, shape us, and are spiritually useful in ways we may not yet understand or appreciate. Furthermore, often these minor traditions reveal and express deep spiritual realities and reflect profound truths. They certainly shape our Orthodox phronema.

The unchanging and consistent faith and life of the Church is expressed through these little actions we call "traditions." They find expression in many different ways that vary with time and culture, such as specific foods, ways of celebrating various feasts, ways of honoring local saints, and so forth. The faith, liturgy, basic practices, and phronema are the same in Greek Orthodoxy, Russian Orthodoxy, Romanian Orthodoxy, and every form of Orthodox Christianity regardless of the language, country, or cultural expression. The language and customs that function as Orthodox Christianity's expression in a specific cultural context can change, but the *substance* of the faith (Tradition) remains unchanged. Tradition is that which is essential for our salvation, whereas customs are the actions by which our faith is expressed and lived in a given time and culture.

We should not ignore or scoff at small "t" traditions in the Church, since they are expressions of the essential and timeless Tradition. Yet at the same time we should not magnify customs and little traditions to the extent that we equate them with Holy Tradition. Human traditions in various cultural contexts can be vehicles that convey the universal and enduring expression of true Orthodoxy. These traditions are not unimportant, because they express the Faith and allow us to fully live our faith, although they are not the Faith *itself*, which was "once for all delivered to the saints" (Jude 3).

Even though they are useful and meaningful, we must be careful not to overemphasize those little traditions to the point that we make them indispensable and elevate them to the position of divine, unchanging, eternal truth. They should not become the focus of our activity and attention to the point that they replace our relationship with Christ Himself. They should not be reduced to superstition, nor be observed in a ritualistic or legalistic manner, but should be practiced as an expression of our faith and of true Orthodoxy. While we embrace, respect, and esteem Tradition, we must be careful not to lapse into a rigid observance of customs, which is traditionalism.

TRADITION VERSUS TRADITIONALISM

TRADITION IS A CONTINUOUS, DYNAMIC, and living experience, with the flexibility to adapt as the Church faces new eras and new cultural situations. If we have an Orthodox phronema, we will recognize Orthodox Tradition in diverse cultural contexts as the same Orthodoxy, yet presented and adapted to a different cultural context. Traditionalism, on the other hand, is a slavish and stiff insistence on the observance of external, small "t" traditions, equating observance of these practices with Tradition itself. As the great scholar and theologian Jaroslav Pelikan observed, "Tradition is the living faith of the dead; traditionalism is the dead faith of the living."[39]

Meyendorff recognized that the Orthodox Christian faithful "often feel

---

39 Jaroslav Pelikan, *The Christian Tradition: A History of the Development of Doctrine* (5 vols.), vol. 1, *The Emergence of the Catholic Tradition* (Chicago: University of Chicago Press, 1971), 9. Pelikan became an Orthodox Christian in 1998 and often said that he had not as much converted to Orthodoxy as "returned to it, peeling back the layers of my own belief to reveal the Orthodoxy that was always there." Timothy George, "Delighted by Doctrine," *Christianity Today International, Christian History & Biography*, no. 91 (2006): 43–45.

themselves responsible for the integrity of the faith. They tend to identify their Orthodoxy as an integral whole, where doctrinal beliefs are inseparable from worship, customs, language, and cultural attitudes."[40] They can find it difficult to distinguish between Holy Tradition and human traditions, between the "absolute firmness" required for dogmatic teachings and essential practices and "absolute catholicity and balance."[41] Orthodoxy rejects both relativism and one-sidedness, maintaining balance between extremes while preserving absolute truth.

Many schismatic and non-canonical Orthodox groups fall victim to the lure of traditionalism. Convinced of the righteousness of their cause, they have broken off from the Church and then proudly identify themselves as the "genuine" or "pure" or "true" Orthodox when in fact they are schismatics and extremists. They perceive themselves as the righteous remnant and label the other hundreds of millions Orthodox Christians in the world as "traitors" against Orthodoxy. They justify their schism by condemning what *they* deem to be heresy: a new calendar, a bishop they refuse to recognize, a decision made by a bishop, or some practice they have labeled as "modernist." For such groups, any change or deviation from their particular practice(s) is denounced as a betrayal of the faith, as though true Orthodoxy depended on a particular language or calendar, head coverings, beards, or cassocks. Like the Pharisees in the time of Christ, these Orthodox "strain out a gnat and swallow a camel" (Matt. 23:24 [NKJV]) by focusing on the letter of the law rather than on its spirit, placing importance on the precise observance of a tradition rather than on its purpose.

The pious observance of certain customs and rubrics, the choice of old or new calendar, or the use of a particular liturgical language is perfectly acceptable and part of Orthodox life. But elevating such details to absolutes or essentials is idolatry and a sin, particularly when the result is schism. Adherence to specific externals or customs of Orthodox Christianity, even out of sincere and zealous devotion to "true" Orthodoxy, while condemning others who do not observe these practices in fact distorts and diminishes the faith and does not reflect Orthodoxy at all.

---

40   Meyendorff, "Doing Theology," 90.
41   Bouteneff, *Sweeter Than Honey*, 64.

Sometimes converts to Orthodoxy are attracted to extremist or schismatic groups because those groups present an appearance of piety. Their zealotry seems compelling, and they hold up clear standards that offer an appearance of certainty based on strict structure and rules. Converts to Orthodoxy from religious traditions that emphasize conformity to specific norms might be uncomfortable without clear guidelines and precise definitions. They want to know what they must do to be "good" Orthodox Christians. Seeking the comfort and fallacy of certainty, they have simply replaced the rigidity or liberalism of Western Christianity with other rules with an Orthodox veneer.

Father Thomas Hopko observed that today's radical individualism has produced a reaction of flight from the modern world into a world of romantic reconstructions of the past. "Those making this flight often create or join cultic communities in which they hope to fulfill their fantasies. They surrender their personal freedom and responsibility and blindly follow the commands of leaders or appoint themselves leaders, who guarantee safe and secure protection against the evils of the modern world."[42]

Orthodoxy is not about following rules but about inner transformation. Extremists and schismatic Orthodox are not Orthodox, in spite of any Orthodox appearance and rigorous observances, because they lack an Orthodox phronema. The practices may be well intentioned, but they are misguided. When conformity to outward forms, disciplines, and practices takes on primary importance, we have forgotten the purpose of those observances. They then do not benefit us at all but rather can lead to our condemnation, especially if the result is pride and self-righteousness. Saint Nicodemus commented on this trap: "Thinking of their external pious works and deeming them good, they imagine they have already reached perfection and, puffing themselves up, begin to judge others."[43]

Traditionalism can degenerate into a pharisaical form of Orthodoxy,

---

42 Thomas Hopko, "Theological Education and Modernity," academic paper presented at the Fifth International Consultation of Orthodox Theological Schools, Halki, Turkey, 1994, 5–6. "Many who take this flight are burned-out refugees of radical individualism who have overdosed on individual choices, decision and actions."

43 Nicodemus of the Holy Mountain, *Unseen Warfare as Edited by Nicodemus of the Holy Mountain and Revised by Theophan the Recluse* (Crestwood, NY: St. Vladimir's Seminary Press, 1978), 79.

almost becoming an idolatry of outward forms, when it becomes a purely external piety, when one believes oneself to be pious but the motions of the *metania* (prostrations) are done without the repentant heart. It is a reductionist response to a real longing for authentic Orthodox Tradition and spirituality.

> Among the other positions upheld by the traditionalists are, variously, support for the Old (Julian) Calendar, or criticism of liturgical renewal (seeing frequent or regular communion as a decline in Eucharistic discipline), or espousal of head coverings for women, or emphasis on the monastic experience and ascetical literature. . . . The difference between traditionalists within the canonical Churches and the promoters of traditionalism in uncanonical churches is in ecclesiological perspective. In the uncanonical churches there is obviously a readiness to condemn the canonical Churches as modernist and heretical. Consequently, separation from the canonical Churches is seen as courageous and as a necessary act of confessing the true faith. In the canonical Churches, the traditionalists do not propose to leave their Churches, and do not espouse divisions or schisms. They are simply determined to "return" the Churches to the days prior to ecumenism and prior to what they define as modernism.[44]

TRADITION IS NOT LEGALISM

A SIGNIFICANT CHALLENGE FACES THE Orthodox Church today: freeing itself from Western theological attitudes, constructs, and categories. Florovsky remarked that "Russian theology had been entirely disfigured by Western influences."[45] Western-style legalism, which to some degree has also influenced many Orthodox, can still be seen in both theology and praxis and

---

44   Fr. Leonid Kishkovsky, Director of External Affairs and Interchurch Relations, "Orthodoxy Today: Tradition or Traditionalism?" *Orthodox Church in America* website, 2005, https://oca.org/holy-synod/statements/fr-kishkovsky/orthodoxy-today -tradition-or-traditionalism.

45   See Georges Florovsky, "Western Influences in Russian Theology," *Aspects of Church History*, 157–182.

often manifests itself in a spirit of severity and exactness which is promoted in many Orthodox circles as authentically Orthodox but which is actually quite foreign to Orthodoxy. Western Christianity greatly influenced Russian Orthodoxy well before the twentieth century. One may be rigorous in one's own observance, but the observances must not be more important than love shown to others. Saint Paisios rejected the legalism embraced by extremist Orthodox Christians:

> The way of the Church is love; it differs from the way of the legalists. The Church sees everything with loving forbearance and seeks to help each person, no matter what he has done, or how sinful he may be.[46]

Extremism or legalism can be very harmful to ourselves and others. It is a special trick of the evil one to tempt us to become judgmental toward others and to cultivate a spirit of pride within ourselves. Saint Paisios warned against fanaticism and harsh judgment of others and counseled us that a spirit of legalism is not the spirit of God.

> A Christian must not be a fanatic but must have love for everyone. Whoever hurls indiscreet words, even when he may be in the right, does harm. . . . Whoever censures publicly someone who has sinned, or whoever speaks with animosity about someone, such a person is not motivated by the Spirit of God; he is moved by another spirit. . . . I notice in some devout people a rather strange type of logic. Their devotion and good intentions are all very well, but they need to be spiritually discerning and broadminded, so their devotion is not accompanied by narrowmindedness and hardheadedness, that is, a stubborn and closed mind. The premise is to be in a spiritual state, to have spiritual discernment, otherwise one remains at the level of the "letter of the law," and the "letter of the Law kills."[47]

---

46 Paisios, *Spiritual Counsels of Elder Paisios* (5 vols.), vol. 2, *Spiritual Awakening*, Peter Chamberas, trans., Anna Famelios, ed. (Thessalonika: Holy Monastery of the Evangelist John the Theologian, 2008), 89.

47 Paisios, 2:89. He is quoting St. Paul (2 Cor 3:6).

TRADITION IS NOT RETREAT FROM THE WORLD

ORTHODOX CHRISTIANITY'S SPIRITUAL ORIENTATION CAN inspire a desire to escape the modern world, to retreat to Byzantium or to Mother Russia, or to identify so much with heavenly worship that we choose not to face the modern world. But Orthodoxy is fully equipped to face the modern world, and, in fact, the modern world is in desperate need of Orthodox Christianity—of its emphasis on the value of each individual human person, on a loving God who wishes to save and heal everyone, on the potential in each person to become godlike. "Panaceas are always being suggested for our troubles, but what the world really needs is saints."[48] Nothing is more powerful than Orthodox Christianity as an antidote to the despair and loss of meaning in modern society, not as a set of beliefs, but as a way of life promoting healing, wholeness, and holiness. John McGuckin correctly observes that Orthodoxy neither abhors human culture nor embraces it, neither stands apart from it nor is hostile toward it.[49] As usual, Orthodoxy presents a balanced approach, not an extremist one.

One manifestation of the retreat into the past by traditionalist Orthodox is the rejection of science, secular learning, technology, and even theological education. But that is also not the Orthodox tradition. Saint Basil was fully educated in the science of his day and used it to explain Genesis in *The Six Days of Creation*. The Fathers were highly educated within a pagan Greek or Latin framework and engaged the world by responding to it daily in their sermons. Their knowledge of the culture, along with their secular education and deep spirituality, allowed them to respond to the prevailing culture so effectively. We are not called to be like the Amish in America, who turn their backs on modernity for some ideal that equates spirituality with complete disengagement from the world. Rather than seeking to disengage from modern life and culture, devout Orthodox Christians need to bring the Church's transforming presence to the world. This in fact is the Orthodox Tradition. Many saints were not educated, and they retreated from the surrounding culture,

---

Moore, *Sacred Tradition,* 12.
John McGuckin, "Orthodoxy and Human Culture," *The Orthodox Christian World,* Augustine Casiday, ed. (New York: Routledge, 2012), 412.

usually as monastics. However, the greatest Fathers, to whom we owe the precise exposition of our doctrine and way of life, lived in the world and shepherded parishes. They employed their education for the benefit of the faithful and responded to the culture around them.

The Effect of Tradition: Cohesiveness and Wholeness

Orthodox Christianity manifests a cohesiveness, a wholeness, a strong connectivity between various aspects of Orthodox faith and life. Nothing is in disagreement or disharmony. This reality strengthens our confidence in Tradition, because Orthodoxy is "a single harmonious whole. No part of the Tradition is in conflict with any other part, nor could be," and this harmony "is a sign and proof of the health and authenticity of the tradition."[50] The liturgy, hymnology, theology, iconography, spirituality, daily practices, and prayers all have the same message, the same "melody of theology," and operate in concert with each other.[51] Furthermore, the unity of faith among believers, theologians, clergy, and monastics is striking. This is the result of centuries of Tradition and our strong dedication to it, which has molded and shaped the Orthodox phronema. Tradition both contributes to and perpetuates the phronema.

By contrast, Western Christianity is highly fractured. Among Protestants, the divisions are quite observable and exist for obvious reasons. While there is much more unity among Roman Catholics, nonetheless a wide variety of liturgies, spiritualities, practices, and observances exist even there. Students who study Catholic theology often receive a specific type of formation. Approximately one thousand different Catholic religious orders exist, each with its own theological emphasis, based on the spirituality, writings, and teachings of the founder of that order or movement. These include the well-known Jesuit, Franciscan, and Dominican orders along with many others.

The Orthodox embrace cultural plurality but not spiritual or theological plurality. There is one theology, one spirituality, one Lord, one faith, one

---

50   McGuckin, *Orthodox Church*, 91.
51   Jaroslav Pelikan, *The Melody of Theology: A Philosophical Dictionary* (Eugene, OR: Wipf and Stock, 1988).

baptism. All the elements of Orthodox Christianity work together and cannot be understood apart from one another. Scripture is understood through Tradition, but Tradition is also scriptural. Apostolic teaching is expressed by the Fathers, but one cannot be a Father unless he reflects Tradition. Icons are not mere religious art but complex expressions of theological teachings in which every detail has meaning. Orthodox hymns are deeply theological expressions rooted in Scripture, life, and Tradition.

The wholeness of Orthodoxy is "not simply in some cumulative sense, but in an organic way in which the reality of each element is defined only in the interplay of all of the elements in their relationship."[52] Orthodox Christianity can be truly understood only from within. A convert to the Orthodox Church once commented, "When you are outside it, you can't understand it, and when you are in it, you can't explain it."[53]

The Effect of Tradition: Stability, Constancy, Reliability, Confidence

WHAT IS TAUGHT IN ORTHODOX Christianity today is what has always been taught. What is lived by Orthodox Christians today is what has always been lived. This gives Orthodoxy dependability, stability, and a timeless character that constantly reinforces the phronema.

Some years ago I was the sponsor (godparent) at an adult baptism. A mutual friend who was a Coptic Orthodox Christian came to the baptism. The Eastern Orthodox are not in union with the Copts (the Egyptian Orthodox) since a schism that developed after 451.[54] After the baptism, my new goddaughter asked what to do with the towels and sheets that had been used

---

52 Harakas, "Tradition," 161.
53 The original source of this comment is unknown, but the comment went viral over the internet some years ago because it so perfectly encapsulated the challenge of explaining Orthodox phronema.
54 A schism occurred because the Copts did not accept the decision of the Fourth Ecumenical Council at Chalcedon. They are among the "Oriental Orthodox," a designation which includes the Ethiopian, Indian, and Armenian Orthodox. The Eastern Orthodox and Oriental Orthodox have not been in communion for over fifteen hundred years. Recently, however, encouraging signs suggest that union may be possible in the future.

in the service. I replied, "Take them to the ocean and wash them out. Then you can wash them at home."

Our Coptic friend smiled and exclaimed, "We are the same! We are the same!" She recognized in my reply a shared Orthodox phronema in the form of a very simple practice. Because some of the holy chrism would likely have been on the sheets, towels, and baptismal garments, we do not wash them in a washing machine, since the holy chrism would then enter the sewer system. Instead, we wash them in the ocean or other natural body of water first.

I know this, but I cannot say how or why I know it. Did I learn it from my mother? My grandmother? Did a priest mention this once? Did I read it in a book? How did I know about this? But now my goddaughter knows it, and she will also observe this practice and instruct others in it.

Actions like this shape phronema but also reveal our phronema. This tradition is observed not because it is a tradition. It is observed because the holy chrism is sacred and does not belong in the sewer. It was a simple statement of instruction, but in that simple reply our Coptic friend recognized the fact that Greek Orthodox preserve Tradition just as the Copts do. If we preserve Holy Tradition in small ways, we will certainly preserve it in even more important matters. Such experiences give us confidence in the reliability of Holy Tradition, as we see the same care and reverence expressed in little actions such as this that have been perpetuated across time and culture.

Recognizing Orthodox Phronema by Devotion to Tradition

THE ORTHODOX CHURCH HAS BEEN separated from the Catholic Church for a thousand years, but the Coptic Orthodox have been separated from the Eastern Orthodox for much longer, for over fifteen hundred years. Why are the Eastern Orthodox much closer to Coptic Christians in our beliefs and practices than we are to Catholics? How do we recognize Orthodoxy in each other?

The Catholic Church has deviated from the ancient Tradition significantly. But the Copts and other Oriental Orthodox have kept the same phronema that the Eastern Orthodox have, and because of that we recognize Orthodox phronema even when the Liturgy or particular customs are not exactly the same. What matters is the attitude the practice reveals. Unwavering fidelity to Tradition creates and sustains our Orthodox phronema. Tradition creates stability and constancy in the Church across cultures and across generations. "This identity and permanence, from apostolic times, is indeed the most conspicuous token and sign of right faith."[55]

The Orthodox Church manifests an unbroken historic continuity. What is most specific or distinctive about Orthodox Christianity is its changelessness, its sameness across time and cultures. This is why Orthodox Christianity is the ancient, apostolic faith.

> In other words, she is not *a* Church, but *the* Church. It is a formidable, but a fair and just claim. There is here more than just an unbroken *historical continuity*, which is indeed quite obvious. There is above all an ultimate *spiritual and onto-logical identity*, the same faith, the same spirit, the same ethos. And this constitutes the distinctive mark of Orthodoxy.[56]

Confidence in Tradition

IT IS WELL KNOWN AMONG Cypriots, not to mention a matter of national pride, that St. Lazarus lived on the island of Cyprus after the Lord's Resurrection. Saint John's Gospel tells us that the Jewish leaders had resolved to kill both Jesus and Lazarus. They considered it necessary to kill Lazarus because belief in Jesus as the Messiah increased after he raised Lazarus to life when he had been dead for four days (John 12:9–11). Lazarus was literally living proof of this extraordinary miracle. The New Testament itself does not tell us that Lazarus went to Cyprus later, but this was known in the tradition of the Church of Cyprus. The gospel message came to Cyprus very early, and the Church was established there even before St. Paul became a missionary (Acts 11:19–21).

My husband, Fr. Costas, was born and lived on the island of Cyprus when it was still a British colony. He related to me that the Cypriots would boast

---

55 Florovsky, "Patristic Theology and the Ethos," 15.
56 Florovsky, 14. Emphasis in the original.

about St. Lazarus to the British there. But the British would often scoff at this claim, saying there was no proof that Lazarus had ever come to Cyprus.

A very old church dedicated to St. Lazarus, dating back to the 800s,[57] is located in Larnaca, Cyprus. In 1972 a fire caused serious damage to the church building. The subsequent renovation required digging beneath the church to support the structure during reconstruction. In the process of digging, workers uncovered the relics of St. Lazarus located directly below the altar in a marble sarcophagus engraved with the words "Lazarus, the four-day dead and friend of Christ."

No written proof existed that Lazarus had ever come to Cyprus, but the tradition was preserved orally and passed along among the faithful of that island for almost two thousand years. Occasionally, Tradition receives indirect historical verification such as this, but the Orthodox have never relied on documented verification. The rediscovery of the relics of St. Lazarus exactly where one would expect them to be found—directly under the altar of the church that bears his name—is an example of the many experiences we have that support our confidence in Tradition.

We trust Tradition because we have experienced its reliability in countless ways. We do not have confidence in Tradition on the basis of faith alone. We do not keep Tradition for Tradition's sake. We do not need a pope or magisterium to tell us what to believe or do. We do not need rationalistic explanations or historical verification. Our experience confirms the power and reliability of Tradition. We trust Tradition because of our *personal experience* with it in tiny moments such as this, which have occurred time and again, not necessarily to us as individuals but through the lived experience of all those who came before us in the Church. Our experience confirms the power and reliability of Tradition. We have confidence that what we know, what we believe, what we do is *true*. We know that we have preserved the true faith generation after generation, back to the time of the apostles, because we have preserved Orthodox phronema.

---

57 The Byzantine emperor Leo IV had constructed the church to replace the small edifice that had stood over the burial site of St. Lazarus, according to long-standing tradition.

CHAPTER 8

Orthodox Theology and the Shaping of Phronema: Scripture

The Importance of the Scriptures in Orthodox Christianity

THE HOLY SCRIPTURES ARE INSPIRED and authoritative, peerless in historical and theological importance, and a priceless treasure. The New Testament is especially revered as the written remnant of the living voice of Christ and the apostles. The book of the four Gospels, the verbal icon of the Incarnate Word of God, is embellished, decorated, kissed, honored, used for blessing baptismal waters and wedding rings and crowns, carried in triumphal procession through the congregation, and always placed on the center of the altar in an Orthodox church when the altar is not in use. Scripture readings are an expected part of an Orthodox Christian's daily rule of prayer. The hymns, prayers, and divine services of the Church overflow with Scripture readings, expressions, and quotations.

The Scriptures are valued not simply as a historical record or a source of inspiration, but as the ultimate standard by which we measure theological truth. As the Word of God, the Scriptures also sanctify and transform us by orienting us toward God and cementing our relationship with Him. The apostles were important in the life of the Church not because they knew a lot *about* Christ, but because they *knew* Christ. And so we read the Scriptures because through them we encounter the living Christ. This is complementary to our understanding of the purpose of theology itself: knowing God. Just as the

Scriptures were based on the apostles' experience of Christ, our theology is grounded in the experience of God. We encounter Christ every time the Gospels are read.

INSPIRATION AND SYNERGY

THE SCRIPTURES ARE THE WORD of God in human language and expression. Not every word is intended to be understood literally. They are inspired but not dictated by God. Some Christians are uncomfortable with this and would insist that only dictation could account for biblical inspiration. But this is a naïve and simplistic view. The presumption that the Bible is Scripture because God dictated every word leads to an interpretive problem: how do we explain the variety of literary styles and perspectives in the Bible? Sometimes the same story is told more than once and with different details. Insistence that dictation is the only way to explain inspiration is based on fear that if the Bible is not dictated, then it is not inspired at all.

The dictation view of inspiration suggests that God acts on a passive human author. God is the sole actor, the sole contributor to the Scriptures, and the human author is the passive recipient of the action, like a lifeless tool or instrument utilized by God. It is not surprising that such a view of the Bible is more prominent in religious traditions that do not recognize the need for the human being to partner with God, to be an active participant in his or her own salvation. A dictation view of biblical inspiration contradicts the basic Orthodox understanding of the relationship between human beings and God. The dictation model is not the only way to explain inspiration or to affirm the truth and proclaim the divine character of the Bible.

From an Orthodox perspective, and from that of the Holy Fathers, dictation does not represent the dynamic and mysterious relationship between the human author and God. Inspiration is understood in Orthodox Christianity as divine illumination. God illuminated the minds of the human authors of Scripture, who expressed the stories and message of the Bible in their own style and language, with the images and concepts of their particular culture. The Bible is the inspired word of God, but it was written by humans in human language.

For Orthodox Christians, the Bible is the result of a cooperation (synergy) between God and the human authors. This is consonant with the Orthodox view of salvation: we must cooperate with God for our salvation. God has done and continues to do His part: He created us, He saved us, He gives us grace in countless ways. But we must respond to His offer of salvation and continue to respond to that grace throughout our lives. God will never compel us to accept Him, to love Him, or to be in a relationship with Him. God does not force Himself on us, just as He did not overpower the biblical authors and dictate how they would express themselves. The biblical authors were not deprived of their personhood or their humanity. They enjoyed the freedom to express biblical stories and concepts in their own manner, yet the Holy Spirit gave them special insight, illuminating their minds and inspiring their writings.

The Scriptures are an excellent example of God's synergy with human beings. The Bible is a divine-human product. Therefore, to properly interpret the Scriptures we must take into consideration both authors: the human, with his particular style, personality, purposes, and culture; and the Divine, with the saving purpose and message the human words were intended to convey. The Holy Spirit inspired the human author, and even the tiniest detail can contain great meaning. But exactly how the interaction between God and the human author operated as the two co-operated we cannot know and would never attempt to explain. We only know that the Bible reveals its human quality as well as its divine character as the inspired Word of God. The human contribution does not diminish the holiness of the Bible nor negate its inspired character. Likewise, the divine contribution does not nullify the human reality and human contribution to the Scriptures.

SCRIPTURE IN THE PRIMITIVE CHURCH

WHAT ROLE DID SCRIPTURE PLAY in the primitive Church? Initially there were no apostolic writings. The Jewish Scriptures were the only Scriptures of the first Christ followers, since Christianity did not even exist as a separate religion. Christ's followers were simply Jews who believed that Jesus was the Messiah and the Lord. They began a *movement*, not a religion. They never imagined that their movement would become an entirely different religion with a significantly different focus and character. The first Christians pored over the Jewish Scriptures, read them in worship services, taught them, interpreted them, preached about the Son of God as revealed in the Jewish Scriptures, and sang the psalms as prayers. The Jewish Scriptures had moral authority, provided guidance, and affirmed basic concepts about the nature of God, humanity, sin, and God's interaction with the world, especially His covenant and His relationship with the people of Israel.

The Jewish Scriptures held particular importance for the first Christians due to the messianic prophecies they contained. The promises in the Jewish Scriptures were fulfilled in Jesus Christ. The apostles and Christians who came after them continually claimed that Jesus was Messiah because He had fulfilled the prophecies. Jewish followers of Jesus saw in the Scriptures a specific message that other Jews rejected: Jesus of Nazareth was the Christ, the promised and long-awaited Messiah.

For a few decades, the Church enjoyed the dynamic presence of the apostles themselves, living eyewitnesses to all that the Lord had said and done. The oral transmission of their teachings became Holy Tradition. Some of the apostolic teaching, originally exclusively oral, was written down and became the books of the New Testament. The apostles often reminded their communities of their oral teaching (1 Cor. 11:2; 15:3; 2 Thess. 2:15; 2 Tim. 1:13; 2 John 12). The early Church did not depend on Scripture in the way that the doctrine of sola scriptura demands. The reality was quite the opposite: the words and stories about Christ continued to be conveyed orally into the third century.[1]

After the death of the apostles and their immediate disciples, the Church faced significant internal and external difficulties and needed to express specific beliefs in the form of more precise dogmatic definitions. The leaders of the Church, the bishops, were responsible for preserving the original deposit of Tradition and passing it on unaltered to subsequent generations.[2] The

---

1   For example, by Clement of Alexandria and Origen. Oral transmission of the Lord's words was actually preferred, as we have seen in chapter 7 and as expressed by Papias, the second-century bishop of Hierapolis.

2   Saint Paul reminds Timothy, whom he had placed as bishop of Ephesus, to "guard the truth that has been entrusted to you" (2 Tim. 1:14; also 1 Tim. 6:20).

bishops opposed heresies, and the Scriptures were the means by which heresies were routed—but not by the Scriptures *alone*. Heretics also quoted the Scriptures in defense of their falsehoods. Since both sides cited Scripture, whose interpretation was correct? The proper interpretation of the Scriptures, the ability to distinguish truth from falsehood, and the capacity to formulate precise doctrine all depended on Tradition.

Scripture scholars today from all faith backgrounds increasingly recognize that both the Old and New Testaments are based on an underlying oral tradition. The Church is the foundational reality behind both Scripture and Tradition. Father Theodore Stylianopoulos astutely observed, "Memories and traditions neither arise nor endure without a community."[3] For this reason, the Scriptures are correctly understood and interpreted only *within* the Church and do not stand as a body of knowledge or teaching separate or apart from the Church or from Tradition.

THE INTERPLAY BETWEEN SCRIPTURE AND TRADITION

THE RELATIONSHIP BETWEEN SCRIPTURE AND Tradition is "vivifying and dynamic." Tradition

> may be likened to a great river, whose main current is Scripture. Scripture is the normative or "canonical" witness which serves as the touchstone by which all traditions are measured and all authentic Tradition is discerned. Orthodoxy sees the relationship between the two in a way that cannot be described as Scripture *or* Tradition, or Scripture *and* Tradition, but Scripture *in* Tradition. This is because Scripture *is* Tradition in the sense that New Testament writings are a part of Tradition and constitute its normative element.[4]

---

3   Stylianopoulos, "Scripture and Tradition," 24.
4   John Breck, *Scripture in Tradition: The Bible and Its Interpretation in the Orthodox Church* (Crestwood, NY: St. Vladimir's Seminary Press, 2001), 3.

Since Tradition includes content, it is difficult to avoid conceptualizing it as a source of information or a deposit of beliefs and practices. Furthermore, the faith was at times described as a "deposit" to be carefully guarded and preserved (2 Tim. 1:14).[5] One cannot deny that something is being conveyed or handed down, but Tradition should not be understood simply as a complement to the Scriptures—a separate, supplemental, or alternative body of information that proves doctrines or practices which cannot be explicitly located in Scripture. Tradition is much more than that.

When Protestants insisted on sola scriptura, the Catholic Church responded that both Scripture and Tradition are sources of information or authority. This explanation has often been adopted by Orthodox Christians as an easy or handy response. But it is actually inaccurate from an Orthodox perspective, because Scripture and Tradition as two sources of "information" suggests an artificial distinction between the two and does not account for the way Tradition is understood and lived in Orthodoxy. Tradition and Scripture cannot be separated, because Tradition is more than just information. A dynamic interplay animates the relationship between Scripture and Tradition. Scripture *is* Tradition in written form, and Tradition *includes* and *interprets* Scripture.

Conceptualizing Tradition as an additional source of information to stand alongside Scripture creates another issue: the need to determine or delineate the relative importance or authority of each. The oral tradition existed *before* the Scriptures, and yet Tradition does not stand over the Scriptures, because they are mutually interdependent and equally necessary. Scripture is the written expression of Tradition, but Scripture does not include the totality of Tradition. Scripture is neither subject to Tradition nor below it. Likewise, Tradition is not something added to Scripture. Tradition does not compete with Scripture. Tradition is both the foundation of the Scriptures and an interpretive lens through which the Scriptures are properly understood, because Tradition is the context in which the Scriptures were created.

---

5   The RSV reads "Guard the truth that has been entrusted to you," but the Greek word there is not "truth" (*aletheia*) but "deposit" (*paratheke*).

Tradition and Interpretation

SCRIPTURE, TRADITION, AND THE CHURCH exist in a dynamic, complex, intertwined relationship that is impossible to untangle, define, or precisely articulate, and yet it is a completely natural and symbiotic relationship. Scripture is both part of Tradition and the criterion for the proper functioning of Tradition. Tradition is the means by which the Scriptures are interpreted and properly understood, since Tradition includes and interprets apostolic teaching.

Since Tradition is an entire way of life and phronema, it is a critical component for the correct interpretation of the Bible. By living and believing according to Tradition, we have conformed our minds to the Mind of Christ, the mind of the early Church, and those who composed the Scriptures in the first place. The phronema of the apostles continues to direct the Orthodox Church because of our unwavering fidelity to Tradition. Our adherence to Tradition, not as a set of facts but as an entire way of life, shapes the phronema by which we properly understand the Scriptures.

> Without the simple and continuous tradition of the Church, which has its very foundation in the teachings of the apostles, no other authentic interpretation of Holy Scripture is possible. There is no other security against heresies which can devastate Christian truth. There is no unity of faith and life; there is no unified spirit of Christian truth without the Tradition of the historical Church.[6]

Around AD 200, apostolic books were finally accepted as Scripture by Christians and called the New Testament. The Jewish Scriptures became known as the *Old* Testament. But for about 170 years after the birth of the Church, "Scripture" for Christians was the Jewish Scriptures only.

The apostles and other early Christians had no New Testament. They employed the Jewish Scriptures to convincingly establish that Jesus Christ was the Messiah who had fulfilled the prophecies. The Jews, however, reading and relying on those same Scriptures, did not accept that Jesus was the Messiah. Why not? Only within the Church, within the community of faith, were the messianic prophecies correctly interpreted and understood. Saint Paul

---

6   Papadopoulos, "Revelatory Character," 55.

described the "veil" over the Scriptures (2 Cor. 3:14–16) that hindered their correct understanding by the Jews:

> But their minds were hardened; for to this day, when they read the old covenant, that same veil remains unlifted, because only through Christ is it taken away. Yes, to this day whenever Moses is read a veil lies over their minds; but when a man turns to the Lord the veil is removed.

That passage reflects Paul's direct experience of countless discussions and debates with his fellow Jews in which he "argued with them from the Scriptures" that Jesus is the Messiah (Acts 17:2). Some Jews were open to the message and responded by accepting Christ, but most did not, which confirms the limitations of human reasoning. Paul's reasoning alone could not convince those Jews, and he concluded that a "veil" remained over their minds that obscured their correct understanding. The correct interpretation of the Jewish Scriptures was only possible in the Church and through faith in Christ.

This was the belief of the early Church and has remained foundational in Orthodox Christianity. It remains the conviction of Orthodox Christianity that proper interpretation of the Scriptures is rooted in Holy Tradition, which is the continuous faith and life of the Church from the beginning. Our interpretation reflects our phronema, which we have acquired through the apostles from Christ Himself.

CHRIST AS THE SOURCE OF CHRISTIAN BIBLICAL INTERPRETATION

CHRIST HIMSELF BEGAN THE CHRISTIAN tradition of Scripture interpretation in His own lifetime with His interpretations of specific passages, such as "The LORD said to my Lord, / 'Sit at My right hand, / Till I make Your enemies Your footstool"[7] and "The stone which the builders rejected / Has become the chief cornerstone."[8] On the Day of Pentecost, Peter gave the

---

7   Mark 12:36; Matt. 22:44; Luke 20:42 [NKJV], interpreting Ps. 109:1/110:1.
8   Mark 12:10; Matt. 21:42; Luke 20:17 [NKJV], interpreting Ps. 117:22/118:22.

same interpretation of the verse "the LORD said to my Lord" as he preached to the crowd (Acts 2:34). When he was taken before the Sanhedrin, Peter explained who Jesus was by giving the same interpretation Jesus had given of the verse "the stone which the builders rejected" (Acts 4:11).

Christ Himself used typology in his "sign of Jonah" statement, interpreting Jonah emerging from the fish after three days as foreshadowing His Resurrection.[9] Even after His Resurrection, Christ instructed disciples on the road to Emmaus when "beginning with Moses and all the prophets, he interpreted to them in all the scriptures the things concerning himself" (Luke 24:27).

The Christological key to unlock the Jewish Scriptures was given to the Church by Christ *Himself*. These interpretations were repeated continually in apostolic testimony while the apostles were alive and then preserved within the Tradition of the Church. Today, remnants of those Christological and apostolic interpretations find expression in many subtle details that go unnoticed by most Orthodox Christians: phrases in hymns, the appearance of certain details in iconography, the use of specific readings for feast days, the use of certain psalms for particular feasts or services. The first Christians knew all these passages and how they were fulfilled by Christ. Today, we hear the hymns but do not always recognize the allusions or nuanced imagery. We hear the readings, but we do not know why we are hearing those specific readings on those feast days. Even though most Orthodox Christians do not understand how a particular passage was employed in the early Church to express the ancient Church's interpretation of that passage as fulfillment of messianic prophecy, nonetheless, the memory is preserved and expressed in the divine services. We may not have been taught about those messianic prophecies, but we absorb them in the life of the Church, and this experience frames and shapes our phronema.

Other factors, such as the destruction of the Jewish Temple, the self-identification of the Church as the New Israel, and even some traditional rabbinic interpretive techniques would also influence early Christian biblical interpretation. But the New Testament itself describes the apostles

---

9   Matt. 12:39,16:4; Luke 11:29–30, referring to Jon. 1:17. His interpretation is explicit in Matthew 12:40: "For as Jonah was three days and three nights in the belly of the whale, so will the Son of man be three days and three nights in the heart of the earth."

consistently speaking in the synagogues and elsewhere, attempting to convince their fellow Jews that Jesus was the Messiah by opening the Scriptures and showing them that Jesus had fulfilled the messianic prophecies.

From the inception of the Church, Christ had established, and the apostles had continued, a specifically Christian understanding of key passages as well as a specifically Christian approach to the Scriptures in general. The New Testament itself is a theological interpretation of the person and ministry of Christ. It never pretends to be an objective account of historical events. For this reason, attempting to interpret the New Testament apart from the Church and Tradition is quite unnatural and will fail to uncover the true purpose and meaning of the text. Christ did not establish Scriptures, but a Church. The Church existed before the New Testament, and the apostolic Tradition, preserved by Orthodoxy as a sacred treasure, is the only context in which the Scriptures are correctly understood.

THE FATHERS AND SCRIPTURE INTERPRETATION

Every Church claims to have the truth. How do we know what is true? Irenaeus of Lyons faced the same question. When heretics, long ago and today, promote their teachings by citing passages of Scripture, the Church responds with its interpretation of those passages. The correct interpretation cannot depend on anyone's reasoning, faith, piety, education, opinion, or sincerity. Our confidence that we possess the truth relies on Tradition, just as St. Irenaeus appealed to the "rule of faith" or the "rule of truth" back in the second century. By *rule* (or "canon," *kanon*) he meant "a standard, a criterion" for measuring what was correct and true. The standard was apostolic Tradition. Heretics quoted and appealed to the Scriptures to support their heresies, but their interpretation was not supported by the continuous Tradition of the Church. Only within the Church, the community of true belief, of right faith, of "Orthodoxy," can the Scriptures be correctly understood and interpreted, because the Church has preserved the apostolic teaching and Tradition unchanged. Holy Tradition remains the standard for testing biblical interpretation in Orthodox Christianity through our continuous connection to the Christians of the past and an unbroken phronema and interpretive tradition.

169

The best guides for the interpretation of the Holy Scriptures are the Fathers of the Church, first because they stand within that unbroken interpretive tradition, preserving it, expressing it, and passing it down to us. Second, they are the premier interpreters because of their holiness, intellect, and education, which shine through their interpretations. Their relationship with God illumined their understanding as to the deeper meaning of the biblical text and its application to our lives.

The Fathers interpreted the Bible according to the continuous stream of Tradition. This does not mean they could not or did not have their own insights, but their interpretation was consistent with what had been said before, reaching back to the time of the apostles. They did not use their imagination, express personal views, or violate the norms of apostolic Tradition. The Fathers provided a balanced interpretation of the Scriptures, addressing the historical and literary context and details as well as the spiritual meaning of a passage and its pastoral application.

The Orthodox custom of looking to the Fathers for Scripture interpretation can never be reduced to the practice of *catenae*—citing strings of patristic quotations. This violates the very spirit of Scripture interpretation the Fathers exemplified. Orthodox Christians who are untrained in Scripture interpretation will simply search for patristic quotations to repeat. But our goal should not be simply to quote the Fathers but to have the mind of the Fathers, whether we specifically quote them or not. Being able to quote the Bible, even copiously, does not mean that one understands it correctly, just as simply quoting the Fathers does not make one Orthodox. The Fathers, just like the Scriptures, can be distorted and misinterpreted. An Orthodox theologian need not quote the Fathers to express the mind of the Fathers, and everyone with an Orthodox phronema will recognize that.

MODERN BIBLICAL SCHOLARSHIP AND ORTHODOX CHRISTIANITY

MODERN BIBLICAL SCHOLARSHIP HAS CONTRIBUTED greatly to our understanding of the Bible. The Fathers of the Church themselves applied many of the same techniques. Today we know more about biblical times and cultures, and this information contributes to our understanding of the Scriptures.

The Orthodox Church supports the academic study of the Bible, but limiting biblical interpretation to academic, intellectual, or scholarly analysis is impoverished and insufficient from an Orthodox perspective, for many reasons. First, it is impossible to interpret the New Testament accurately apart from Christ, since the entire New Testament is saturated with theology and presumes faith in Christ. A purely objective or historical understanding cannot be achieved. To understand the biblical author, one must acquire the mind of that author, his phronema. New Testament authors had the phronema of the ancient Church, not the mentality of the Reformation, the theology of scholasticism, the perspective of the Enlightenment, nor the obsession with scientific or historical proof found in the modern age.

Second, no one can interpret any Scripture with complete objectivity, even if he or she claims to offer a nondenominational or unbiased interpretation. All of us bring biases, presuppositions, and assumptions to the text. We cannot remove ourselves from our own heads nor escape the influence of our education, our personal experiences, or our background. All these factors and more are destined to affect how we read the biblical text, whether we are aware of that influence and admit it or not. This is why Orthodox interpreters do not rely on themselves but remain rooted in the Tradition.

Third, the Bible is not simply a historical record. An attempt to interpret the New Testament apart from Tradition ignores the very purpose of the Bible, which was written to express God's relationship to humankind and His saving actions, not merely to record historical events. No interpretation is correct if the interpreter ignores or violates the book's very purpose and message. Removing the Bible from its context as a product of the people of God only leads to error and a distortion of the biblical message, since the Scriptures were never intended to be interpreted or understood apart from the community of faith.

Scholarly analysis of the biblical text has been part of the tradition of the Church at least since the time of Origen in the early third century and is perfectly compatible with the Orthodox phronema. But discovering more information about the text, about biblical times and thought, or even about the biblical author's intended meaning does not exhaust the role and purpose of the Orthodox biblical scholar, and certainly not the message of the Bible. Andrew Louth makes an excellent point that as a living text, the Bible has a meaning that extends beyond its original meaning and purpose, even into the future.

> Scholarly interpretation has been governed by an overriding concern to estab-lish the original text and meaning. But there are many circumstances in which this is either not appropriate or not the whole story. For the Scriptures do not simply belong to their original context: they have been read and re-read over the centuries. When we venerate the book of the Gospels we are acknowledg-ing it as something that belongs to the present: it embodies Christ now . . . we can discern Christ's voice speaking to us now. The recognition that we are dealing with a living text, a text that, in some sense, is contemporary, not just to the time of its composition but to the time of its reading, suggests consid-erations that even the driest scholarship should be able to take into account.[10]

ORTHODOX INTERPRETATION AND THE BIBLE AS A LIVING DOCUMENT

AT ONE TIME, ZOOS CONSISTED of animals in cages. People went to zoos and circuses to look at them. Many decades ago, the San Diego Zoo removed the animals from cages and placed them in open enclosures with no bars. Only a deep moat separated the visitors from the animals. The animals had more freedom of movement and were not behind bars, but the enclosure was made of poured concrete. It was cold, artificial, lifeless. Today, the zoo houses its animals in enclosures that mimic their natural habitat, with grass, rocks, flowing water, trees, and often other animals sharing the same enclosure. Now visitors observe animals in a more natural environment—in their original context, if you will.

This is the difference between a detached and purely rational or schol-arly study of the Bible and the Orthodox interpretation, which preserves the

---

10   Louth, *Introducing Eastern Orthodox Theology*, 9.

original context of the Scriptures through the living Tradition of the Church. The Orthodox Church participates in and supports the academic study of the Bible. That is part of our tradition, because the Fathers engaged in the scholarly study of the Bible. But we never interpret the Bible apart from the totality of its context. Context includes not only the historical and cultural setting and textual elements such as literary arrangement and relationship of the words. Context includes the original setting in which the Scriptures were written—the Church. The author belonged to the community of faith, as did his anticipated audience.

To ignore the living context of a New Testament book—being composed and received within a faith community—puts the Bible, as it were, behind bars. This occurs when Scripture is interpreted purely rationally or according to "what it means to *me*," with no consideration of anything outside the reader's own mind. Considering the historical and literary context is a great improvement. This is like viewing the animal in a concrete enclosure where no bars obscure the view, but the animal still is not in a natural environment. The most natural interpretation is that of the Orthodox Church, which considers the entire "habitat" of the Bible in its totality and complexity: its historical and literary context, its liturgical use, its continuous theological interpretation, its spiritual use and application—in short, its unbroken use and understanding within the community of faith. This is why the Orthodox Church is confident that it has preserved the true interpretation of the Scriptures.

The original context and purpose of the Bible was always communal and theological. To separate the Bible from its theological and spiritual setting renders an interpretation that is cold, artificial, and tells us very little about the original meaning. Without the life and dynamism of the Church, this approach to the Scriptures can only succeed in presenting a pale, weak understanding of the bare word of Scripture. Thankfully, Scripture scholars and many ordinary Christians today have a growing appreciation for the original context of the Bible. However, without the phronema of the ancient authors, they will never begin to comprehend it fully. The phronema is only acquired by embracing the totality of the Tradition of the Orthodox Church, the uninterrupted faith and way of life of the ancient Church.

Reading the Scriptures as an Orthodox Christian

ON ONE LEVEL, EVERYONE CAN understand the Scriptures. They were written in ordinary human language. The Bible is not formal, fancy, or stuffy. An education is not needed to comprehend most of it. It was written in common, ordinary Greek and Hebrew so that everyone could understand what they read or heard on a basic level and could benefit from it. Gospel stories about Jesus, for example, are easily understood. But other parts of the New Testament, such as the Book of Revelation, are much more challenging. The Bible is yet another theological paradox: understandable by everyone on some level, while at the same time impossible for anyone to fully plumb or comprehend. Understanding the Scriptures *well* requires study and effort.

Just as God the Word condescended to become a human being for our salvation, He also showed His great condescension (*synkatabasis*) to humanity by giving us the Holy Scriptures. All human language is insufficient to describe or even to discuss God. And yet God has given the Scriptures to us in our weakness and frailty to aid in our salvation. He "condescends," or accommodates Himself, to our human needs and weakness. He allows Himself to be discussed and described in human language and concepts, all of which are unworthy of God, who is beyond all human comprehension or expression. This is important to remember because, as highly as we regard the Bible, ultimately what it says is very limited, because God cannot be comprehended or described. God is infinite and eternal Truth. The Bible points to what we can know *about* God, but it never describes God. The limitations of human language and the peculiarities of biblical expressions must be kept in mind whenever we interpret the Bible.

The Bible is like a gold mine, Chrysostom observed. Some of the treasure is near the surface and easy to uncover (this is the "easily understandable" part), but most of it lies at great depth (the part that requires study and effort). Like a buried treasure, it requires practice, effort, skill, and tools to uncover it.[11] Among the tools that are needed to properly understand the Bible are actual knowledge about it: its geography, culture, idioms, authors, language, and so

---

11   Chrysostom, *Homilies on Genesis* 21.1–2, FOTC 82:50–51.

forth. The Bible is a product of *synergy*, divine-human cooperation. In order to understand it, we also are expected to contribute our human efforts, which should not be limited to learning facts, reading books, or acquiring information about the Bible. Equally important is the spiritual aspect: a pure heart, a good life, prayer, silence. Since the Bible is a spiritual book, spiritual insight is needed to understand it.

The Scriptures are spiritual and can only be understood spiritually. Our level of understanding is dependent on our spiritual level. The Bible has many layers of meaning, and what we draw out of it depends greatly on our spiritual life and our relationship to God. As we contribute our efforts and show our desire, the Holy Spirit—the divine Author—illumines our mind to understand the Scriptures more deeply. This too is synergy. The Fathers mention many factors that contribute to a deeper spiritual understanding of the Bible, including prayer, diligence, persistence, meditating on what we read, paying attention in church, silence, humility, acquiring a pure soul, and living a virtuous life.

RESPECT FOR THE SCRIPTURES IN ORTHODOXY

FROM THE BEGINNING, THE CHURCH translated the Scriptures into the language of the people. The faithful were encouraged to read the Bible even when books were extremely expensive. Because of this, early translations were quickly made in Syriac, Coptic, Latin, and Armenian. But as time passed and Latin ceased to be widely used as a common language, it came to be viewed in the West as a "sacred" language. Ordinary people were unable to read the Bible in Latin, and its translation was resisted in the West. The Reformation led to a flood of Scripture translations into the vernacular languages of Western Europe.

But the Eastern Church facilitated and supported Scripture reading by everyone and encouraged translation of the Bible into other languages from the beginning. The Scriptures were considered so important that whenever the Church sent missionaries out to evangelize other lands, those missionaries always prioritized the translation of the Scriptures into the language of the people. When no alphabet existed for a language, missionaries created one so the people could worship and read the Scriptures in their native tongue. This has been the consistent tradition of the Orthodox Church and reflects the premier importance the Church places on the Scriptures and their accessibility to the faithful.

Orthodox Christians kiss the Gospels and have great respect for the Bible, yet they can be unfamiliar with it and often neglect personal Bible reading. They may have a lower rate of general biblical literacy than Protestants and typically are not challenged to memorize Scripture verses. This should not be interpreted to mean that the Bible is not important in Orthodoxy, or that the lack of Bible reading and knowledge is acceptable. A number of historical and cultural factors account for the deficiency.

First and foremost, Orthodox Christianity emphasizes relationship with Christ through the totality of life in the Church, especially the liturgical life, not primarily through the reading of Scripture. The emphasis in Orthodoxy was never on the Scriptures *alone*, in spite of their importance. Furthermore, the Scriptures were always available in the language of the people and heard at every church service. The faithful were not denied access to the Scriptures or prevented from hearing or reading the Bible, which was one of the factors that prompted the Protestant Reformation in the West.

HISTORICAL FACTORS CONTRIBUTING TO THE NEGLECT OF SCRIPTURE READING

OTHER SIGNIFICANT CULTURAL AND HISTORICAL factors also contribute to the lack of Scripture knowledge, especially among those born into the Orthodox faith. Until the invention of the printing press, books were hand-copied and extremely expensive. But when the printing press was invented, most traditional Orthodox lands, such as the Balkans and the Middle East, were under Muslim rule. No Christian printing presses operated in Greece until modern times.

In Western Europe an entirely different set of circumstances and attitudes toward the Scriptures contributed to the Protestant Reformation. The Bible was forbidden fruit, the subject of curiosity. Secretly translated and published pages were smuggled into areas where possessing the Bible in one's own language was illegal.[12] Western obsession with Bible translation into vernacular languages was not shared by the East, since the Scriptures had already been translated into various languages centuries before.

In the sixteenth century, when Protestant Reformers emphasized Scripture reading, copies of the Bible in vernacular languages became the craze in Western Europe. But for Orthodox Christian nations under Muslim occupation, the goal was literally survival. They were pressured and sometimes forced to convert to Islam or penalized with high taxes if they did not. Their daughters were taken as sex slaves, and young sons were taken and raised to become janissaries—trained soldiers sent back to fight against their own people. Many, many thousands of Orthodox Christians were martyred, at times even in mass genocides. The Greek island of Chios and the Armenian nation are only two well-known examples of this historical reality. Under such circumstances, Bible reading and basic education were not a priority or even an option. The faithful had no Bibles, and even if they did, most people could not read, including many priests.[13] The reality of life for Orthodox Christians in traditional Orthodox lands stood in sharp contrast to the relative freedom and advanced intellectual life in Western Europe, with its proliferation of Bibles. Even in Russia, where Christianity was the official religion, literacy was not widespread.

Millions of Orthodox Christians suffered under Muslim rulers for several hundred years. By the time Greece became a modern nation in the twentieth century, Western Europe had already enjoyed hundreds of years of access to books, ideas, and education. Ottoman Turkish occupation ended in Greece only about a hundred years ago, after World War I. Some Greek islands did not

---

12   In England, for example, where copies of the Bible in English were forbidden and associated with "heresy" in the late fourteenth /early fifteenth centuries. See *The Cambridge History of the Bible* (3 vols.), G.W.H Lampe, ed., vol. 2, *The West from the Fathers to the Reformation* (Cambridge: Cambridge University Press, 1969), 393–94. See also Beryl Smalley, *The Study of the Bible in the Middle Ages* (Notre Dame, IN: University of Notre Dame Press, 1989).

13   Saint Cosmas Aitolos was a Greek missionary in Greece during the eighteenth century. He established many churches and schools and also taught priests to read. See Constantine Cavarnos, *Saint Cosmas Aitolos*, Modern Orthodox Saints, vol. 1 (Belmont, MA: Institute for Byzantine and Modern Greek Studies, 1985).

become part of modern Greece until after World War II. The twentieth century brought the end of the Ottoman Empire, but other struggles and deprivations came to the Balkans, including severe economic depressions, another world war, civil wars, and military coups. As Greece was just emerging from hundreds of years of Turkish slavery, the rest of the Balkan nations and Eastern Europe were falling under the dark shroud of communism.

I mention all of this because the lack of biblical knowledge among "cradle" Orthodox is often criticized and equated with a lack of respect for the Bible. The hardships and persecution Orthodox Christians endured for hundreds of years in traditional Orthodox nations should be taken into consideration before ordinary believers are condemned for paying insufficient attention to the Scriptures. This is not an excuse for widespread biblical illiteracy today, but the mentality and focus of Orthodox Christians has not caught up with modern conditions and opportunities. It fair to say that while the Bible is extremely important in the Orthodox Tradition, *personal* Bible reading and knowledge is not a priority for Orthodox Christians in the same way it is for Protestants. Orthodox Christians tend to have a liturgical and sacramental relationship with the Bible: they encounter it when it is read in church.

THE PURPOSE OF THE SCRIPTURES

THE PURPOSE OF READING THE Scriptures is to acquire the grace of the Holy Spirit, to grow in our relationship to God, to commune with God, to open ourselves to the presence of God, to improve our moral behavior, and to imitate Christ and the saints. But all of this is possible even without the Scriptures. The Bible exists for our salvation, but our salvation is not *dependent* on the Bible. Reading the Scriptures is important because it contributes to our growth in holiness, but countless believers were illiterate and yet became saints.

Orthodoxy has survived for hundreds of years, even when subject to severe oppression and persecution—something we have seen even in recent years. Today, the rapid revival of Orthodoxy in Russia and parts of Eastern Europe is stunning. Greece and the Middle East did not experience the cultural and educational transformations that occurred in Western Europe during the past few hundred years. And yet, in spite of persecution and the general lack of education, Orthodox Christians maintained the Orthodox faith not because of book learning, but because they had the Orthodox phronema and preserved Tradition.

ORTHODOX PHRONEMA AND MODERN BIBLICAL STUDIES

WITH THE RISE OF MODERN biblical studies, emphasis in universities shifted away from any spiritual interpretation of the Bible to that which can be studied and learned objectively or scientifically through historical and literary analysis. In academic institutions, such analysis was expected to be dissociated from any faith perspective. Many biblical scholars were convinced that the truth about Jesus could only be uncovered if the theological layers were stripped away.

In the twentieth century, a dichotomy was created between the historical Jesus and the Christ of faith. Academic conclusions today are based on personal analysis and scholarly standards of objectivity and historical verification. The Bible is no longer presumed to be a reliable and historical source of Christian doctrine. This attitude of skepticism among many Bible scholars is actually understandable. Without ever experiencing unbroken Tradition, continuity in belief and practice in the ongoing life of the Church, even scholars who have a faith perspective doubt that they can rely on Tradition, because they know they cannot rely on *their* faith tradition. Their phronema is founded on the belief that truth must conform to science, reason, and logic or receive historical verification. Coupled with an attitude of skepticism in the culture at large, which is celebrated as "objectivity" and "open-mindedness," doubts about the Bible among biblical scholars have trickled down to ordinary Christians, who have become skeptical of the veracity of biblical stories. Jesus becomes a Milquetoast philosopher with a socially palatable message. Accounts of His miracles and Resurrection are considered nothing more than myths.

When I was a college student, I took a course on the Gospel of Mark. When we reached the section describing the Baptism of Christ, the professor said matter-of-factly, "Jesus came to be baptized. Obviously, he had sins." I was stunned by the comment. I was at a Catholic university, listening to a Catholic professor. It made no difference to the professor that Matthew's Gospel explained why Jesus came to be baptized, "to fulfil all righteousness" (Matt. 3:15).[14] "Obviously" this could not be historically accurate in her opinion because it was a theological layer that had been added on by the Church to promote the idea that Jesus had no sins.

I looked incredulously at the other students, expecting a reaction. They did not react in the least but busily continued taking notes. I was a mere college student, and regardless of how logical that explanation might have appeared to others, I could never accept that Jesus had sins. I did not write down that comment. I was twenty years old, but I had the Orthodox phronema.

Since the purpose of the Bible is to aid our salvation, to bring us to an encounter with the living Christ, and to attract the grace of the Holy Spirit, it is quite impossible for an Orthodox Christian to read or interpret the Bible without Christ, as a mere piece of literature. We know that from the inception of the Church, the interpretation of the Scriptures was initiated by Christ, taught by the apostles, and preserved in Tradition. Orthodox Christian biblical scholars also study, analyze, discuss, or consider the original historical and literary context of a book or passage. They read, study, and employ techniques and knowledge of modern biblical scholarship. But rigorous analysis or the additional insight gained by the scholarly approach does not replace nor obviate Tradition.

CHRIST IN THE OLD TESTAMENT

OLD TESTAMENT INTERPRETATION THAT IGNORES Christ is unnatural for Orthodox Christians, as it ought to be for all Christians, because Christ Himself gave the Church the key to the interpretation of the Jewish

---

14 The Baptism of Christ is celebrated on January 6 as the feast of Epiphany or Theophany. This feast was extremely important in the early Church. It remains very important in Orthodox Christianity because it revealed the identity of Jesus Christ as the Son of God and the Triune nature of God. For a discussion of the Western Christian ambivalence to its importance, see William Bush, *The Mystery of the Church* (Salisbury, MA: Regina Orthodox Press, 1999), 60–65.

Scriptures. The New Testament demonstrates the early Christian conviction that the Son of God was active in the life of Israel and present in Old Testament events before the Incarnation. The remarkable statement in the Gospel of John that "the Word became flesh and dwelt among us . . . and we have beheld his glory" (John 1:14) is an unequivocal affirmation that the pre-incarnate Son of God was the One who accompanied Israel in the wilderness and literally "tented" with them. It was the *Son*, not the Father, who wrestled with Jacob (Genesis 32), appeared to Abraham at Mamre (Genesis 18), and saved the three holy youths from the fire (Daniel 3).

Christ Himself confirmed this on numerous occasions through His "I am" (*ego eimi*) statements, identifying Himself in the Gospels as God (Matt. 14:27; John 6:20), as the One who spoke to Moses in the burning bush (Exodus 3), and by referring to Himself as the "son of Man" who was seen in Daniel's vision seated at the right hand of God (Dan. 7; Matt. 12:8; Mark 14:62). That the *Son*, not the Father, was the member of the Trinity who interacted with the people of Israel in the Old Testament era was uniformly recognized in the early Church but is little known in the West today, even among theologians and Bible scholars.[15] This is due to the lack of patristic knowledge and because biblical studies and theology in the West are entirely divorced from the Tradition of the ancient Church.

That the Son was the member of the Trinity who manifested God to Israel in the Old Testament was not a later Orthodox theological elaboration but the early Church's understanding of Christ from the beginning. To deny that Christ is the key to the Scriptures, including the Old Testament, is to deny

---

15 For example, in commentaries on the Gospel of John 8:58, when Jesus says, "Before Abraham was, I AM," many biblical commentators do not realize that Jesus was identifying Himself as God who was with Israel in the wilderness. They believe Jesus is identifying with the Father or affirming that He is the One who reveals the Father. The reason for this mistaken conclusion is that they are not aware that the early Church always understood the Old Testament appearances, including the revelation of the divine Name to Moses, to be appearances of the *Son*, not the Father. This is *precisely* what the Fourth Evangelist is expressing throughout the Gospel. John repeatedly links the Son to those Old Testament manifestations. This is not John's theological innovation or elaboration. Rather, this understanding of the Son was the belief of the early Church from the beginning. It is well known in Orthodoxy, expressed in our iconography and hymnology, because we have preserved the traditional interpretation of the early Church.

that Christ and the message about Him are the foundation of all Christian teaching. Even before the Gospels were composed, when St. Paul commented on the Exodus experience of Israel, he identified Christ as the One who was with Israel in the wilderness:

> I want you to know, brethren, that our fathers were all under the cloud, and all passed through the sea, and all were baptized into Moses in the cloud and in the sea, and all ate the same supernatural food and all drank the same supernatural drink. For they drank from the supernatural Rock which followed them, and the Rock was Christ. (1 Cor. 10:1–4)[16]

Some biblical scholars would say that many words and deeds attributed to Christ in the Gospels were invented by Jesus' followers after His death. According to that theory, Jesus never claimed to be God. His disciples themselves decided that Jesus was the Son of God and added details into the stories about Him to make it appear that He had fulfilled those prophecies. Jesus was nothing more than a first-century rabbi with a small band of followers. These scholars would have us believe that there was nothing particularly extraordinary about Him, and yet in spite of His premature and scandalous death by crucifixion, His movement survived and grew into the largest religion in the world.

Some people may find that conclusion logical, but it is extremely unlikely and quite illogical. The evidence is overwhelming that Christ believed Himself to be the Son of God and taught that fact to His disciples, who witnessed countless miraculous events that confirmed His claims. Basic beliefs about the Person of Christ are consistent throughout the New Testament among all

---

16   Here again, the reference to Christ as the "Rock" (*petra*) is the ancient Christian interpretation that is preserved and well known in the Orthodox Church because of our phronema. Christ is the Rock (*petra*) upon which the Church is built, not St. Peter (*Petros*): "You are Peter (*Petros*), and on this rock (*petra*) I will build my church" (Matt.16:18). The early Church never considered Peter to be the foundation of the Church because the early Church knew that the word *petra* in both the Septuagint Old Testament and New Testament referred to the Son of God. This is confirmed by Peter himself. See 1 Peter 2:6-8, which refers to Christ as both "stone" (*lithos*) and "rock" (*petra*). The popular Catholic interpretation, that the Church is founded on Peter as the rock, was first promoted by Pope Leo the Great in the fifth century.

its authors. This includes St. Paul, whose writings were composed only about twenty to thirty years after the Resurrection, when thousands of eyewitnesses to Christ were still alive. Claiming that Christ never performed miracles and never claimed to be God is less rational than accepting the historical record that Jesus was condemned to death precisely for claiming divinity. He claimed the prerogative of God by forgiving sins, changing the Sabbath rules, rejecting ritual cleanliness, and so forth. In these details and others, the Gospels are absolutely consistent.

I was recently challenged in class by a Catholic graduate student of theology about whether Jesus really said, "If any man would come after Me, let him deny himself and take up his cross and follow me" (Matt. 16:24; Mark 8:34; Luke 9:23). He doubted it because he had been told by other professors that Jesus could not have known that He would die by crucifixion; therefore, He could not have told His disciples that they must follow Him to the cross. What the student had previously been taught seemed logical to him, the result of analyzing the Scriptures and Christ in a purely human manner. But such a conclusion virtually denies the divinity of Christ.

Orthodox phronema rejects both biblical fundamentalism and a rationalistic and skeptical interpretation of the Bible that does not permit a faith perspective. Even though Orthodox biblical scholars effectively employ the tools of modern biblical interpretation, Orthodox biblical interpretation is too often dismissed as fundamentalism or narrow-mindedness, or as lacking scholarly rigor, because we would never accept heretical interpretations, regardless of how rational they might seem to others.

Many years ago, I heard a lecture by then-Bishop Demetrios Trakatellis, a New Testament scholar who would later become the Greek Orthodox Archbishop of America. I had never met an Orthodox biblical scholar. We certainly have excellent biblical scholars who are known within Orthodoxy, but they not well known outside the Church. After his talk, I asked Bishop Demetrios why there were no famous Orthodox Bible scholars, only Protestant and Catholic ones. His simple reply stung: "Because they don't respect us." It stung because I knew instantly that it was the truth, and I also knew why it was true: We do not share the phronema. The West does not understand that we even *have* a phronema, so how can they appreciate it? Orthodox Christian theologians have a unique perspective that *should* be appreciated in the West, since Orthodoxy has preserved the mind of the early Church. But it is not appreciated, because our phronema does not comport with that of the West.

Many brilliant Western Christian Scripture scholars today are supremely confident in their analysis but constrained by their own phronema. They believe they are open-minded, and they sincerely seek the truth, convinced that their methodology leads to the discovery of truth. But they are far removed from the phronema of the early Church, and that seriously inhibits their ability to understand the text. Tradition as the basis for the interpretation of the Scriptures is more reliable, because the interpretation of the early Church is closer in time to when the events actually occurred. Tradition is more reliable because the apostles knew Jesus, what took place and what it meant, and their apostolic knowledge of Jesus was passed on to us. Tradition gives Orthodox Christians confidence, because our interpretation is the uninterrupted and consistent teaching of the ancient Church.

CHAPTER 9

Orthodox Theology and the Shaping of Phronema: The Fathers

Who Are the Fathers of the Church?

ALONG WITH SCRIPTURE AND TRADITION, critical to Orthodox thought and life are the writings of the Holy Fathers of the Church. As with the other key components of Orthodoxy, the role of the Fathers can never be correctly understood separately from Scripture and Tradition. The Church is not only apostolic and scriptural; it is patristic.

The Fathers are those who preserved, expressed, and bore witness to the ongoing rule of faith in the life of the Church. They were the brilliant thinkers and writers who faithfully expressed the teachings and Tradition of the Church, defended her against heresy, interpreted the Scriptures, and preached and wrote on matters of doctrine and morality. They were men of great intellect, excellent education, and deep prayer who were illumined by the Holy Spirit. Doctrinal statements made by church councils often began with the words "Following the Holy Fathers . . ." This is not a mere formality or poetic formula. It is a statement indicating that the decision of the council is consistent with the Fathers and therefore consistent with Tradition. The Fathers are the "recognized defenders of truth against heretical distortions and have therefore become the privileged spokesmen of the authentic Christian tradition."[1]

---

1   Meyendorff, "Doing Theology," 83.

185

The Importance of the Fathers

THERE IS NO ORTHODOX THEOLOGY without the Fathers. They are not relegated to a corner of church history, to icons or footnotes as a reminder of the past. The opposite is true. The writings of the Fathers occupy a central place in Orthodox theology almost for the same reason that the Bible does: because they are relevant, contemporary, inspired, deep, and profound. The Fathers were brilliant, holy men whose writings inspire and guide us today because those qualities were recognized by the faithful who came after them.

The Fathers function as a kind of authority in Orthodoxy, but not in any formal or rigid sense. The Fathers offer guidelines. The authority is really the Tradition. The Fathers are its universally recognized representatives and spokesmen because they faithfully and accurately preserved and articulated Holy Tradition. Only for this reason are they considered Fathers. Orthodox Christians are confident that we if follow the Fathers, we are in line with Tradition and Scripture. The Fathers are those who interpret Scripture and articulate Tradition for each generation. Their work and life authentically expressed the consciousness of the Church.

The Fathers have an intimate and inseparable relationship with Scripture and Tradition. When heretics used Scripture to support their heresy, the Fathers explained the verses correctly according to the unbroken apostolic Tradition and the totality of the life of the Church. Time and again, as the Church was confronted with new heresies, issues, controversies, and challenges, the Fathers did not create new theology but accurately articulated what the consistent belief of the Church has always been, even if precise terminology had not yet been established or was still being discussed.[2] The Fathers are not

---

2   The correct terminology is important, but more important is the acceptance of what the term means as it is used in the Church. When the Church was laboring to precisely express the divinity of the Son of God, it chose the word *homoousios*. The Son is "one in essence" with the Father, meaning completely equal to God the Father, of the same "substance." Saint Basil knew that the correct terminology alone was not enough, and he rejected those who used the term but did not believe it as it was understood by the Church. "It is therefore desirable to receive them with the confession not only that they believe in the words put forth by our fathers at Nicaea, but also according to the sound meaning expressed by those words." Basil the Great, *Letters*, Letter 125, NPNF-2, 6:194. Conversely, if someone did not want to accept the actual term *homoousios* and yet his

simply literary vocalizations of a historic period, but something beyond it, spokesmen of the spirit of Christianity, bearing a message that has as much weight today as it did at the time when they lived. If, finally, it is they who composed the canon of the New Testament, articulated the dogmas and shaped the liturgy, the importance of the study of their works is obvious as assisting the exact and orthodox interpretation of Scripture, the analysis of Church Dogmatics and the understanding of Christian worship, and furthermore as bearing witness to the faith and life which they promote.[3]

The Fathers had the ability to express and defend the Faith due to their education, knowledge, oratorical and literary gifts, and especially their deep spiritual life of prayer. This is why they were truly theologians—they knew God from *experience*. Patristic theology is rooted in the actual spiritual experience of the Fathers. They were educated, but their writings and sermons were not based on clever argumentation. In fact, they objected to the use of Aristotelian methodology in the pursuit of theological truth. Ironically, that philosophy became foundational for theology in the West, especially under the influence of Thomas Aquinas. This also contributed to the gulf between Eastern and Western Christian thought, since the West embraced this form of argumentation and the East rejected it. Even during the critical debates of the fourth century, when theological terminology was being fleshed out, Fathers such as Gregory the Theologian rejected the use of clever argumentation and Aristotelian syllogisms, preferring the philosophy of the fisherman, the Tradition of the Church.

To be Orthodox is to have the Orthodox phronema. Our phronema exists because the faithful—whether famous or unknown, clergy or laity, men or women, now or in the past—have preserved it, and that includes the Fathers. They expressed the phronema for all of us, and this is why they were recognized as Fathers—not because they were clever or innovative but because

---

belief about the Son was correct, St. Basil did not insist that the person employ that precise term. He was willing to allow people to accept the term gradually so long as their faith was orthodox.

3   Panagiotis K. Chrestou, *Greek Orthodox Patrology,* George Dion Dragas, ed. and trans. (Rollinsford, NH: Orthodox Research Institute, 2005), 7.

they expressed true Orthodoxy. Reading and relying on the Fathers establishes and reinforces the phronema for us and among us.

HOW ONE IS RECOGNIZED AS A FATHER OF THE CHURCH

MOST CHURCH FATHERS ARE MEN who served the Church as bishops, since they, as successors to the apostles, were entrusted with preserving sound doctrine. Some Fathers were presbyters and monks, such as St. Jerome and St. Symeon the New Theologian, but clerical status was never a requirement to be considered a Father of the Church. One could even be a layman, such as St. Justin the Philosopher and Martyr. Because the Orthodox Church is consistent, timeless, and changeless in its phronema, we recognize what is Orthodox and what is not, what is part of the Tradition and what is not, and we honor those who preserved Tradition and expressed it accurately. One is not recognized as a Father through any formal process but when members of the Church begin to cite him as a patristic authority after his death. The Church as a whole, with its phronema, has recognized that he has accurately expressed and faithfully preserved Tradition in his writings and that he has lived a life of holiness.

Certain factors have typically been cited as necessary for one to be considered a Father of the Church: (1) orthodoxy of doctrine, (2) brilliance of mind, (3) holiness of life, and (4) ecclesiastical approval, meaning that the Church recognizes him as a Father. The West also adds the requirement of antiquity, which will be discussed below.

Western Christians emphasize brilliance of mind and antiquity as the primary characteristics. Ecclesiastical approval is not necessarily shared in common between East and West. Catholics recognize men as Fathers whom we reject, such as Clement of Alexandria, Tertullian, Eusebius of Caesarea, and Origen; and, conversely, they reject Fathers whom we accept, such as Photios the Great and Gregory Palamas. Clement of Alexandria, Origen, and Tertullian are important for historical purposes, but they would not be considered Fathers by Orthodox theologians, nor are they cited as authorities. The end of Clement's life is not known, and therefore he cannot be considered a saint.

Tertullian died outside the Church as a Montanist schismatic, and Origen's writings were condemned centuries later by a church council. These men cannot be considered "Fathers" by the Orthodox because Fathers are not merely witnesses to antiquity but witnesses to *truth*.

THE SPECIAL CASE OF ST. AUGUSTINE

AT THIS POINT, A WORD must be said about St. Augustine, who is by far the most important Father in the Catholic Church but is almost entirely ignored in Orthodox Christianity. Augustine is at the root of the deviation of the West from the ancient Tradition. This was well established by twentieth-century Orthodox theologian John Romanides.[4] Augustine made significant theological errors and deviated from the consistent Tradition of the Church. He also introduced an entirely new phronema to the West, primarily the emphasis on faith and reason. The Greek Fathers maintained an unwavering continuity with ancient apostolic Tradition in language, thought, and phronema, never yoking faith and reason. Augustine was a prolific writer, and the Latin West came to rely almost exclusively on him for its theology and phronema. On the other hand, the East enjoyed many notable Greek Fathers and never depended heavily on any single one of them. Augustine dominated and shaped the Western Christian mind. Western Christian theology is founded on the phronema of Augustine. The East did not acquire the mind of *one* Father, but the mind of the *Fathers*.

Augustine's writings were not translated into Greek until the high Middle Ages, when theological issues had already divided East and West. Prior to those translations, the Orthodox had no knowledge of Augustine's phronema or his theological errors. He had already been accepted as a saint and a Father in the East, based on his reputation in the West, long before the Great Schism, but he was never cited in the East, since knowledge of Latin was uncommon there. Today, Augustine is rarely cited by Orthodox theologians, and never for dogmatic purposes. If he is used at all, he would be cited only with

---

4   See for example, *Franks, Romanism, Feudalism and Doctrine* (Brookline, MA: Holy Cross Orthodox Press, 1982); and *The Ancestral Sin*, George S. Gabriel, trans. (Ridgewood, NJ: Zephyr Publishing, 1998).

extreme caution and probably more for historical purposes or Scripture interpretation. In other words, Augustine has the title "Father" but is not treated
as one by the Orthodox.

Some Orthodox Christians argue that St. Augustine is not even a saint,
because in Orthodox circles he is routinely referred to as "the Blessed Augustine." But St. Augustine is on the Church's canon of saints, and there is no
such thing in the Church as someone who is "sort of a saint." Titles such as
"Blessed" or "Venerable" (*Hosios*) are simply descriptive or honorific. They do
not indicate that someone is not exactly a saint or somehow occupies a lower
position than other saints. Other Orthodox Christians argue that Augustine
should not be considered a Father because of his errors. But such a stance is
contrary to Orthodox phronema. Augustine is a Father because he has been
regarded as one for hundreds of years, and it is unorthodox to individually
oppose the position of the Church.

Since Augustine's writings have become more accessible in translation and
on the internet, they are facing greater scrutiny and widespread disapproval
among Orthodox faithful and theologians. In many instances, Augustine does
faithfully express the ancient tradition of the Church, common to East and
West. But the title "Father of the Church" requires that one faithfully preserve
apostolic teaching unchanged, and the Orthodox overwhelmingly concur
that Augustine deviated from Tradition and committed serious theological
errors.[5] Since no formal process exists for declaring someone to be either a
Father or not a Father, it is very possible that in the future Orthodox Christianity will not recognize Augustine as a Father. However, this cannot be based
on the opinion of individuals. It will require the consensus of the Church over
a long period of time.

---

5   Augustine changed the understanding of the Fall and original sin from that of the early
    Church, forever influencing the West's conception of sin, forgiveness, and spiritual
    perfection. See Romanides, *Ancestral Sin*, 155–169. Augustine was also responsible for
    introducing the idea that the Holy Spirit proceeds from the Son, as well as belief in the
    progress or development of dogma. He furthermore changed theological methodology
    by the application of imagination and conjecture and the conformity of theology to
    reason, which had never been the practice of the Greek Fathers. See chapter 9 below and
    Romanides, *Dogmatike kai Symboliki Theologia tes Orthodoxes Katholikes Ekklesias*, vol. 1
    (Thessaloniki: Pournaras Press, 1973), 28–32.

The High Patristic Standards in Orthodoxy

THE STANDARDS FOR AN ECCLESIASTICAL writer to be considered a Father are much higher in Orthodoxy than in the West for two reasons. First, we rely on the Fathers, and they hold an importance in Orthodoxy that far exceeds what they mean to the West. The Fathers are cited and used by the Orthodox as the dependable expression of the apostolic faith, assurance that a theologian's teaching is consistent with Tradition. It would be inconceivable to cite someone who died as a schismatic, such as Tertullian, or who accepted Arianism, such as Eusebius of Caesarea, as a trustworthy guide and expositor of the Tradition.

Second, we require saintliness of the Fathers. They are cited as authorities primarily because of their holiness of life as true theologians. Therefore, if we are not certain that a man died as a saint, how could he possibly be considered a Father? But because the West values primarily mental acumen, reason, and logic over prayer for its theology, the West can accept ecclesiastical writers as Fathers primarily on the basis of their witness to antiquity and their brilliance of mind. Although personal holiness is recognized, it appears less important, if important at all.

Theology cannot be separated from the life of prayer and the practice of virtue. This is why the Fathers are the greatest and only *true* theologians of the Church. We value not only their consistent witness to the Tradition but the authority with which they proclaim it, an authority based not on external approval, formulas, or definitions but on their lives, which were perfected through prayer and the acquisition of virtue. The Fathers are not only the preservers of Orthodoxy, that is, true faith and true worship, but "the transmitters of 'Orthopraxy,'" the true practice of that faith.[6]

Was There a Patristic Era?

WESTERN CHRISTIANS TYPICALLY ADD ANTIQUITY as a requirement for being regarded as a Father, but there is no agreement as to what date marks the end of antiquity.[7] The Orthodox, however, do not require antiquity,

---

6   Harakas, "Tradition," 158.
7   Constantine Tsirpanlis, *Introduction to Eastern Patristic Thought and Orthodox Theology*,

nor do they recognize any chronological limitation for the Fathers, because the teachings of the Fathers were never superseded by later theological developments.

> From the Western point of view "the Age of the Fathers" has been succeeded, and indeed superseded, by "the Age of the Schoolmen," which was an essential step forward. Since the rise of Scholasticism, "Patristic theology" has been antiquated, has become actually a "past age," a kind of archaic prelude. If the East accepts that there was an Age of the Fathers then either one has to regret the "backwardness" of the East which never developed a "Scholasticism" of its own, or one should retire into the "Ancient Age" . . . and practice what has been described . . . as a "theology of repetition." The latter, in fact, is just a peculiar form of imitative "scholasticism."[8]

Restricting the patristic age to a specific date is "totally arbitrary" and unnatural, since the Fathers are "the bearers of the divine grace of the Spirit." The Church "has never restricted this appearance to any particular period of her history." Because of the "Orthodox ecclesiastical consciousness," the Church "attributes the title of father in every epoch."[9] We have Fathers from every era of the Church, including some from the early second century (e.g., St. Ignatius of Antioch), and some from more recent times, such as St. Nicodemus of the Holy Mountain in the nineteenth century and St. John of Kronstadt, who reposed in the twentieth.

The Church is patristic and will always be patristic, not because we live in the past but because the Fathers expressed the timeless and continuous Tradition of the Church. For that reason, every era can produce Fathers. Since we reject development of doctrine, what the Fathers expressed in the past is just as true and complete today as it was for their time. There are also Holy

---

Theology and Life, vol. 30 (Collegeville, MN: Liturgical Press, 1991), 21. Although Catholics tend to accept "antiquity" as a criterion, most would also recognize Bernard of Clairvaux (d. 1153) as a Church Father. The Fathers proposed as marking the end of the patristic era have ranged from Gregory the Great (d. 604) to John of Damascus (d. 750), but some place the end as early as the Fourth Ecumenical Council (451).

8 Florovsky, Bible, Church and Tradition, 110.

9 Chrestou, Greek Orthodox Patrology, 15–16.

Mothers of the Church; however, we have few writings by saintly women. Until recently, women were not usually educated, and since women were never priests or bishops, they did not often preach or produce many writings.

The Interrelatedness of Scripture, Tradition, and the Fathers

TRADITION, SCRIPTURE, AND THE FATHERS cannot be separated. They have no defined spheres. Each relies on the others and reflects the others. The books of the New Testament are not "something outside the tradition, according to the scheme that distinguishes Scripture from Tradition, nor something higher than the Tradition, because they are the written part of the Tradition of the Apostles."[10] The Fathers function as authority in the Orthodox Church because they express Holy Tradition and the correct interpretation of Scripture. By articulating these, the Fathers became part of that Tradition as those who knew, understood, defended, strengthened, perpetuated, promoted, and clarified the Scriptures and Tradition.

The Fathers are a trustworthy, consistent, and stable expression of both Scripture and Tradition, regardless of when or where they wrote. "Tradition for them was not the enumeration of quotations from the Scriptures or the previous Fathers; it was the offspring of the Incarnation of the Word of God which took place in space and time. Thus Tradition was a continuous extension into history of the Incarnation of the Son of God."[11] Their writings resonate within the Church and are accepted instinctively and intuitively as the Faith the Church has always taught.

FREEDOM, AUTHORITY, AND THE FATHERS

IT IS NOT AN EXAGGERATION to say that to be in agreement with the Fathers is to be Orthodox. Conversely, if one is not in agreement with the Fathers, one is not Orthodox. This is not to say that the Fathers agreed perfectly among themselves on absolutely everything, but they are consistent on

---

10   Chrestou, 91.
11   George S. Bebis, "The Concept of Tradition in the Fathers of the Church," *Greek Orthodox Theological Review* 15, no. 1 (Spring, 1970): 22–55, 50.

matters of doctrine, morality, and the spiritual life. They function as authorities because when we read them, we recognize that what they express is *true*. We know it to be true because we share with them the phronema of the ancient Church. We are not obligated to follow them like mindless robots. The Fathers do not impose their views on us, and they have no authority over us, over Scripture, or over Tradition. No one insists that we comply or obey. Archimandrite Vasileios, Abbot of the Iveron Monastery on Mt. Athos, wrote simply:

> In the Church you do not receive external, mechanical orders which turn you into a puppet; nor do you improvise for yourself, making the people under your pastoral care into guinea pigs. You are free, you move spontaneously and you obey one truth and life. You die and are buried with Christ.[12]

Orthodoxy rejects compulsion and treasures freedom. Orthodoxy treasures and insists on freedom because it is "an essential element of our likeness to God."[13] Conformity to the Fathers or any other authority, even ecclesiastical authority, is never a matter of obedience or submission in the way that Vatican documents require Catholics to submit to the Roman pontiff and the decisions of the magisterium.

> The opinions of the Fathers are accepted not as a formal subjection to outward authority, but because of the inner evidence of their catholic truth. The *whole body* of the Church has the right of verifying, or to be more exact, the right and not only the right but the duty, of *certifying* the truth.[14]

Submission to ecclesiastical authority is not required of us because in Orthodoxy, the *people* are the "guardians of piety,"[15] and the Fathers give words

---

12   Archimandrite Vasileios, *What Is Unique about Orthodox Culture?* Elizabeth Theokritoff, trans. (Montreal: Alexander Press, 2001), 42.
13   John Meyendorff, "Historical Relativism and Authority in Christian Dogma," in *The New Man: An Orthodox and Reformed Dialogue* (New Brunswick, NY: Agora Books, 1973), 87.
14   Florovsky, *Bible, Church and Tradition,* 53. Emphasis in the original.
15   Encyclical Letter of the Eastern Patriarchs, 1848.

to what we instinctively know and experience. We love the Fathers and willingly seek to conform our minds to their mind, because we recognize in them
the mind of the Church, the mind of Christ. The teaching of the Fathers is "a
constant and ultimate measure or criterion of right belief. In this sense, again,
Fathers are not merely witnesses of the old faith, but above all and primarily
witnesses of the true faith."[16] The Fathers embody what Orthodox Christianity
represents and cherishes: truth, stability, constancy, timelessness. Our goal in
reading them is to do as they do, to think as they thought, to live as they lived,
and to pass on to the next generation what we have received from them exactly
as they have preserved it for us because of their faithfulness to Holy Tradition.

WHAT IS MEANT BY "ACCORDING TO THE FATHERS"

IN ORTHODOXY THERE ARE NO different types of theology such as we see
in the West: feminist, progressive, womanist, natural, liberation, fundamentalist, traditional, etc. Our theology is pure, consistent throughout time. It is
deep but relatively uncomplicated. It is the theology of the apostolic Church
as preserved and expressed by the Fathers. There is no other way to be Orthodox. There is no other way to think as an Orthodox Christian. For this reason,
conciliar statements begin with the expression, "Following the Holy Fathers."

> "Following the Holy Fathers" . . . is not a reference to abstract tradition, to for-
> mulas or propositions. It is primarily an appeal to persons, to holy witnesses.
> The witness of the Fathers belongs, integrally and intrinsically, to the very struc-
> ture of the Orthodox faith. The Church is equally committed to the kerygma of
> the Apostles and to the dogmata of the Fathers. Both belong together insepa-
> rably. The Church is indeed *"Apostolic."* But the Church is also *"Patristic."* And
> only by being *"Patristic"* is the Church continuously *"Apostolic."*[17]

The Fathers exude Orthodoxy, and we imbibe them deeply. They are never
far from us; like familiar friends, we turn to them again and again. They are

---

16   Florovsky, *Aspects of Church History*, 16.
17   Florovsky, 16. Emphasis in the original.

our most important resource, and good Orthodox theologians read them lav-
ishly and incessantly, whether our field is dogmatics, church history, patristics, the canons, spirituality, or Scripture. Turning to the Fathers consistently
and extensively shapes us and forms us to think as Orthodox Christians, provided we also live a completely Orthodox life in the Church. Our objective is
to acquire the mind of the Fathers, and by reading them persistently, we do.
This is deeply ingrained within us. Jaroslav Pelikan noted:

> A twelfth-century theologian observed that "the Romans (that is, the Byzan-
> tines) are exceedingly manly in other respects; but when it comes to trans-
> gressing the boundaries of the holy fathers, they are extremely cowardly."[18]

This peculiar attitude toward the Holy Fathers has always been quite puzzling to the West. Those of us who have extensive discussions with Western
Christians have experienced their frustration when we refuse to contravene
Tradition and the Fathers. "The norm of orthodoxy, the requirement that a
doctrine be one that has been always believed, referred with special force to
the 'doctrines of the fathers who spoke of God' from which it was wrong to
deviate."[19] We simply follow the Fathers.

> To follow does not mean either to return or to walk forward. To follow means to
> come after, and the one who comes after does not determine his course by him-
> self but is set on the course of him or them whom he comes after. "Following
> the holy Fathers" then, means "coming after the holy Fathers," not returning to
> the past of their historical presence, nor transforming them into archeological
> treasures in the present and future. "Following the holy Fathers" means accept-
> ing the living presence of the holy Fathers as members of the single body of

---

18 Theorianus, *Disputations with Narsai* IV.2, P.G. 133:289, Pelikan, *Christian Tradition*,
    vol. 2, *The Spirit of Eastern Christendom (600–1700)* (Chicago: University of Chicago
    Press, 1974), 9. The term "Byzantine Empire" is a construction of the West. People who
    lived in what is today called the "Byzantine Empire" would never have recognized that
    term. They proudly called themselves "Romans" because their empire was an unbroken
    continuation of the ancient Roman Empire.
19 Pelikan, *Christian Tradition*, 1:336.

Christ, to which we also belong, and being led by their life teaching, by their manner and mind. This is the sole duty of the Orthodox.[20]

Orthodox Christians interpret the Bible according to the Fathers, but this does not mean that we can only parrot the Fathers and are not permitted insights of our own. It is not Orthodox to insist that if the Fathers did not already say something, it is not valid. A theology of repetition would virtually deny the presence and action of the Holy Spirit in the life of the Church. The Fathers did not exhaust the meaning of the Bible, nor did they comment on every issue the Church will ever face. "According to the Fathers" means that we are in agreement with the Fathers and that they would have been in agreement with us, because we share the same phronema. "Following the Fathers" means expressing the phronema of the Fathers, but this can occur in a fresh way that is inspired by the Holy Spirit and responds to the needs of the Church today.

The Fathers responded to the heresies, challenges, and situations of their time and articulated the beliefs of the Church for their times. Their statements were accepted by the Church because they reflected the phronema of Orthodox Christianity. They spoke according to the Fathers who had come before *them.* They were in line with sacred Tradition. Our era also has its unique challenges, and Orthodox theologians must express the Tradition of the Church on issues that the Fathers themselves never addressed—such as climate change, social media, pollution, feminism, reproductive technology, and gender identity. It is not sufficient simply to find some appropriate quotation from the Fathers. If we have the mind of the Fathers, we will be able to address those issues in the same manner they would have done.

Theological arguments that appear rational and irrefutable to Western Christians often rely on deductive reasoning, which is not persuasive to Orthodox Christians. Conversely, Western Christians are not persuaded by what we believe to be the strongest and most important position in every controversy: the consistent, unwavering belief and practice of the Church. This is Holy Tradition, that which the Orthodox Church has continually known,

---

20   Giorgios I. Mantzarides, *Orthodox Spiritual Life,* Keith Schram, trans. (Brookline, MA: Holy Cross Orthodox Press, 1994), 5. Emphasis added.

lived, adhered to, and preserved from the beginning as expressed in the writings of the Fathers. No artfully reasoned argument can overcome or replace this ultimate standard for Orthodox theologians. The criticism expressed by Humbert of Romans toward Greek theologians—"they do not understand what is said to them with reasons, but always adhere to some councils or other, and to what has been handed down on to them by their predecessors"[21]—is a badge of honor and a tremendous compliment to any Orthodox Christian. The Fathers are important to Catholics as well, to a limited degree, but not for the same reason. The Fathers do not function methodologically or theologically in the Catholic Church as they do for the Orthodox. The Orthodox Church truly is "the Church of the Fathers."

Patristic Infallibility and Patristic Fundamentalism

THERE ARE LIMITATIONS EVEN FOR the Fathers and our use of them. Furthermore, we must not overexaggerate their role or authority out of piety or zeal. Heresies were present in antiquity, and even some Fathers of the Church occasionally expressed ideas that were not universally accepted.

Some Protestant Christians today advocate millennialism, the belief that when the Lord returns, He will establish an earthly kingdom and rule for a thousand years. They defend this belief on the basis that some early Christians held this view, such as Justin Martyr, an early Father of the Church. But millennialism was not universally accepted, nor was it apostolic. Saints and Fathers sometimes made mistakes.

As much as we respect the Fathers, we do not elevate their opinions to the level of infallibility, nor should we apply their statements in a fundamentalist manner. The Fathers were human beings with their own weaknesses and flaws. They made no mistakes on matters of dogma or morality—otherwise they would not be Fathers—but they were men of their times, just as we are people of our times. None of us can entirely separate ourselves from who we are. Our culture, education, family, nation, and religious background affect the way we view the world. We all accept as true many common presumptions

---

21   Every, *Misunderstandings,* 993.

of our era and culture. They are so deeply ingrained that we do not recognize them as cultural presumptions that may in fact *not* be true.

The Fathers often reflected many of the prevailing attitudes of their times as they addressed issues such as gender roles. Their personal life experiences and education also influenced their opinions. In chapter 8 we discussed how the Bible is a product of synergy. God illumined the biblical authors, but they were not removed from their times and cultures. When we interpret the Bible, we must consider its cultural context to understand it correctly. Similarly, when we read the Fathers of the Church, we must remember their historical milieu.

Sometimes the Fathers are criticized and accused of misogyny or anti-Semitism. Their fiery rhetoric can also seem extremely harsh to us, since our culture prefers a respectful tone rather than the exaggerated and emotional style popular during their times. Impassioned rhetoric was the norm in the early centuries of the Church, and people were not easily offended as we are today. People in earlier eras also did not expect dispassionate, detached objectivity from a speaker or that a writer present both sides of an issue.

We should not judge the people of the past by applying the standards of our times (as though our judgments and values were flawless!), but neither should we take patristic comments out of context or accept every comment as though it were automatically sanctified because it came from a Father. A proper understanding of the Fathers sometimes requires discernment, spiritual maturity, and knowledge of their theological, historical, and cultural context.

ERRORS AND *THEOLOGOUMENA* IN THE FATHERS

As MUCH AS WE RESPECT them, the Fathers are not infallible in Orthodoxy. This is accepted by the Fathers themselves. Saint Photios the Great discussed this issue and was not troubled by "error (even 'godless error,' *dyssebema*)" which might occasionally be found in the writings of the Fathers. In spite of a rare error, they "were admirable by reason of many other qualities which manifest virtue and piety."[22] We benefit from historical hindsight, and

---

22 Augustine Casiday, "Church Fathers," 180, citing Photios, *Mystagogy* 75 and *Letter* 24.21.

because of this "we are obliged to be charitable." Saint Photios also believed that even venerable Fathers were "not *ipso facto* inerrant, that a saint can be in error and that holiness is distinguishable from accuracy even amongst the Greek Fathers."[23]

Occasionally, a Father or two takes a theological position that is not shared by the rest of the Church. This does not mean that he is no longer to be regarded as a Father. We simply recognize that in this particular area, his view is not consistent with the Tradition of the Church or is not universally recognized. We call this a *theologoumenon*,[24] which is the opinion of one Father or a small group of Fathers. Such irregular patristic statements, which deviate from the patristic norm, are not cited by Orthodox theologians as authority[25] or used to guide the faithful, even if they were expressed by a highly respected Father of the Church. It matters not who said it but whether it is consistent with the Tradition and universally accepted within the Church. So, generally speaking, that type of patristic opinion is ignored or overlooked among the Orthodox.[26] Even if a highly regarded Father wrote it, that position does not become the basis for expanding theology or developing other ideas, because it is a deviation from the Tradition of the Church. This shows the limits of patristic authority.

It is clear that the Fathers are not in complete agreement on everything. This serves as an important model for us in our discussions within the Church. Orthodoxy accepts a certain amount of freedom in theologizing. Conformity is not demanded of us on all matters. It is unfortunate when Orthodox Christians repeat the erroneous idea that the Fathers are in agreement on absolutely everything. It is far better to realize that the Fathers disagreed at times and yet were in agreement on the crucial matters of dogma and morality. Andrew

23 Casiday, 180.
24 Pronounced "theh-oh-loh-GHOU-meh-nohn." *Theologoumena* is the plural.
25 *Theologoumena* are discussed by Orthodox theologians but would not be cited to support an idea, since we recognize that the opinion is not universally held within the Church.
26 The most commonly cited example of this is St. Gregory of Nyssa, who reportedly expressed the belief that ultimately everyone would be saved. Some Orthodox theologians think that he never taught this but rather that what he wrote was misunderstood. But even if he actually held this view, it would not be accepted or promoted as a teaching or alternative teaching of the Church, because it deviates from the unbroken Tradition of the Church.

Louth expressed it well: "We should beware of trying to iron out the differences between them. What we should hear from the chorus of the Fathers is rich harmony, not a thin unison."[27]

THE WESTERN APPROACH TO THE FATHERS

THE ORTHODOX CARE DEEPLY ABOUT the Fathers, and Orthodox schools of theology devote a significant amount of time and attention to them. By contrast, Catholic theologians may learn about the Fathers in graduate school, but they quickly move on to scholastic theology and then to more modern trends. Many university theology departments and graduate schools, even at Catholic institutions, have no courses at all on patristics. Catholic theologians are generally not oriented toward the Fathers, and familiarity with them is not emphasized. I cannot recall ever hearing a lecture or presentation by a Catholic scholar or student who ever cited even a single Father, with the possible exception of St. Augustine.

This is not to say that the Fathers are expendable for Catholics, only that Catholics seem to look chiefly to papal documents as the primary expression of the tradition of the Catholic Church. Papal documents, canon law, and catechisms often contain brief citations or quotations from the Fathers to support theological developments that the Catholic Church has created, which were often not patristic teachings at all. The Fathers are distant, filtered through the lens of papal documents and a thousand-plus years of Catholic history and culture. They are faint echoes, important for their time and for their contribution to the development and exposition of doctrine. They are valued as witnesses to the traditions and thought of the early Church, but they have been superseded in the Catholic tradition to the extent that they have little impact on Catholic theology today.

In recent decades, interest in the early Church and an appreciation for our common Christian history has steadily increased in some Protestant circles. This development is not shared among all Protestants, most of whom have no orientation to the early Church other than the Book of Acts.

---

27 Louth, *Introducing Eastern Orthodox Theology*, 13.

Increasing Protestant awareness of the importance of the patristic tradition and an appreciation for the writings of the Church Fathers is evidenced today by the growing number of Protestant publishers that are printing English translations of patristic works. This development is most welcome, and many Western Christians have discovered Orthodoxy and the early Church through exposure to the writings of the Fathers.

UNDERSTANDING AND MISUNDERSTANDING THE FATHERS

KNOWLEDGE OF THE CONTEXT OF the Fathers—their historical situation, the controversies of their day, their audience in a given writing, etc.—is critical to understanding patristic writings. Too often Orthodox Christians make vague general statements that begin, 'The Fathers say . . ." followed by some theological point. One wonders whether this is simply an opinion or impression formed by the speaker, who now buttresses his argument by ascribing it to some anonymous throng of Fathers. The Fathers do not say anything as a group, except for decisions issued as a council. Individual Fathers made statements at certain times for certain purposes and to specific audiences. Consensus exists among the Fathers as to dogma, spirituality, and morality, but if we truly value the Fathers as we claim to do, we should be able to say who said what and why he said it. If we acquire only general notions about the Fathers, we produce weak and useless statements prefaced by "The Fathers say . . ."

Vague generalities about the Fathers do great injustice to the Orthodox Tradition. We give the impression of "imitation and immobility."[28] We have sometimes been criticized by other Christians because they have the impression that Orthodoxy really has nothing to offer, nothing to say. Everything worth saying has been said already by the Fathers, and now we simply repeat them. We are not called to be parrots but "reason-endowed sheep." Finding patristic quotations and reciting them to support our opinion is unacceptable if we do not understand the Fathers or if we take them out of context.

---

28   Savas Agourides, "Teaching Scriptures," a paper presented at the Second Consultation of Orthodox Theological Schools (New York: 1982), 1–10, 3.

It is utterly misleading to single out particular statements of the Fathers and to detach them from the total perspective in which they have been actually uttered, just as it is misleading to manipulate with detached quotations from the Scripture. It is a dangerous habit "to quote" the Fathers, that is their isolated sayings and phrases, outside of that concrete setting in which only they have their full and proper meaning and are truly alive. "To follow" the Fathers does *not* mean just *"to quote"* them. "To follow" the Fathers means to acquire their "mind," their phronema.[29]

Piling up patristic quotations rather than actually understanding the Fathers is a distortion and a type of Orthodox scholasticism. In our zeal for the Fathers we have imitated the West by making statements and quoting the Fathers as proof texts, depriving them of their life and spirit rather than standing in the stream of Tradition along with them. When we fail to understand the Bible in its context or simply quote isolated verses, we distort it. Likewise, quoting isolated patristic statements and ignoring their context in the patristic writings distorts and misuses the Fathers.

One particularly unfortunate example of citing the Fathers without understanding them is Orthodox Christian creationists who imitate fundamentalist Protestants by insisting on a literal interpretation of the Genesis creation accounts—because the Fathers said that Genesis must be understood literally. They proudly claim to prove their Orthodoxy by insisting on their misguided patristic interpretation of Genesis. Unfortunately, they have read enough of the Fathers to *mis*understand them but not enough to understand them.[30] It is much easier to fling a few patristic quotes at a theological opponent and assume a posture of Orthodox triumphalism than it is to be quiet and humble,

---

29 Florovsky, *Bible, Church and Tradition*, 109.
30 By saying that the creation accounts must be understood "literally," the Fathers were not advocating a Protestant-style fundamentalist interpretation. They recognized that the Scriptures are not "literally" true as a description of events, since God cannot be described. Rather, the Fathers were opposing the allegorical interpretation of Genesis by heretics who said that God did not create the world and that the creation stories must be understood "allegorically," as symbols of something else. By insisting on the "literal" truth of Genesis, they were affirming that God indeed created everything in the universe.

read deeply, study the principles of patristic interpretation, and enter into the mind of the Fathers.[31]

USING AND MISUSING THE FATHERS

Even worse than misreading the Fathers is purposely misquoting them to support one's position. On one occasion, I pointed out to a supposedly Orthodox internet disputant that his theological understanding was incorrect. His arrogant dismissal of my explanation compelled me to point out that he was unqualified to give theological opinions, since he had no theological education. He quickly posted a quotation from St. John Chrysostom: "Wait for no other teacher—you have the word of God."[32] Clearly my disputant was implying that no education is needed to theologize or to correctly interpret the Bible, and he misused Chrysostom to make his point.

This is certainly not what Chrysostom intended to convey. Chrysostom did not make that statement to encourage his congregation to theologize without training. He was encouraging them to read the Bible and not to be intimidated by it. He told them that the books of the Bible were composed by simple people in simple Greek so that no person could say he could not understand it. Chrysostom never promoted ignorance in the Scriptures or theology. He often spoke of the importance of learning about and defending correct doctrine, learning about the Scriptures, their language, style, tools for interpretation, and so on. Quoting Chrysostom saying "wait for no other teacher" to defend ignorance or to suggest that theological education is not necessary is a distortion and a misuse of his teachings.

Moreover, the Lord also, by urging the Jews to "search the Scriptures" (John 5:39) made our study of them still more imperative. Indeed, He would not have spoken thus if it were possible to grasp them at once and from the first reading. No one would ever search out the meaning of what is evident, but only the

---

31 The same lazy and misinformed approach is applied to the holy canons, which also can be properly understood only in their historical context and require even greater theological knowledge and spiritual discernment.

32 Chrysostom, *Homilies on Colossians*, Homily 9.1.

meaning of what is obscure and found only after much seeking. It is for this reason, also that he said, that they are a hidden treasure: so spur us on to the search. Now, He said these things to us in order that we might not approach the words of the Scriptures casually, but with great care. For if someone should listen to what is written in them without examining into the meaning and should accept everything in its literal sense, he would get many strange notions about God. For example, he would learn that He is a man, and made of bronze, and angry and hot-tempered and many ideas of Him still stranger than these. But by examining the sense that lies hidden deep within he will rid himself of all these strange doctrines.[33]

The statements by Chrysostom about the need for serious study of the Bible are numerous. Chrysostom encountered many people who claimed that serious study was unnecessary, just as Orthodox armchair theologians today defend themselves by quoting the maxim "the theologian is the one who prays." Commenting on Colossians 3:16, "Let the word of Christ dwell in you richly," Chrysostom mentioned the scriptural excuses some gave for their ignorance:

But what do those who are more irrational than drones say in reply? "Blessed be every simple soul" and "He that walks in simplicity walks confidently" (Prov. 10:9). Now, it is the cause of all kinds of evils that many do not know how to use the testimony of Scriptures rightly. "Simple" here does not mean "irrational" and does not refer to the man who knows nothing, but the blameless, the man who does no evil, the prudent. If it were otherwise, it was vain to hear, "Be therefore wise as serpents and simple as doves" (Matt. 10:16). But why should I say these things since this discussion is beside the point? In addition to what we have mentioned, other things are not right with us, I mean those pertaining to our life and conduct.[34]

It is dishonest and reprehensible for an Orthodox Christian who claims to respect the Fathers to deliberately distort them or to cherry-pick their

---

33 Chrysostom, *Homilies on the Gospel of John*, Homily 15, FOTC, 33:141.
34 Chrysostom, *Homilies on John*, Homily 17, FOTC, 33:172.

statements to find something that suits his purposes. We are called to acquire the mind of the Fathers, not to quote isolated statements from them.

ACQUIRING THE MIND OF THE FATHERS

WE CANNOT ACQUIRE THE MIND of the Fathers if we do not read them and understand them in their historical and theological context. Knowing their context means knowing about the life of a specific Father, his background, education, controversies, writings, and place in church history, as well as basic Orthodox doctrine. The Fathers continually refuted heresies, and their points escape our understanding if we do not realize what they are referring to or why they are making a particular statement.

For example, Chrysostom frequently paused to emphasize that the Old Testament is Scripture. Why? Was the congregation so uninformed that they needed to be reminded that the Old Testament is Scripture? Chrysostom almost always stops to comment on the word "through" (*dia*). Again, why would he stop to call their attention to a simple word like "through"?[35] If we read Chrysostom and do not understand such things, then we do not fully understand Chrysostom.

We are not expected to be patristic experts, and no one is born with theological knowledge. Each of us must apply effort to continue to grow in our understanding. But we should realize that if we do not understand Chrysostom's motivation and context, or those of any Father—whether pastoral, theological, moral, or personal—we certainly do not understand him well enough to quote him, nor should we imagine that we can theologize or

---

35 Chrysostom emphasized that the Old Testament is Scripture because the heretic Marcion rejected the Jewish Scriptures, and Marcion had founded many heretical "Marcionite" churches. The Manicheans also rejected the Jewish Scriptures, and the pagans mocked the Old Testament as crude. Chrysostom almost always stops to comment on the word "through." The Arian heretics claimed that the Son was not equal to the Father because the Gospel of John states about the Son/Logos, "All things were made *through* him" (John 1:3). The Arians used that word to argue that this indicated that the Son was an intermediary for the Father and not equal to the Father. So, every time the word "through" is used in reference to the Father or the Spirit, Chrysostom stops to point that out to the congregation to show that the Arian argument, that the use of "through" proves the inferiority of the Son, is baseless.

206

represent ourselves as knowledgeable. We cannot acquire the mind of the Fathers if we do not understand the reasons for their statements. Without the mind of the Fathers, we cannot apply their thought to our times, and we cannot effectively bring the gospel to the world. We cannot carry the Tradition forward and keep it alive and relevant. We have much more work to do if we wish to theologize.

I have explained the importance of the Fathers in Orthodox Christianity. But the majority of Orthodox Christians have never read the Fathers and never will. While the Fathers are important for our theology, and Orthodox theologians must know them well, acquiring an Orthodox phronema does not require any particular academic knowledge of the Fathers or any direct familiarity with their works. The Fathers often focused on complex theological and scriptural issues, matters that are often over the heads of most Orthodox Christians and would not be very useful. Reading the lives of the saints, spiritual works, or even introductory materials about the Orthodox Church or the Bible would be more beneficial for most Orthodox Christians.

Many things shape our phronema. Because the mind of the Fathers expresses the Tradition of the Church, even if we never read the Fathers, we can still have the mind of the Fathers—an Orthodox phronema.

CHAPTER 10

Characteristics of the True Orthodox Theologian

WE HAVE DESCRIBED PHRONEMA, THEOLOGY, the theologian, and how the foundations of Orthodox theology shape our phronema. What characterizes a true Orthodox theologian? An Orthodox theologian adheres to apostolic teaching as expressed in the Bible and Tradition and uses the Fathers as trustworthy guides. Generally speaking, the Orthodox theologian embraces the totality of life in the Church, and his or her manner of life should reflect the Orthodox phronema. What is particularly distinctive about Orthodox theologians in the approach or attitude they bring to the act of theologizing?

Orthodox theologians, regardless of their different institutions and areas of specialization, "feel and think within a given framework of concern which unifies us," writes Nikos Nissiotis. He identified three areas of consensus among Orthodox theologians as they define theology.[1] First, "theology is the articulate expression of the event of the ecclesial faith as it is lived within an Orthodox ecclesial communion." In other words, the theologian must be accurate, not simply in an academic or technical fashion, but must express the Orthodox faith as it is *lived* within the Church.

Second, "theology expresses the unbroken historical continuity of the

---

1   Nikos Nissiotis, "Orthodox Theological Education: Reality and Perspectives" (academic paper), July 12–19, 1977, Syndesmos Consultation on Orthodox Theological Education, Geneva, Switzerland, 2.

apostolic faith as it is clearly stated basically in the Bible and consistently explained, expounded and systematized by the Church writers of all centuries." Therefore, the theologian must be faithful to Tradition, which includes the Bible, the Fathers, and the faith as understood through the totality of the life of the Church throughout the ages.

Finally, theology "is the reasonable interpretation of the liturgical experience of the continuously worshipping community of faith." That is, theology is experience rooted in liturgy and is ultimately doxological, aimed at the glory of the Triune God. The theologian does not attempt to conceptualize but to describe and express the truth of the Orthodox faith, based essentially on his or her experience. This is not something that can entirely be taught. It must also be lived.

This book has frequently referred to the Orthodox maxim, "The true theologian is the one who prays." But other qualities also characterize a true theologian, and it is toward those that we shall direct our attention.

The True Theologian Is Pastoral

THEOLOGY IS ESSENTIALLY PASTORAL. THE theologian serves the Church. The Church as the Body of Christ is composed of human beings on their journey to salvation. Each is made in the image of God, and the role of the theologian is to assist them with great pastoral sensitivity to each person's particular capacity and situation. Theology is not an intellectual pursuit but a spiritual one, and ultimately all theology is pastoral in purpose.

Some of the qualities needed for this pastoral disposition are discussed below, but the primary quality is discernment. This is discussed in the chapters that follow, chapters 13 and 14 on "When to Speak" and "When Not to Speak." We must never forget that each member of the Body of Christ is capable of absorbing only certain things and only at certain times.

Not all people can "endure" hearing the whole truth to the same degree. This is why we will give it gradually and carefully, so that they are not scandalised. This is also what the Fathers always meant when they said "the greatest of virtues is '*discernment.*'" If Christ Himself recognised at one point the inability even of His disciples to understand Him, and "interrupted," saying, "I still have many things to say to you, but you cannot bear them now" (John 16:12), how much more is the modern theologian obliged to evaluate the "endurance" of an audience in each situation, even when there is a well-informed and mature congregation.[2]

Saint Paul wrote, "I have become all things to all men, that I might by all means save some" (1 Cor. 9:22). Those words may sound arrogant to modern ears, but the theologian must have pastoral sensitivity, because everything done in the Church is for the purpose of salvation. Nothing is purely theoretical. This means that what we say, when we say it, how and to whom we say it are all extremely important, including above all our personal attitude, which must always be pastorally oriented.

The True Theologian Practices Humility and Recognizes His Limitations

WHEN A THEOLOGIAN IS ALSO a clergyman, he expresses his unworthiness as a celebrant during the Divine Liturgy. He turns toward the congregation, bows, and asks the people for forgiveness. They bow in response. An attitude of humility when theologizing is essential. The theologian's work is offered to God for the people of God. We must always theologize with an awareness of our own sins, faults, and shortcomings.

> A truly humble person never behaves like a teacher; he will listen, and, whenever his opinion is requested, he responds humbly. In other words, he replies like a student. He who believes that he is capable of correcting others is filled with egotism.[3]

The good theologian knows his or her limitations, not only spiritual weaknesses but intellectual and academic ones. When St. Paul wrote that he had

---

2   Harkianakis, "Theologian in Modern Society," 124. Emphasis in the original.
3   Paisios, *Spiritual Counsels*, 2:51.

"become all things to all people" (1 Cor 9:22), he was not saying that he knew everything, only that he shaped his message to suit his audience and used various methods to present his message. This might include references to the Jewish Scriptures or even to pagan beliefs, such as the Athenian belief in an "unknown god" (Acts 17:22–31).

Pride in a theologian inhibits the ability to theologize for the edification of others, since in that instance the theologian is motivated only by his own desire for glory. He imagines himself to be greater than he is and has no grasp on reality. Pride precludes true theology, just as it prevents the acquisition of virtue. Saint Gregory the Theologian observed:

> This is a state of mind which demands, in special degree, our tears and groans, and has often stirred my pity, from the conviction that imagination robs us in great measure of reality, and that vainglory is a great hindrance to men's attainment of virtue. To heal and stay this disease needs a Peter or Paul, those great disciples of Christ, who in addition to guidance in word and deed, received their grace, and became all things to all men, that they might gain all. But for other men like ourselves, it is a great thing to be rightly guided and led by those who have been charged with the correction and setting right of things such as these.[4]

No Father of the Church wrote more explicitly on the work of theology than St. Gregory the Theologian. Before explaining the task of theology, he began by focusing on the character of the theologian. In a subsequent oration, he briefly reviewed what he had discussed.

> Last time we used theology to cleanse the theologian. We glanced at his character, his audience, the occasion and range of his theorizing. We saw that his character should be undimmed, making for a perception of light by light; that his audience should be serious-minded, to ensure that the word shall be

---

4   Gregory, *Or.* 2.51, *On Defense of His Flight to Pontus. Select Orations of Gregory Nazianzen*, NPNF-2, vol. 7, *Cyril of Jerusalem, Gregory Nazianzen.* Charles Gordon Browne and James Edward Swallow, trans., Philip Schaff and Henry Wace, eds. (Grand Rapids, MI: William B. Eerdmans, 1893), 215–16.

no sterile sowing in sterile ground, that the right occasion is when we own an inner stillness away from the outward whirl, avoiding all fitful checks to the spirit; and that the range should be that of our God-given capacity.[5]

Notice that St. Gregory first discussed the character of the theologian himself, followed by other factors: the nature of the audience, the occasion of his speech, and finally, the "range" of the topic, which "should be that of our God-given capacity." It is a sign of pride—not to mention ignorance and folly—to attempt to discuss matters that exceed the limits of our capacity.

Saint Gregory employed the image of Moses ascending Mt. Sinai to express the idea that we are at different levels. We must accept in humility that most of us are not on the level of Moses. This does not mean that we cannot ascend to a higher level later, only that we must know ourselves and honestly assess our abilities before we theologize. Saint Gregory expressed this reality with very striking and poetic imagery:

I eagerly ascend the mount—or, to speak truer, ascend in eager hope matched with anxiety for my frailty—that I may enter the cloud (Ex. 24:18) and company with God (for such is God's bidding) (Ex. 24:12). Is any an Aaron? He shall come up with me (Ex. 19:24). He shall stand hard by, should he be willing to wait, if need be, outside the cloud. Is any a Nadab, an Abihu, or an elder? He too shall ascend, but stand further off (Ex. 24:1–2,9–10, 14), his place matching his purity. Is any of the crowd unfit, as they are, for so sublime contemplation? Utterly unhallowed?—let him not come near, it is dangerous (Ex. 19:12). Duly prepared?—let him abide below. He shall hear but the voice and the trumpet, true religion's outer expressions; he shall see the mount in smoke with its lightning-flashes (Ex. 19:16–20), warning and wonder to those who cannot ascend it.[6]

---

5   Gregory, *Or.* 28.1 (also known as the "Second Theological Oration"), *On God and Christ. The Five Theological Orations and Two Letters to Cledonius*, Lionel Wickham and Frederick Williams, trans., Popular Patristics, no. 23 (Crestwood, NY: St. Vladimir's Seminary Press, 2002), 37.

6   Gregory, *Or.* 28.2, *On God and Christ*, 37–38.

The True Theologian Is Authentic and Honest

THE THEOLOGIAN MUST BE AUTHENTIC. Phoniness, false piety, feigned humility, or a life of hypocrisy not only draws the judgment of God but in time becomes apparent to all. This can lead others to despair and loss of faith, just as in the case of a clergyman who falls and becomes the subject of a scandal. The clergyman and the theologian who cause scandal are responsible for the souls of those who are scandalized and fall away. Clergy and theologians are the special targets of the evil one. He seeks to destroy us by our own egos, by the false belief that we know better than others, that we would never fall away, when in fact we can deny Christ by our words and our deeds—and many have done so.

The theologian must be honest, not by indiscriminately admitting his or her sins so as to scandalize others, but by recognizing his or her own failings and shortcomings and admitting them when appropriate. The call to theologize must be accepted only with humility and even with reluctance to leap into the fray. It requires regular introspection, self-examination, and confession so that we avoid judging others and falling under our own self-created sentence of condemnation. "For with the judgment you pronounce you will be judged, and the measure you give will be the measure you get" (Matt. 7:2).

Without honesty we do not speak in an authentic manner. But honesty also requires discernment and humility. We will be called to account for the way we present the teachings of the Church and the way we interact with others. Being honest does not require being insensitive, cruel, or judgmental. A gentle explanation does not compromise the faith. An honest reply, especially in personal matters, need not be callous or hurtful. At the same time, the theologian must not shy away from saying what must be said, even if it is difficult. Above all, theology requires love and discernment, since the goal of everything in the Church is to cure spiritual illness, not to inflict wounds.

Theology should never forget that it operates not only on books, but also on living examples and people who voice the word of God for reconciliation and judgment, of salvation and crisis to the world. In other words, theology cannot forget its prophetic function preparing future Church leaders, preachers, charismatic persons and educators. Prophecy is the consciousness that one has, as a committed Christian, to speak and act on behalf of God's word to the world. This consciousness urges theologians of all kinds as described above, to be ready to place the world under the judgment of God, boldly and frankly, against all nationalistic, racial or economic discrimination.[7]

The True Theologian Is Spiritually Vigilant

THE TRUE THEOLOGIAN IS SPIRITUALLY vigilant and struggles against spiritual complacency. It is only in this way that any progress in spiritual enlightenment can occur. Without it, there is no true theology. Without struggle and repentance, we are merely parrots. Our words and lives lack authenticity. We are a sham and a fraud. Father Andrew Louth described how a Russian Orthodox nun, Mother Thekla, expressed the work of her convent following Orthodox Tradition in the environment of contemporary England. It was

> "the innermost battle cry of the monastery, the austere demand of refusing to discuss what is not lived, and the impossibility of living this ourselves: back on to the revolving wheel of repentance: Face God, not man." The sense of theology as rooted in experience, and yet the idea that this experience is beyond us, so that we are constantly pushed back to repent, to turn again to God. This seems to me to be absolutely central to the Orthodox experience of theology, of coming to know God.[8]

Louth chose to relate the quotation because it eloquently captured the endless cyclical encounter between God and humans, the emphasis on experience, the continual seeking of God, the return to repentance, and—especially important for theology—"refusing to discuss what is not lived."

---

7   Nissiotis, "Orthodox Theological Education," 8.
8   Louth, *Introducing Eastern Orthodox Theology*, 7, citing Mother Thekla, *The Monastery of the Assumption: A History*, Library of Orthodox Thinking, pamphlet no. 8 (Whitby, England: Greek Orthodox Monastery of the Assumption, 1984), 16.

The True Theologian Acts from Love and Has Pure Motives

SAINT PAUL'S ADVICE TO THE congregation in Corinth is useful for reflecting on our attitude when theologizing. The Corinthian Christians disputed with each other over who had the superior wisdom: "I belong to Paul, I belong to Apollos, I belong to Cephas," etc. (1 Cor. 1:12). As he instructed the community about leadership, food that had been offered to idols, behavior at worship services, divorce, sexual immorality, and several other issues, St. Paul repeatedly emphasized that "'knowledge' puffs up, but love builds up" (1 Cor. 8:1). It was in *that* context that he penned his famous hymn on love: "Love is patient and kind; love is not jealous or boastful; it is not arrogant or rude," etc. (1 Cor.13:4–5).

Saint Paul was not writing about romantic love but about the attitude each of us, especially clergy and theologians, must have toward others. Without love, our words are nothing more than "a noisy gong or a clanging symbol" (1 Cor. 13:1). Saint Maximos the Confessor commented on the necessity for love when advising his fellow monks: "Since 'knowledge makes boastful but love edifies,' (1 Cor. 8:1) link up love with knowledge and you will not be puffed up but rather a spiritual architect building up yourself and all those around you."[9] He warns against being motivated by glory or pride.

> The one who seeks after the virtues out of vainglory obviously seeks after knowledge as well out of vainglory. Clearly such a person neither does nor says anything for the sake of improvement but is in all circumstances pursuing the approval of the onlookers or hearers. The passion is detected when some of these people impose censure on his deeds or his words and he is enormously grieved thereby, not because he did not edify, for such was not his purpose, but because of his own disgrace.[10]

Hence, the motivation of the theologian must not be ego, otherwise our words have no effect—or if they do, they result in our own condemnation and

---

9 Maximos the Confessor, *Four Hundred Chapters on Love* 4.58, *Maximus the Confessor: Selected Writings*, George C. Berthold, trans., Classics of Western Spirituality (New York: Paulist Press, 1981), 81.

10 Maximos, *Chapters on Love* 3.75, *Selected Writings*, 71–72.

215

destruction, because our motive is to glorify ourselves, not God. Saint Maximos explains:

> This is the reason why love edifies, because it neither envies nor grows angry
> with those who do envy, nor does it make a public display of what is the object
> of envy, nor think that it has already apprehended (Phil.3:12), but confesses
> unabashedly its ignorance of what it does not know. In this way it renders the
> mind modest and constantly prepares it to advance in knowledge.[11]

The True Theologian Is Not Disputatious

THE THEOLOGIAN WHO IS MOTIVATED by love, not ego, will not have a
spirit of disputation nor engage in pointless arguments and ridiculous debates
such as those frequently found on the internet. Pride is at the root of these discussions; the participant is "inspired by self-confidence and the faith that the
theologian has in his or her own abilities."[12] Saint Symeon the New Theologian encourages us to direct our attention toward those subjects that are profitable for our salvation and avoid subjects that are not spiritually profitable.
This advice is useful even for those who do not attempt to theologize, but St.
Symeon wrote specifically "against dabblers and meddlers without experience
or faith."

> Let us therefore put aside every vain and unprofitable disputation, and let us
> not seek ahead of time to learn what is proper to that hour, i.e., the Second
> Coming, but instead let us be persuaded by the Master Who says "Search
> the Scriptures" (John 5:39). Search, that is, and do not meddle! Search the
> Scriptures and do not busy yourselves with disputes which lie outside the
> sacred writings. Search the Scriptures so that you may learn about faith,
> hope and love.[13]

---

11 Maximos, *Chapters on Love* 4.60, *Selected Writings*, 81–82.
12 Harkianakis, "Theologian in Modern Society," 123.
13 Symeon the New Theologian, *The Ethical Discourses: St. Symeon the New Theologian
    on the Mystical Life,* (3 vols.), Alexander Golitzin, trans. *First Ethical Discourse 12: On*

The True Theologian Has Discernment

DETERMINING WHAT IS PROFITABLE TO say and when it is profitable to speak requires spiritual discernment, which is a gift of the Spirit. This is not a quality that can be acquired by study, nor can it be acquired quickly. Furthermore, the ability to theologize and interpret the Scriptures correctly requires time, patience, and perseverance. Saint Gregory the Theologian was amazed at how people were eager to comment on the Holy Scriptures, unaware of the difficulty of Scripture interpretation or their inability to evaluate the accuracy of their conclusions. Pride motivated them to assume tasks and to address matters that were beyond their abilities.

> In regard to the distribution of the word, to mention last the first of our duties, of that divine and exalted word, which everyone now is ready to discourse upon; if anyone else boldly undertakes it and supposes it within the power of every man's intellect, I am amazed at his intelligence, not to say his folly. To me indeed it seems no slight task, and one requiring no little spiritual power, to give in due season to each his portion of the word, and to regulate with judgment the truth of our opinions, which are concerned with such subjects as the world or worlds, matter, soul, mind, intelligent natures, better or worse, providence which holds together and guides the universe, and seems in our experience of it to be governed according to some principle, but one which is at variance with those of earth and of men.[14]

The True Theologian Observes Balance

CHANGES WITHIN THE WORLD AND society at large are occurring at an exponential rate. Dramatic societal changes of the most astonishing nature, affecting every aspect of human life, are accelerating even more

---

Searching Out the Mysteries of the Kingdom of Heaven, "Against Dabblers and Meddlers without Experience or Faith" (Crestwood, NY: St. Vladimir's Seminary Press, 1995), 1:63.

14 Gregory, *Or.* 2.35. NPNF-2, 7:212.

rapidly now than when Fr. Thomas Hopko observed the trend nearly thirty years ago.

> Our modern world is also a time when virtually all Orthodox Churches and communities are experiencing a breakdown of the Church's living Tradition while also experiencing an explosion of information about Orthodox theology, history, liturgy and spiritual life. This ironic situation has produced a loss of balance and integrity in Orthodox thinking and activity.[15]

Orthodox responses to the challenges posed by our present times can be an overreaction. Some are tempted to modernize, to change the Church traditions, teaching, and practices to remain "relevant." But due to the basic Orthodox character, which values Tradition, this reaction is less common than its opposite. The Orthodox are more likely to recede into the comfort of an ossified conservativism, much as Protestant fundamentalists reacted to scientific discoveries in the late nineteenth century.

Retreat and withdrawal from the world may seem safe and even Orthodox, but that is not the correct response either. Although Orthodoxy has a timeless quality, it is incorrect to say that the Orthodox Church has *never* changed. Nonetheless, it has changed *very little* in comparison to other forms of Christianity. The changeless or timeless character of Orthodox Christianity is its most recognizable characteristic.

Finding a balance between what is essential and unchanging and what is temporary and cultural is a great challenge, requiring both spiritual discernment and actual knowledge. Some Orthodox theologians describe balance as among the most important characteristics in Orthodox Christianity. Panagiotis Bratsiotis observed that Orthodoxy maintains a balance "between the human element (stressed in Roman Catholicism) and the divine element (which predominates in Protestantism)."[16]

---

15 Hopko, "Theological Education," 2–3.
16 Bratsiotis, "Fundamental Principles," 24. Bratsiotis notes specifically that he did not include "either *nationalism* or *ritualism*, which are only aberrations from the genuine spirit of Orthodoxy." Bratsiotis, 30.

The True Theologian Exercises Freedom with Faithfulness

BRATSIOTIS ALSO REMARKED THAT BALANCE manifests itself in another fundamental principle of the Orthodox Church, which he describes as the *"harmonious blending of authority and freedom,* which are equally balanced, as they were in the early Church."[17] Balance and freedom intersect as the Church recognizes the special role and involvement of the laity in a way that differs from the extremes that have been seen in both the Roman Catholic and Protestant traditions. The clergy, and especially the bishops, retain their traditional role in Orthodoxy, since the hierarchical nature of the Church was present from the beginning. The balance Orthodoxy has managed to achieve in contrast to the West is the harmony and cooperation between the clergy and laity, with mutual respect for their unique roles. Many Protestants reject hierarchy altogether in favor of a church dominated by the laity. By contrast, the Roman Catholic tradition overemphasizes the clergy, especially the pope and bishops, with the consequence often being clericalism.

> Here it should be noted that the Orthodox people as a whole, the body of the Church, are regarded as the guardians of Orthodoxy. . . . The Orthodox view that the *laity* constitute an essential part of the body of the Church is supported by their place in worship. Neither the holy liturgy nor the sacraments may be performed in the absence of lay [people]. Furthermore, in accordance with the principles and the ancient tradition of Orthodoxy, the lay element plays an important part in the appointment of the clergy and in the administration of the Church, as it did in the early Church . . . for since the very foundation of the early Church the laity have played an important part in every aspect of Church life and in Church administration.[18]

I happened on an Orthodox internet site on which an Orthodox priest insisted that Orthodox Christians must believe everything the Church teaches: "You must believe everything the Church teaches or none of it!" This is a Western Christian phronema and does not reflect true Orthodoxy. I am

---

17 Bratsiotis, 26. Emphasis in the original.
18 Bratsiotis, 28–29. Emphasis in the original.

not saying we are free to exercise personal choice in doctrine, that we may believe or do whatever we wish. However, Orthodoxy is freedom. Certain behaviors and beliefs are expected but never demanded. We are encouraged, but we are not obligated, especially not in an all-or-nothing way.

Peter Bouteneff astutely observed that some Orthodox Christians "seek refuge" in the "absoluteness" of Orthodoxy, especially if they are fleeing relativism or other faith traditions. But Orthodoxy is not "absolute" about everything. Rather, it is a "strange yet realistic blend of absolute firmness in dogmatic teachings and practices and absolute catholicity and balance."[19] Dogma is quite limited in Orthodox Christianity. Very few teachings are actually considered "dogma," doctrines essential to salvation. Some examples of dogma are the Trinity, the Virgin Birth, the Incarnation, and the Resurrection of Christ. These matters are essential to salvation, since not to believe dogma is to fall into heresy, which threatens our salvation. Other teachings, however, are not essential to salvation but part of Tradition—for example, that the Virgin Mary lived in the Holy of Holies. The Church does not demand that we accept this.

In fact, the Church does not demand that we accept even what is considered essential to our salvation, because the Church does not make demands. We ought to believe, and we are encouraged to believe. But just as God never demands that we have a relationship with Him but leaves it to our free will, the Orthodox Church never demands that we believe anything. But this does not mean that the Church encourages personal opinion. Rather, we are encouraged to use our freedom to conform our minds to that of Christ, as St. Paul advised: "Do not be conformed to this world but be transformed by the renewal of the mind" (Rom. 12:2).

Freedom is an essential characteristic of the Christian life. Christ promised that the truth would set us free (John 8:32), not that we would be enslaved to it. The theologian is acutely aware of the balance between our God-given freedom and the authority of Tradition.

An Orthodox theologian, although he necessarily defines himself as a consistent follower of the patristic and conciliar tradition of the early Church, and

---

19   Bouteneff, *Sweeter Than Honey,* 64.

although he is inevitably respectful of the present positions of his Church as they are expressed in the consensus of the episcopate, is fundamentally free in his expressing of the faith. Of course, he is also responsible since freedom entails the risk of error.[20]

For the theologian, the exercise of personal freedom within the Church can be challenging to navigate. Theologians must always remember their responsibility and the fact that they are accountable to God and to the Church. This is not freedom as it is understood by the world. Freedom in Orthodoxy is freedom from compulsion, not freedom to do as we please.

Hopko described the exercise of this freedom as the "narrow way which leads to life" (Matt. 7:14), a type of freedom that is "generally incomprehensible to the modern (and post-modern) mind."[21] Orthodox theologians are answerable to Scripture and Tradition. Each is "a fully free person, entrusted by God to learn the truth and to communicate it to others. This freedom can be restricted only by the truth itself." Christ, who is the Way, the Truth, and the Life, does not restrict human freedom by imposing obligations; rather, He sets us free. "You will know the truth, and the truth will make you free" (John 8:32). Saint Paul made the same point numerous times in his epistles, distinguishing between law and grace. "Where the Spirit of the Lord is, there is freedom" (2 Cor. 3:17).

The Church recognizes and affirms our individual freedom. "The early Church did not know—and the Orthodox does not know today—any automatic, formal or authoritarian way of discerning truth from falsehood."[22] Discerning truth from falsehood is possible only if one possesses the Orthodox phronema. The Roman Catholic Church issues statements and imposes obligations on the faithful, who are expected to believe and comply. Not surprisingly, Protestant Christianity reacted against the heavy imposition of Roman ecclesiastical authority and swung to the other extreme, toward

---

20 Meyendorff, "Doing Theology," 92.
21 Hopko, "Theological Education," 6. Some Orthodox theologians describe this freedom as "freedom with authority" (*eleutheria met' authentias*). See Bratsiotis, "Fundamental Principles," 24.
22 Meyendorff, "Doing Theology," 86.

complete independence from the church and the rejection of ecclesiastical parameters.

But in Orthodoxy, the Church is "not an authority just as God is not an authority, since authority is something external to us. The Church is not authority . . . but Truth."[23] Since Christ lives within us, He cannot be an external authority that is imposed on us. Meyendorff observed that in Western Christianity "authority became an external power" and "knowledge of religious truths [was] cut off from religious life."

> Obedience to authority became the content of Church life in Roman Catholicism, whereas Scripture as a compendium of written propositional truths replaced Church authority in Protestantism. "The premises are identical."[24]

The Orthodox faithful are neither told nor required to submit to the Church. If we conform to the teaching of the Church, we do so because we choose to obey—to hear and to accept—the Tradition, not because it is demanded that we submit to it as an authority.

The True Theologian Accepts Creativity but Not Speculation and Innovation

AN ORTHODOX THEOLOGIAN DOES NOT employ speculation or imagination in theology. Speculative theology is foreign to Orthodox Christianity, because theology is not a mental exercise or purely intellectual pursuit. The proverbial "How many angels can fit on the head of a pin?" type of question is not part of the Orthodox Tradition. Speculation serves no purpose except to allow one to engage in intellectual gymnastics as a display of intelligence and education or to feed the ego. Hence, Orthodox Christians who engage in debates over questions such as "Which is greater, God's sovereignty or man's free will?" or "How can we explain the death of the dinosaurs before the

---

23 Meyendorff, 87, quoting Alexei Khomiakov, *Quelques mots d'un chrétien orthodoxe sur les confessions occidentales* (Paris, 1853), in *Ultimate Questions*, A. E. Morehouse, trans. (Crestwood, NY: St. Vladimir's Seminary Press, 1975), 50–51.

24 Meyendorff, 87, quoting Khomiakov, 50–51.

appearance of human beings and the Fall?" are revealing a complete absence of Orthodox phronema.

Theology is for the glorification of God and for service to the Church. It is intended to be therapeutic, for the spiritual healing of the human person. Theological speculation is useless and is avoided by the true Orthodox theologian. Speculative theology is not patristic nor part of the ancient Church. Speculation and imagination are absent in the canonical tradition as well. Canons were never written to address problems that might arise in the future but only to address actual problems in the Church at that time.

The Orthodox theologian does not attempt to change the Faith to reflect current norms, values, or attitudes, nor does he or she promote a private opinion over that of the Church. And yet the good Orthodox theologian finds a way to be creative without being innovative. Creativity is allowable, since the gospel must continually be preached at all times and in every place. As times and cultures change, the gospel of salvation must be presented in a way that speaks to each new location and generation—in a manner that nonetheless remains timeless and authentic. Preaching the gospel in a fresh manner without innovation or speculation requires theological and spiritual discernment to apprehend the limits of that creativity.

Saint John Chrysostom agreed that in spite of our fidelity to Tradition, the gospel message can always be fresh:

> How many persons, do you suppose, have spoken upon the Gospels? And yet all have spoken in a way which was new and fresh. For the more one dwells on them, the more insight does he get, the more does he behold the pure light.[25]

Since the Spirit is continuously at work in the Church, the Spirit inspires a creative action within the Church as it witnesses to the world. This is especially evident in missionary activity, but such theologically appropriate creativity should be equally expressed in modern Western culture, which needs the gospel just as urgently as those who have never heard of it.

---

25 Chrysostom, *Homilies on Acts of the Apostles*, Homily 19, NPNF-1, 11:127.

The True Theologian Does Not Rely on Individual Conscience

THE ORTHODOX CHURCH DOES NOT demand assent, submission, or compliance. Freedom of opinion is allowed in certain matters, but this freedom is not to be misapplied or misunderstood. We have freedom in Orthodoxy, but this does not mean we should rely on our own mind and individual reasoning or that we should take positions based on our individual conscience.

Catholics place their confidence in their Church because they rely on Rome, the papacy and the magisterium, as the guarantee of truth. For the Orthodox there is no such structure. Certainly, the bishops of the Church are charged with "rightly handling the word of truth" (2 Tim. 2:15), but Orthodoxy preserves the dynamic and palpable sense that the faith is preserved by the people themselves. We know that intuitively, and we believe that preserving the faith is the serious and sacred responsibility of all of us.

The Protestant Reformation began with Martin Luther's expression of his conscience. Luther famously cited his conscience in refusing to recant his teachings when called on to do so by the Catholic Church at the Diet of Worms: "I cannot and I will not recant anything, for to go against conscience is neither right nor safe."[26] Individual conscience is important and foundational for the entire Protestant Reformation. Even secular Western society places the highest value on following one's own individual conscience.

Conscience is an important and indispensable guide given by God, but it is a fallacy to believe that one's well-formed and reasonable opinion or conscience is more reliable or more important than the continuous ancient Tradition of the Church. Phronema is not the same as conscience.

> For while phronema is identified as super-subjective with the "mind of Christ" and unites us with those of like faith who came before us and will come after, conscience is the sum total of completely subjective ethical and spiritual powers, i.e., the most individual part of a person.[27]

---

26 Martin Luther, "Luther's Final Answer," in *Documents of the Christian Church,* Henry Bettenson and Chris Maunder, eds., 4th ed. (Oxford: Oxford University Press, 2011), 214.

27 Harkianakis, "Theologian in Modern Society," 121. Emphasis in the original.

Phronema is a collective understanding and mentality. It is corporate and objective (i.e., it reflects that which the Body of Christ has universally believed), whereas conscience is individualistic and subjective, based on what *I* believe. Conscience is God-given and extremely important, particularly in matters of morality and behavior, but it is not a reliable guide without the proper phronema. In Orthodox Christianity conscience is never a basis for theological opinion.

The True Theologian Reflects the Mind of Christ, Not Personal Opinion

NOT SO LONG AGO, SOMEONE might be asked to give an opinion when he or she had real knowledge, experience, or information about an issue. In modern times, especially since the advent of the television age, a great deal of emphasis is placed on the value of personal opinion, regardless of whether the person queried has any actual knowledge or expertise in the subject at all. Opinion polls are a common feature on news reports, and even little children are encouraged to give their opinion.

The result is that today the general public believes that nearly everything is simply a matter of personal opinion, especially the Bible, religion, and theology. On matters of faith we are told "let's agree to disagree" since "your opinion is as good as mine." Somehow, treating all opinions as equally valid has become virtuous, because opinion is treated as synonymous with truth. Suffice it to say that Orthodox phronema does not equate personal opinion with truth. Opinion is similar to conscience in that it is entirely subjective and individualistic.

A theologian's ability to render an *informed* opinion is necessary, however. A theologian might be asked for an opinion when an issue is not clear or when people are divided as to an interpretation or current application. For example, I was recently asked whether or not eating something that contained blood, such as English blood pudding, is a sin, because of the prohibition against the eating of blood in the Old Testament (Lev. 17:10–14) and in Acts 15:20. Biblical prohibitions exist, but those might be considered Judaic and no longer necessary. Canons exist, but those might also be reconsidered or might be disciplinary canons, the specifics of which were appropriate for the culture of their time. Ultimately, my response would be an opinion, since no clear church teaching exists on the issue, and reasonable Orthodox theologians might disagree.[28]

An Orthodox theological opinion, however, is not a mere *personal* opinion, but an *informed* opinion based on theological education, thought, prayer, and study. The theologian considers what the Fathers may have said on the issue, whether any canons discuss it, the historical circumstances at the time that restriction was placed on believers, and so on. He or she then gives an informed theological opinion rooted in and reflecting the Tradition of the Church.

Florovsky noted that opinions on such matters require theological discernment because

> not everything in the historical institutions of the Church is equally important and venerable; not everything in the empirical actions of the Church has even been sanctioned. There is much that is only historical. However, we have no outward criterion to discriminate between the two. The methods of outward historical criticism are inadequate and insufficient. Only from within the Church can we discern the *sacred* from the *historical*. From within we see what is catholic and belongs to all time, and what is only "theological opinion," or even a simple casual historical accident.[29]

The True Theologian Accepts Mystery and Paradox

WE CANNOT COMPREHEND GOD, AND furthermore, all human language about God fails. Such a statement seems obvious on its face, and yet even Orthodox Christians sometimes engage in theological discussions on such questions as how God's mercy correlates to His justice, or the extent of an action needed to appease God's "wrath." Such debates immediately reveal the lack of an Orthodox phronema. Such disputes are pointless exercises, usually

---

28 Theologians have indeed disagreed on this subject. Orthodox theologian and biblical scholar Edith Humphrey effectively analyzes this question and discusses why the strict apostolic prohibition seems to have faded and the historical factors that may have contributed to that, as well as how other traditions were shaped. Edith Humphrey, *Scripture and Tradition: What the Bible Really Says* (Grand Rapids, MI: Baker Academic, 2013), 144–45.

29 Florovsky, *Bible, Church and Tradition*, 50. Emphasis in the original.

designed to demonstrate one's biblical, philosophical, or intellectual rigor. Such speculation is not only futile, but its foundation is pride, especially if the one speculating is convinced that he or she can somehow solve or logically explain the conundrum. Such debates are not Orthodox, because they reinforce carnality rather than spirituality.

Orthodox theology defines only what is necessary and always leaves unspoken that which cannot be explained. This approach was part of the Christian faith from the beginning. But the Western phronema often suppresses, dismisses, minimizes, or ignores this stance. The Western mind is compelled to define and explain everything, since without a rational explanation a concept or fact cannot be considered true, or, conversely, all truth can be proven rationally.

Paradox and mystery are everywhere in Orthodoxy and are part of the very essence of Christianity itself. Jesus Christ died to defeat death. Through death He gave us life. He who humbles himself will be exalted. If one tries to save his life, he will lose it. The Christian faith is built on paradoxes such as these.

Seeking rational explanations for divine mysteries—how the bread and wine become the Body and Blood of Christ, exactly how God created the world, and so forth—is not Orthodox. If we are asked whether we believe that the bread and wine become the actual Body and Blood of Christ, the answer is "Yes." If we are asked whether we believe in transubstantiation, the answer must be "No," because that is a Catholic attempt at a rational explanation for how the bread and wine change into the Body and Blood of Christ and yet still look and taste like bread and wine. We do not feel compelled to explain such things, nor did the early Church. These rational explanations developed in Western Europe during the Middle Ages and are the product of Scholastic theology, which is foreign to the Orthodox mind.

The True Theologian Has Unwavering Commitment to Tradition

BEFORE I BECAME A HARVARD student, I met with a few professors who welcomed me into their offices and answered my questions as I considered applying to the Divinity School. In our conversations, I received the distinct impression that Orthodox students at Harvard Divinity were sometimes perceived as difficult, although that word was not used. One professor told me they had one Orthodox doctoral student at that time who was not always "cooperative." He refused to draw certain conclusions or make certain statements in his Ph.D. dissertation. I did not know who the student was, but I immediately realized that he must have an Orthodox phronema. This was the source of the problem for the professors. They could not understand why he would not "cooperate," because they did not realize that they expected him to abandon his Orthodox phronema.

Later, I learned who the student was, came to know him, and found I was correct. He would not violate Holy Tradition by reaching certain conclusions in his dissertation because he had the Orthodox phronema. His difference of opinion might have been respected if he had been a Buddhist or Muslim. But since he was an Orthodox Christian, his refusal to reach a conclusion the professors believed to be entirely rational was perceived as mere stubbornness.

True Orthodox theologians will not allow themselves to be pressured to violate Tradition. They won't follow the crowd. They won't just go along and capitulate to Western Christian norms and ideas. The West claims to value diversity, but it does not value diversity in religious perspectives among Christians if the beliefs do not align with what "logic" demands. Orthodox scholars have experienced this on numerous occasions. When no effort is made to understand the Orthodox phronema—since the West does not even understand that we *have* a phronema—the Orthodox perspective is easily dismissed as uneducated, ignorant, stubborn, uninformed, difficult, irrational, and rooted in denominational bias.

The Orthodox phronema is the mind of the ancient Church, but that is unrecognizable to Western Christianity in spite of our common roots. After nearly two thousand years of theological development, both Protestant and Catholic Christianity no longer resemble the early Church in thought or behavior.

The True Theologian Accepts Tradition over Human Rationality

Saying something about God is not the same as encountering him. Speaking of God requires that you pronounce words, and perhaps that you have some skill with them, if you are not just to have knowledge but to make use of it and pass it on. It also requires all sorts of logical reasoning, compelling arguments and worldly examples, all or most of which are gathered by seeing and hearing, and are the prerogative of people who spend their lives in this world. They may be acquired by the wise men of this present age, even though their lives and souls may not be completely pure. It is absolutely impossible, however, to truly encounter God unless, in addition to being cleansed, we go outside, or rather, beyond ourselves, leaving behind everything perceptible to our sense, together with our ability to perceive, and being lifted up above thoughts, reason and every kind of knowledge, above even the mind itself, and wholly given over to the energy of spiritual perception.[30]

In the quote above, St. Gregory Palamas eloquently reminds us that being able to talk about God has nothing to do with knowing God. The true Orthodox theologian ought to remember that skillful rhetoric, compelling arguments, and logical explanations ultimately fail to convey any true knowledge of God, who is above all human reasoning and outside all sense perception. This is why the Church does not rely on human deductive reasoning for its theology and places the highest emphasis on spiritual experience. The true theologian is the one who prays, whose words are based on direct experience of God. Since few of us achieve this, in the alternative, the theologian is also one who follows Tradition and the Fathers and accepts the experience of the saints, as explained in chapter 11. The true theologian accepts Tradition and observes it, even when it defies rational explanation.

It is significant that Palamas's words are taken from a sermon on the Entry of the Theotokos into the Holy of Holies. The ancient Tradition of the Church is that after Mary was dedicated to God and taken to the Jewish Temple by her parents, Joachim and Anna, she lived in the Holy of Holies. It can be said that this is historically impossible. This tradition is difficult for many Orthodox Christians, especially converts. How could the Theotokos literally live in the Holy of Holies?

---

30   Gregory Palamas, *On the Entry of the Theotokos into the Holy of Holies,* Homily 53.51, *Gregory Palamas: The Homilies,* 437.

We could say that St. Gregory did not know enough about first-century Judaism to know that this was not possible. Or we can say that it is a poetic expression of a much deeper mystery. She literally became the Holy of Holies since she contained God Himself in her womb, just as the Holy of Holies of the Temple building was the place where God dwelt. We could also ponder this with an Orthodox phronema and contemplate the mystery this tradition is trying to convey. Trying to historically or rationally justify it is pointless, and it is ultimately of no importance whether it is historically defensible. The question for us always is: What spiritual lesson is the Church presenting for us?

Should these stories be discarded because we "know better" now? Did they remain part of the life of the Church only because people were ignorant? Although these stories are embraced by most Orthodox faithful on the lowest level of meaning, as literal history, they have a spiritual value and resonate on a deep spiritual level. This is why they continue to capture the imagination of the Church. They draw the mind upward from the mundane to the sublime. They invite us to contemplate the mystery of the Incarnation of the Son of God, the extraordinary life and character of the Theotokos, and her role in making the Incarnation a reality.

That which is spiritually beneficial is beyond reason, beyond explanation. Saint Gregory encouraged his monks to *contemplate* the entry of the Theotokos into the Temple. He acknowledged that it is "difficult to understand and cannot easily be comprehended by those whose minds lack concentration." Nonetheless, he said, "I do not think such words should be banished from the holy precincts, for we do not avoid the narrow way which leads to life simply because it is difficult to follow." This type of mystical contemplation that leads the mind upward toward divine things is not like "easily earned dust," he said, but, rather, it is like "hard-won gold." The spiritual ascent to divine things requires that we leave worldly knowledge, historical realities, and human reasoning behind if we are to ascend to spiritual heights.

Let each of you gather his mind within itself, just as men going along narrow passageways gather up their cloaks, and ascend intently towards the majesty of this thought; for there is no accessible means of ascent to so highly exalted a meaning for those who creep along the ground. Once, however, you have lifted your minds above material concerns and resolved to meditate on the Mother of God's divine way of life in the holy sanctuary, eager to understand something of what happened there and to emulate her as far as possible, then perhaps you will soon receive that blessed gift of those purified in heart (cf. Matt. 5:8) and invisibly observe the honours proper to the immortal world.[31]

Most of us are not monastics and rarely contemplate such sublime matters as St. Gregory addressed. But we can adopt the same attitude he encouraged in his monks. It is not enough to learn about the Orthodox Church. Indeed, there is much to learn about the Scriptures, theology, the liturgy, feasts and fasts, how to live the Christian life, and so on. But mere knowledge is insufficient without correct phronema.

If all this remains at the level of knowledge, of information, it is all rather pointless. This is true of any system of belief that issues in a way of life, but it seems to me to be radically true of Orthodoxy: The only knowledge that counts, the only *theology* that is *truly* Orthodox, is *participation* in God's movement in love towards us in creation and Incarnation by our response of love.[32]

Our emphasis on faith and Tradition should not be used to silence inquiry. Faith is critical if we are not to remain earthbound. Divine matters cannot be comprehended with the mind, but we are conditioned in our Western society to believe that the highest level of comprehension is intellectual. Some Orthodox struggle with intellectual questions: "If I could only understand how the Theotokos could live in the Holy of Holies, then I would accept it." But the highest level of understanding is not intellectual but spiritual, and spiritual realities are beyond reason, since God's ways are beyond human comprehension. Whether or not Mary literally lived in the Holy of Holies is not important, and focusing on whether or not that is historically accurate leaves us earthbound, unable to sprout spiritual wings and contemplate, or even be open to, mystery.

---

31 Gregory Palamas, *On the Entry of the Theotokos into the Holy of Holies*, Homily 53.54, *Palamas: The Homilies*, 438–39.

32 Louth, *Introducing Eastern Orthodox Theology*, 122. Emphasis added.

Intellectual answers are limited and partial at best. It is truly tragic if we willingly remain at that level our entire lives, choosing to accept only that which we can intellectually comprehend. Saint Gregory Palamas hints at the amazing world of spiritual experience that awaits those who are willing to make the ascent he describes above, leaving behind earthly realities and being open to spiritual possibilities.

I once read a beautiful example of being open to the truth of Tradition regardless of how unlikely it seems. It is the personal experience of a Greek Orthodox convert and nun, Mother Nectaria McLees, in her book, *Evlogeite! A Pilgrim's Guide to Greece*. I am grateful that she shared her experience, because we can all benefit from her example. She described a particular struggle she had with certain details in the lives of the saints:

> After my conversion to Orthodoxy, I, like many others, struggled with misgivings about some of the details of traditional hagiography, in particular with stories like the one in the life of St. Nicholas the Wonderworker, where, as an infant he refused his mother's breast on Wednesdays and Fridays, the weekly fast days of the Church. It went against every bit of rational, logical, common sense thing I knew about babies, and yet I was reluctant to take the easy way out and dismiss it as a pious legend.[33]

Mother Nectaria explains that she decided to simply pray "that God would enlighten me." Her prayer was answered. On a subsequent trip to Greece, she met a nun who was the great-niece of St. Philomenos, a Greek Orthodox monk who was martyred at Jacob's Well in the Holy Land. He had a brother who was an abbot and also known for his upright life. When speaking of their lives, the nun mentioned to Mother Nectaria that as infants these two brothers refused to nurse from their mother on Wednesdays and Fridays. The other children "behaved quite normally, but these two simply would not nurse on fast days." The entire village knew about this problem and tried various schemes to get the babies to eat, but to no avail.

---

33 Mother Nectaria McLees, *Evlogeite! A Pilgrim's Guide to Greece* (Maysville, MO: St. Nicholas Press, 2002), 22–23.

Mother Nectaria was given the phone number of their elderly aunt, who was still alive and had lived in the village when the saintly monks were infants. She could verify this. Later, Mother Nectaria was told a similar story by the nuns at the Annunciation convent on the island of Patmos regarding their spiritual father, who had also refused his mother's breast on Fridays when he was a baby.

What is important for our purpose and edification is not that Mother Nectaria was able to verify something that was against all reason, common sense, and scientific knowledge about infants. What we should remember is her phronema. Rather than dismissing the stories as pious legends or attempting to resolve the question intellectually, she decided to pray "that God would enlighten me." And He did. God enlightened her, not because she was a nun but because she asked and was open-hearted. God hears such prayers and always responds to them.

This story is a beautiful example of how we ought to respond to stories or details in Church Tradition that we find difficult to believe—we respond by adopting the correct phronema.

CHAPTER 11

Theological Education

Zeal without Knowledge: The Armchair Theologian

AMATEUR THEOLOGIANS SEEM TO HAVE proliferated in Orthodoxy since the rise of the internet and social media (or perhaps they have simply become more visible). I rarely become involved in online Orthodox discussions, but on one occasion, I saw that an Orthodox discussion site administrator had given an incorrect response to a question. I jumped in to offer clarification about the meaning of a particular theological word. The error was so significant that I believed it should be corrected. I made a quick comment about the meaning of the Greek word, anticipating a brief, polite discussion. It was anything but that. I supported my point with indisputable ancient and patristic sources, liturgical references, and scholarly citations, but the site administrator vehemently rejected my explanation.

I then looked at his Facebook page to learn about the background of this administrator since I did not know him. He had no role in the Church or academia. He had no education or expertise in theology or any related field, such as history, philosophy, philology, archeology, etc. He was not ordained and had no pastoral experience. He was *entirely unqualified* to answer theological questions. His opinion would be irrelevant—except that he was a site administrator on a public forum answering theological questions for people seeking information about Orthodox Christianity. That is a problem.

He was completely dismissive of my explanation, and since he repeatedly

234

insisted that he was correct, I finally explained to him that I was an Orthodox Christian theologian, a professor with forty years of experience and five
degrees in theology, including a Ph.D., and that what he was saying was a significant theological error. His response was contempt. He curtly informed me
that the Orthodox Church has only had three theologians and I am not one.

We will return to the story in a moment, but for now let us consider his
point. I typically do not refer to myself as a theologian, out of deference to
those great three who have been accorded the title "the Theologian." I usually describe myself as a professor or a biblical scholar. Indeed, I have heard
other Orthodox Christians like my Facebook debater assert that no one else
can ever be called a theologian because that title was only given to Ss. John,
Gregory, and Symeon the New. If a spirit of humility motivates a theologian to
decline such a description, this is commendable. But the fact that the Church
conferred the *title* "the Theologian" on those three does not mean that the
term "theologian" is never applied to anyone else. This is typical of an exaggeration motivated by piety that results in error.

Someone might consider that a minor point, but the misperception that no
one else is a theologian in the Church has become an excuse for uneducated
and unqualified people to give theological opinions. Our precious Orthodox
Tradition is being abused and distorted. Our reverence and respect for the
theologian saints is now a pretext for propagating ignorance and error.

Many theologically uneducated individuals become involved in discussions and attempt to answer questions about Orthodox Christianity, whether
in private conversations or on the internet. In fact, they are posing as theologians, speaking about God, regardless of whether they claim the title. They
proudly and righteously defend their refusal to recognize anyone else as a
theologian, blissfully unaware of their own hypocrisy as they casually and
carelessly theologize without the title. The number of wannabe theologians,
theologizing with neither the training nor the education, let alone the spiritual qualifications necessary, seems to be increasing. The internet is anonymous and gives everyone a platform. This is problematic since people who go
to Orthodox internet sites for information rarely investigate whether those
providing answers are actually qualified to do so. Some discussions are little
more than the blind leading the blind.

Although the pseudo-theologians purport to believe no one can now be called a theologian, they behave as though anyone can theologize, since this is precisely what they are doing. Their behavior implies that no theological education is needed, that no one serves the Church today as a theologian, and that uninformed answers are just as reliable as explanations coming from a person who has spent years in an Orthodox school of theology. This reveals a spirit of pride and self-righteousness, not to mention self-delusion.

WHO CAN BE CALLED "THEOLOGIAN"?

IT IS FALSE THAT NO one besides the three titled Fathers is a theologian in the Orthodox Church. Such a statement itself shows ignorance. In fact, "theologian" is a common noun and not exclusive to John, Gregory, and Symeon, even among the Orthodox. Only those three saints have received the *title* "the Theologian" affixed to their names. But the distinct honor accorded to those three specific saints does not forbid referring to someone else as "*a* theologian" in the ordinary sense. To say that no one else can be called a theologian is to disagree even with the holy Fathers and their use of the term "theologian."

If it were true that literally no one else could ever be referred to as a theologian, then not even St. Athanasius or St. Cyril the Great, who were responsible for the defeat of the worst heresies faced by the Church, could be called a theologian. Saint Basil, who laid the groundwork for the Second Ecumenical Council by explaining the divinity of the Holy Spirit, could not be called a theologian. Saint Gregory Palamas, who defended the holy hesychasts, affirmed the practice of the Jesus Prayer, and defined the theology of the essence and energies of God, could not be called a theologian. The same applies to countless other great Fathers of the Church.

The Fathers were theologians in the truest sense of the word. They knew God and spoke about Him. They defined, explained, and defended the deepest theological truths. They embodied the very definition of "theologian": one who speaks about God.

Among the millions of Orthodox Christians throughout history, there are very few whom we call "Fathers." The Church survived two millennia because of countless Orthodox priests, teachers, authors, professors, catechists, and ordinary believers who faithfully taught, preserved, and defended Orthodox Christianity. They were theologians too. Most of them are not remembered by history, only by God. They spoke about God and conveyed divine truths. The Church would not exist without these nameless servants who quietly worked and served the Church as faithful guardians and teachers of our precious and holy Tradition.

Orthodoxy has honored only three saints with the title "the Theologian," but this does not mean the Church never uses the noun "theologian" to refer to anyone else. Just as the term "saint" (holy one) is actually appropriate for all Christians, and we are called to the chalice with the words "holy things for the holy," the word "saint" as a *title* is used only for those whom the Church has specifically recognized as such. Metropolitan Kallistos discussed the issue of whether it was appropriate to refer to anyone besides Ss. John, Gregory, and Symeon as a theologian. Of course, he turned to the Fathers for an answer. He noted that St. Gregory Palamas applied the term "theologian" not only to saints but to those who "trust the experience of the saints," meaning those who teach Orthodoxy by faithfully following the Tradition of the Church.[1] This is *truly* the Orthodox tradition and actual practice.

We recognize that the term "theologian" in the truest sense belongs to the one who prays, but those who have an advanced theological education are also routinely called theologians in Orthodox Christianity. Many Orthodox Christians have faithfully served the Church as theologians through the centuries, and even today countless individuals are involved in the task of theology. It is a common practice in the Church to recognize as theologians those who have a high level of theological education, those who are engaged in the work of catechism, preaching, teaching, and writing about God and the Orthodox Faith. The term "theologian" is often applied to both men and women, clergy and laity, who are qualified by their education and their life, who piously preserve and impart the Faith, who are recognized by their local bishop and by the faithful in general as authentic teachers of true Orthodoxy.[2]

---

1   Ware, "Theological Education," 8, citing A. M. Allchin, "The Appeal to Experience in the Triads of St Gregory Palamas," *Studia Patristica* viii (Berlin, 1966), 323–28.

2   My husband, Fr. Costas, has a Ph.D. in theology. For a few months while he served the Church of Cyprus, his bishop told Fr. Costas that he had permission to preach, "since

"UNFAITHFUL" THEOLOGIANS?

IN TRUTH AND IN FACT, an Orthodox theologian is recognized by the Orthodox faithful not only because of his or her theological education but because of his or her phronema. If someone does *not* reflect the phronema, he or she finds no acceptance in the Church.

In recent decades, some Catholic theologians have promoted teachings contrary to Catholic doctrine. This has become a significant concern in the Catholic Church, to the extent that papal documents have been issued regarding Catholic theological education and requiring Catholic theologians to be faithful to Catholic teaching.[3] Catholic theologians cited academic freedom, but Rome was concerned about the propagation of heresy and has taken measures to prevent it.

I was asked once what the Orthodox Church does when an Orthodox theologian gives theological opinions that conflict with Orthodox teaching— something that occasionally happens but seems to be increasing due to the influence of Western phronema. The answer is simple: the so-called theologian would be ignored, not in a vindictive or shunning manner. An Orthodox theologian who teaches something that is not Orthodox would simply become irrelevant, because the Orthodox who might hear him or read his books would recognize that he does not represent the Orthodox Tradition. His or her ideas might be discussed among theologians, but the Orthodox laity will typically react quite sharply in condemning such a theologian. The theologian would lose respect, and his or her opinions would thereafter be viewed with suspicion by other Orthodox Christians.

The Orthodox Church has no process or procedure for censuring or controlling a theologian, other than perhaps denying him permission to preach

---

you are a theologian." Many priests in Cyprus do not have any degree in theology, and therefore they do not have permission from their bishop to preach. This does not mean that there is no sermon. Instead, the bishop publishes a weekly sermon that is read to the faithful in parishes in which the priest himself does not preach.

3   John Paul II issued an Apostolic Constitution *Ex Corde Ecclesiae* (1990), specifically directed to Catholic universities. An Apostolic Constitution was issued by Pope Francis in 2017, *Veritas Gaudium*, reinforcing and largely repeating an earlier document by John Paul II, known as *Sapientia Christiana* (1979). These documents gave very specific instructions regarding teaching in Catholic institutions.

in church. We need no statement from any patriarch. There are no credentials to be denied or removed. Other Orthodox theologians would respond to the false statements of a pseudo-theologian and correct the errors. But generally speaking, a false Orthodox theologian would simply be regarded by the rest of the Church as "not Orthodox," despite his position or education, and his opinions would eventually be ignored. Such a person would exercise little to no lasting influence in the Church. This is due to our phronema. We recognize true Orthodoxy in others and pay no attention to those who claim to be Orthodox but by their words and actions reveal otherwise.

A theologian might be a clergyman, but the Orthodox Church also has many lay theologians, including many women around the world. "Lay professors," men and women, "are a majority in the theological faculties in Greece and they represent a sizable minority in the theological schools of Russia and Serbia."[4] In America, Orthodox priests have a theological education, and for this reason they routinely preach at the divine services and sacraments. But in other parts of the Orthodox world, such as Greece and Cyprus, most men who are ordained to the priesthood do *not* have a theological education. They complete two years of education after high school, consisting of training for their priestly duties, but this is far less than the seven years or more of higher education most Orthodox priests have in America.[5]

Priests who do not have a theology degree usually do not preach because

---

4   Meyendorff, "Doing Theology," 92.
5   Most Orthodox clergy in America have a bachelor's degree (four years after high school) and also a master of divinity, which is an advanced theology degree that requires at least three additional years to complete after the bachelor's degree. A master of divinity (M.Div.) consists of academic courses (theology, Scripture, canon law, church history, dogmatics, New Testament Greek, etc.) and also more "practical" classes (pastoral care, hospital and prison ministry, liturgics, chanting, parish administration, etc.). Those who study theology but are not preparing for the priesthood typically do not take the "practical" classes. A degree that focuses on theology alone is often called master of theological studies (MTS) and requires two years to complete, after a four-year university degree. But other master's degrees may actually be higher than a master of divinity and require additional years of study, such as a master of theology (Th.M.) or a doctorate (Ph.D. or D.Min., doctor of ministry). Other countries have different names for these types of degrees, but there are thousands of Orthodox Christians around the world who are engaged in advanced theological studies and will be considered "theologians" when they complete their education.

they are not qualified; they are not theologians. However, a qualified lay theologian, whether a man or woman, can preach with the permission of the local bishop. Metropolitan Panteleimon Rodopoulos, a well-known professor and canonical expert, writes that the bishops are canonically obligated "to retain the revealed teaching and bear witness, unfailingly and unerringly, to the truth." But qualified priests, deacons, and even laypeople, with the consent of the bishop, have this responsibility to "transmit the truth of the word of God through preaching, through publications and through any available means such as radio, television and so on."[6]

"ONE WHO PRAYS" AS AN EXCUSE FOR IGNORANCE

LET US RETURN TO THE story about the administrator on the Orthodox discussion site.

My online critic wanted to have the last word in our conversation. Since he was a site administrator, he blocked me from the discussion site so that I could not reply to his statements. I appealed to another administrator's sense of fairness. He removed the block, and I rejoined the conversation.

---

6   Panteleimon Rodopoulos, *An Overview of Orthodox Canon Law* (Rollinsford, NH: Orthodox Research Institute, 2007), 159. The basic qualification to preach is usually an advanced degree in theology from an Orthodox institution and the permission of the local bishop. The teaching responsibility in the Church historically belongs to the bishops, who have been ordained and charged with preserving apostolic Tradition and "rightly proclaiming the word of truth." Just as no priest can perform a sacrament without the permission of the local bishop, lay theologians do not preach in church without episcopal permission and the permission of the parish priest. Not all Orthodox jurisdictions or bishops allow laypeople to preach in the Church, but many do. This reflects the attitude of the Church from the earliest years through today. The Orthodox Church has always had lay preachers and teachers, including women, and always encouraged the laity to be involved in the Church to the greatest extent possible. The important work and large number of women Orthodox theologians in Greece and elsewhere should not be overlooked. In Asprovalta (northern Greece), for example, laywomen have organized as the Sisterhood of St. Lydia. They are not nuns, but many are theologians. They operate the largest printing press in the Balkans and publish excellent books on the Orthodox faith. They also operate a radio station and television station in Thessalonika known as "4E" with continuous religious programming in the Greek language. It is the first television station in the world dedicated to the Greek Orthodox faith. It can be live streamed at http://www.tv4e.gr/livestreaming.php.

I told my critic that he was not qualified to give theological responses because he had no theological education. Another participant leapt to his defense, defiantly informing me that "one need not be educated to be a saint." Of course. Many saints were uneducated, but they did not presume to function as theologians. The question is not about sainthood or salvation but about whether one ought to be qualified if one is to respond to theological questions. My critic was uninfluenced by my contributions, undeterred in his activities, and unconvinced that any real education was needed by one who answered theological questions. I chided myself for wasting so much precious time on a quixotic mission.

My Facebook disputant, his defender, and countless other online armchair theologians distort the very Orthodox Tradition that they wrongly believe they are defending. They may express falsehoods, make harsh judgments, slander and scandalize, misrepresent and distort Orthodoxy, confidently emboldened by the maxim that the theologian is the one who *prays*, not the one who is *educated*. They smugly dismiss any need for genuine expertise, either in the form of an education or in the classic Orthodox understanding of a deep personal relationship with God.

Ironically, while he rejected my description of myself as a theologian, my critic was *posing* as a theologian, assuming the mantle of knowledge with no education, no training, no qualifications, no experience, and probably (judging by his attitude and the hours he spends on the internet) lacking a deep relationship with God. Zeal without knowledge is damaging and dangerous. A little knowledge can be worse than complete ignorance, especially when we become wise in our own conceits. A little knowledge without humility is the worst of all.

While we maintain that the theologian is "one who prays," this maxim must not be misconstrued and distorted to mean that no education is needed to teach theology or to answer theological questions. One can be illumined with knowledge of God through prayer alone, but this is exceptional, and such saints did not spout their opinions on the internet or casually discuss theology in other settings. They may have offered advice to a few faithful who sought them out for spiritual guidance, but that is not theologizing. It was the educated saints, the Fathers of the Church, who wrote treatises and scripture commentaries and responded to questions about complex matters of theology.

Not merely *some* prayer is needed to be considered "one who prays" but a life devoted to prayer and an intimate knowledge of God, which is rarely seen among those of us who live in the world. Saint Symeon the New Theologian railed against those who theologized without any qualification to do so. His sharp words are thought-provoking for all of us but should be especially so for those who believe that no qualifications are needed to theologize. They babble about theology, and when they are confronted with their error, they smugly retort that "the theologian is one who prays." Saint Symeon's standards for spiritual qualification as "one who prays" were extremely high.

> Do you not shudder and put your hand over your mouth and discipline your tongue not to chatter about matters that you have not yet experienced, the knowledge of which your reason has not yet grasped, which you have not seen with your eyes, whose grandeur has not entered into your hearing? Do you not know that they who have had the experience of these things in deed and word laugh at you as a fool whenever you try to talk about them and babble on about one thing and another? If, though, you have been made worthy of the grace from above, then speak freely about what concerns it and theologize without hindrance about him Who is God by nature. . . . But, if you admit that, while doing what is good, you have not partaken of grace, nor felt yourself become dead to the world, nor have known yourself to have ascended up into Heaven so as to be hidden there alone and nowhere else, nor have gone like Paul outside the whole world, whether in the body or without the body, nor have discovered yourself to have been completely changed and, as it were become spirit by the putting off of the flesh and comparing spiritual things with the spiritual, then why do you not embrace the beauty of silence and try, with repentance and tears, to receive and learn these things instead of vainly talking about matters about which you have no true knowledge and wanting to be called a "saint" without having fulfilled these conditions and carry on as if you have already been saved while daring to pick up strange notions and teach them to others?[7]

---

7   Symeon the New Theologian, *Sixth Ethical Discourse: On Dispassion and a Virtuous Life*, "Against False 'Practitioners' and Spiritual Quacks," *On the Mystical Life*, vol. 2, 76–77.

Very few people could ever meet that standard, but at the very least those who theologize ought to have a theological education.

I am not suggesting that it is wrong to learn theology or talk about God. Far from it. We ought frequently to discuss Bible stories, the Sunday Gospel reading, and the lives of the saints. Such discussions are positive, useful, and important. But those subjects are basic matters of catechism. One should not answer questions or give advice even in those subjects unless one is truly well informed.

The Education of the Fathers

THE FATHERS OF THE CHURCH spent many years pursuing an advanced education, both secular and theological, which prepared them to discuss theology and to refute heresy.[8] They studied oratory, Greek philosophy, grammar, history, science, mathematics, literature, and logic. They read the Fathers who came before them and also received instruction from actual teachers who guided and mentored them. They learned apostolic Tradition, Israel's history, church history, philology, doctrine, the Bible, and biblical interpretation.

Chrysostom's teacher for scriptural interpretation was a famous biblical interpreter, Diodore of Tarsus, and his pagan teacher of rhetoric was the most famous rhetorician in the world, Libanius. Saint Gregory the Theologian affectionately refers to his many teachers, both pagan and Christian, who were well known in their day and contributed to his knowledge and skills. Gregory initially studied for two years in Nazianzus, where he received a basic education. He then spent two years in higher studies in Caesarea of Cappadocia. This was followed by a year of study in Caesarea of Palestine, another year in Alexandria, and a full ten years studying in Athens—which amounts to a total of fifteen years of advanced education.

The Fathers of the Church did not simply pray and then begin to theologize. They trained themselves by sharpening their abilities. They possessed the spiritual qualifications but were also well prepared for the task of theologizing through their formal education, both sacred and secular. Saint Basil

---

8   Beeley, *Gregory of Nazianzus*, 7–9.

noted the need for both theological education and spiritual experience; he points out the foolishness of self-appointed critics with no knowledge of the subject matter. In his assessment of unqualified theologians, Basil applied the same standard to those who would ignorantly theologize.

> The critic ought really to set out with much the same training and equipment as the author. A man ignorant of agriculture is quite incapable of criticizing husbandry, and the distinctions between harmony and discord can only be adequately judged by a trained musician. But anyone who chooses will act as a literary critic, though he cannot tell us where he went to school, or how much time was spent in his education, and knows nothing about letters at all. I see clearly that, even in the case of the words of the Holy Spirit [the Scriptures], the investigation of the terms is to be attempted not by everyone, but by him who has the spirit of discernment, as the Apostle has taught us, in the differences of gifts.[9]

Although theologizing is a spiritual task, St. Basil acknowledged that expertise in the form of actual knowledge and training was required, just as it is to become a farmer or musician. That the true theologian is one who prays is the Orthodox tradition, but it is a perversion of Tradition to cite this maxim as an *excuse* to neglect the academic or scholarly foundation or preparation theology requires. It is truly dangerous and irresponsible to discuss theology without a theological education.

Theology has always required education. The Church has schools of theology. Why not simply teach men how to pray, ordain them, and send them off to parishes? In fact, that is very close to the model often seen in the Protestant world: relying on oneself and one's relationship to God. In many Protestant denominations and churches, no education is required to preach, teach, or lead a parish. Many famous Protestant preachers never attended any seminary, or even a Bible college, and it shows. Is this what those who would present themselves as the teachers and defenders of Orthodoxy wish to imitate? It

---

9   Basil, *Letters*. Letter 204.5 to the Neocaesareans, NPNF-2, vol. 8, *Basil: Letters and Select Works*, Blomfield Jackson, trans., Philip Schaff and Henry Wace, eds. (Grand Rapids, MI: William B. Eerdmans, 1894), 244.

matters not at all that we think we are Orthodox or call ourselves Orthodox, or that we only intend to be helpful. It is morally wrong to teach simply because one believes that he or she is qualified to answer theological questions.

We must also recognize that as a practical matter, the Church expects persons assuming specific roles in the Church to be qualified. The Church is a place of order where norms, standards, and procedures exist for everything. We have a lectionary that tells us the readings of the day; we have set prayers for daily devotions and services. Clergy are educated, trained, and ordained, in addition to being required to be free of certain canonical impediments. They follow rubrics that direct them in how to perform the services. Chanters are trained and tonsured by the bishop and may chant only with the permission of the priest. They sing specific hymns for specific feast days and at specific points in the service. Particular musical tones and melodies are appointed for the hymns. Even parish council members and those who wish to serve as sponsors at a wedding or baptism must meet certain spiritual and canonical standards and receive permission to serve in that role. Can it be that it is only when theologizing that no standards are necessary, expected, or required?

Excuses for Ignorance

THIS SEEMS VERY OBVIOUS, BUT we must remind ourselves that the Church is not a free-for-all. If everything and everyone else has procedures, training, requirements, permission, and expectations, how can anyone assume that he can answer theological questions with no education or ecclesiastical approval at all?

The Church needs theologians. It has people today who function as theologians: parish priests, professors, writers, preachers, teachers, and so on. Orthodox theologians must be properly trained and educated; they must have an upright spiritual life as well as the proper phronema. This need for education, training, and permission to serve in this capacity is acknowledged—by priests who are responsible for our parishes, by bishops who oversee our parishes, by Orthodox schools of theology, and by the faithful themselves, who intuitively recognize when a theologian manifests an Orthodox phronema and when he or she does not.

In times when the Church was in hiding or under persecution, people were called by God and did serve the Church without meeting standards that might be expected today. But generally speaking, unless an extraordinary situation exists, the Church expects that an individual who comes forward to serve in a particular capacity combines an appropriate moral and spiritual character with proper training and preparation. What education or training has the armchair theologian received? None. What hierarchs or ecclesiastical institutions recognize the qualifications of the untrained internet "theologian" to give theological answers or opinions? None. Our Holy Orthodox Tradition, which emphasizes the spiritual foundation of theology, is distorted and abused by amateur theologians to justify their activities. Yet amateur theologians offer many excuses for giving theological opinions.

- *"I rely on the Fathers."* But the Fathers would not approve of what you are doing. The Fathers would tell you *not* to theologize; therefore, you betray the Fathers whom you claim to honor.
- *"One need not be educated to be a saint."* But we are not discussing sainthood or salvation; we are discussing whether you are qualified to theologize and be responsible for the spiritual welfare and direction of those people whose questions you are answering.
- *"All one needs is prayer and a spiritual life."* What kind of spiritual life? If theology is actual knowledge of God acquired through prayer, would you place yourself in the same category as the saints and Fathers? If not, then why shouldn't you at least have a theological education before posing as a theologian?
- *"I know enough to grasp the concepts."* This means you actually know very little. Theology requires accuracy and precision. It requires depth of knowledge, not shallow understanding. Are you prepared to be judged by God for what you say?
- *"I've read a lot of books on Orthodox theology."* But is your understanding correct? How would you know that you are correct? Has your knowledge and understanding been tested by those with expertise? What knowledge have you retained? Have you engaged in deep research? Written lengthy papers? Have you spent years immersed in the subject?

Because you have read a few books, are you now qualified to assume the
role of theologian by presuming to teach others?

- *"Even experts can be wrong and have biases."* Because others can also be
  wrong, do you—with no education—now presume to discuss such matters? Who is more likely to be wrong, you or those who have at least some
  established level of expertise? If one seeks to be a theologian, even on the
  "secondary" level,[10] how can one know whether or not one is being faithful to Holy Tradition, correctly explaining doctrine, or properly interpreting Scripture if one is completely lacking in theological training?

These are typical of the excuses given by amateur theologians to justify
their actions and to negate the importance of academic study. A student of
theology would be held accountable by professors by means of exams, research
papers, grades, and so forth. In short, one is evaluated and is proven competent and capable in Orthodox theology by some objective standard. This takes
years, and with it comes a serious responsibility.

It is much easier to look something up on Wikipedia, type in a quick
response on Facebook, and thereby feel important, knowledgeable, and competent. But this is a falsehood. Christ is truth. Orthodoxy is truth. Statements
about the Orthodox Christian faith must be *true*. Our presentation of ourselves must be true and not misleading.

Without an Orthodox education, one should not pretend to know theology and function as a theologian. Education is important because the Faith is
not simple. People with general knowledge of any subject do not appreciate or
understand it thoroughly. Yet within their own minds they believe they have
some understanding and that this is enough. They hold this false belief precisely because they are not aware of the complexity of the subject. This is true
for virtually every profession or area of expertise. What's worse, amateur theologians are entirely unaware of the dangers inherent in their actions, because
what is being discussed is God Himself, and what is at stake is eternal salvation.

---

10 As mentioned in chapter 6, Ware observed that the true theologians are the saints who
   have direct experience and knowledge of God. But one could be considered a theologian
   on a lower, or "secondary" level, if one has the education, trusts the experience of the
   saints, and believes and teaches the Orthodox Faith. Ware, "Theological Education," 8.

The Church and Orthodox Theological Education

WHEN WE REPEAT THE MAXIM "the theologian is one who prays," is the *purpose* of that proverb to suggest that theological education is unnecessary? Certainly not. It expresses the Orthodox phronema, that true theology is not based on human knowledge or mental constructs. Did the Church *ever* believe that theological education is unnecessary? Absolutely not. Before becoming a member of the Church, catechumens are catechized—they are taught the faith. During the earliest decades of its existence under the Roman Empire, the Church lived under conditions in which catechism and theological education were suppressed and even forbidden. But religious education was still considered necessary. Classes were held in secret, and countless early Christians literally risked their lives to teach the faith to others. Their activities were illegal for well over two hundred years. Education has always been important in the Church, and the Church did its best under difficult circumstances.

Every Greek knows about the "secret schools" created during the four hundred years when Greece suffered under Turkish occupation. Children were taught secretly at night, often by the village priest. Similar stories abound for those faithful who suffered under Muslim rule in other countries, such as Serbia, or under communist oppression in the Soviet Union and elsewhere, when religious education was forbidden. Not long ago, the Turkish government forced the closure of Halki, the most celebrated Greek Orthodox school of theology in the world, which for generations produced the best theologians and bishops of the Church.[11] The Ecumenical Patriarchate continues to push for the reopening of Halki against Turkish government opposition and oppression.[12]

---

11   The closure was forced in 1971 by the Turkish government as part of a decades-long campaign to suppress Orthodoxy and Greek culture in Turkey. The Ecumenical Patriarchate has continued to push for the reopening of Halki. See "The Re-opening of Halki Seminary: A Great Opportunity for Turkey's Image!" by Justine Frangouli Argyris, https://www.huffpost.com/entry/the-reopening-of-halki-se_b_5681617.

12   The closure of the Greek Orthodox School of Theology at Halki is considered a violation of human rights. Since 1992, Human Rights Watch, an organization created to promote and monitor compliance with human rights provisions in accordance with the Helsinki Accord of 1975, has been formally calling on the Turkish government to allow the reopening of Halki. *Denying Human Rights and Ethnic Identity: The Greeks of Turkey* (New York: Human Rights Watch, 1992), 41.

Regardless of the sacrifice or danger involved, up to and including death, the Church has always encouraged theological education on every level and attempted to educate its clergy and its people as best it could. This continues today.

Orthodoxy preserves balance in theology between the spiritual and the academic:

> Research is always necessary when the human mind tries to grasp the deepest roots of truth and when it is concerned with the intellectual and spiritual development of human personality. It is the necessary presupposition of all educative endeavors envisaging the integral personality of an educated person who has put himself at the service of truth without prejudices and fanaticism. Theology without academic research is seriously crippled and sooner or later it will prove to be unable to serve its educative purposes.[13]

"GO FORTH AND BAPTIZE ALL NATIONS, TEACHING THEM . . ."

IN THE ORTHODOX CHURCH, WE catechize converts, organize Sunday schools, send young men to the seminary, and offer parish Bible studies. We expect the parish priest himself to be educated. But what about the absolute necessity for advanced theological education for others who wish to teach theology or answer questions? How many hapless enquirers—sometimes Orthodox, sometimes investigating Orthodoxy—ask a question on an Orthodox site or chatroom only to receive erroneous, improper, or extreme responses from those eager to display their scant knowledge and assume the mantle of "Instructor in the Faith" or "Defender of Orthodoxy"? Even worse, at times the response to an online question is harsh and unchristian, even condemnatory. These are the Cliff Clavins of Orthodox websites: know-it-alls motivated by a need to feel important or intelligent.[14]

---

13 Nissiotis, "Orthodox Theological Education," 7.
14 Cliff Clavin was a character on the popular 1980s television show *Cheers*, which was set in a bar and featured various regular characters. Cliff was an ordinary mailman, but to feel important and intelligent, he frequently offered unsolicited opinions and

We are all called to learn our faith, discuss our faith, and share our faith. But let discussions be limited to what is appropriate and spiritually useful. As Socrates famously said, "Know thyself." Let those who wish to expound theology get an education.

"EVERYONE'S AN EXPERT"

PEOPLE SOMETIMES ASSUME THAT THEOLOGY or religion is simply a matter of opinion. But theology and religious studies are academic subjects like any other. They require knowledge of history, languages, Scripture, terminology, and theological thought. In the field of religion and theology it seems that everyone is an expert. If one were to go to any gathering of ordinary Orthodox Christians and ask, "Is confession necessary?" "How ought one prepare for communion?" Rarely does anyone hesitate to offer an opinion. Even when people know the actual teaching of the Church, they often contradict it with a private opinion or give a response based on their family practices, which are often not correct.

People ordinarily recognize when they are outside of their area of expertise, or in over their heads. In many other fields—law, engineering, medicine, construction, accounting—we seek out experts. People recognize that training, education, and expertise are important. One would not ordinarily attempt to give accounting advice or answer engineering questions without the proper education. Not so with theology, even though it is an academic discipline and requires expertise, just as any other field does.

Theology is deep and complex. It is not simple, shallow, or a matter of opinion. On the internet, all voices seem equal. It can be difficult to distinguish truth from falsehood, canonical Orthodox churches from schismatic groups, sound teaching from extremism. More reliable sources of information are your parish priest; books written by qualified Orthodox theologians; or church websites such as those of the major archdioceses, Ancient Faith Radio, and other trustworthy sites.[15]

---

dubious "facts" as the bar "know-it-all." Interestingly, the actor who brilliantly played Cliff Clavin, John Ratzenberger, is himself an Orthodox Christian and a benefactor of Orthodoxy, having donated land for a monastery in Washington State.

15 See goarch.org, antiochian.org, oca.org, and ancientfaith.com.

The problem created by amateur theologians is not new. In the late fourth century, St. Jerome bemoaned the fact that people believed themselves to be capable of rendering an opinion on the Holy Scriptures, regardless of their education or spiritual condition. Everyone seemed to fancy himself or herself an expert, although they were completely unaware of the complexities of the Bible or the training necessary to understand it properly:

> The art of interpreting the scriptures is the only one of which all men every-where claim to be masters. To quote Horace again, "Taught or untaught we all write poetry." The chatty old woman, the doting old man, and the wordy soph-ist, one and all take in hand the Scriptures, rend them in pieces and teach them before they have learned them. Some with brows knit and bombastic words, balanced one against the other philosophize concerning the sacred writings among weak women. Others—I blush to say it—learn of women what they are to teach men; and as if even this were not enough, they boldly explain to others what they themselves by no means understand. I say nothing of persons who, like myself have been familiar with secular literature before they have come to the study of the holy scriptures. Such men when they charm the popular ear by the finish of their style suppose every word they say to be a law of God. They do not deign to notice what Prophets and apostles have intended but they adapt conflicting passages to suit their own meaning, as if it were a grand way of teaching—and not rather the faultiest of all—to misrepresent a writer's views and to force the scriptures reluctantly to do their will. . . . It is idle to try to teach what you do not know, and—if I may speak with some warmth—is worse still to be ignorant of your ignorance.[16]

---

16   Saint Jerome, Letter 53.7 to Paulinus, Bishop of Nola, *Jerome: Letters and Selected Works,* W. H. Fremantle, trans., Philip Schaff and Henry Wace, eds., NPNF-2, vol. 6 (Grand Rapids, MI: William B. Eerdmans, 1892), 99. Jerome's comments here about women should not be misunderstood. Women were not educated to the extent that men were, if at all, and therefore were rarely qualified to teach. This does not mean that Jerome was opposed to the education of women. As a matter of fact, he was tremendously popular among wealthy aristocratic women in the city of Rome, who flocked to his Bible studies. His comments here caution against the interpretation of Scripture by anyone who is untrained, whether male or female.

PART III

The Application of Orthodox Theology

CHAPTER 12

The Fathers on Those Who Would
Dabble in Theology

THE FATHERS OF THE CHURCH frequently warned against the practice of dabbling in theology as an occasional pastime, attempting to discuss matters beyond one's actual abilities. Amazingly, those whom the Fathers
were admonishing against theological dabbling were not necessarily people
living in the world, with secular careers, jobs, and families, as most dabblers
are today. Saint Gregory the Theologian sometimes refused to discuss theology with his own bishops! Saint Symeon the New Theologian sharply criticized both monks and clergy for discussing theological matters about which
they had no real experience. If such warnings can be issued to monks, priests,
and bishops, how foolish it is for the rest of us to dabble in theology!

In the comment below, St. Symeon the New Theologian criticizes some
dabblers who theorized and philosophized about the nature of life in the
Kingdom of heaven.

> I would really like to hear you tell me what use this is to you! As I said, you
> are already condemned by your own conscience since you have not kept the
> commandments ordered by Christ and on this account have no portion in
> him. There is no profit for you at all if you should learn from our teaching what
> the pleasures and glories and delights and restorations are which are in His
> Kingdom. On the contrary, you contrive a greater condemnation for yourself

255

because, once having learned about these matters, you hold them in contempt, and want neither to put aside your own conceit nor acquire humility. Now I want to ask you something in all meekness, so please answer me peaceably. If a little child who has not yet learned its letters were to ask someone to interpret the rules of grammar and rhetoric, would anyone who does know put up with it for an instant, or think the child's foolishness worthy of a single word in reply? Would he not instead dismiss the child as foolish and its question as puerile, as asking senselessly after something which exceeds its abilities? And if this is the case, and right and proper concerning matters of grammar, how much the more so is it not true when the issue touches on what transcends words and reason and intellect?[1]

Chrysostom likewise criticized those who attempted to comprehend the incomprehensible. Even the Evangelist John did not attempt to explain divine things but only accepted them.

John, son of Thunder, as he sounded forth on his spiritual trumpet, did not enquire further. . . . And you, who do not share in his grace but merely give voice to your weak reasonings, strive contentiously to surpass the measure of his knowledge? For this reason you will never be able even to approach the measure of his knowledge.[2]

Saint Gregory the Theologian suggested framing an argument to convince people that actual theological knowledge and training were necessary before theologizing.

Now, if we were to speak gently to one of them, advancing, as follows, step by step in argument: "Tell me, my good sir, do you call dancing anything, and flute-playing?" "Certainly," they would say. "What then of wisdom and being wise, which we venture to define as a knowledge of things divine and human?" This also they will admit. "Are then these accomplishments better than and

---

1   Symeon the New Theologian, *First Ethical Discourse* 12, *Ethical Discourses*, 1:66–67.
2   Chrysostom, *Homilies on John*, Homily 7, FOTC, 33:75–76.

superior to wisdom, or wisdom by far better than these?" "Better even than all things," I know well that they will say. Up to this point they are judicious. "Well, dancing and flute-playing require to be taught and learnt, a process which takes time, and much toil in the sweat of the brow, and sometimes the payment of fees, and entreaties for initiation, and long absence from home, and all else which must be done and borne for the acquisition of experience: but as for wisdom, which is chief of all things, and holds in her embrace everything which is good, so that even God himself prefers this title to all the names which He is called; are we to suppose that it is a matter of such slight consequence, and so accessible, that we need but wish, and we would be wise?" "It would be utter folly to do so."[3]

But as Gregory continued, he bemoaned the fact that most dabblers will not be convinced even by an indisputable argument such as this. They would accept the logic that ordinary arts and academic subjects require great effort, training, and years of preparation, and yet this would not discourage the theologically uneducated from theologizing. Clearly, in his experience people who theologize without appropriate preparation will not be convinced of their incompetence. Saint Gregory attributes this to ignorance and pride.

If we, or any learned and prudent man, were to say this to them, and try by degrees to cleanse them from their error, it would be sowing upon rocks, and speaking to ears of men who will not hear, so far are they from being even wise enough to perceive their own ignorance. And we may rightly, in my opinion, apply to them the saying of Solomon: "There is an evil which I have seen under the sun, a man wise in his own conceit" (Prov. 26:12), and a still greater evil is to charge with the instruction of others a man who is not even aware of his own ignorance.[4]

Divine truths cannot be comprehended, pictured, envisioned, or conceived. Human analogies and constructs have limited usefulness and can

---

3   Gregory, *Or.* 2.50, NPNF-2, 7:215.
4   Gregory, *Or.* 2.50, NPNF-2, 7:215.

actually lead us to become enamored with our own ideas and to rely on our thoughts and imaginings as though we actually understood something about God. Saint Symeon the New Theologian stated that we cannot speak about God, even from the Scriptures. One must accept doctrines on the basis of faith, accepting what has been written by the Fathers and not seeking to dabble or meddle in divine things.[5]

It is much better to focus on what benefits us spiritually than to attempt to discuss matters about which we have no real knowledge or expertise. How can we seek to enquire into such matters when by doing so we reveal that we do not even know ourselves? Self-knowledge, especially the awareness of one's own limitations, must come first, St. Gregory the Theologian advises.

> Why do you fly off to heaven, earthling that you are? Why do you build "a tower" if you do not have "enough to complete it"? (Luke 14:28–30). Just why do you measure "the waters in the hollow" of your "hand" and mark off "the heavens with a span, and enclose all the earth in a measure" (Is. 40:12), those primal elements that can be measured only by Him who created them? Know thyself, first of all. Comprehend the things that immediately concern you.[6]

Theology is dangerous, since it concerns eternal life and eternal death. For this reason it is imperative that the theologian have the spiritual foundation and education to be equipped for the task. Saint Gregory the Theologian tried to direct the energies and ambitions of the dabblers toward other, less risky subjects. If the dabblers felt compelled to speak on theology because they were too ambitious to confine their discussions to other topics, at least they ought to restrict their theological talk to certain subjects, such as the Resurrection or the universe.

> If however, you reject these subjects as unworthy of your intellect, being petty and often refuted, and you wish to move in your own field, and fulfill your ambitions there: here also I will provide you with broad highways. Speculate

---

5   Symeon the New Theologian, *Ninth Ethical Discourse*: "That True Knowledge Comes from Purity and Grace from on High," *Ethical Discourses*, 2:113.

6   Gregory, *Or.* 32.27, FOTC, 107:210.

about the Universe—or Universes, about matter, the Soul, about Natures (good and evil) endowed with reason, about the Resurrection, the Judgment, Reward and Punishment, or about the Sufferings of Christ. In these questions to hit the mark is not useless, to miss it is not dangerous. But of God himself, the knowledge we shall have in this life will be little, though soon after it will perhaps be more perfect.[7]

Gregory had little patience for those who refused to refrain from speaking about matters beyond themselves and did not accept his advice to be silent on theology. Their compulsion to theologize revealed the serious spiritual illness of pride, which necessarily was coupled with sharp criticism of others:

You do not accept this; your tongue knows no curb. You are unable to control your impulsive behavior and so are doomed to run amuck, refusing to be subject to the highest powers (though of course there is a limit even to their own knowledge) and assuming a level of self-importance that is not to your advantage. You swear that you are a decent person. Then do not condemn your brother, or call his lack of resolution a disregard of God, or be so quick to turn your back on him in disapproval or dismissal. Instead, show humility on this earth while you can; on this earth honor your brother above yourself—you will not regret it—where to condemn in disgrace is to cast out from Christ, our only hope, and to cut down along with the weeds wheat we cannot see, wheat perhaps more precious than you. Instead, set him on the right path, and do so gently and lovingly, not as an enemy or brutish physician who knows one thing alone, how to cauterize and cut; at the same time take note of yourself and your own infirmity. . . . Yes, what if you think everything is spinning because you happen to be nauseous or drunk and impute your own disorientation to others? You must live long and suffer much before you can accuse another of impiety.[8]

---

7   Gregory, *Or.* 27.10, *On God and Christ,* 33–34.
8   Gregory, *Or.* 32.29, FOTC, 107:212.

Theology is not for those who dabble. It requires an actual education, St. Gregory cautions. Christians should not despise even secular education, which can be useful when used appropriately.

> I take it all intelligent men agree that among human advantages education holds first place. I refer not only to our nobler form of it which disdains all the ambitious ornaments of rhetoric and attaches itself only to salvation and the beauty of spiritual contemplation, but also to that external culture which many Christians by an error of judgment scorn as treacherous and dangerous and as turning us away from God. The heavens, the earth, the air, and all such things are not to be condemned because some have wrongly interpreted them and venerate the creatures of God in place of God. On the contrary, we select from them what is useful both for life and enjoyment and we avoid what is dangerous, not opposing creation to the Creator, as the foolish do, but acknowledging the Maker of the world from his works, as the holy Apostle says (2 Cor. 10:5).[9]

Saint Gregory offered St. Basil as an example of the correct use of secular education. He used his education in this world to acquire the heavenly life. Basil used what is below to gain what is above through "philosophy," "the love of wisdom." When the Fathers of the Church praised "philosophy," they did not mean human intellectual constructs but the love of Holy Wisdom, the Holy Trinity. Christ was also identified with wisdom, and the Fathers often referred to the Christian faith as "true philosophy." Speaking of Basil, St. Gregory praised his worldly education and how he used it to acquire that which is "above."

> But philosophy was his pursuit, as he strove to break from the world, to unite with God, to gain the things above by means of the things below, and to acquire, through goods which are unstable and pass away, those that are stable and abide.[10]

---

9   *Funeral Oration for St. Basil* 11. *Funeral Orations by Saint Gregory Nazianzen and Saint Ambrose,* Leo McCauley, John Sullivan, Martin McGuire, and Roy Deferrari, trans., FOTC, vol. 22 (Washington, DC: Catholic University of America Press, 1953), 35–36.

10   Gregory, *Funeral Oration for St. Basil* 13, FOTC, 22:38.

Those who disdain education wish to hide their own lack of knowledge and personal deficiencies, St. Gregory concluded, but Basil's example ought to be followed. Basil was highly educated but avoided the errors in pagan education and skillfully appropriated what was useful to strengthen his ability to defend Christian doctrine.

> So also from the pagans we have received principles of inquiry and speculation, while we have rejected whatever leads to demons, and error, and the abyss of perdition. And from such material we have drawn profit for piety, by learning to distinguish the better from the worse, and from its weakness we have made our own doctrine strong. Therefore we must not dishonor education because certain men are pleased to do so. Rather, we should regard such men as ignorant and uncultured who would have all others be like themselves, that their own deficiencies might be hidden in the general mass, and their want of culture escape reproach. With this premise made and acknowledged, contemplate the life of Basil.[11]

Those who theologize ought to continue to receive instruction eagerly and to give way cheerfully to those with greater knowledge. But above all, spiritual purification is most necessary.

> This, my brothers, is the order we should respect, this the order we should preserve. Let one man serve as an ear, another as a tongue, a third as a hand and another in some further capacity. Let one man teach and another learn and yet another do "honest work with his hands" that he may give to him that is poor and needy (Eph. 4:28). Let one man rule and preside and another be justified in his service; and let him who teaches do so in a dignified way.... But if another has been enlightened, let the first yield. And let him who learns be receptive to instruction; and him who ministers do so with cheerfulness, and him who attends, with eagerness. Let us not all try to serve as a tongue, that most facile medium. Let us not "all" try to be "apostles, all prophets, all interpret" (1 Cor. 12:29–30). Do you think talking about God is important? It is more important

---

11   Gregory, *Funeral Oration for St. Basil* 11, FOTC, 22:36.

to purify yourself before God because "wisdom will not enter a deceitful soul" (Wis. 1:4).[12]

Saint Symeon is even more passionate than St. Gregory in his denunciations of those who speak about God and teach theology, meddling in matters of which they have no knowledge. Their bold attitude is arrogant and presumptuous, since not only do they think more highly of themselves than they ought and attempt to teach others about matters beyond their knowledge, but they have not even acquired the most basic of virtues.

> Have you, O brother, renounced the world and what is in the world? Have you become one who possess nothing and submissive and a stranger to your own will? Have you acquired meekness and become humble? Have you fasted to the supreme degree, and prayed, and kept vigil? Have you acquired perfect love for God and have you regarded your neighbor as yourself? Do you intercede with tears for those who hate and wrong you, and are hostile to you, and do you pray that they may be forgiven those offenses, having first had compassion on them from your soul? Or have you not yet been led up to this height of the virtues?
>
> . . .
>
> If you have not yet been deemed worthy of such great gifts, nor have attained to so great a height of the deifying virtues, how then do you dare at all even to open your mouth and speak? How, being still a catechumen, do you decide to teach, and try to meddle in matters about which you neither know nor have heard, and then, as if you know about divine things, proceed to argue boldly about such matters? . . . Stung by my argument, what you say you know nothing about and admit that you have neither seen, nor heard, nor been found worthy of receiving in your heart, these things you have no shame in interpreting and clarifying as if you did know nor do you blush at men's laughter.[13]

---

12 Gregory, *Or.* 32.12, FOTC, 107:199–200.
13 Symeon the New Theologian, *Ninth Ethical Discourse. Ethical Discourses*, 2:117–119. Saint Symeon was speaking to monks. None in his audience were literally catechumens. His point was that they were still in need of basic instruction (by which he meant spiritual experience), and none of them were qualified to theologize.

Just as Symeon had explained to his monks that spiritual struggles and acquisition of virtue must precede theology, Gregory also insisted on the same preliminary steps. Before we can theologize and "smooth the theologian within us, like a statue, into beauty," we must "look at ourselves" and remove "all alien elements."

> But first we must consider, what is this disorder of the tongue which leads us to compete in garrulity? What is this alarming disease, this appetite which can never be sated? Why do we keep our hands bound and our tongues armed? Do we commend hospitality? Do we admire brotherly love, wifely affection, virginity, feeding the poor, singing psalms, nightlong vigils, penitence? Do we mortify the body with fasting? Do we through prayer take up our abode with God? Do we subordinate the inferior element in us to the better—I mean the dust to the spirit, as we should if we have returned the right verdict on the alloy of the two which is our nature? Do we make life a meditation of death? Do we establish our mastery over our passions, mindful of the nobility of our second birth? Do we tame our swollen and inflamed tempers? Or our pride "which comes before a fall" (Prov.16:18), or our unreasonable grief, our crude plea-sures, our dirty laughter, our undisciplined eyes, our greedy ears, our immod-erate talk, our wandering thoughts, or anything in ourselves which the Evil One can take over from us and use against us, "bringing in death through the windows" (Jer. 9:21/20), as Scripture has it, meaning through the senses? No. We do the very opposite.[14]

But dabblers are not dissuaded, Gregory lamented, and having learned a few expressions from two or three authors, not from real study but only pick-ing up a few comments in order to impress others, they proceed to theologize. They know little about the Scriptures and yet cultivate an appearance of learn-ing and piety. Rather than recognizing that they themselves need to learn, they are eager to teach others and expect to be lauded. Ego motivates the dabblers, Gregory observed, and truly pious or spiritual men abandon them. Gregory levels a devastatingly accurate critique:

---

14   Gregory, *Or. 27.7, On God and Christ*, 30–31.

Among us, however, there is no boundary line between giving and receiving instruction, like the stones of old between the tribes within and beyond the Jordan: nor is a certain part entrusted to some, another to others; nor any rule for degrees of experience; but the matter has been so disturbed and thrown into confusion, that most of us, not to say all, almost before we have lost our childish curls and lisp, before we have entered the house of God, before we know even the names of the Sacred Books, before we have learnt the character and authors of the Old and New Testaments. . . . If, I say, we have furnished ourselves with two or three expressions of pious authors, and that by hearsay, not by study; if we have had a brief experience of David, or clad ourselves properly in a cloak, or are wearing at least a philosopher's belt, or have girt about us some form and appearance of piety—phew! how we take the chair and show our spirit! Samuel was holy even in his swaddling-clothes; we are at once wise teachers, of high estimation in Divine things, the first of scribes and lawyers; we ordain ourselves men of heaven and seek to be "called Rabbi by men" (Matt. 23:7); the letter is nowhere, everything is to be understood spiritually, and our dreams are utter drivel, and we should be annoyed if we were not lauded to excess. This is the case with the better and more simple of us: what of those who are more spiritual and noble? After frequently condemning us, as men of no account, they have forsaken us, and abhor fellowship with impious people such as we are.[15]

The serious responsibilities inherent in theologizing are unrecognized by the dabblers, sometimes even by those who are educated in theology. The chapters that follow will reflect on the practice of discerning when to speak and when not to speak.

---

15   Gregory, *Or.* 2.49, NPNF-2, 7:215.

CHAPTER 13

Theological Discernment: When to Speak

P ERHAPS NO QUALITY IS MORE important to the theologian than discernment. As we have seen, the Fathers of the Church taught that theology is not for all people at all times and in all places. One ought to think about God constantly, but not always speak about God, St. Gregory advises.[1] In this chapter we will address several conditions under which it is appropriate for a theologian to speak.

Long Experience in the Church

WHEN IS IT APPROPRIATE TO theologize? First, one must have an Orthodox phronema. This requires many years of participation in the life of the Church. The holy canons forbid the ordination of a recent convert.[2] By extension and analogy, it can safely be said that a recent convert should not theologize, advise, or teach theology, for, according to the words of the canon, "it is wrong for one without experience to become the teacher of others."[3] This has been the tradition of the Church since the beginning. Saint Paul advised Timothy not to ordain recent converts (1 Tim. 3:6).

---

1   Gregory, *Or.* 27.4, *On God and Christ*, 27–28.
2   See Canon 2 of the 20 Canons of the First Ecumenical Council at Nicaea, Canon 80 of the 85 Canons of the Holy Apostles, and Canon 3 of the 60 Canons of Laodicea.
3   Canon 80 of the 85 Canons of the Holy Apostles. *The Rudder*, D. Cummings, trans. (Chicago: Greek Orthodox Christian Educational Society, 1957), 139.

One cannot be Orthodox without the proper phronema, and this simply requires time. Converts enthusiastically wish to share what they have learned, teach, theologize, or even become priests. Their zeal is understandable but unwise if employed too quickly. A certain level of spiritual maturity is needed that can only be attained through experiencing the life of the Church, ecclesiastical year after ecclesiastical year, season after season—the divine services and sacraments, the prayers, the practices, the life of the community. Orthodoxy is not a set of intellectual precepts but a way of life that can only be learned by living it. A convert who thinks he knows enough and does not wish to wait until he is mature in the faith also shows a lack of humility, and this is not a good sign.

Furthermore, it goes without saying that no one should theologize, whether cradle or convert, who is not currently active in the total life of the Church. This includes consistent attendance at the Divine Liturgy, participation in the sacraments, a regular prayer life, receiving ongoing direction from a spiritual father, giving to the poor and needy, living an ethical life, pursuing virtue, and avoiding immorality in word and in deed. The theologian can only be one who strives to apply what he or she has learned toward his or her own spiritual improvement first of all. Just as it is inappropriate to receive Holy Communion and then use that same mouth for foul language, curses, and slanders, it is unimaginable that one would even consider theologizing while he or she is not struggling to live an Orthodox Christian life to the fullest extent possible. Theology is not a purely intellectual pursuit. Most of all, rather than growing in *self*-confidence over time, a true theologian becomes increasingly aware of his or her unworthiness to theologize at all.

An Orthodox Theological Education

AS WE HAVE SEEN, THE advice given by the Holy Fathers and the custom of the Church affirm that one who theologizes by preaching or teaching should have an Orthodox theological education with actual expertise and basic qualifications to perform this service in and for the Church. "Theology," St. Gregory the Theologian reminds us, "is not for all people, but only for those who have been tested and have found a sound footing in study, and more importantly, have undergone, or at the very least are undergoing, purification of body and soul."[4]

An Appropriate Audience

ASSUMING THE THEOLOGIAN IS PROPERLY prepared academically and is basically healthy spiritually, then the theologian must discern whether it is appropriate to speak in light of the situation and audience. The Fathers of the Church often advise that the setting be taken into serious consideration before theologizing. Saint Gregory advises:

> Discussion of theology is not for everyone, I tell you, not for everyone—it is no such inexpensive or effortless pursuit. Nor, I would add, is it for every occasion or every audience; neither are all its aspects open to inquiry. It must be reserved for certain occasions, for certain audiences, and certain limits must be observed.[5]

Saint John Chrysostom occasionally commented on the limitations of his audience. At times he restricted his remarks because they had grown tired, were bored, or were not paying attention. Rather than being helped by the sermon, their attitude would contribute to their condemnation. In such cases, sometimes after upbraiding the congregation, he stopped preaching.[6]

Other factors affected his decision regarding what to say and for how long to speak, including time constraints, the weather, and the ability of the congregation to remember what he had said.[7] Chrysostom was keenly aware of the limitations of his congregation. "Indeed, teachers do not say all things as they

---

4   Gregory, *Or.* 27.3, *On God and Christ*, 27.
5   Gregory, *Or.* 27.3, *On God and Christ*, 26–27.
6   Chrysostom, *Homilies on Acts of the Apostles*, Homily 19, NPNF-1, 11:127–28.
7   Chrysostom, *Homilies on John*, Homily 4, FOTC, 33:43–44. "I also wished to attack other questions, but perhaps our minds have become weary.... I realize that many of you have become listless because of the length of my sermon." *Homilies on John*, Homily 2, FOTC, 33:22–23. "The reason we are giving our interpretation a little at a time is that all things may become easily intelligible for you, and may not escape your memory." FOTC, 33:25.

desire, but say many things as the dispositions of imperfect listeners demand."[8] On another occasion, Chrysostom restrains himself by noting the inability of his listeners to comprehend his comments: "I would add our own explanation, but I fear that I shall overwhelm your minds."[9] Moderation should be observed in all things, including discussions of theology, St. Gregory advises:

> Yet I am not maintaining that we ought not be mindful of God at all times— my adversaries, ever ready and quick to attack, need not pounce on me again. It is more important that we should remember God than that we should breathe; indeed, if one may say so, we should do nothing else besides. . . . So it is not continual remembrance of God that I seek to discourage, but continual discussion of theology. I am not opposed either to theology, as if it were a breach of piety, but only to its untimely practice, or to instruction in it, except when this goes to excess. Fullness and surfeit even of honey, for all its goodness, produces vomiting, and "to everything there is a season" (Eccl. 3:1), as Solomon and I think "and what's well is not well if the hour be ill." . . . Are we then to neglect "the due season" only in the discussion of theology, where observing the proper time is of such supreme importance?[10]

Appropriate Subject Matter

THE SUBJECT MATTER MUST ALSO be considered. Not all topics are appropriate to every audience or situation. The purpose of theology is the spiritual improvement of the faithful. Not everything is beneficial to all people. Gregory the Theologian compares inappropriate subject matter to food that injures the health, or a load that is too heavy for someone to carry. Discussing topics that are beyond the ability of the audience to understand might actually be harmful to them.

> What aspects of theology should be investigated, and to what limit? Only aspects within our grasp, and only to the limit of the experience and capacity

8   Chrysostom, *Homilies on John*, Homily 30, FOTC 33:293–94.
9   Chrysostom, *Homilies on Philippians*, Homily 6, NPNF-1, 13:209.
10   Gregory, *Or.* 27.4, *On God and Christ*, 27–28.

of our audience. Just as excess of sound or food injures the hearing or general health, or, if you prefer, as loads that are too heavy injure those that carry them, or as excessive rain harms the soil, we too must guard against the danger that the toughness, so to speak, of our discourses may so oppress and overtax our hearers as actually to impair the power they had before.[11]

Gregory maintains that silence is best and should be preferred above speaking.

Go ahead and speak if what you have to say is better than silence, for, as you know, it is commendable to impose order on one's tongue, but try to cherish quiet when silence is preferable to speech, and be content sometimes to speak up and sometimes to listen, sometimes to express your approval and some- times to withhold it, though not in an ill-tempered way.[12]

A Spiritually Disposed Audience

NOT ONLY IS THEOLOGIZING CHALLENGING due to the difficulty of expression, but its effectiveness also depends on the disposition of the hearers. Spiritual purity is required for the listener to properly understand the message.

You cannot know how great a gift from God is silence and not having to speak on every occasion, thus to have it within ourselves, as keepers over both our speech and our silence, to choose what to say and what to suppress. For all speech is by nature loose and inadequate and, because it is open to chal- lenge, vulnerable, and speech about God all the more so as the subject is more important and the emotion runs higher and the venture is more difficult. What shall we fear? And where then place our trust? Human reason? Speech? The things we hear? We oscillate precariously between three poles: the difficulty of forming a conception of him, the near impossibility of expressing it in words, and the still greater task of finding an ear to receive it in purity.[13]

---

11   Gregory, *Or.* 27.3, *On God and Christ*, 27.
12   Gregory, *Or.* 32.13, FOTC, 107:200–201.
13   Gregory, *Or.* 32.14, FOTC, 107:201.

Responsibility to Speak

SILENCE MAY BE PREFERRED, BUT at times the theologian has a responsibility to speak, which St. Gregory also recognized. Silence would be acceptable if the theologian lacked the capacity to theologize adequately, but he is "culpable" if he refuses to become involved when he does have the capability.

> One does better to contribute what one can than not to make the effort at all. A person should certainly not be held responsible if he lacks an aptitude for such things; culpable, however, he is if he refuses to involve himself be it in matters divine or human.[14]

Saint Basil agreed with his dear friend Gregory. There are times when the theologian must speak, even though all theological language is insufficient to express the thoughts of the speaker. Even when it is difficult to respond, it "looks like a betrayal" when the theologian will not "give an answer about God to those who love the Lord." Basil himself had encouraged the introverted Gregory to devote his talents and God-given intellectual energies to advocate for truth:

> When I wrote to you, I was perfectly well aware that no theological term is adequate to the thought of the speaker, or the want of the questioner, because language is of natural necessity too weak to act in the service of objects of thought. If then our thought is weak, and our tongue weaker than our thought, what was to be expected of me in what I said but that I should be charged with poverty of expression? Still, it was not possible to let your question pass unnoticed. It looks like a betrayal, if we do not readily give an answer about God to them that love the Lord. What has been said, however, whether it seems satisfactory, or requires some further and more careful addition, needs a fit season for correction. For the present I implore you, as I have implored you before, to devote yourself entirely to the advocacy of the truth, and to the intellectual energies God gives you for the establishment of what is good. With this be content, and ask nothing more from me. I am really much less capable than is supposed, and

---

14   Gregory, *Or.* 32.1, FOTC, 107:191.

am more likely to do harm to the word by my weakness than to add strength to the truth by my advocacy.[15]

Cyril of Alexandria refuted Arian heretics, who denied the equality of the Father and the Son based on a misinterpretation of Scripture. He offered guidance to those "who cling to truth" in formulating responses to heretics. The Orthodox must "follow the footprints of the Fathers," meaning they must explain the correct interpretation of the scriptural passage and then investigate how they might equip themselves to counter the arguments of heretics. It would be acceptable to be silent if no harm would ensue by not responding, but someone might be persuaded by the arguments of heretics to accept their dogmas.

> If we could pass over them in silence and see that no harm would enter the mind of the simple from them, we would rightly conclude that their vain arguments are not worth spending time on, and we would proceed to the consideration of the next passage. But since it would do no small damage if such dogmas were accepted by someone, does it not follow that we, moved by zeal and love for God, should engage the battle with arguments and words? In this way the villainy of the opponents may easily be detected.[16]

Having considered the situation, the subject matter, the audience and their capacity, and the general preference for silence, perhaps it might nonetheless be necessary for the theologian to speak. Saint Basil the Great offers beautiful advice regarding how a theologian ought to speak. One ought not to be ambitious, not seek to make a display, be willing to learn, not begrudge giving information but also not take credit for ideas that are not his or her own. The theologian must be courteous, gentle, amiable, modest, and humble. Harshness should never be used, and if a rebuke is necessary, it should be given in such a clever way that the listener condemns himself, as David did after

---

15   Basil the Great, *Letters*, Letter 7 "To Gregory," NPNF-2, 8:115.
16   *Commentary on John* 10.2, *Cyril of Alexandria: Commentary on John* (2 vols.), David Maxwell, trans., Ancient Christian Texts, Joel Elowsky, ed. (Downer's Grove, IL: IVP Academic, 2015), 2:213.

Nathan's story about the lamb (2 Sam./2 Kg. 12:1–15). Such was the advice St. Basil gave to Gregory the Theologian:

> This, too, is a very important point to attend to—knowledge how to converse; to interrogate without over-earnestness; to answer without desire of display; not to interrupt a profitable speaker, or to desire ambitiously to put in a word of one's own; to be measured in speaking and hearing; not to be ashamed of receiving, or to be grudging in giving information, nor to pass another's knowledge for one's own, as depraved women their supposed children, but to refer it candidly to the true parent. The middle tone of voice is best, neither so low as to be inaudible, nor to be ill-bred from its high pitch. One should reflect first what one is going to say, and then give it utterance: be courteous when addressed; amiable in social intercourse; not aiming to be pleasant by facetiousness, but cultivating gentleness in kind admonitions. Harshness is ever to be put aside, even in censuring. The more you show modesty and humility yourself, the more likely are you to be acceptable to the patient who needs your treatment. There are however many occasions when we shall do well to employ the kind of rebuke used by the prophet who did not in his own person utter the sentence of condemnation on David after his sin, but by suggesting an imaginary character made the sinner judge of his own sin, so that, after passing his own sentence, he could not find fault with the seer who had convicted him.[17]

---

17 Basil the Great, *Letters*, Letter 2.5 "To Gregory," NPNF-2, 8:111–112.

CHAPTER 14

Theological Discernment: When Not to Speak

I N ADDITION TO THE GENERAL recommendation to prefer silence, there are certain situations in which the theologian ought especially to refrain from the discussion of theology.

> It is pious to keep God in mind without ceasing, and the soul who loves God finds no satiety in this, but it is audacious to expound upon God in speech. For our mind has fallen quite far from the dignity of the true realities and moreover our speech communicates our thoughts obscurely. So then, if our mind is so distant from the grandeur of the true realities and our speech is even more inadequate than our mind, how are we not compelled to keep silent, so that the wonders of theology do not seem to be diminished by the poverty of our words?[1]

When should the theologian refrain from speaking? He or she must consider the subject matter to be discussed, the disposition and capacity of the listeners, his or her own ability to answer, the possible motives of the questioner, his or her own motives in choosing to speak, and whether a superior theologian is present.

---

1   Basil, *Homily on Faith* 1, *On Christian Doctrine and Practice*, Mark DelCogliano, trans., Popular Patristics, vol. 47 (Crestwood, NY: St. Vladimir's Seminary Press, 2012), 234.

The Subject Matter Is Inappropriate for the Audience or Forum

THE THEOLOGIAN MUST CONSIDER WHO is present for the discussion. Where is this discussion taking place? Is it a parish Bible study? A parish retreat? A clergy meeting? On the internet?

If the location is a school of theology, then almost any subject would be open to discussion (but even then, not at all times or with all people), because the purpose of gathering at a school of theology is for instruction in theology, and the students are known to the professor. They have been recommended and admitted for the study of theology. The classroom is private, and the level of understanding of the students is higher than most, or at least they are on a trajectory of growth in theological understanding. Their commitment to the Church has already been established. Theology students spend hours in the classroom over a period of years, during which misunderstandings would presumably come to light and be corrected. It is only in this type of setting, or perhaps at a conference of Orthodox theologians, that one should discuss such deep and complex topics as theosis, the essence and energies of God, or the procession of the Holy Spirit. This is true theology, talking directly about God, and such topics should not be discussed casually.

And yet such profound topics are discussed every day on the internet, where anyone can read and participate in the discussion, even though the background, lives, motivation, and psychological or spiritual conditions of the people engaged in such discussions are unknown.

An internet site is more appropriate for questions about the Bible and basic information about the faith. Saint Gregory the Theologian remarked that only those for whom theology is a serious subject ought to discuss it. But he did not mean to include dabblers who consider themselves serious students of theology but who actually have never formally studied.

> Who should listen to discussions of theology? Those for whom it is a serious undertaking, not just another subject like any other for entertaining small-talk, after the races, the theater, songs, food and sex. For there are people who count chatter on theology and clever deployment of arguments as one of their amusements.[2]

---

2   Gregory, *Or.* 27.3, *On God and Christ,* 27.

The Questioner Is Incapable of Understanding

SOMETIMES PEOPLE SIMPLY CANNOT UNDERSTAND a theological explanation. They may be very devout and pious, but their faith is extremely simple. When the theologian perceives this, he or she must moderate the response rather than pushing to persuade the questioner to accept a deeper or more complex answer. This is particularly true in the area of the creation accounts of Genesis. Some people can understand creation only on a very basic level. They should be left alone rather than disturbed with sophisticated explanations that are likely to scandalize or distress them. This calls for discernment.

Even in a theological classroom, at times students are not ready to hear what they need to hear. They come to the school of theology with their own ideas, perhaps instilled by a parish priest or relative, or perhaps formed by their own reading. Theology students are likely to be quite enthusiastic about theology but may also be rigid in their opinions. They may fear that moderating their views to accept something deeper or more nuanced is tantamount to betraying Tradition, even when the professor supplies numerous patristic witnesses to support his or her teaching.

My first year as a New Testament professor was at Holy Cross Greek Orthodox School of Theology. I was teaching a course on the Gospel of Matthew, and I realized that a small group of rather conservative students in the back of the class did not trust my orthodoxy. I was new, and they did not know me. The fact that I was a woman contributed to their distrust. They often whispered among themselves during class.

One day the subject of the lesson was the Sermon on the Mount, Matthew 5—7. Chrysostom's analysis of this section of the Gospel is so brilliant that I told the students at the very beginning of the session that everything I said that day would come from Chrysostom unless I told them otherwise. As the lesson proceeded, eventually we arrived at the place where the Lord said that it was not enough to avoid committing actual adultery; one should not even look at a woman with lust (Matt. 5:28). I said, "If you wish to look at a woman with lust, look at your wife. That is not lust."

Immediately a voice rang out from the back of the classroom proclaiming, "That is *not* according to the Fathers!" I simply smiled, and after a moment of silence the entire class burst out in laughter. The guardians of Orthodoxy in the back of the classroom had forgotten that I was quoting Chrysostom for the entire class period, including that apparently unpatristic and objectionable statement.

Sometimes people are not prepared to receive even what a well-intentioned theologian wishes to convey to them, especially on difficult theological matters. We must be sensitive to that. This requires serious discernment, because the role of the theologian is not to harm, not to scandalize or create barriers to faith, but to teach, encourage, edify, and inspire. At times this can only be done gradually, whether at a parish, at a graduate school of theology, or in private conversation. It is more important that we affirm and strengthen someone's faith than that we display how educated or intelligent we are. If the result is that one seeking answers becomes disillusioned or scandalized and falls away, we have not achieved our purpose.

Chrysostom recognized that his congregation's capacity was limited. On one occasion he directly commented about the need to introduce ideas to them slowly, comparing his progress to laying the foundation of a house so that it will be strong and secure.

Dearly beloved children, the reason why we have fed you little by little with thoughts from the Scriptures and have not poured them all out at once, is that we might make it easy for you to hold fast those already given to you. And I say this for, in constructing a building when the first stones are not yet firmly fastened together, if a man sets others upon them, he renders the wall altogether unsound and easy to throw down. But, if he waits for the cement to set first, and then places the rest upon it gradually, he completes the whole house with safety, making it not a temporary structure or easily destroyed, but durable. Let us also imitate these builders and let us build up your souls in the same way. For we are afraid lest, when the first foundation has just been laid, the adding of the next teachings may weaken the former, because your understanding is not sufficiently strong to hold all together firmly.[3]

---

3   Chrysostom, *Homilies on John*, Homily 7, FOTC, 33:74–75.

Just as a doctor does not treat every person with the same medicine, recognizing that healing may require different remedies and differing lengths of time, the theologian must accept the spiritual and psychological limitations of his audience. Most Orthodox Christians have received only a basic Sunday school education, if even that—especially the cradle-born Orthodox. Many Christians, Orthodox or not, never receive any religious education beyond elementary school age and effectively remain on a child's level in terms of religious knowledge. They may have always attended church and are happy as Orthodox Christians, but unless they took the initiative to learn more about their faith or had an exceptional parish priest, they most likely do not know their faith well. They have a simple faith.

A deeper understanding would be wonderful; however, some people may never be able to conceptualize at a deeper level. Doing so is not necessary if they have no desire for it, and it may actually be harmful if they become scandalized or confused. Theologians must accept that and remember the Lord, who said that unless we become "like children" we "will never enter the kingdom of heaven" (Matt. 18:3). Becoming more knowledgeable about the faith is important for everyone, but complex concepts can be off-putting. A simple but deeply held, sincere faith may define the limit of a person's capacity, but that person may enter the Kingdom of heaven before some theologians do.

Furthermore, the Lord warned that "whoever causes one of these little ones who believe in me to sin, it would be better for him to have a great millstone fastened round his neck and to be drowned in the depth of the sea" (Matt. 18:6). The theologian cannot be the cause of others falling away simply because he or she would like them to advance in their understanding. We cannot force people to grow intellectually or spiritually. We are unaware of their particular fears, limitations, and life experiences.

We should also recognize that these "little ones" may have insights we lack. The Lord thanked the Father for having "hidden these things from the wise and understanding and revealed them to babes" (Matt. 11:25; Luke 10:21), because it was not the learned and wise who believed in Christ but the simple and uneducated. Remembrance of the Lord's words should help us to cultivate humility.

The Questioner Does Not Understand or Respect the Orthodox Faith

WE MUST RECALL AND TAKE very seriously the Lord's instruction not to "throw your pearls before swine" (Matt. 7:6), which means not to give something precious to a person who will not appreciate or respect it. When questioners simply do not understand the Orthodox faith, they may not be able to receive what is said, even if they are willing. But when the person enquiring does not even respect the Orthodox faith, the theologian should exercise the greatest discernment, since his or her comments may be misused to misrepresent, oppose, or even ridicule the Orthodox faith.

The teachings of the Orthodox Church are precious pearls and should not be shared with those who do not believe or who lack the ability to understand our words. I have seen the faith ridiculed and mocked by unbelievers. We speak about the faith as "mystery," but we do not actually treat it as though it were a mystery. If we openly share our doctrines with everyone, we neither guard the faith nor protect it but cast our pearls before swine. When we do not treat these holy mysteries of the faith with reverence, we do not encourage others to do so either.

> It is not appropriate for what pertains to the truth—that is, the mystical doctrines to be told to just anyone, but only to the neighbor (Eph. 4:25). In other words, it is not appropriate to divulge them to whoever happens to be around but only to those who have come to share in the mysteries.[4]

Saint Basil lists many common Christian practices that were never written down. They were unwritten not because people could not read but because these things were secrets and considered inappropriate for discussion among the unbaptized. Saint Basil distinguished between *dogma*, or the essential teachings of the Church that are known only by the initiated (baptized), and the *kerygma*, the preaching, which is the public proclamation of the gospel. After listing many unwritten practices or traditions Christians observed, he continued:

---

4   Basil the Great, *First Homily on Psalm 14*, Homily 1 on Ps. 14.3, *On Christian Doctrine and Practice*, 96.

What about baptizing a man with three immersions and other baptismal rites, such as the renunciation of Satan and his angels? Are not all these things found in unpublished and unwritten teachings, which our fathers guarded in silence, safe from meddling and petty curiosity? They had learned their lesson well; reverence for the mysteries is best encouraged by silence. The uninitiated were not even allowed to be present at the mysteries; how could you expect these mysteries to be paraded about in public documents? . . . Moses was wise enough to realize that triteness and familiarity breed contempt, but the unusual and the unfamiliar naturally commands eager interest. In the same way, when the apostles and Fathers established ordinances for the Church, they protected the dignity of the mysteries with silence and secrecy from the beginning, since what is noised abroad to anyone at random is no mystery at all. . . . Dogma is one thing, kerygma is another; the first is observed in silence, while the latter is proclaimed to the world.[5]

Saint John Chrysostom also warned against sharing mysteries of the faith with unbelievers, pointing out that even believers have not been given complete knowledge and understanding by the Lord. If some aspects of the faith remain mysteries even to believers, why should everything be told to those who have no appreciation for our holy doctrines or are incapable of understanding them?

So we have been also charged, "not to give the holy things unto dogs nor to cast our pearls before swine" (Matt. 7:6). For some are carnal and do not understand; others have a veil upon their hearts and do not see; wherefore that is above all things a mystery, which everywhere is preached, but is not known of those who have not a right mind; and is revealed not by wisdom but by the Holy Spirit, so far as is possible for us to receive it. And for this cause a man would not err, who in this respect also should entitle it a mystery, the utterance of which is forbidden. For not even to us, the faithful, has everything been committed with entire certainty and exactness. As Paul also said, "We know in part, and we prophesy in part: for now we see in a mirror darkly; but then face to face" (1 Cor. 13:12).[6]

---

5   Basil, *On the Holy Spirit* 66, Popular Patristics 42:99–100.
6   Chrysostom, *Homilies on First and Second Corinthians*, Homilies on First Corinthians, 7.3, NPNF-1, 7:35.

A Christian hears and accepts a religious concept in one sense, whereas the same teaching might be misunderstood or taken in an entirely different sense by an unbeliever. Not only would this be the case for Christians and non-Christians, but we must recognize that this applies to conveying Orthodox doctrines to non-Orthodox Christians who lack the phronema to understand Orthodox doctrine correctly. Chrysostom commented on this reality:

> I, for instance, feel differently about these subjects than an unbeliever. I hear, "Christ was crucified" and immediately I admire His loving-kindness to men. The other hears and esteems it as weakness. I hear, "He became a servant" and I wonder at his care for us. The other hears and counts it as dishonor. I hear, "He died" and I am astonished at His might, that He was not held in death, but even broke the bands of death. The other hears and surmises it to be helplessness. He, on hearing of the resurrection, says the thing is a legend. I, aware of the facts which demonstrate it, fall down and worship the dispensation of God. . . . For not by the sight do I judge the things that appear, but by the eyes of the mind. I hear of the "Body of Christ." In one sense I understand the expression, in another sense the unbeliever.[7]

Saint Gregory also emphasized the need to discern the audience, not only to avoid exposing sacred doctrines to unbelievers but even to avoid disputes and dissensions among Christians in the presence of unbelievers. Unbelievers should not witness quarrels between Christians, since they might exploit the controversies and use them against the faith.

> Let us not "sing the song of the Lord in a foreign land" (Ps. 137/136:4) by which I mean before any and every audience, heathen or Christian, friend or foe, sympathetic or hostile. These keep all too close a watch on us, and they would wish that the spark of our dissentions might become a conflagration. They kindle it, they fan it, by means of its own draught they raise it to the skies, and without our knowing what they are up to, they make it higher than those

---

7   Chrysostom, *Homilies on First and Second Corinthians*, Homilies on First Corinthians 7.2, NPNF-1, 7:34.

flames at Babylon which blazed all around (Dan. 3:20). Having no strength in their own teaching, they hunt for it in our weakness, and for this reason, like flies settling on wounds, they settle on our misfortunes—or should I say our mistakes? Let us be blind to our doings no longer and let us not neglect the proprieties in these matters. If we cannot resolve our disputes outright, let us at least make this mutual concession, to utter spiritual truths with the restraint due to them, to discuss holy things in a holy manner, and not to broadcast to profane hearing what is not to be divulged. . . . We must recognize that, as in dress, diet, laughter, and deportment there are certain standards of decency, the same is true of utterance and silence, particularly as we pay special honor to "the Word" among the titles and properties of God. Let even our contentiousness be governed by rules.[8]

The Questioner Is Unwilling to Believe or Understand

THE LORD HIMSELF OFTEN REFUSED to respond to the questions of Jewish leaders when He knew they were insincere. "If you are the Christ, tell us plainly," they demanded. He replied, "I told you, and you do not believe" (John 10:24–25). Even at His trial, when He was asked whether He was the Christ, He stated, "If I tell you, you will not believe" (Luke 22:67). Sometimes response to the gospel is a matter of whether people are willing to hear, not whether they are physically able to hear. For that reason He repeatedly said, "He who has ears to hear, let him hear."[9]

Gregory the Theologian expressed concern about exposing mysteries of the faith to unbelievers, not only because pagans were opposed to the Christian faith or would use the words of Christians against them, but because the immoral pagan lifestyle hindered them from properly comprehending Christian doctrines. Certainly the same thing can be said today, even though we rarely find ourselves disputing with pagans. But atheists, members of other religions, and other Christians who oppose the Orthodox Christian faith lack an Orthodox phronema. Furthermore, to the extent to which they are carnally

---

8   Gregory, *Or. 27.5, On God and Christ,* 28–29.
9   Matt. 11:15, 13:9, 13:43; Mark 4:9, 4:23; Luke 8:8, 14:35. He also says this in the Book of Revelation at the end of each of the letters to the seven churches in chapters 2 and 3.

rather than spiritually minded, they will likewise be unable to comprehend Orthodox doctrine.

It is truly outrageous that Orthodox Christians are discussing the essence and energies of God, the procession of the Holy Spirit, theosis, and other profound matters of faith on the internet in the presence of anyone who might happen to read it. To expose sacred doctrines in the same manner as any common or profane discussion borders on blasphemy. Gregory the Theologian would condemn this and admonish us to refrain from theologizing in that type of situation, regardless of our good motivations to defend the faith or explain Orthodoxy:

> Why do we allow audiences hostile to our subject matter to listen to discussion of the "generation" and "creation" of God, or of God's "production from non-being" and such dissections, and distinctions and analyses? Why do we appoint our accusers as our judges? Why do we put swords into our enemies' hands? How, I ask you, will such a discussion be interpreted by the man who subscribes to a creed of adulteries and infanticides, who worships the passions, who is incapable of conceiving anything higher than the body, who fabricated his own gods only the other day, and gods at that distinguished by their utter vileness? What sort of construction will he put on it? Is he not certain to take it in a crude, obscene, material sense, as is his wont? Will he not appropriate your theology to defend his own gods and passions?[10]

Among believers, however, the problem in the audience is not necessarily hostility toward our doctrine but laziness. In that case, it may still be prudent to refrain from speaking, since the audience lacks the proper appreciation for what is being presented. Chrysostom expressed frustration that even though his congregation was capable of learning, they were lazy. He considered it pointless to continue to instruct them about the Scriptures when they were indifferent and indolent. At one point he refused to explain anything after they complained that his sermons were always about the same thing. His reply was that in spite of his repetition, they still had not learned anything. He chastised them for their complaints and laziness. To demonstrate that they still

---

10 Gregory, Or. 27.6, *On God and Christ*, 29.

knew nothing after hearing numerous sermons, he challenged them to answer questions of basic knowledge about the Scriptures:

> Look, what a number of things I am going to speak of—Say, what is a narrative? what is prophecy? what is parable? what is type? what is allegory? what is symbol? what are gospels? Answer me only to this one point, which is plain: why are they called gospels, "good tidings"?[11]

He persisted at length, asking them many more questions. He blamed himself for contributing to their laziness by not requiring any effort from them and told them he would not explain these things to them, since preaching to them was like pouring water into a sieve. The judgment of God upon them for their neglect of such matters would be worse if he continued to preach and they continued to learn nothing:

> Where are they that say, "Always the same things"? If you knew these things— though a man should live a thousand years, they are not the "same things," you would not say this. Believe me, I will not tell you the answers to any of these questions; not in private, not in public; only, if any find them out, I will nod my assent. For this is the way we have made you good-for-nothing, by always telling you the things ready to your hands, and not refusing when we ought . . . but now we will hold our peace. For if what has been spoken has done you no good, much less would it, should we add more. We only pour water into a vessel full of holes. And the punishment too is all the greater for you.[12]

The Questioner Is Not Genuinely Interested in Learning

WHEN A QUESTIONER IS NOT truly interested in learning, the theologian should refrain from speaking. Sometimes the person is simply disputatious. When St. Basil presented homilies against certain heresies, he was forced to cope with a contentious audience. They themselves were not heretics but

---

11   Chrysostom, *Homilies on Acts of the Apostles,* Homily 19, NPNF-1, 11:127–28.
12   Chrysostom, *Homilies on Acts of the Apostles,* Homily 19, NPNF-1, 11:128.

orthodox Christians who wanted him to speak on matters he refused to discuss, especially about the Holy Spirit. Basil complained that he was being constantly challenged, as though he were in court, because they would not accept his words and sought to be taught what pleased *them*, rather than being satisfied with "what is acceptable to the Lord, consonant with the Scriptures and not in conflict with the Fathers." His audience, a congregation, insisted on being told more about the Spirit than was known from the Scriptures, Tradition, and the Fathers. Saint Basil refused to speculate or say anything about the Holy Spirit beyond what he had received from Holy Tradition. This is Orthodox phronema.

> But for quite some time now I have realized that what I am saying bores you. And it seems to me that you have all but stopped listening to me because I dwell upon points of agreement and do not touch upon the questions on everyone's mind. For all ears these days are eager to hear debates about the Holy Spirit. Now I especially wish that, just as I received the tradition without qualification, just as I agreed to it without refinements, so too may I hand it on thus to my audience, without being constantly challenged on these issues, but having disciples persuaded on the basis of one confession. But since you stand around us more like judges than disciples, wanting to test us and not seeking to learn anything, we are obligated, as if in a court of law, to respond to objections, to submit over and over again to questioning and to state over and over again what we have received. But we exhort you not to seek to hear from us only what pleases you, but rather what is acceptable to the Lord, consonant with the Scriptures and not in conflict with the Fathers.[13]

Chrysostom encouraged the congregation to avoid arguments and empty talk in favor of acts of love and hospitality.

> Persevere in listening to the divine Scriptures and do not enter into argumentation where it is not necessary. Paul also urged Timothy to this course of action, even though he was already possessed of a great store of wisdom and had the

---

13   Basil the Great, *Homily against Sabellians, Anomoians, Pneumatomachians* 4. *On Christian Doctrine and Practice*, 297.

power to work miracles (2 Tim. 2:14). Well, then, let us obey him and putting aside empty talk, let us occupy ourselves in good works—I mean brotherly love and hospitality.[14]

The Purpose of Speaking Is Not Godly

THERE ARE OCCASIONS WHEN THE subject matter is appropriate and the audience is acceptable, but the theologian's purpose in speaking is not godly. The theologian should not speak in that case. This requires introspection, self-restraint, and self-examination. If the impetus to speak is not the edification of others but other motives such as ego, criticism of others, the desire to appear intelligent, to be admired, to win an argument, to prove a point, and so forth, this is a spiritual snare. It is better to be silent. Saint Gregory lamented the fact that Christians not only carelessly exposed the holy mysteries of the faith to unbelievers, but even worse, as they argued among themselves, they used their talents to attack each other:

All fear has been banished from souls, shamelessness has taken its place, and knowledge and the deep things of the Spirit are at the disposal of anyone who will; and we all become pious by simply condemning the impiety of others; and we claim the services of ungodly judges, and fling that which is holy to the dogs, and cast pearls before swine, by publishing divine things in the hearing of profane souls, and, wretches that we are, carefully fulfil the prayers of our enemies, and are not ashamed to go a-whoring with our own inventions. Moabites and Ammonites, who were not permitted even to enter the Church of the Lord, frequent our most holy rites. We have opened to all not the gates of righteousness, but, doors of railing and partisan arrogance; and the first place among us is given, not to one who in the fear of God refrains from even an idle word, but to him who can revile his neighbor most fluently, whether explicitly, or by covert allusion; who rolls beneath his tongue mischief and iniquity, or to speak more accurately, the poison of asps.[15]

---

14   Chrysostom, *Homilies on John,* Homily 66, FOTC, 41:225–26.
15   Gregory, *Or.* 2.79, NPNF-2, 7:221.

Saint Paisios commented on the importance of the demeanor and attitude of a theologian. Humility is necessary, and the theologian should refrain from believing that he or she is in a position to correct others:

> He who has humility never takes on the air of an instructor; he listens, and when asked of his opinion he speaks humbly. He never says "I," but rather, "my thought tells me," or "the Fathers tell us." He speaks like a student. He who thinks that he can correct others thinks far too highly of himself.[16]

The Matter Is in the Realm of Mystery

SOME SUBJECTS ARE ALWAYS INAPPROPRIATE because they can never be explained, and expounding on these shows a lack of an Orthodox phronema. Orthodox theologians are less likely to succumb to this temptation. Speculating about that which cannot be explained is more typical of the Western Christian tradition and phronema. If the matter is an appropriate subject for theological inquiry, it could be discussed at the appropriate time and place and for a valid purpose, but never simply as conversation. That ought to be avoided, for, as St. Paul explained, we are "stewards" of mystery: "This is how one should regard us, as servants of Christ and stewards of the mysteries of God" (1 Cor. 4:1).

As "stewards" we are responsible for the mysteries and accountable to God for our handling of them. We are not only stewards but "servants of Christ"; that is, we are to serve Him and not our own egos. A theologian should not speak about matters that simply cannot be explained. Nonetheless, because of the influence of the Western phronema, some Orthodox are engaged in pointless discussions, casually and unsuitably discussing the deepest mysteries, even extremely unspeakable ones, such as how the Theotokos remained a virgin during her birth-giving. Such inappropriate conversations on the internet remind me of St. Symeon the New Theologian's condemnation of such talk:

> You who ignore everything we have been saying, and who have not arrived yourselves at the perception and knowledge and experience of divine

---

16 Paisios, *Spiritual Counsels,* 2:89–90.

illumination and contemplation, how can you talk or write at all about such things without shuddering? For, if we are obliged to render an account for every idle word, how much the more shall we not be tried and convicted as vain babblers when our words touch on matters such as these?[17]

The Theologian Does Not Know the Answer

PRESVYTERAS (PRIESTS' WIVES) OCCASIONALLY MEET for fellowship and mutual support. On one occasion, a new presvytera[18] came to such a meeting and asked us for feedback about some advice she had been given after her husband's recent ordination. "I was told," she said, "never to say 'I don't know.'" Every single presvytera in the room told her that was *not* good advice. I had never heard of a priest's *wife* being given that advice, since she is not responsible for the parish. However, I have heard people advise a new priest, "Never say 'I don't know' "—advice that is frankly ridiculous.

At times we *must* say "I don't know" when in fact we do *not* know. No one knows everything, and there is no shame in that. Perhaps the advice never to say "I don't know" is based on fear that if a priest should admit that he does not know something, the congregation will lose confidence in his abilities. But in fact, priests or theologians who are unwilling to acknowledge that they do not know the answer to a question actually create *less* confidence rather than more. When someone asks the priest a specific question and receives a long, rambling response that never actually provides the answer, no one is fooled. It is obvious that the priest does not know the answer and has simply talked and talked until the listeners were relieved that he finally stopped talking. Politicians are quite expert at talking a lot and saying nothing at all, especially in answer to a difficult question. This is never appropriate for a clergyman or theologian. If he does not know or cannot comment, he should

---

17   Symeon, *First Ethical Discourse* 12, *Ethical Discourses*, 1:79.

18   "Presvytera" or "Presbytera" is a title used by the Greek Orthodox for the priest's wife, the wife of the presbyter. Other Orthodox have different titles for the priest's wife, such as "Matushka" in the Russian tradition and "Khouria" among the Arabic-speaking Orthodox. Addressing the priest's wife by a title is a very old custom. The Jews have a similar title for the wife of the rabbi: "Rebbetzin."

simply say "I don't know" and try to find the answer, if the question is deserving of an answer.

A parish is well aware of its priest's level of knowledge and commitment. Does he prepare for his Sunday sermon, or does he simply ramble on and on, talking off the top of his head? If he rambles, it is clear that he was unprepared for the sermon, in spite of the fact that he knew Sunday was coming. He did not even take ten minutes to prepare an outline for a sermon. No one is fooled. Even if the congregation never complains to him directly, they complain to each other and to people outside the parish about how terrible his sermons are. By his lack of preparation, the priest or theologian not only has wasted an important opportunity for religious education, but he gives a bad impression of himself to the congregation.

A lack of knowledge or the inability to give an immediate answer to a question is excusable if the question is difficult or obscure, or even simply outside one's scope of knowledge. Priests and theologians have a sacred responsibility to prepare for sermons, theological discussions, Bible studies, and presentations. Lack of preparation is a serious omission and a sin because the spiritual needs of the congregation are not met, and that specific opportunity to minister to those for whom Christ died is lost forever.

Chrysostom advised his congregation, which consisted of ordinary believers, not to discuss theological issues with heretics, not because they were not theologians but because they were unprepared. He said he would relish seeing them "plunge into the fray" and debate with heretics or pagans whose teaching were at such a low level that the pagans did not even know the simplest truths that every Christian knew. But Chrysostom warned them not to "plunge into the fray," saying, "I dread the struggle," since his parishioners were "unarmed." In other words, they were unprepared for the battle against heretics should they engage in theological discussions.

> Let us not heed them [the heretics]. I say this to you, for we, indeed, shall not beg off from the combat against them. But he who is unarmed and defenseless will easily be captured, even if he falls in with the weak and though he may be stronger than they. Indeed, if you had paid attention to the Scriptures and thus sharpened your powers each day, I would not be advising you to avoid

battle against them, but would counsel you, on the contrary, to plunge into the fray. I say this for truth will prevail. But since you do not know how to use the Scriptures, I dread the struggle, lest they may find you unarmed and vanquish you. Indeed, nothing, nothing is weaker than those who are deprived of the help of the Spirit. Further, if they cite pagan philosophy, you ought not to be in awe, but to laugh them to scorn because they are making use of stupid teachers. For those philosophers could discover no sound teaching either about God or about creation, but Pythagoras did not yet know things which even the widow among us understood (Mark 12:41-44).[19]

An Ulterior Motive Is Suspected

IT CAN BE USEFUL TO ask the questioner why he or she is posing a particular question. Discernment and caution are required, because the circumstances behind the question are unknown. It could be that the inquiry is intended to elicit a response that will contradict something the questioner's parish priest has said or done. A theologian should not speak when he suspects an ulterior motive behind the question. The questioner may be seeking to covertly involve the theologian in undermining the priest. A theologian or visiting priest should take care not to support or encourage undercutting the parish priest or local bishop, especially since the theologian would not be aware of all the facts. The questioner may himself be unaware of all the facts or may have intentionally distorted the facts to present the parish priest or local bishop in a bad light.

This sometimes happens when a canonical issue is involved. "Why is Father doing *this*?" or "How can the bishop allow *that*?" The difficulty in such a situation is that the circumstances that may have warranted *oikonomia* (relaxation of canonical standards) are personal, confidential, and known only to three people: the person who came to the priest for help, the parish priest himself, and the bishop. Neither the priest nor the bishop can discuss the matter, since it is confidential. The priest can never explain or defend himself to the congregation. It is important for the theologian not to comment

---

19   Chrysostom, *Homilies on John*, Homily 66, FOTC, 41:224.

on pastoral matters or denounce the violation of the canon, if indeed there was one, since he or she is not aware of the pastoral circumstances that have allowed for an exception, and he or she is not responsible for that decision or for the care of that person's soul.

The Bishop or One with Superior Knowledge Is Present

WHEN A BISHOP IS PRESENT, a theologian should defer to him out of respect and in recognition of the fact that as successors to the apostles, the bishops are entrusted with preserving the Orthodox faith. Likewise, when the parish priest is present, it is important not to contradict him or undermine his authority in the parish, which could contribute to conflict, cause people to fall away from the faith, or contradict spiritual direction that was given by the priest. The bishop or priest will most likely invite or welcome a comment by the theologian, but it is best to exercise extreme caution, not to insert oneself into the situation, and to remember the patristic advice to observe silence.

Silence is also advised when a theologian with greater knowledge or expertise is present to answer the question that was posed. Theologians have different areas of expertise, and the wise theologian defers to others with greater or deeper experience in that subject. This also allows the less-informed theologian to benefit from the knowledge or experience of the more learned. Gregory the Theologian explains the benefit of learning about what one does not know from a more experienced theologian rather than attempting to teach others what one does not know himself:

> We are aware that it is better to offer our own reins to others more skillful than ourselves, than, while inexperienced, to guide the course of others, and rather to give a kindly hearing than stir an untrained tongue. And after a discussion of these points with advisers who are, I fancy, of no mean worth, and, at any rate, wish us well, we preferred to learn those canons of speech and action which we did not know, rather than undertake to teach them in our ignorance.[20]

---

20 Gregory, *Or.* 2.47, NPNF-2, 7:214.

At all times the theologian should exercise discernment, show restraint, and cultivate humility, especially in remaining silent, yielding to others, and recognizing the greater spiritual progress of another:

> Do you realize that humility is judged not so much in small matters—this would be the case with a false, but flashy, show of virtue—as it is put to the test in great ones? In my opinion, the humble-minded man is not the one who says little about himself, and this only to a few and rarely, nor the one who addresses his inferior in a humble way, but the one who shows restraint in discussing God, who knows what to say and what to keep to himself and in what to admit his ignorance, who yields to the one who has been charged with speaking and accepts the fact that another is more spiritually endowed and has made greater progress in contemplation.[21]

---

21   Gregory, *Or.* 32.19, FOTC, 107:205.

CHAPTER 15

Theological Dangers: Conceptual

I think it is dangerous to either accept the responsibility
for other souls or to take up theology.[1]
—St. Gregory the Theologian

THEOLOGIZING IS DANGEROUS NOT ONLY for actual, trained and educated theologians who function in a professional capacity, but also, and perhaps especially, for the dabblers, those who engage in theology without real training and knowledge. In their enthusiasm to discuss the mysteries of God, they cannot heed St. Gregory's warning about the dangers of theology, since they do not realize any danger.

Two main categories of danger exist. The first consists of conceptual, intellectual, or mental theological errors—that is, mistakes of the mind in theological conception, explanation, reasoning, and so forth. These errors always necessarily harm the one who theologizes, but they also affect those who read or listen to the erring theologian. The second category consists of spiritual dangers, which are extremely serious and threaten the eternal salvation of the one who theologizes. The spiritual dangers are similar to those faced by the clergy and are perils always inherent in the task of theology.

Conceptual dangers are errors in speech or writing that result from errors

---

1   Gregory, *Or.* 20.1, FOTC, 107:108.

in ideas or expression of thought. All theological errors have a spiritual component and are always spiritually dangerous, but I have described the first category as "conceptual" because they are theological mistakes—often of a technical nature, but not necessarily so—and the danger manifests itself as a mistake in theological expression, stance, or opinion. These errors usually stem from inadequate theological education, but they can also happen to a trained theologian who, for example, has chosen to ignore what he has learned or has deviated from the Tradition of the Church to embrace his or her own individual ideas. These conceptual errors include heretical beliefs and other errors less serious than heresy: imprecision and carelessness, expansion, innovation, speculation and ignoring Tradition, compromise, reliance on human reasoning, narrow-mindedness and zealotry, rigidity and extremism, individualism, and private opinion.

The Danger of Heresy or Other Theological Errors

ONE CAN EASILY LAPSE INTO heresy through ignorance. The most frightening fact about heresy is that those who hold heretical opinions are unaware that they are expressing heresy. No one intends to commit heresy, and yet church history is littered with examples of those who are remembered for their heresy rather than their orthodoxy, including countless bishops.

Internet discussions often result in heretical statements when the participant is a dabbler, one who is untrained in theology but who holds a high opinion of himself and his ability to theologize. I recently witnessed an example of this. In explaining the importance of the Incarnation and the full divinity of the Son of God, St. Athanasius famously wrote, "God became man that we might become gods." It was a clever, poetic expression of a deep theological truth. He was expressing the fact that when the Son of God became a human being, He sanctified human nature and made it possible for us to become godlike, to acquire holiness and be transformed. Saint Athanasius did not mean that we *literally* become gods, and those with proper education and phronema do not misinterpret it that way.[2] In a Facebook discussion, an Orthodox

---

2   Today Mormons are perverting the Fathers and using that statement to support their

dabbler was discussing theosis, union with God, and he insisted that one actually becomes "God" when we are united to God. The dabbler had no theological education, but having read a little about the subject, he believed he was in a position to discuss theosis and the essence and energies of God. I explained that to say that we actually *become* God is blasphemy. He retorted that since St. Athanasius said that we become gods, *I* was accusing St. Athanasius of blasphemy.

Saint Gregory the Theologian might have said the following about this dabbler:

> We certainly do not condemn impassioned feeling, without which no great accomplishment in piety or any other virtue is possible—but rather those whose intensity of feeling is accompanied by folly and ignorance and its vile offshoot, rashness, for rashness is the child of ignorance.[3]

I could quote numerous statements by countless Fathers about observing silence and refraining from theologizing on matters about which we have no knowledge or experience. Dabblers would not accept that simply reading a few books on theology does not give one knowledge sufficient to theologize. Saint Gregory the Theologian emphasized the need to insist on clear dogma and to refrain from discussing other matters:

> We must recognize one God, the Father, without beginning and unbegotten, and one Son, begotten of the Father, and one Spirit who takes his existence from the Father. . . . These are the doctrines that we must acknowledge; these we must confess; on these we must take our stand and leave their garrulous nonsense and godless chatter to those with nothing better to do. What is it that provoked all these ideas of theirs? A passion that has no logical foundation and no connection with knowledge and a faith that sails along with no one at the helm.[4]

---

heresy that God the Father was once a man and that humans can *literally* become gods, equal to God the Father.

3   Gregory, *Or.* 32.3, FOTC, 107:192.

4   Gregory, *Or.* 32.5, FOTC, 107:194.

Not only dabblers but trained theologians and pastors can fall into heresy if they approach theology in the wrong way. Nestorius, once the archbishop of Constantinople, was eventually condemned as a heretic. Nestorius taught that there could be no real union between the humanity and divinity of Jesus Christ, because divine nature and human nature are too different to be united. He sincerely believed that he was correct to separate the human Jesus from the divine Son of God. He claimed the Virgin Mary should not be called "Theotokos" (birth-giver of God) since she did not give birth to the eternal Son of God but only to the human Jesus.

In response, St. Cyril of Alexandria championed the Tradition of the Church, saying that it is appropriate to call Mary "Theotokos." She did give birth to God, because the person to whom she gave birth, Jesus Christ, is both God and man. By saying that Mary gave birth only to Jesus' humanity, thus separating the humanity and divinity of Christ, Nestorius logically believed he was preserving the two natures, but in fact he was denying the Incarnation. The deep, insidious danger of heresy is how logical it often seems on the surface. This is why we do not depend on human reasoning for our theology but on the Tradition of the Church.

The Danger of Imprecision, Sloppiness, and Carelessness

ANOTHER THEOLOGICAL DANGER IS IMPRECISION, which includes sloppy and careless statements. The Fathers of the Church spent a great deal of time discussing terminology; however, they recognized that correct *belief* was more important. If a bishop did not like a particular term but held the correct belief, the Fathers, such as Basil the Great, were willing to accept that rather than become combative over terminology. Conversely, if someone accepted the correct term but did not believe what it *meant* as defined by the Church, that attitude was unacceptable. Using correct theological terminology is essential. Theological terms have acquired a specific meaning within the Church, and it is assumed that one who uses a term understands its precise meaning. Using correct terminology is the way we differentiate truth from falsehood. Using a term incorrectly suggests heresy or a less serious theological error.

The Church fathers had good reason for devoting so much attention to problems of terminology. They were trying to find and establish words that would be adequate to their conceptions of God and which would precisely express, and thus protect, the truths of their faith. Their concern for terminology was not excessive. A word gives outer form to a thought and verbal precision is necessary for the full expression of intellectual conception. The patristic theologians tried to formulate their creeds with clarity because they hoped to establish the living traditions of the Church by expressing them in a versatile system of theology.[5]

On an Orthodox internet site, an amateur armchair theologian was using the term "sinless" to describe the Virgin Mary, the most holy Theotokos. This is a significant error, since the term "sinless" (*anamartitos*) is used theologically in the Tradition *only* for God or Christ.[6] The holiness of the Theotokos is beyond our comprehension. We use many words to describe her—pure, immaculate, spotless, all-holy, and so on—but the Fathers of the Church did not use the term "sinless" for the Virgin Mary. This does not mean that she was just an ordinary person or a "sinner" as we are. Her holiness is unparalleled, so much so that she exceeds the holiness of the bodiless powers. In fact, we say she is "more honorable than the cherubim and more glorious beyond compare than the seraphim." She is holier than the angels. Out of recognition of this, some Orthodox Christians might refer to her as "sinless," but technically speaking it is theologically incorrect to use that term for her.[7] As a matter of fact, in prayers addressed to Christ we say, "*You alone*, O Lord, are without sin."[8]

---

5   Georges Florovsky, "Basic Features of Theology in the Fourth Century," *Eastern Fathers of the Fourth Century*, vol. 7 in *Collected Works*, 35.

6   According to *Lampe Patristic Lexicon, anamartetos*, meaning "free from sin" or "sinless," is used only to describe God or Christ. Regarding human beings, in patristic writings "the possibility is denied" that a human can be described as without sin. The word was occasionally used in a restricted or very limited sense for infants, for Adam before the Fall, for "penitents" and for saints when they are refraining from sin, but not in a truly theological sense.

7   Some Fathers say that the Theotokos received purification at the Annunciation when she conceived Christ by the Holy Spirit, but the question here is whether we can or should use a term the Church and the Fathers used only for God and apply it to the Theotokos out of piety or a desire to honor her.

8   For example, in the Trisagion service for the dead, when asking for God's mercy for the departed, the priest prays, "God of spirits and of all flesh . . . give rest to your servant . . .

This is an important theological point. It is not a disparagement of the Theotokos in any way but an affirmation of the uniqueness of the person of Jesus Christ, something that can never be compromised. Insisting that the Theotokos was "sinless" is zeal without knowledge (Rom. 10:2), and unchecked zeal develops into false doctrine. This is exactly how the Catholics arrived at the erroneous doctrine of the Immaculate Conception, by expanding on their doctrines. Out of piety, they have elevated the Theotokos almost to the level of Christ by saying that she, by a "unique prerogative," was preserved "without sin." This may go even further, as many Catholics, including popes, have referred to Mary as Co-Redemptrix and have been pushing for this to be proclaimed as a dogma for many years.[9]

Watching such developments in Catholic theology over the past 150 years, including the expansion of Marian dogmas and papal claims, Orthodox Christians should recognize the danger in making exaggerated statements and refrain from making them, even when motivated by piety or a desire to honor the Theotokos. Although it may seem that the word "sinless" *should* be used for the Theotokos, since she refrained from sin, the term is not used for her in the Greek patristic writings.[10] That is significant, because it shows that the term "sinless" was "protected" by the Fathers and was limited, as is proper, to Christ/God alone. The numerous adjectives we have to describe the exceptional holiness of the Theotokos may have developed over time due to the fact that we do *not* apply the term "sinless" to her. As much as we Orthodox honor

---

pardon every sin which he has committed . . . for there is no man who lives and sins not, *for you alone, O Lord, are without sin."*

9   Mark Miravalle, "Pope Francis' Guadalupe Homily and Mary as Co-Redemptrix," *National Catholic Register*, December 21, 2019. The Catholic Church attempted to cite the Fathers in support of their dogma of the Immaculate Conception of Mary, citing descriptions of her that we Orthodox use as well, such as "pure," "all-holy," and "immaculate." But those adjectives are not the same as "sinless." The Fathers never used "sinless" for the Theotokos, but Catholic doctrine does, significantly minimizing the uniqueness of Christ.

10   From Clement of Rome (first century) through Theodore the Studite (ninth century), according to *Lampe Patristic Lexicon,* which covers Greek patristic writings to the ninth century. It is unlikely that any Father would have used the term "sinless" for the Theotokos after the ninth century either, since it was not applied to her by earlier Fathers. For a very good discussion of this question, see Christopher Veniamin, *The Orthodox Understanding of Salvation* (Dalton, PA: Mount Thabor Publishing, 2016), 45–59.

the Theotokos, we must not go beyond the ancient boundaries the Fathers have established.

Theology must be accurate if it is to express the truth. The use of the wrong term or the misunderstanding of a word can result in theological errors. This is dangerous because one is "misrepresenting God." Maximos the Confessor explains:

> Many of us talk, but few of us act. But no one should falsify the word of God by his own carelessness. Rather, he should confess his weakness and not hide from God's truth, lest he be charged with transgressing the commandments and misrepresenting God.[11]

Saint Maximos noted that spiritual vigilance is needed even after acquiring theological knowledge, because carelessness can lead the theologian to commit errors, thereby proving himself unworthy to theologize. He used King Saul[12] as an example of potential deviation from truth by spiritual laxity and carelessness:

> Knowledge of divine things without passion does not persuade the mind to disdain material things completely, but rather resembles the mere thought of a thing of sense. Thus one finds many men with considerable knowledge who yet wallow in the passions of the flesh like pigs in mud. For in reaching through their diligence a certain degree of purification and in acquiring knowledge but later growing careless they can be compared to Saul, who after being given the kingship conducted himself unworthily and was dismissed from it with terrible wrath.[13]

---

11   Maximos the Confessor, *Chapters on Love* 4.85, *Selected Writings*, 85.
12   Saul, the king of Israel, was to wait for Samuel, the high priest, to offer sacrifice to the Lord. But after waiting for seven days, Samuel still had not yet arrived, and Saul offered the sacrifice himself. Since Saul had arrogantly and inappropriately taken the role of the high priest by offering sacrifice, Samuel told him that his kingdom would not be confirmed by God (1 Samuel/Kingdoms 13).
13   Maximos the Confessor, *Chapters on Love* 3.66, *Selected Writings*, 70.

The Danger of Expansion, Innovation, and Speculation

ONE WHO IGNORES TRADITION OR the Orthodox phronema effectively betrays the Orthodox Faith. A favorite biblical quotation among the Fathers was, "Do not move the ancient boundaries which your fathers have established" (Prov. 22:28), frequently cited to encourage maintaining Tradition and not going beyond it.

When St. Augustine was attempting to explain the relationship of the Holy Spirit to the Father and the Son, he said that the Spirit is neither from the Father alone nor from the Son alone, but that both the Father and the Son share a reciprocal love which is identified with the Holy Spirit.[14] The person and mode of existence of the Spirit are extremely difficult to discuss. In his treatise *On the Trinity*, Augustine employed tremendous effort to analyze and explain the Persons of the Trinity and their relationship to each other. But he applied logic and philosophical techniques to the question, which led to his errors and eventually to a theological rift between the East and the West.

Augustine lacked precision in his use of terminology. He also lacked a precise understanding of the meaning of the Greek terms—not only the Greek terms used in the New Testament, but the explanations of them given by the Greek Fathers who preceded him. Augustine relied on the application of his mind rather than on the Scriptures and Tradition because he believed that faith could not conflict with reason. This led to his innovation and expansion on the Tradition beyond the established boundaries. It was typical of Augustine to analyze every issue exhaustively and eventually arrive at a logical conclusion, and that style is seen in this treatise on the Trinity. His approach planted the roots of the Western Christian theological method.

Augustine expanded church doctrine by developing the *Filioque*, the Catholic doctrine that the Holy Spirit proceeds from the Father "and the Son," which in Latin is rendered by the word *filioque*. Augustine was fighting the Arian heresy in the West. The Arians denied the full divinity of the Son,

---

14   Augustine, *On the Trinity* 17.27. "And the Holy Spirit, according to the Holy Scriptures, is neither of the Father alone, nor of the Son alone, but of both; and so intimates to us a mutual love, wherewith the Father and the Son reciprocally love one another." *On the Holy Trinity, Doctrinal Treatises, Moral Treatises*, NPNF-1, vol. 3, Arthur West Hadden, trans., Philip Schaff, ed. (Grand Rapids, MI: William B. Eerdmans, 1887), 215.

saying that He is not equal to the Father. Augustine replied that the Son *is* equal to the Father—so much so that the Spirit proceeds (has its origin) not only from the Father but from the Son as well.

Since Augustine disliked Greek, he did not read the Fathers who came before him, especially the Cappadocian Fathers (Ss. Basil, Gregory the Theologian, and Gregory of Nyssa), who had already articulated the Trinitarian doctrine of the Church. It had also been enshrined in the Creed. Rather than countering the Arians by simply affirming the equality of the Father and the Son, Augustine attempted to bolster his position that the Son is equal to the Father by attributing to the Son something new: that the Spirit proceeds from the Son also, not from the Father alone.[15] It was also a mistake on Augustine's part because the Scriptures are clear: Jesus said that He would "send" the Spirit *"who proceeds from the Father"* (John 15:26). There is a difference between the Son *sending* the Spirit to the world within time and the eternal origin of the Spirit *proceeding* from the Person of the Father alone.

The Holy Trinity is a great mystery and a very difficult subject to discuss. It is enough to recognize that a serious theological error was introduced by expanding on doctrine beyond that which the Church had already established. While the filioque may seem trivial, since the addition consists of only three little words in English and one word in Latin, it remains a serious point of disagreement between Western and Eastern Christianity. Eventually the Western Church added the word filioque to the Creed, solidifying the error by unilaterally adding something to the Nicene Creed. Most first-millennium popes were aware of the error and refused to add the filioque to the Creed, but eventually it was accepted by all in the West. The filioque became a major issue when St. Photios was Patriarch of Constantinople, and the disagreement resulted in a brief schism.[16]

---

15 Augustine, *On the Trinity* 26.45.
16 See Francis Dvornik, *The Photian Schism* (Cambridge: Cambridge University Press, 1948), and A. Edward Siecienski, *The Filioque: History of a Doctrinal Controversy* (Oxford: Oxford University Press, 2010). In the Photian Schism, Photios opposed the filioque and was condemned by a council initiated by Pope Nicholas I in 869. This decision was reversed in 879 by another council called by his successor Pope John VIII, who rejected the filioque. Photios was reinstated. But today, the Catholic Church accepts the first council, which deposed Photios, and rejects the second, which reinstated Photios

Saint Augustine's error and its unintended consequence show the danger of expansion, going beyond the ancient boundaries of Tradition, even though his motivation was to support the divinity of the Son and fight the Arian heresy. Vladimir Lossky believes that the filioque is actually the most serious difference between East and West because it concerns doctrine about God. It is theology in the highest sense.

> Since the dogma of the Trinity is the keystone of the arch of all theological thought and belongs to the region which the Greek Fathers called Theologia *par excellence,* it is understandable that a divergence in this culminating point, insignificant as it might seem at first sight, should have a decisive importance.[17]

It would have been better for Augustine not to elaborate on the Person of the Holy Spirit and not exceed the "ancient boundaries" established by the Fathers. By contrast, Basil the Great and Gregory the Theologian consistently refused to elaborate on the Person of the Holy Spirit. They taught only what is clear from the Scriptures and Tradition and then remained silent, regardless of pressure or encouragement to comment or speculate further.

The tendency among Western theologians to engage in theological elaboration and speculation is rooted in Augustine's phronema—a methodology that encourages the application of the mind, analysis, and rational deduction to determine theological truth. Saint Basil was not impressed by the application of human reasoning:

---

and denounced the filioque. Both councils were approved by the popes at the time, so there is no question that the second council is ignored, because the Catholic Church decided later to accept the filioque. Saint Photios's classic work on the subject of the Spirit is *On the Mystagogy of the Holy Spirit* (Brookline, MA: Holy Transfiguration Monastery, 1983).

17 Lossky, *In the Image and Likeness,* 80. Lossky analyzes how the different ways of explaining the relationship of the Persons of the Trinity reflect a fundamental difference in theological presumptions and approach—basically, a different *phronema.* "The difference between the two conceptions of the Trinity determines, on both sides, the whole character of theological thought. This is so to such an extent that it becomes difficult to apply, without equivocation, the name of theology to these two different ways of dealing with divine realities." Lossky, 80.

Let the Tradition shame you into not separating the Holy Spirit from the Father and Son. This is what the Lord taught, the Apostles preached, the Fathers preserved, the Martyrs confirmed. Be satisfied with speaking as you have been taught, and do not bother me with these sophistries.[18]

One argument being made about the Holy Spirit during St. Basil's era was that the Holy Spirit is a creature. Heretics denied the divinity of the Holy Spirit based on the reasoning that there are only two modes of existence: either unbegotten, like the Father, or begotten, like the Son. If the Holy Spirit is unbegotten, He is the Father. If He is begotten, He is the Son. If He is neither, then He must be a creature.

This was being discussed prior to the composition of the final portion of the Nicene Creed,[19] which affirms that the Holy Spirit is "Lord"—in other words, He is God, like the Father and the Son; He is the Creator of Life and proceeds from the Father.[20] When St. Basil wrote his treatise *On the Holy Spirit,* defending the divinity of the Spirit, the final part of the Creed had not been written. Basil's response was based solely on Scripture and Tradition, whereas the heretics based their position on human reasoning. Basil replied:

So then, here I am neither generating innovative formulations nor denying His dignity, but rather I bewail those who dare to designate Him a creature and I mourn the fact that through their petty sophisms and spurious reasoning they cast themselves into the pit of perdition. For they say: "Our intellect has

---

18 Basil the Great, *Homily against the Sabellians, Anomoians, Pneumatomachians* 6. *On Christian Doctrine and Practice,* 299.

19 The last section of the Nicene Creed, which begins, "And in the Holy Spirit, the Lord . . ." was actually composed at the Second Ecumenical Council in 381. Saint Basil had already died in 379, but his treatise *On the Holy Spirit* was very important in clarifying the Person of the Spirit and how dogma concerning the Spirit should be expressed in the Creed. On the other hand, Augustine's treatise *On the Trinity* was composed around AD 400, *after* the Creed had been written and statements about the Person of the Holy Spirit had been definitively established by the Church. Augustine's statement that the Holy Spirit proceeds from the Father *and the Son* (Filioque) deviates from and contradicts the Scriptures, the decision of the Council, and the Creed itself, which states that the Holy Spirit proceeds "from the Father."

20 The Spirit "proceeds from the Father." That is the Spirit's "mode of existence," and because He comes from the Father, it is clear that He is not a "creature" like us.

comprehended these three, and among existents there is nothing that does not fall under the category of existents." . . . Have you investigated everything? In your thoughts have you placed everything in a category? Have you left nothing unexamined? With your intellect have you grasped everything? With your mind have you comprehended everything? Do you know what is under the earth? Do you know what's in the deep? That's what the demons brag about: "I know the number of the sands and the measure of the sea."[21] Now if you are ignorant about many things, and if what you don't know infinitely surpasses what you do know, why not put your shame aside and along with everybody else admit your ignorance about the way in which the Holy Spirit exists, seeing that such ignorance is not fraught with danger? As for me, I do not have the leisure to refute your stupid ideas, nor to point out how many existences there are which have escaped the comprehension of your thoughts.[22]

Orthodox Christianity rejects theological innovation and speculative theology, since they are useless and often ego driven. The purpose of theology is salvation, not mental gymnastics. Theology is nothing but "meaningless, empty words if it does not reflect our Christian life and experience. . . . A theologian whose theology is purely theoretical and not at all experiential is not a true theologian."[23] Maximos the Confessor advised against speculation and venturing beyond the limits of Tradition and our human comprehension. In fact, speculation can result in disaster, as evidenced by the rift between East and West created by the filioque and other Western innovations.

Seek the reason why God created, for this is knowledge. But do not seek how and why he only recently created, for that question does not fall under your mind since while some divine things are comprehended by men others are not. As one of the saints has said, "Unbridled speculation can push you over the precipice."[24]

---

21 Here Basil cites a Pythian oracle as recorded by the Greek historian Herodotus 1.47.
22 Basil, *Homily against the Sabellians* 6. *On Christian Doctrine and Practice,* 300.
23 Maximos Aghiorgoussis, *In the Image of God* (Brookline, MA: Holy Cross Orthodox Press, 1999), 114.
24 Maximos the Confessor, *Chapters on Love* 4.5, *Selected Writings,* 76. The exact saint he is referring to is uncertain, possibly Gregory's Oration 27.7, in which he described the Eunomians, who did not respect the fact of God's mystery but believed they could

Gregory the Theologian endured significant frustration with those who attacked him by misrepresenting his statements. He continued to repeat what he had said about the relationship between the Father and the Son. Like Basil, Gregory consistently refused to speculate beyond that which can be said with certainty, in spite of pressure to do so. Theological speculation is risky because it can lead to heresy.

> And let no one sneer at my words. I am not suggesting that the Son derives his being from the Father in that he first existed in the Father and later made his way into being, nor that he was first unformed and then formed, as is the case with human generation. These are the views of malcontents, the views of those who are quick to jump on every word. They are not our thoughts or beliefs. . . . I am repeating myself because your crassly materialistic cast of mind frightens me. . . . I am satisfied with the declaration that he is Son and that he is from the Father, and that the one is Father and the other Son; and I refuse to engage in meaningless speculation beyond this point. I have no wish to be like the man who loses his voice from overuse or his eyesight from staring directly into the sun; the more fully and sharply one wants to see, the more he damages his eyes and is blinded altogether, for his vision is overwhelmed by the magnitude of the sight if he insists on taking in the whole instead of only that portion which is without risk.[25]

The Danger of Compromise

WHEN THE FATHERS OF THE First Ecumenical Council at Nicaea were discussing how to express the idea that the second Person of the Trinity, the Son, is equal to God the Father in His divinity, they chose to use the word *homoousios*. This means that the Son has the "same essence" or "same substance" as God the Father. The Arians rejected the decision at Nicaea and said the Son is *not* God, *not* the same substance as the Father but a completely different substance. The Arians used the term *heteroousios*. Long after the decision at

---

comprehend God.
25 Gregory, *Or.* 20.9–10, FOTC, 107:113–14.

Nicaea, the empire remained divided, as the two sides could not agree. Some suggested a compromise: the Son is not exactly the *same* essence as the Father, *homoousios*, nor entirely *different* from the Father, *heteroousios*, but he is "like" the Father—*homoiousios*. The compromise was not accepted.

Other attempts at theological compromise have been seen in church history, including the *Henotikon*, an attempt to heal the schism between Christians who accepted the decision of the Fourth Ecumenical Council at Chalcedon (451) and those who did not—variously called the non-Chalcedonians, monophysites, or miaphysites. They refused to accept the decision that said Jesus Christ was "one person in two natures" (two *physis*). The non-Chalcedonians were convinced that this council had betrayed and changed the decision of the previous council at Ephesus (431), which had said that the Incarnate Logos was one *physis*, meaning one unified person. But the term *physis* could mean "nature," as in "essence" or characteristic qualities, which was how the Fourth Ecumenical Council used the term. The non-Chalcedonians were convinced that the Chalcedonians had essentially divided Jesus Christ into two people, because they understood *physis* as "person" instead of "nature."

In the early seventh century, the Patriarch of Constantinople Sergius I and the Emperor Heraclius were anxious to resolve the schism between those who accepted Chalcedon and those who did not. Sergius proposed a compromise: first, that Jesus Christ had only one energy (*monoenergism)*, and later, another idea, that Jesus had only one will (*monothelitism*). Sergius and Heraclius promoted the ideas to foster Christian unity, and the Pope of Rome, Honorius, agreed to the idea as well. However, monothelitism and monoenergism were condemned as heresy by Maximos the Confessor and later by the Sixth Ecumenical Council in 680, because those teachings effectively denied the full humanity of Christ by saying that He had no human will or energy.

These examples from church history remind us that although unity is important, it is never more important than truth, and no compromise to the Faith is ever acceptable. Theological compromise, St. Maximos said, might unite human beings, but it separates us from God. Maximos was accused of heresy and tortured for refusing to accept these doctrines. At his trial he said:

But if the saving faith should be removed along with heresy for the sake of an arrangement, then the arrangement is a thorough separation from God and not a unity with God. For tomorrow the Jews will say, "Let us arrange a peace with one another and unite, and let us remove circumcision and you baptism and we shall not dispute anymore with each other." Once the Arians put this forward in writing at the time of the great Constantine, saying, "Let us remove the *Homoousion* [same essence] and the *Heteroousion* [different essence] and let the churches unite." Our God-fearing Fathers did not consent to this; but rather they preferred to be pursued and put to death than to pass over in silence a term indicating the one supersubstantial Godhead of the Father, Son and Holy Spirit. And the great Constantine concurred with those who were putting such suggestions forward, as is recounted by many who diligently wrote of these matters at the time. No emperor was able to convince the inspired Fathers to come to an agreement with the heretics of that time through the use of equivocal terms. Rather they employed clear and fixed terms corresponding to the dogma inquired about.[26]

The Danger of Reliance on Human Reasoning

WE HAVE ALREADY DISCUSSED WHY the Orthodox Tradition rejects the use of human reasoning to arrive at theological truth. The Orthodox Faith does not entirely reject reason; in fact, it frequently refers to human beings, made in the image and likeness of God, as "reason endowed." However, as we have seen, overreliance on the human mind and human logic in reaching theological conclusions has led Western Christianity in an entirely different theological direction, far from the early Christian Tradition. This Tradition has been faithfully preserved in Orthodoxy because Orthodoxy has resisted reliance on deductive reasoning.

Many aspects of our faith are beyond human logic and comprehension, including the cross itself, which St. Paul described as contrary to human wisdom: "For the Lord knows the reasonings of the wise (Ps. 94:11), that they are vain" (1 Cor. 3:20 [ERV]). Commenting on that verse, St. John Chrysostom remarked,

---

26   Maximos the Confessor, "The Trial of Maximus the Confessor," *Selected Writings,* 20–21.

Now when the Wisdom which is boundless pronounces this edict concerning them, and declares them to be such, what other proof do you seek of their extreme folly? For men's judgments, it is true, in many instances fail, but the decree of God is unexceptionable and uncorrupt in every case.[27]

The weakness of heretics was due to reliance on their own reasoning, which extended beyond the "ancient boundaries" and ignored human limitations. We cannot understand the Holy Scriptures by the application of human reasoning alone, Gregory the Theologian remarked: "What can your conception of the divine be, if you rely on all the methods of deductive argument? To what conclusion will closely-scrutinized argument bring you, you most rational of theologians, who boast over infinity?"[28] Human reasoning is faulty because it is earthly and must be illuminated by divine grace. Chrysostom stated:

Now, nothing makes one so dizzy as human reasoning, which says everything from an earthly point of view, and does not allow illumination to come from above. Earthly reasoning is covered with mud. Therefore, we have need of streams from above, so that, when the mud has fallen away, whatever part of the reason is pure may be carried on and may be thoroughly imbued with the lessons taught there. This takes place when we manifest both a well-disposed soul and an upright life. For it is possible, it is possible, I repeat, for the mind to be darkened also by corrupt habits, and not only by untimely curiosity.[29]

Chrysostom recognized that scriptural language was inadequate to express divine truths. He continually encouraged the congregation not to attempt to understand the stories of creation through human reasoning but to focus on the spiritual message they contained:

Since we therefore listen to these words not as the words of Moses but as the words of the God of all things coming to us through the tongue of Moses, so,

---

27 Chrysostom, *St. Chrysostom: Homilies on the Epistles of Paul to the Corinthians,* Homily on First Corinthians 10.3, NPNF-1, 12:55.
28 Gregory, *Or.* 28.7, *On God and Christ,* 41.
29 Chrysostom, *Homilies on John,* Homily 24, FOTC, 33:240.

I beg you, let us heed what is said and part company with our own reasoning. Scripture, after all, says, "the thoughts of mortals are deceptive, and their thinking unreliable" (WSir 9:14).[30]

Saint Maximos the Confessor described the "perfect mind":

The perfect mind is the one that through genuine faith supremely knows in supreme ignorance the supremely unknowable, and in gazing on the universe of his handiwork has received from God comprehensive knowledge of his Providence and judgment in it, as far as allowable to men.[31]

Knowledge is limited, especially knowledge of God, since God is beyond all human understanding. Archbishop Vasileios, abbot of the Iveron Monastery on Mt. Athos, expressed the paradox of the progression from human ignorance to human knowledge, after which "ignorance" (un-knowing) is required. "We advance from ignorance to knowledge. And our knowledge seems little. So we go beyond knowledge, into the ignorance, the unknowing higher than any knowledge."[32] Saint Gregory remarked:

All truth, all philosophy, to be sure, is obscure, hard to trace out. It is like employing a small tool on big constructions, if we use human wisdom in the hunt for knowledge of reality. We do not abandon the senses, they go with us, when we look at supra-sensible realities. But by these same senses we are perplexed and led astray. We cannot get nearer the truth by meeting things in their naked reality with naked intellect. Our minds cannot receive direct and sure impressions. Now theology is fuller, and so harder, with more counter-arguments, tougher solutions, than other philosophy. Every slightest objection bars, hinders, the course of the argument and checks its progress. It is like applying the reins suddenly to galloping horses, making them veer round with the surprise of the shock.[33]

---

30 Chrysostom, *Homilies on Genesis*, Homily 2.5, FOTC, 74:32.
31 Maximos the Confessor, *Chapters on Love* 3.99, *Selected Writings*, 75.
32 Vasileios, *Orthodox Culture*, 65.
33 Gregory, *Or.* 28.21, *On God and Christ*, 52–53.

Metropolitan Vlachos warns against a growing "scholasticism" in Orthodox Christianity. This trend is seen when conclusions are based on reason and conjecture and when the emphasis is on intellectualizing or rationally understanding the faith. This is particularly seen among converts who become trapped in intellectual conundrums or stuck on historical or theological issues in the Church that they cannot rationally resolve. Rather than focusing on such things, what is needed is to live the faith and apply the therapeutic methods of the Church that are designed for our spiritual healing. These practices are what heal the soul and draw us closer to God, not the proper understanding of mental concepts.[34]

Human comprehension will always be inadequate. Saint Symeon the New Theologian wrote that we cannot receive full knowledge of God or comprehend the Orthodox Faith even by the writings of the Fathers and the saints. The insights received through the operation of the Holy Spirit are not the same as what we can achieve through our human reasoning and study.

> We think we will receive the full knowledge of God's truth by means of worldly wisdom, and fancy that this mere reading of the God-inspired writings of the saints is to comprehend Orthodoxy, and that this is an exact and certain knowledge of the Holy Trinity. Nor is this all, but the more august among us foolishly suppose that the contemplation which comes to pass only through the Spirit in those who are worthy is the same as the thoughts produced by their own reasoning. How ridiculous! How callous![35]

"The logic of this world on its own is a coffin," wrote Archimandrite Vasileios, because the "success and happiness" that the world promises "does not conquer death."[36] An emphasis on reason also minimizes the role and importance of faith, which is what Christ expects from us. Commenting on Christ's dialogue with Nicodemus and his question, "How can a man be born when he is old?" (John 3:4), Chrysostom stated:

---

34 Vlachos, *Mind of the Orthodox Church*, 209–10.
35 Symeon, *Ninth Ethical Discourse, Ethical Discourses*, 2:113.
36 Vasileios, *Orthodox Culture*, 60.

For nothing is worse than to relegate spiritual things to human reasoning. This also was what kept him from placing a lofty and sublime interpretation [on the words]. We ourselves are called "faithful" precisely for this reason: in order that, having put aside the weakness of human reasoning, we may come to the sublimity of faith, and that we may entrust the greater part of our welfare to the teaching of faith.[37]

The Orthodox Tradition always emphasizes the ability of the ordinary person to achieve theological insight through prayer. "The true theologian is one who prays." The intellect (nous) is enlightened by experience of God, not through knowledge of philosophy or the application of human reasoning. The practice of the early Church was to baptize and commune even infants and children, rather than waiting until the "age of reason," which became the practice in the West. To require that a child reach the "age of reason" suggests that salvation is dependent on knowledge rather than on purification of the soul. The Holy Mysteries unite us to God through purification of the soul, not through our mental capacity. Saint Gregory the Theologian emphasized that if the Faith were dependent on human reasoning and logic, it would "remain beyond the reach of most persons." He went on to explain:

My brothers, our faith would be the most unfair thing in the world if it applied only to sophisticates and those with a flair for language and logic. It would then of necessity remain beyond the reach of most persons. . . . Take care not to spurn the ordinary or go hunting after novelty to impress the mass. Let Solomon's advice be your guide: "Better is a little with security" than much with uncertainty (Prov. 15:16) . . . that is, the man who is poor in words and understanding, who uses simple expressions and clings to them as to a flimsy raft in his effort to survive, is better than the unctuous fool who in his ignorance takes pride in feats of logic and by his facility with words empties the cross of Christ of its power (1 Cor 1:17) and thereby through logic and its inadequacy degrades the truth.[38]

---

37 Chrysostom, *Homilies on John*, Homily 25, FOTC, 33:243.
38 Gregory, *Or.* 32.26, FOTC, 107:209–10.

Archimandrite Vasileios expressed this same idea in a simple but profound way:

> There is room for everyone in the Church; all are sanctified, that is, there is room for the restless soul. And the simple soul is calmly honoured. The one discovers himself in the simple life of the Church, in practical virtue. And the other, in thought, in philosophy and beyond. The Church does not tire the one with philosophical ideas which he does not need, nor does she leave the other without answers to the problems which torment him. Both the one and the other are looking for the same grace. They stand in need of the same power which has conquered and conquers death. Hence, educated people are not necessarily great saints nor are those of little education necessarily minor figures. The ones who are great are the humble—whether illiterate or learned—who have shone forth, filled with the Holy Spirit.[39]

Purity of soul, not human reasoning, is the key to enlightenment. We are indeed "reason endowed," and this differentiates humans from animals. Our reasoning capacity and intellect (nous) were implanted in us in order that we might know God. But the Fathers continually remind us that divine truths are known through prayer, grace, and the experience of God, not by conjuring mental constructs. Saint Symeon the New Theologian cites Christ's words, "No one knows the Son except the Father, and no one knows the Father except the Son and any one to whom the Son chooses to reveal Him" (Matt. 11:27).

> With these and similar sayings He therefore shuts up the shameless and flapping mouths of those people who say and think that by exterior wisdom and book-learning they know the whole truth, know God Himself, and possess knowledge of the mysteries hidden in God's Spirit. For if no one knows the Son except the Father, neither does anyone know the Father except the Son and whomever the Son may wish to reveal the Former's depths and mysteries to. In effect, He says that "My mystery is for Me and My own." Who then among men on earth, wise men, or rhetoreticians, or mathematicians, or others, save

---

39   Vasileios, *Orthodox Culture*, 68–69.

those who have cleansed their intellect by the supreme philosophy [the Christian faith] and asceticism, who thus bring to the task a soul whose perceptions have been thoroughly stripped, could ever know the hidden mysteries of God from merely human wisdom and without the revelation which comes through the Lord from on high? These are mysteries which are unveiled through an intelligible contemplation enacted by the operation of the Holy Spirit in those to whom it has been given—and is ever given—to know them by virtue of the grace from on high. Knowledge of these things is for them whose intellect is illumined daily by the Holy Spirit on account of their purity of soul, whose eyes have been clearly opened by the rays of the Sun of righteousness, whose word of knowledge and word of wisdom is through the Spirit alone, whose understanding and fear of God, through love and peace, are preserved firmly in faith by the sanctity and goodness of their way of life.[40]

The Danger of Narrow-mindedness and Zealotry

NARROW-MINDEDNESS AND ZEALOTRY ARE SOMEWHAT related to rigidity and extremism, which will be discussed in the section that follows. Rigidity is the fruit of narrow-mindedness and zealotry, which often have their origin in a sincere piety and a desire to practice or preserve Orthodoxy. But the sincerity and good intentions can become enflamed by ego into narrow-mindedness and zealotry. These dangers can become deadly when they develop into spiritual delusion and pride.

Saint Gregory the Theologian recognized the danger in zealotry and narrow-mindedness. He referred to a rule observed by the Jews that some Scriptures were not to be given to the young because they lacked the discernment to know how to apply or interpret them. Out of enthusiasm and ambition they could become more zealous than they should be. His comments reveal his true pastoral considerations.[41] We would be wrong if we were to assume

---

40   Symeon, *Ninth Ethical Discourse, Ethical Discourses,* 2:114–115.
41   In our class on canon law at Holy Cross Greek Orthodox School of Theology, zealous theology students sometimes argued with our gentle professor, Dr. Patsavos, who had devoted his life to the holy canons. When the professor raised pastoral considerations that might call for the easing of canonical standards (*oikonomia*), students sometimes

that the Fathers of the Church were strict and rigid. In fact, this is not the case at all, and Gregory in particular is known for emphasizing the "middle way," taking a position not too far to the right nor too far to the left. Narrow-mindedness and zealotry do not "commend us to God," as St. Paul wrote, nor are they are a litmus test of our Orthodoxy. In fact, Gregory commented that such zealotry was irresponsible and could actually be harmful.

> We should in fact have a rule similar to the one laid down by the Hebrew sages of old to the effect that there are some holy books that are to be kept out of the hands of the young on the grounds that minds still tender and impressionable are unable to derive any benefit from them. In the same way, the right to discourse on the faith should not be granted to everyone nor always, but only to some and on some occasions; I mean it should be given to those persons who are not completely irresponsible and uncomprehending as well as to those who can control their enthusiasm and ambition and are not more zealous than they should be for true doctrine. These groups should be put into a position where they can neither harm themselves nor others; and those persons who exercise restraint in discourse and who comport themselves in a truly decent and prudent manner should enjoy liberty of expression. We should, however, direct most people away from this path and the now raging fever of garrulity, and interest them in some other, less dangerous form of achievement where not only will irresponsible behavior work less harm but boundless fervor is more a mark of piety.[42]

The Danger of Rigidity and Extremism

OUR EMPHASIS ON TRADITION LEADS some Orthodox Christians to focus so much on preserving the faith—a laudable and important goal—that they become not only traditional but rigid in their views and practices. In

---

challenged him and argued that the canons should be applied strictly. But they were only students, and the discussion was "theoretical," not a situation faced by a real person with a soul. The zealous students had difficulty appreciating the flexibility of the canons because they lacked the *phronema* that comes with time, maturity, and pastoral responsibilities.

42   Gregory, *Or.* 32.32, FOTC, 107:214.

chapter 7, we have already seen that the Fathers of the Church did not equate Tradition with antiquity or custom. Tradition has a living quality. As such it is dynamic and flexible. Rigidity can lead to traditional*ism*, which is "the dead faith of the living" rather than the "living faith of the dead."[43]

One can have "zeal for God, but not according to knowledge" (Rom. 10:2 [NKJV]). Zeal can be misplaced and become idolatry. It can lead to pride when a person begins to style himself or herself as the authentic guardian of Orthodoxy, a modern-day St. Athanasius or St. Mark of Ephesus. Such a person proudly believes he is "contending for God," St. Gregory the Theologian remarked. But what such people are actually clinging to and insisting on are their private opinions and customs. Their fervent faith makes them hostile, and they assume that any flexibility in their position is not humility or piety but "treason to the truth."

> For having undertaken to contend on behalf of God, the Supreme Being, and of salvation, and of the primary hope of us all, the more fervent they are in the faith, the more hostile are they to what is said, supposing that a submissive spirit indicates, not piety, but treason to the truth, and therefore they would sacrifice anything rather than their private convictions, and the accustomed doctrines in which they have been educated.[44]

Such people can be forgiven since they are acting out of piety, Gregory states. He concludes that there is hope for them, if they are moderate.

> I am now referring to those who are moderate and not utterly depraved in disposition, who, if they have erred in regard to the truth, have erred from piety, who have zeal, though not according to knowledge, who will possibly be of the number of those not excessively condemned, and not beaten with many stripes, because it is not through vice or depravity that they have failed to do the will of their Lord; and these perchance would be persuaded and forsake the pious opinion which is the cause of their hostility.[45]

---

43 Pelikan, *Christian Tradition*, 1:9.
44 Gregory, *Or.* 2.40, NPNF-2, 7:215.
45 Gregory, *Or.* 2.40, NPNF-2, 7:215.

It can be difficult to know what is changeable and what is unchangeable in Orthodox Christianity. It requires discernment, and this is one reason the Church is exceedingly slow to change. Father Hopko commented that what is changeable and unchangeable is not always obvious. It

> really has nothing to do with antiquity or novelty as such. It is not about what is old-fashioned or modern, traditional or innovative, conservative or liberal. For as Christ has said, "every scribe who is made a disciple for the kingdom of heaven is like a man who is a householder who brings forth from his treasure things new and old" (Matt. 13:52).[46]

If the Church were rigid, we would see no blending of old and new. Many traditions and customs in the Church are Jewish in origin, while other practices reflect the newness of the gospel. Rigidity is not a virtue. Something may appear to be new that is not new at all. It may be a "recovery of something old which has been lost, forgotten, obscured or misunderstood."[47]

A good example of this is the life and work of St. Symeon the New Theologian. Hopko reminds us that the Lord, the prophets, and the apostles were all killed for being "innovators." Many Church Fathers and other saints also suffered because of this accusation, including Gregory Palamas, Symeon the New Theologian, Tikhon of Moscow, and Silouan of Mt. Athos. We should not immediately react against everything we perceive as "new." Many customs and practices that we treasure and assume to be quite old are not actually as ancient as we believe.[48] Saint Cyprian of Carthage said in the mid-third century that "antiquity is not truth (*antiquitas non est veritas*), and that ancient custom may be nothing more than ancient error."[49]

Truth is not simply a matter of quoting the Scriptures, the Fathers, and the canons. Without discernment and the proper phronema, these important

---

46   Hopko, "Theological Education," 3.
47   Hopko, 4.
48   For example, the Orthodox love the Lamentations service of Great and Holy Friday, but the lamentations we sing for Christ are not very ancient. They first appear in ecclesiastical service books around the thirteenth or fourteenth century. *Threskeytike kai Hethike Egkyklopaideia,* 12 vols. (Athens, 1967), s.v. "Engomia."
49   Hopko, "Theological Education," 3.

authorities of the Church will be misunderstood, misapplied, and distorted. "Many who are mistaken and create schisms and heresies in the Church may be 'conservatives' who mindlessly repeat the good words of the Scriptures, councils and saints while they distort the content of the teaching and fail to live by its truth."[50]

Saint Paisios presented the iconoclast controversy as an example of extremism that manifested itself in church history. Some Orthodox considered the icons so sacred that they took bits of paint from them and put them in the communion chalice, while others rejected the icons entirely and destroyed them. The saint was asked why people start out with good intentions but go to extremes. Notice that Paisios identifies the root of extremism as personal ego.

> Pride has infiltrated his activity but he does not realize it because he does not know himself yet and that's why he goes to extremes. People often start out piously but get lost. This is what happened during the iconoclast controversy between the iconodules and the iconoclasts. Extremes on one side, extremes on the other. The iconodules went so far as to scrape the paint off the Icon of Christ and put it into the chalice to improve Holy Communion! The Iconoclasts would either burn the Icons or throw them away. This is why the Church was forced to put the icons high up and, once the controversy subsided, the icons were lowered for the people to venerate them and render honor to the persons they represented.[51]

The Danger of Individualism and Private Opinion

YET ANOTHER PARADOX IN ORTHODOX Christianity is the place of the individual. The importance and value of the individual person is not only recognized; it is emphasized. This is evident in that the Church does not require or demand that everyone conform to the same standards or practices in matters such as a rule of prayer or fasting. It is also evident in the application of the holy canons, which are tailored to a specific situation, and in the fact that

50   Hopko, 3.
51   Paisios, *Spiritual Counsels,* 2:90.

allowances are made for individual circumstances. The value of each individual person is seen perhaps most simply in that when we approach the chalice for Holy Communion or participate in other Mysteries, the priest always says our name. We are part of the Body of Christ, but never as anonymous members.

And yet, while the Church emphasizes the value of the individual, an individualist mentality is unacceptable. Just as the Church recognizes freedom rather than demanding submission or imposing authority over us, there is a similar tension between recognizing our uniqueness as individuals and rejecting individualism. Meyendorff remarks that the experience of the Holy Spirit in the Church is always personal and liberating. The Christian life is free. Authority in the form of canons, hierarchy, and conciliar decisions exists to *protect* our freedom, not to replace it. "The personalism of the faith does not result in charismatic subjectivity or individualism; it initiates each person to think and to act as a responsible member of the body."[52]

Individualism and private opinion might be influenced by ego, by the values of the world, or by a desire not to conform to the teachings of the Church. Saint John Chrysostom remarked:

> You see, whenever people are unwilling to take the consequence of following the norms of Sacred Scripture, wishing to make room for the vagaries of private reasoning, they upset their sense of balance and undermine the solid orthodoxy of dogmas with endless disputes and questioning.[53]

Chrysostom's remark also reveals one of the by-products of individual opinion: disputes and dissensions. Even when the theologian does not consciously recognize his or her personal motivation, the private opinion serves his or her need or desire. He or she supports and defends the opinion and may even find a clever way to distort the Tradition to "prove" that this opinion is Orthodox. But it is not. The theologian has become enamored by his or her own ideas and finds a way to justify them, believing that Orthodoxy can embrace a personal opinion even if it stands outside the boundaries of Tradition.

---

52 Meyendorff, "Doing Theology," 94.
53 Chrysostom, *Homilies on Genesis,* Homily 14.6, FOTC, 74:184.

Recently, a theologian has argued quite adamantly that there is no such thing as eternal punishment. He is certainly not the first person to make that argument. His premise is that we can affirm the existence of human free will *or* eternal punishment, but not both, since no one would willingly choose to be in hell. Therefore, there is no hell. He is enamored with his opinion and insists that his position is unassailably "logical." He presents his arguments in an extremely sophisticated and philosophical manner, challenging others to find any flaw in his reasoning. But this is precisely why our theology is not based on human reasoning. Shall we choose someone's individual reasoning, or the consistent Tradition and teaching of the Christian faith—not to mention the very words of Christ, who often warned us about hell?

Freedom in the Church does not mean expressing or promoting personal opinion. We must recognize that we have our limitations—in knowledge, in spiritual experience, in discernment, in wisdom—and we should seek to understand the teaching of the Church as it has been expressed throughout its history, to acquire the mind of Christ. The theologian must first "master his subjectivity," that is, be free from his own limitations and standards, and second "must live in spiritual sympathy with, and understand, the Church's historical completeness."[54]

In the Orthodox Church, "personal opinions cannot and should not exist," because that spirit violates the catholicity of the Church and Holy Tradition, which is the standard by which we measure and determine theological truth.[55] And yet, Fr. Hopko notes that even people who consider themselves conservative can have a modern, individualist spirit—something they would vehemently deny because they are conservative.[56] Therefore, the individualistic spirit can be recognized not only in those who are perceived to be promoting something new but also among some who seem to be quite the opposite. Such people appear to be insisting on Orthodox doctrine and practice but are in fact individualists, because they decide for themselves what constitutes true Orthodoxy. They do this on a very narrow, often uninformed basis and then reject everything else. As Hopko astutely comments:

---

54   Florovsky, *Bible, Church and Tradition*, 54.
55   Florovsky, 54.
56   Hopko, "Theological Education," 5.

Individualists basically recognize no authority other than themselves. Not being anarchists, they usually admit the need for civil and ecclesiastical "authorities" but they seek those who agree with them and enforce their opinions and desires. When such people are religious they follow the god of their choosing . . . and when they go to church, even to an Orthodox church—even as pastors, monks, professors or teachers—they go to the church (or jurisdiction) of their choice, based on their subjective opinion and desire of what the "true church" and "true Orthodoxy" are and should be. And they interpret the authoritative witness to the Church's faith and life through the lenses of their predetermined and prejudiced predilections.[57]

The spirit of individualism is a spirit of ego and pride. This is why it is sinful even when the person believes he or she is striving to be Orthodox and preserve true Orthodoxy. Hopko sadly observes that at times those who are infected with the individualist spirit are actually leaders in the Church—bishops, priests, theologians, elders, and monks. They even attract a following and "victimize their disciples with an 'Orthodox' theology, liturgy and piety of their own making."[58] As St. Paul observed, they have zeal without knowledge and substitute their own righteousness for that of God (see Rom. 10:2–3). It is "not according to knowledge" even if they are educated people, monastics, or theologians, because their ego has misled them. They lack discernment and accurate spiritual knowledge of themselves and their true motivation. They are not aware that the evil one is prompting their ideas in order to inflame their egos and sow dissension in the Church.

The Danger of Creating Doubt

THEOLOGIANS MUST TAKE GREAT CARE to discern the appropriateness of their comments in light of the ability of their audience to understand them. It is especially important not to contribute to a loss of faith by creating doubt. This can easily happen, especially when a theologian seeks to make a display

---

57 Hopko, 5.
58 Hopko, 5.

of knowledge or does not exercise discernment. The theologian will certainly be answerable to God for that soul who falls away because of doubt that he or she created.

Saint John Chrysostom believed that his congregation should be capable of explaining and defending the faith. Of course, they were not. And yet they were capable of explaining in detail the various abilities of popular dancers, actors, and charioteers, a fact that agitated their pastor tremendously. He held them responsible for the lack of faith of the pagans.

On one occasion, when he was chastising the congregation regarding their inability to respond to pagan critics of the Christian faith, Chrysostom posed a series of questions to which they could not reply. He abruptly stopped when he realized that by only posing the questions and not giving the responses, he might actually cause some of them to lose their faith. "But it is not expedient to ask many questions in succession and be silent about the answers, lest in this way we harm the more simple [among you]."[59]

Elsewhere he cautioned against asking too many questions regarding matters that are beyond comprehension and that might lead to doubt. In discussing the dialogue between Christ and Nicodemus, who asks, "How can a man be born when he is old? Can he enter a second time into his mother's womb and be born?" (John 3:4), Chrysostom warns the congregation about the word "how." Expecting to understand spiritual matters rationally has led many to fall away.

This word "how" is the expression of doubt and does not belong to those whose faith is firm but to those who are still of the earth. Sara, for example, was offering derisions by her question, when she said "How" (Gen. 18:10–14); and many others who used this question have fallen away from the faith. In this way, also, heretics persevere in heresy, hunting down this expression everywhere. Some say: "How was He made flesh?" while others: "How was He born?"—subjecting that infinite Being to the weakness of their reasoning. Therefore, they who are aware of this must flee such untimely curiosity. Those who so question will not know the "how" and they will fall away from the true faith.[60]

---

59   Chrysostom, *Homilies on John*, Homily 17, FOTC, 33:171.
60   Chrysostom, Homily 24, FOTC, 33:238.

It is pointless to ask "how?" since by doing so we are subjecting divine things to the "order prevailing among us," meaning the natural world. But God is not part of the natural world, and it is foolish to expect that we can comprehend spiritual things by applying human reason.

> Do you see how, when a man wrests spiritual things to his own reasoning, he both utters absurdities and seems to be raving and intoxicated, since he is unduly examining the words, beyond what is pleasing to God and does not accept the deposit of faith? He has heard of spiritual generation, but did not understand that it was of the Spirit. Instead, he dragged what was said down to the lowliness of the flesh and thus made a great and sublime teaching depend on the natural sequence [of birth]. So, in the end, he trumped up foolish trifles and ridiculous questions. Therefore, Paul also has said: "The sensual man does not perceive the things that are of the Spirit of God." (1 Cor. 2:14) . . . Therefore, since we know these things, let us not examine into the things of God by reasoning and let us not submit divine things to the order prevailing among us, nor subject them to the necessity of nature, but let us think of them all reverently, believing as the Scriptures have said.[61]

Doubt can be created not only by those who seek to understand the spiritual and sublime matters on a human level, but by theologians expressing or promoting theories or explanations to solve biblical questions or theological conundrums. The theologian must recognize where human reasoning ends and divine mystery begins, and encourage the faithful to accept this as well.

---

61 Chrysostom, Homily 24, FOTC, 33:239.

CHAPTER 16

Theological Dangers: Spiritual

THE PRACTICE OF THEOLOGY IS fraught with significant spiritual dangers that should not go unrecognized. Saint Gregory the Theologian, speaking about the responsibilities of the clergy, expressed the danger of being insufficiently trained and, even worse, not recognizing one's own ignorance.

> Accordingly, to undertake the training of others before being sufficiently trained oneself, and to learn, as men say, the potter's art on a wine-jar, that is, to practice ourselves in piety at the expense of others' souls, seems to me to be excessive folly or excessive rashness—folly, if we are not even aware of our own ignorance; rashness, if in spite of this knowledge we venture on the task.[1]

The same could certainly be said about the dangers of theologizing since, in each case, both clergy and theologians essentially act as spiritual guides. The theologian may not explicitly be providing spiritual advice and direction, but effectively he or she is doing so, since the theologian speaks about God and everything pertaining to the Church and salvation. This responsibility is even more serious than that of a physician, attorney, engineer, airline pilot, bus driver, or any other person to whom we entrust our physical safety. We expect them to exercise the utmost care and concern for our physical welfare. But the words and deeds of clergy and theologians affect the eternal destiny of

---

1   Gregory, *Or.* 2.47, NPNF-2, 7:214.

the soul. Not only are such people responsible, but they are answerable to God for their statements and actions. It is no wonder that St. Gregory proclaimed theology and the shepherding of souls to be quite dangerous.

Gregory recognized the danger and knew that the discussion of theology attracted those who wished to display even their scant knowledge for honor and glory. He noted that even Moses did not receive what he requested from God, but everything that did occur happened in the order and manner set by God.

> But we, once we get our hands on a little glory, and often not even that, by managing to memorize at random two or three phrases of Scripture, and these hopelessly out of context . . . we are forced into the impossible position of rejecting Moses and identifying with the godless scoundrels Dathan and Abiram (Ex. 28:1; Num. 3:2). Let us avoid their impudence and keep from imitating their folly and bringing their end upon ourselves.[2]

The spiritual dangers are many. They especially arise when one is theologizing without a genuine and consistent spiritual life. This distorts everything and leads to many problems. Maintaining a rule of prayer, an active liturgical life in the Church, and a relationship with a spiritual father is essential. Worldly success certainly can be experienced by a theologian or a priest—awards, important positions, accolades, publications, admirers, and so forth. This can lead to complacency but also to triumphalism and gloating, not to mention pride. When we avoid one trap, the evil one actively plots to lure us into another. Vigilance is ever necessary, as it is for the spiritual life in general.

The Danger of Pride, Egoism, and Self-Importance

LET US BEGIN WITH THE most obvious and probably the most serious danger: pride. It can fairly be said that all the other dangers to be enumerated are related to this one, but they manifest themselves in different forms. Chrysostom noted the "strategy of the Devil" is to "entice us" with hopes of

---

2   Gregory, *Or.* 32.17, FOTC, 107:203.

greater things. He specifically mentions "knowledge and honor," alluding to the Fall of Adam and Eve from Paradise. In the pursuit of theological truth, it is worthwhile to remember that our first parents fell because they believed they could be like God.

Chrysostom comments on John 1:9 (the Logos is the "true light") and reminds us in the excerpt below about the limitations of our understanding. By seeking to go beyond what is appropriate, being enticed by the false promise of greater knowledge and honor, we might lose even what we already have.

> Such as this indeed is the strategy of the Devil: he leads those who are obedient to him beyond the bounds given to us by God, as if to much greater things. But when, having enticed us by these hopes, he has divorced us from the love of God, then not only does he add nothing more for the future (for how can he, since he is the Devil?), but he does not even permit us to return to the former circumstances where we lived safely and securely, but leads us wandering about everywhere, unable to come to rest anywhere. In this way, he also caused our first parent to be deprived of the abode of Paradise. After puffing him up by the promise of greater knowledge and honor, he forcibly separated him even from those things which he then had the right to enjoy with complete freedom.... In order that we, too, may not have something similar happen to us, let us be obedient to God, and let us remain faithful to those things which He has commanded us. Let us not beyond that be unduly inquisitive, that we may not be separated from the good things already granted to us, even as they were.... Let us not change the ancient boundaries which our fathers set, but let us yield everywhere to the laws of the Spirit. And when we hear: "It was the true light," let us seek to find out nothing more. In fact, it is not possible to penetrate the meaning of these words further.[3]

Saint Gregory the Theologian compares the reverent attitude and restraint a theologian must display to the reverence God expected to be shown toward the ark of the covenant, the temple, and temple offerings. Rather than approaching divine things with an attitude of pride, we should remember that

---

3   Chrysostom, *Homilies on John*, Homily 7, FOTC, 33:76–77.

no one could touch even the walls of the sanctuary, and only deserving persons at the proper time could consume the sacrifices. We should take this as a model when discussing God, always remembering our unworthiness and the need for purity.

> No one so much as dreamed of entering the Holy of Holies and looking upon or touching the curtain or the mercy seat or the ark. So, knowing these things, and that no one can be worthy of our great God, who was both victim and high priest, unless he first presents himself to God as "a living sacrifice" (Rom. 12:1), or rather becomes a living "holy temple of the living God" (2 Cor. 6:16) how could either I myself blithely launch into a discussion about God or countenance anyone who, without further ado, does the same? That is not a commendable ambition; the attempt is fraught with peril. In fact, this is why one must purify oneself and then enter into converse with the pure if we are not to share the fate of Manoah, and, when we have beheld the vision of God declare, "We are destroyed, dear wife, we have seen God" (Judg. 13:22) or, like Peter, urge Jesus to leave the boat because we are unworthy of so great a presence (Luke 5:8), or like the centurion in the Bible, seek healing but decline to receive the healer. So long as any one of us is a centurion, with more than his share of wickedness and still in the service of Caesar, the universal ruler of creatures that creep on the ground, let him likewise say, "I am not worthy to have you come under my roof" (Matt. 8:8).[4]

Rather than being proud of whatever theological insights we manage to achieve, we should recognize that it is not a reason for pride, since no theological insight comes from us. Acknowledging that all comes from God hinders spiritual delusion or *prelest*. If it comes from God, how can we be proud of it? It is not our achievement.

The Corinthians were very proud of their "wisdom." Saint Paul scolded them for being "puffed up" and explained that no one has a reason to boast, since all comes from God: "Let no one deceive himself. If any one among you thinks that he is wise in this age, let him become a fool that he may become

---

4   Gregory, *Or.* 20.3–4, FOTC, 107:109.

wise. For the wisdom of this world is folly with God" (1 Cor. 3:18–19). He pointed out that the Corinthians had not acquired spiritual gifts by their own efforts or skill; therefore, they had no reason to be proud of them: "What have you that you did not receive? If then you received it, why do you boast as if it were not a gift?" (1 Cor. 4:7).

The Danger of Self-Reliance

THE FIRST EPISTLE OF ST. Paul to the Corinthians contains many lessons for the pursuit and practice of theology, as Paul compares human wisdom with divine wisdom. The Corinthians' pride demonstrated that rather than being advanced, in fact they were not spiritual at all. Divine things cannot be perceived by the "natural man," one who is controlled by the passions. Paul was using the term "natural man" to draw a contrast with a spiritual person, who behaves and perceives differently. Saint Paul explained to the arrogant Corinthians, "The natural man does not receive the things of the Spirit of God, for they are foolishness to him; nor can he know *them*, because they are spiritually discerned" (1 Cor. 2:14 [NKJV]). Chrysostom comments that a "natural man" is one:

> who attributes everything to reasonings of the mind and considers not that he needs help from above; which is a mark of sheer folly. For God bestowed it [the mind] that it might learn and receive help from Him, not that it should consider itself sufficient unto itself. For eyes are beautiful and useful, but should they choose to see without light, their beauty profits them nothing; nor yet their natural force, but even does harm. So if you note, any soul also, if it chooses to see without the Spirit, becomes even an impediment unto itself.[5]

Chrysostom notes that St. Paul gave other reasons for rejecting human wisdom: "that no flesh should glory," "that he might confound the wise," and "lest the cross of Christ be stripped of its power." But Paul concludes with what Chrysostom considers the primary reason for rejecting worldly wisdom: so

---

5   Chrysostom, *Homilies on Paul's Epistles to the Corinthians*, Homily 7.9, NPNF-1, 12:38.

that we would realize that reason is ineffective for comprehending spiritual things and that all comes from God.

> In this way we most easily see from Whom we may have the means of learning even high things, and things secret, and things which are above us. For reason was absolutely made of no effect by our inability to apprehend through Gentile wisdom the things above us. You may observe, too, that it was more advantageous to learn in this way from the Spirit. For that is the easiest and clearest of all teaching. "But we have the mind of Christ" (1 Cor. 2:16). That is, spiritual, divine, that which has nothing human. For it is not of Plato, nor of Pythagoras, but it is Christ Himself, putting His own things into our mind.[6]

Maximos the Confessor explained why we become enamored with our own reasoning and fall into the trap of relying on ourselves and our opinions rather than on God and the Tradition of the Church. In fact, we might sincerely believe our opinions and reasonings are coming from God. The wise man does not trust his own judgment, recognizing that he can deceive himself. He trusts other wise men to judge his opinions. Those others whom we can trust are the Fathers, the saints, and our spiritual fathers. Saint Maximos explains:

> Just as parents have affection for the offspring of their bodies, so also is the mind naturally attached to its own reasonings. And just as to their parents who are emotionally attached the children appear as the fairest and handsomest of all even though in every way they might be the most hideous of all, so it is with the foolish mind. Its reasonings, even though they might be the most depraved of all, still appear in its view as the most sensible of all. However, this is not the case with the wise man and his reasonings. Rather, when it seems convincing that they are true and correct, then especially does he distrust his own judgment but makes use of other wise men as judges of his own reasonings (so as not to run or have run in vain [Gal. 2:2]), and from them he receives assurance.[7]

---

6   Chrysostom, Homily 7.12, NPNF-1, 12:39.
7   Maximos the Confessor, *Chapters on Love*, 3.58, *Selected Writings*, 69.

Choosing to substitute one's own opinion instead of following Tradition can have serious consequences for the pastor or the theologian, and we must be extremely careful before adopting a practice or belief that contradicts Tradition but seems logical or reasonable to our mind. Conversely, we should not abandon a practice that is part of Church Tradition even though it seems unnecessary or outdated. This has been dubbed "chronological snobbery."[8] We believe we are more intelligent than those who lived in the past. We know better than they do about what to believe or how to behave, despite the fact that we received the Tradition from them and claim to be faithful to it. Reasons for preserving a belief or practice may be much deeper than we realize, and disregarding it can have real consequences.

We ought not to rely on ourselves and our own ideas but follow the Tradition of the Church, which has been established by Christ, the apostles, and the countless saints and faithful who preceded us. Therefore we should have confidence in everything we believe and do in the Church, and it is not safe to disregard it or substitute our own opinions.

The Danger of Arrogance

PRIDE AND ARROGANCE ARE CLOSELY related. Pride is believing oneself to be better than others. Arrogance is having an inflated opinion of oneself. Maximos the Confessor sharply clarified the relationship between arrogance and the true acquisition of knowledge, which is in fact quite simple: if you arrogantly believe that your knowledge is greater than it actually is, you are not open to learning.

If you want to become judicious and moderate and no servant of the passion of conceit, always seek in things what is hidden from your knowledge. You will

---

8   The term was explained by C. S. Lewis. "Chronological snobbery is the uncritical acceptance of the intellectual climate common to our own age and the assumption that whatever has gone out of date is on that account discredited." C. S. Lewis, *A Mind Awake: An Anthology of C. S. Lewis* (Boston: Houghton Mifflin Harcourt, 2003), 221. A similar fallacy is "ethnocentrism," the belief that our cultural values and practices are superior to those of others.

indeed find a great many diverse things which have eluded you, and you will be astonished at your own ignorance and temper your pride. And in knowing yourself you will understand many great and wonderful things, since to think that one knows does not allow one to advance in knowledge.[9]

Pride and arrogance lead to heresy, St. Gregory the Theologian observes. The arrogant either oppose doctrine because they have an inflated self-opinion, or simply out of ignorance they behave boldly and impetuously. Lacking sense, they trample the faith:

> But what is to be said of those who, from vain glory or arrogance, speak unrigh-teousness against the most High, arming themselves with the insolence of Jannes and Jambres,[10] not against Moses, but against the truth, and rising in opposition to sound doctrine? Or of the third class, who through ignorance and, its consequence, temerity, rush headlong against every form of doctrine in swinish fashion, and trample under foot the fair pearls of the truth?[11]

Saint Symeon the New Theologian draws a brilliant mental picture of how to avoid arrogance and pride. We must examine our soul, and if we engage in true self-examination, our conscience will reply honestly.

> You then, who have read this, examine yourself carefully, not with the con-ceit of knowledge falsely-so-called, nor in the concocting of silly opinions, but with fear and trembling. And if you want to learn what condition your life is in, inquire of your soul and ask it: "Soul, have you kept all of God's command-ments or not?" And, opening the mouth of its conscience, it will tell the whole truth. For it will not seek to please you, rather it will reprove you, and whatever you have stored up and keep in yourself, whether good or ill, it will show you. For within the soul's conscience you will discover whether you have loved the

---

9   Maximos the Confessor, *Chapters on Love* 3.81, *Selected Writings*, 72.

10   In both Christian and Jewish tradition, these were the names of Pharaoh's magicians who opposed Moses and Aaron in Exodus 7—9. Their names are mentioned by Paul in 2 Timothy 3:8 as examples of corrupt men who oppose truth.

11   Gregory, *Or.* 2.41, NPNF-2, 7:213.

world; whether you have preferred the world to God; whether you have sought
the glory of men, or whether you have longed for the glory which is God's gift
alone. You will look into yourself as into a chest and will feel around for what
is lying at the bottom, and, tossing out the contents one by one, you will know
everything clearly.[12]

When we examine ourselves deeply, we will realize that our conceited
thoughts are nothing at all and that, in fact, we are not capable of reflecting on
the things of God. Saint Symeon's expertise in the spiritual life shines in this
passage, in which he lays bare what we will find if we look deep into ourselves
and pull the contents out of the box within us one by one:

Allow me to suppose the following contents: first of all love of ambition and of
vainglory, then the sweetness of human praise, a vesture of hypocrisy, a hidden seed of avarice, and, altogether many hidden things, one thing hidden by
and on top of another, and right there on top of everything else let us further
suppose self-importance—"for knowledge," he says, "puffs up" (1 Cor. 8:1)—
and next to it conceited self-opinion, and the supposition that your puffed-up
conceits are really something when, in fact, they are nothing at all. Given that
the latter are present, and adding them to all the other articles which we have
noted, how can you possibly venture to reflect on the things of God? Surely you
must reply: in no way![13]

The Danger of Obsession and Judging God

SOMETIMES PEOPLE OBSESS OVER THEOLOGICAL or biblical issues
which, in their own minds, they believe must be resolved. They fixate on them
and will not cease pondering the problem until they are convinced that they
have arrived at an acceptable solution according to human reasoning. Usually this concerns a passage in the Bible—very often Genesis and the creation accounts, or the killing of the Canaanites in the Book of Joshua. This is

---

12 Symeon, *First Ethical Discourse 12, Ethical Discourses,* 1:69–70.
13 Symeon, *First Ethical Discourse 12, Ethical Discourses,* 1:70.

a particularly difficult section of the Bible, and much of the Old Testament is very violent. We can never understand this or find any explanation that will satisfy our modern minds, which have been shaped according to Christian values. We must begin with the presumption that God is loving and just, and we humans cannot understand His ways. We are in no position to judge God and must accept that there are things we cannot understand.

An obsession can become a spiritual problem because it is a trap the evil one designed to plant seeds of doubt about God. Obsession distracts us from what is truly important and spiritually useful. It can ultimately lead us to lose our faith. This kind of obsession is also ego driven. Countless people have been disturbed by the violence in the Old Testament. After three thousand years, no one has arrived at a satisfactory explanation that will make us comfortable with certain parts of the Bible, but an obsessed person is determined that *he* will find a solution. This type of problem requires spiritual intervention; it cannot be resolved by applying one's own mind.

God allowed actions in the Old Testament that He does not accept in the New.[14] God expects more from us today than He did from ancient, primitive peoples. Our theological and moral understandings and God's expectations for human behavior grow over time. Saint Gregory the Theologian commented that the Holy Trinity was not clearly manifest in the Old Testament because it would have been a burden that people would not have been able to receive. But gradually over time, the truth became manifest, and the Holy Spirit came to dwell in the apostles "according to their capacity to receive him."[15] Chrysostom praised David for having "New Testament values" in the era of the Old Testament because he refrained from killing King Saul when he had the opportunity (1 Sam./1Kg 24:7; 26:11) and displayed other virtues uncommon for the time.[16]

Saint John Chrysostom ignored the harsh application of Old Testament justice and the issues that would obsess the modern mind and instead focused

---

14 Chrysostom, *Homily 1 on David and Saul. Homilies on Hannah, David and Saul,* Robert Hill, trans., St. John Chrysostom Old Testament Homilies, vol. 1 (Brookline, MA: Holy Cross Greek Orthodox Press, 2003), 11.

15 Gregory, *Or.* 31.26–27, *On God and Christ,* 137.

16 See Chrysostom, Homilies 1 and 3, *Homilies on Hannah, David and Saul,* 11 and 43–44.

entirely on the moral lesson to be learned.[17] He did not address the question of apparent "unfairness" or the harsh punishment, because we cannot adequately explain or comprehend this from a human perspective, and therefore it is pointless to discuss it as a matter of philosophical speculation. Chrysostom and other Fathers were very aware of the limitations of biblical language and the fact that the Bible described God in ways that are entirely inappropriate for Him, for example saying that God gets "angry." The Scriptures are God's "condescension" (*synkatabasis*) to our human weakness. He lowers Himself down to our level. The Bible is written with human language and concepts so that we can understand it, but we must not think of God in human terms, nor should we expect to understand His ways by the application of human reasoning.

> Let us accept what is said with much gratitude, not overstepping the proper limit nor busying ourselves with matters beyond us; this is the besetting weakness of enemies of the truth, wishing as they do to assign every matter to their own reasoning, and lacking the realization that it is beyond the capacity of human nature to plumb God's creation.[18]

Saint Cyril of Alexandria took a similar approach when he discussed Christ's healing of the man born blind. When the disciples asked the Lord why the man was born blind, the Lord's reply was "that the works of God might be made manifest in him" (John 9:3). Even if this was the case for this man, because he would be healed by Christ, why should he suffer for his entire lifetime with blindness? Is this fair? What about all the other people who are born with infirmities or illnesses who are never healed? Cyril's response is that Christ was not truly giving an answer by saying that God's work might be manifest; rather, He was deflecting the disciples' question and ascribing this knowledge to God alone. We cannot understand why people suffer through

---

17   Such stories serve as useful warnings to us, according to Chrysostom. Our troubles are the outcome of our sinful actions. We should examine our faults and attribute responsibility not to others, and certainly not to God, but to ourselves. *Homily 1 on Isaiah. Homilies on Isaiah and Jeremiah*, Robert Hill., trans. St. John Chrysostom Old Testament Homilies, vol. 2 (Brookline, MA: Holy Cross Greek Orthodox Press, 2003), 59.

18   Chrysostom, *Homilies on Genesis*, Homily 2.5, FOTC, 74:32.

no fault of their own. Likewise, many other "matters far above us [are] completely inaccessible to the contemplation of our minds." Cyril continues:

> I would advise the prudent to resist even the desire to look into them. That goes for me above all. We should instead think about what we have been commanded, and not search out what is too deep or investigate what is too difficult, or rashly try to dig up what is hidden in the divine and ineffable counsel alone. Rather, we should reverently entrust to God alone the knowledge of matters that are appropriate and distinctive to him, while holding the true belief that since he is the fountain of all righteousness, he would not do or intend anything either in our affairs or in those of the rest of all creation except what is clearly worthy of him and does not depart from what is true and right.[19]

Saint Cyril was advising that we *accept* what is often the most difficult thing to accept: that we cannot explain such things. We can only trust that God is good and then be silent. We must not try to understand what is beyond us, seeking rational explanations to satisfy human sensibilities. Saint John Chrysostom, also commenting on the Gospel of John, censured his congregation for that attitude. We expect to be able to understand everything by employing our weak, human reasoning when even the holy Evangelist John himself did not understand everything.

> Why do you strive contentiously and in vain to compass by your reason this infinite life? It is not possible to do so. Why do you search for the unsearchable? Why do you scrutinize the inscrutable? Why do you seek into the incomprehensible? Inquire into the source of the sunbeams; you will not be able to find it; nevertheless, you do not wax indignant or feel vexed because of your weakness. How is it, then, that you have become rash and impetuous in greater matters than these?[20]

The obsession with solving conundrums is nothing new, either in theology or biblical studies. Gregory the Theologian also warned those who believe

---

19   Cyril of Alexandria, *Commentary on John* 6.1, Ancient Christian Texts, 1:29.
20   Chrysostom, *Homilies on John*, Homily 7, FOTC, 33:75–76.

they know all and can explain all that they are "naïve and pretentious." Their actions are nothing more than an ego-driven display of their intellect, and "they in fact have undermined every approach to true religion by their complete obsession with setting and solving conundrums."

> Such is the situation: this infection is unchecked and intolerable; the "great mystery" (1 Tim. 3:16) of our faith is in danger of becoming a mere social accomplishment.... Do not be surprised if what I say is contrary to your expectations and contrary to your ways, since you profess to know all and teach all—an attitude which is too naïve and pretentious; I would not offend you by saying stupid and arrogant.[21]

The Danger of Conformity, Compromise, and Cowardice

THESE SPIRITUAL DANGERS ARE AMONG the most common faced by all Christians in our era: the pressure to compromise our values, to conform to social norms, or at least to be silent. At the root of this is cowardice—fear of social disapproval, ostracism, or the loss of a job or career if we speak the truth. Because of this we are tempted to soften the moral teachings of the Church in the name of "compassion." We compromise our own values or fail to speak the truth without hesitating, wavering, or vacillating.

This danger manifests itself when ordinary Christians and theologians alike are confronted by moral issues such as abortion, homosexuality, heterosexual couples cohabitating, plural marriage, immodest clothing, violent video games, immoral music videos and lyrics, explicit scenes in popular television shows, gambling, vanity, obsession with physical beauty, the love of money, the widespread use of obscene language—and the list can go on.

Social movements, such as those that initially intended to protect homosexuals from job or housing discrimination, to provide medical benefits for unmarried partners, or to protect women from unsafe abortions, have become aggressive campaigns extending far beyond the legislation that secured certain legal rights. Now various groups demand total, unquestioning acceptance

---

21 Gregory, *Or. 27.2, On God and Christ*, 25–26.

of their activities and lifestyles. They are supported by the media, popular culture, and often the government, so that one cannot voice dissent without expecting retribution. Social and traditional media, governments, entertainment companies, and celebrities have arrayed their massive powers of influence. They number "like the sand of the sea" and "surround the camp of the saints," a veritable army "gathered for battle" (Rev. 20:8–9) against the very Christian values which were once the foundation of our society.

Christ and the apostles warned us not to be of the world. Saint Paul repeatedly wrote against all manner of sin, including sexual immorality. The very idea of choosing a life of holiness rather than pursuit of pleasure and self-indulgence is foreign to modern popular culture. No rational explanation can ever justify or condone immorality, because Orthodox theology is not a matter of clever philosophical arguments. Christians are called not to conform to this world, but to be transformed into something holy and acceptable to God, a living sacrifice. Christians can never excuse or justify sin regardless of social pressure.

Christ warned His followers that they would be hated and rejected by the world, just as He was. "If the world hates you, know that it has hated me before it hated you. If you were of the world, the world would love its own" (John 15:18–19). If the Church becomes secularized and conforms to the values of the world to meet perceived "social needs," it cannot offer spiritual healing or transformation, because it is encouraging humanity to remain in its fallen state. Our duty is not to be popular, not to make concessions, not to compromise, not to prove that we are "loving" or "open-minded," but to present the option of spiritual transformation. "I appeal to you therefore, brethren, by the mercies of God, to present your bodies as a living sacrifice, holy and acceptable to God, which is your spiritual worship. Do not be conformed to this world but be transformed by the renewal of your mind" (Rom. 12:1–2).

Capitulation to societal changes by Christians, or their mere silence, has emboldened and radicalized the enemies of the truth. In fact, the more success they achieve in society, the more aggressive and demanding their positions have become. Anyone who dares to express traditional morals, ethics, and ideals is demonized and denounced as "dangerous" and "hateful."

The words of Christ Himself—such as "love one another" and "judge not"—are being perverted and turned against the faithful. Christians are shamed and silenced simply for expressing traditional moral values. They are accused of violating the Lord's injunction against judging others, reproached for the sin of pride, and charged with believing themselves to be superior to others. The very teachings of our Lord are being used as weapons by the evil one, who mimics and distorts what is good, creating a twisted caricature of Christian teaching to justify sin.

The admonition of Christ to "judge not lest you be judged" has been employed as a weapon to shame, chastise, and even bully any Christian who does not conform to societal norms that accept and promote immorality. But the command to "judge not" does not mean that Christians are not to make judgments about whether a behavior is right or wrong. We *must* distinguish between right and wrong. How can we be expected to do the right thing if we are not allowed to distinguish between right and wrong? "Judge not" means that we are not to condemn another person, since God alone is judge. It is not an order never to acknowledge that an act is a sin. In a pluralistic and worldly society that opposes the phronema of the Church and instead appeals to a distorted Christian ethic as well as to the limited reasoning and rationality of the human mind, the challenge to the theologian is tremendous.

Saint Gregory the Theologian commented on the problem of compromise, conformity, and capitulation to the values of this world, including the fear of social rejection.

> For we are not as the many, able to corrupt the word of truth, and mix the wine, which makes glad the heart of man, with water, mix, that is, our doctrine with what is common and cheap, and debased, and stale, and tasteless, in order to turn the adulteration to our profit, and accommodate ourselves to those who meet us, and curry favor with everyone, becoming ventriloquists and chatterers, who serve their own pleasures by words uttered from the earth, and sinking into the earth, and, to gain the special good will of the multitude, injuring in the highest degree, no, ruining ourselves, and shedding the innocent blood of simpler souls, which will be required at our hands.[22]

---

22   Gregory, *Or.* 2.46, NPNF-2, 7:214.

Christ called on us to be a light to the world and not place our light under a bushel. We should be strict with ourselves but gentle with others. But, as St. Gregory notes, we are responsible for the "innocent blood of simpler souls." We will answer for leading others astray because we sought to curry favor with people rather than speak the truth of God.

We can never condone immorality, but this does not mean that we must be preachy, combative, or antagonistic. We must simply say the truth and stand for it even if we have to endure social, personal, and financial consequences. We expect persecution for being Christ's followers and should rejoice if we are found worthy to suffer for His Name (Acts 5:41). God forbid that we choose to be among those who "love the praise of men more than the praise of God" (John 12:43). Christ will be ashamed of us, and we will be rejected by Him, just as we are ashamed of and rejected Him:

"For whoever is ashamed of me and my words in this adulterous and sinful generation, of him will the Son of man also be ashamed, when he comes in the glory of his Father with the holy angels." (Mark 8:38, Luke 9:26)

"Every one who acknowledges me before men, I also will acknowledge before my Father who is in heaven; but whoever denies me before men, I also will deny before my Father who is in heaven." (Matt. 10:32–33)

Christians are expected to be compassionate, and that expectation is used against us as a weapon. Compassion is misplaced if it results in the condoning of sin. We all have weaknesses that incline us toward certain sins. Whatever our personal weakness, we cannot excuse it by saying that we were "born that way" or, "That's just how I am." Such an attitude is antithetical to our Christian calling and the entire purpose of our lives. It is not enough to accept that Christ has paid for our sins and we are forgiven, as Protestants do, or that we simply need to die in a "state of grace," as Catholics believe. This is not the phronema of Orthodox Christianity at all.

We are not simply to accept that we have been forgiven our failings, sins, and shortcomings. The purpose of the Christian life is *transformation* by the power of the Holy Spirit, which begins with our baptism. We die to sin and rise with Christ, putting off the old and putting on the new. Countless people have overcome temptations and transformed lives of serious, entrenched sin through the power of Christ, the Physician of our souls and bodies. We remember and celebrate sinners who repented and changed their lives. Countless Christians through the centuries were able to overcome tremendous sins and completely change their lives and lifestyles through the power of the Holy Spirit. Our role is not to confront or correct others. However, it is possible to change from a life of sin to godliness, and it is not "compassionate" to encourage others to embrace or accept sin or to give in to temptation. In fact, in such a case, we will be held responsible for the sins of the other.

The ordinary believer is called to remain faithful and to speak and live according to the truth. The task of the theologian is more challenging, since the theologian's purpose is to address contemporary issues with honesty but also with discernment, in the proper way, at the proper time. He or she must truthfully but gently convey the love of God for all people at all times, but also the fact that God "desires all [people] to be saved and to come to the knowledge of the truth" (1 Tim. 2:4). The theologian must live in the world, being sensitive to the pain and struggles of people in the world, but without compromising the gospel. The sweetness of Christ and the transformative power of the Holy Spirit are what the world needs, not philosophical justifications for why a sin is not a sin.

The Danger of Theologizing While Unprepared or Unqualified

ONE WHO THEOLOGIZES UNPREPARED IS risking error, causing harm to others and to himself when he must answer to God for his folly. This shows pride, ambition, a lack of self-knowledge, and a lack of awareness of the danger of theologizing. Saint Gregory the Theologian warned against venturing into theology when one was not prepared or speaking on matters which are outside one's area of competency.

> Do you think teaching important? Yet learning carries no danger. Why do you make yourself a shepherd when you are a sheep? Why do you assume the role of head when it is your lot to be a foot? Why do you try to play the general when

you have been assigned to the ranks? Why do you go after the high but risky profits of the sea when you can, without hazard though with less gain, farm the land? If you are a man in Christ and your faculties have been trained by practice and the light of your knowledge is bright, seek to impart "the wisdom" that is "imparted among the mature" and that is "secret and hidden" (1 Cor. 2:6–7) and do so when you have reached the desired level and are so entrusted.[23]

Theologians who preach or teach beyond their ability or while unprepared cause harm to those who listen. Their information is incorrect, their words ring hollow to the listener, the grace of the Holy Spirit does not accompany them, and an opportunity for the spiritual improvement of the listener is lost. For such things the theologian is answerable to God. The theologian loses the opportunity to learn, to improve his or her own capacity or capability, and to exercise humility by declining to speak about that which he or she is not qualified or prepared to address.

The Danger of Hypocrisy

WE CAN BE KNOWLEDGEABLE CHRISTIANS and even expert theologians, but "purity of life is no benefit if one's doctrines are corrupt, just as, therefore, contrariwise, sound doctrines are no advantage if one's life is immoral."[24]

Christ frequently condemned the Pharisees of His day for hypocrisy. "The scribes and Pharisees sit on Moses' seat," He told His disciples. They had knowledge and authority, but "they preach, but do not practice" (Matt. 23:2–3). The Lord criticized them in a blistering attack for their hypocrisy, love of glory and honor, lack of care for the faithful, corruption, and creation of legal loopholes to avoid their obligations under the Law. Faith and knowledge of the Scriptures are not enough without good deeds and a pure heart. Our theology cannot be merely an intellectual exercise, or we too will be denounced as "whitewashed tombs," for it is not those who say "Lord, Lord" who will enter the Kingdom of heaven but those who do the will of God (Matt. 7:21). It

---

23 Gregory, *Or.* 32.13, FOTC, 107:200.
24 Chrysostom, *Homilies on John*, Homily 66, FOTC, 41:224.

is essential that we not only hear the word of God and speak it, but most of all, that we ourselves do it and keep it.

Saint Symeon the New Theologian describes "vain babble" (Matt. 6:7) or empty words as not simply useless words, but words that are not accompanied by action:

> And vain babble is not, as some might suppose, just unedifying talk. It also applies to talk which is unsupported by practice and the knowledge won from experience. If I do not despise the glory of this world and hold it in contempt with all my soul as injurious to the soul and as depriving me of heaven's glory, and then if I should teach others about the latter and encourage them to abstain from it, will not my words be vain and idle and empty? Shall I not be condemned as a liar? Again, if I do not receive the grace of the Spirit perceptibly and consciously, nor through Him become one who is taught by God, nor receive a word of wisdom and knowledge from on high, yet still set off shamelessly to interpret the God-inspired Scriptures and set myself up in the position of a teacher, plainly depending on false knowledge for this authority, will then God allow me to escape without examination and not demand an accounting from me? Certainly not![25]

The Danger of Scandalizing Others

WE CAN CAUSE SCANDAL BY our words but also by our lives. It is not uncommon among academics to write something extreme or outrageous just to get a reaction or to make a name for themselves. For the Orthodox theologian, this is irresponsible. Gregory the Theologian lamented pointless theological disputes that contributed to scandalizing the people and subjected the faith to ridicule:

> But at the present time there are some who go to war even about small matters and to no purpose, and, with great ignorance and audacity, accept, as an associate in their ill-doing, anyone whoever he may be. Then everyone makes the faith his pretext, and this venerable name is dragged into their private quarrels.

---

25 Symeon, *First Ethical Discourse* 12, *Ethical Discourses,* 1:79.

Consequently, as was probable, we are hated, even among the Gentiles [i.e., the pagans] and, what is harder still, we cannot say that this is without just cause. No, even the best of our own people are scandalized, while this result is not surprising in the case of the multitude, who are ill-disposed to accept anything that is good. Sinners are planning upon our backs; and what we devise against each other, they turn against us all: and we have become a new spectacle, not to angels and men, as says Paul, that bravest of athletes, in his contest with principalities and powers, but to almost all wicked men, and at every time and place, in the public squares, at carousals, at festivities, and times of sorrow. No, we have already—I can scarcely speak of it without tears—been represented on the stage, amid the laughter of the most licentious, and the most popular of all dialogues and scenes is the caricature of a Christian.[26]

The Danger of Judging Others

HYPOCRISY IS OFTEN ACCOMPANIED BY the sin of judging others. We readily choose to overlook our own shortcomings but easily condemn others for theirs. Judgmentalism, lack of love, and lack of pastoral concern for others are great dangers, especially for the theologian.

But what is truly lamentable is that perhaps even most of us do not ourselves realize the weight that every thought and word and deed carries with God; and not only with God but with the majority of men as well, who are slow to judge their own conduct but quick to scrutinize someone else's and would more easily excuse the greatest shortcomings in others than the most trifling in ourselves; and, the more ignorant they are, the more inclined to convict us of impiety than themselves of abject ignorance.[27]

Judging others while comparing ourselves favorably to them reveals self-serving hypocrisy and a lack of love that threaten our own salvation. Saint Gregory the Theologian laments this.

---

26   Gregory, *Or.* 2.83–84, NPNF-2, 7:221–222.
27   Gregory, *Or.* 32.14, FOTC, 107:201.

We observe each other's sins, not to bewail them, but to make them subjects of reproach, not to heal them, but to aggravate them, and excuse our own evil deeds by the wounds of our neighbors. Bad and good men are distinguished not according to personal character, but by their disagreement or friendship with ourselves. We praise one day what we revile the next, denunciation at the hands of others is a passport to our admiration; so magnanimous are we in our viciousness, that everything is frankly forgiven to impiety.[28]

We cannot judge our fellow human beings, since we are all made in the image and likeness of God. The theologian's knowledge of the faith makes him or her more susceptible to this sin since it is all too easy to fall into the trap of rendering judgment on another. If we know better than most what is correct or not correct, we ought to unflinchingly apply the standard to ourselves:

Cutting down a tree or the brief bloom of a flower is not the same thing as cutting down a human being. You are an image of God, your interlocutor is an image of God, and you who pass judgment are yourself being judged (Matt. 7:1); and the one on whom you are passing judgment is the servant of another (Rom. 14:4) and under another's charge.[29]

The Danger of God's Judgment

WHAT WE DO AND SAY affects others, especially the words and deeds of clergy and theologians. Because of our responsibility, the sacredness of the task, and our greater knowledge, we will be judged by God much more strictly. A higher standard is set for the theologian. "Let not many of you become teachers, my brethren, for you know that we who teach shall be judged with greater strictness" (James 3:1).

In one of the silent prayers of the Divine Liturgy, the celebrant prays for "our *sins* and the *failings* of the people." This distinction between the sins of the

---

28   Gregory, *Or.* 2.80, NPNF-2, 7:221.
29   Gregory, *Or.* 32.30, FOTC, 107:212–13.

Clergy and the failings of the people does not of course signify haughtiness. It specifically refers to the words of Christ that "he who knows much will be beaten with many stripes" (Luke 12:47).[30]

The words of the priest indicate that his transgressions are more serious than those of the laity. The same could be said of the theologian. The theologian is the "mouthpiece of God," an awesome responsibility that requires constant awareness of our personal future judgment. It is precisely because the theologian acts as the servant of God, bringing the message of salvation to the people of God, that he or she will be judged more severely.

Bearing in mind the future judgment, we must realize that virtue comes first and is more important than theologizing. Saint Symeon the New Theologian cautions:

Watch that you do not play the shepherd before you have acquired the Good Shepherd as a true friend, since otherwise, you will gain nothing other— be sure of it!—than having to give an account to God not only for your own unworthiness, but as well as the lambs whom you will have lost as a result of your inexperience and passions.[31]

---

30 Harkianakis, "Theologian in Modern Society," 124. Emphasis in the original.
31 Symeon, *First Ethical Discourse* 12, *Ethical Discourses*, 1:78.

Jesus Christ and Orthodox Phronema

O UR PHRONEMA IS OUR MINDSET, but mental attitude can never be separated from behavior. Our phronema is revealed by our manner of life. Conversely, the way we choose to live shapes and reinforces our phronema.

The Gospel of John begins by describing the Son of God with the word *Logos*. "In the beginning was the Logos," or "Word."[1] John's choice of Logos to describe the eternal Son of God is powerful and profound. *Logos* in the Greek language means so much more than simply "word." It also stands for speech, thought, reason, logic, reckoning, explanation, narrative, sermon, verbal expression, subject, cause, and order. It was the word the ancient Greeks used to express the unknown dynamism that ordered and sustained the universe.

By choosing the multifaceted word *Logos*, the Evangelist expressed that Jesus Christ reveals the Person and mind of God the Father. He is the cause and order of creation, the source of life and all that exists. He is the fount of all truth, reason, and thought. Saint John succinctly articulated the purpose of the Incarnation of Christ: to make God known to us, to mediate to us the eternal, omnipotent, uncircumscribed, uncontainable, invisible, ineffable,

---

1   The importance of this passage in Orthodox Christianity is shown in the fact that we read this Gospel at the Divine Liturgy of Pascha as we celebrate the Feast of Feasts, the Resurrection of our Lord Jesus Christ. Our lectionary cycle begins with this Gospel reading, revealing its preeminent theological importance.

inexpressible, inconceivable, incomprehensible God. Jesus identified Himself by using the divine name: I AM. It is not the "name" of God in the usual human sense but a profound expression of what God, beyond all human comprehension or expression, truly is.

Because God is Life and Being Itself, an intimate relationship with God is not only possible; it is our calling. In fact, we were created for that singular purpose: to have a relationship and eternal life with God. This is not simply a future goal but a process that begins in this life and can even be experienced in this life. The Kingdom of God is present here and now, but the extent to which we participate in the life of the All-Holy Trinity depends on us.

But how could we ever relate to God or, even more challenging, truly unite with Him? Of all religions, only Orthodox theology emphasizes union with God—in a real and actual sense—as the goal and purpose of all human life. We rarely speak of "going to heaven," as though it were a destination. We do not speak of experiencing a "beatific vision" of God, as though God could be viewed but remained at some distance from us. Rather, Orthodox Christianity speaks of theosis, the divinization of the human person. We expect, hope, and strive for actual union with the perfect, infinite, eternal, omnipresent, and changeless God. But we are flawed, limited, and come into existence for a brief time; we are confined to one place at one time, and we are constantly changing. So how is union with God possible? The Incarnation, the enfleshment of the Son of God, gave us the ability to truly connect to God and become united with Him, transformed and illumined by Him, not simply because He *died* for us but because of the way He *lived* among us.

The apostles did not study theories, formulas, or theological methods. They experienced the Incarnate Son of God—God Himself, since the Son is fully God. They observed His phronema, and they learned to live it themselves. The uniqueness of Orthodox Christianity is its emphasis on a complete integration of mind and behavior in the same manner that was known and lived in the early Church. This is not something new to us. We did not rediscover something that had been lost. We never needed to correct what was missing by experiencing a reformation. We did not recently come to this understanding or adopt these prayers, practices, or lifestyle by trying to recreate the early Church through study of the Scriptures. We have always lived and believed this way because we have preserved the way of life and way of thought of the apostles—their phronema. They passionately preserved the teachings of Christ, and we passionately preserve what they taught us. This is not merely a set of ideas, beliefs, concepts, or doctrines about Christ, but an actual means of acquiring the mind of Christ and achieving the inner transformation to which we all aspire.

Orthodox Christians follow in the footsteps of millions of Orthodox Christians who came before us, especially the attitude and lifestyle of the saints, because they achieved holiness. In order to follow their path to the Kingdom of heaven, we do as they do, and we aspire to think as they thought. This is why the saints are important and cherished. This is why the ancient prayers and divine services are important—they express the apostolic faith and phronema. This is why the Scriptures are important—they express the mind of the ancient Church. The Fathers of the Church provide us with the proper and ancient understanding of those Scriptures. For this reason, the sacraments are important, and not only the Holy Mysteries. Everything we do in the Church, everything we receive in the Church, is imbued with the grace of the Holy Spirit, who activates the life in Christ, not only impelling us forward toward our goal but beginning the process of spiritual healing and transformation here and now in this life.

Salvation requires tremendous effort on our part. Christ did His part and opened the gates of Paradise to us by His death and Resurrection. But He spoke about the "narrow gate" and warned us that the path would be difficult, and few would find it (Matt. 7:13). He cautioned us through the parable of the sower that most of the seeds sown would not produce a harvest (Matt. 13:1–23; Mark 4:3–20; Luke 8:5–15). We cannot be complacent. It is not enough to simply accept that Jesus saved us and dedicate ourselves to Him. There are no "merits" to acquire, no extra grace from Mary, Jesus, or the saints that we can appropriate for ourselves. We never believe we can earn our salvation, and yet we are solely responsible for our individual salvation. God has already done everything necessary for our salvation and "desires all men to be saved and to come to the knowledge of the truth" (1 Tim. 2:4).

Western Christianity has a wide variety of spiritual practices and traditions, many of them ancient and beautiful. However, Orthodoxy is distinctive in its persistent emphasis on the image of God within each of us. All of us carry the indelible image of God, which is our potential to become godlike. However, it is our responsibility to acquire God's likeness by the help of the grace of God, by responding to that grace and exerting our own efforts. As Christ is the icon of the Father (Col. 1:15), we are all called to become icons of Christ. We are invited to imitate Him—not simply to believe in Him or learn about Him, but to become like Him, to imitate His phronema. He said, "I am the way, and the truth, and the life" (John 14:6). He showed us the Way, taught us the Truth, and gave us Life. He is our example in every aspect of our lives. He spoke to us about God the Father and the Holy Spirit and conveyed God to us in a myriad of ways during His earthly ministry, including in unspoken ways by His entire demeanor—His phronema.

The life of the Lord provides a model for our behavior in general and also for the way we ought to teach and talk about God. All of us who identify ourselves as Christians ought to convey Christ to others by our words and behavior. What can we learn about the Lord's phronema from the Gospels?

We might begin by noting that His teachings were not a radical departure from that which had come before. His teachings were the fulfillment of the Mosaic Law's intent and purpose: to lead the people of a holy God to personal holiness. He promoted inner righteousness and true virtue, not legalistic, ritual cleanliness, since "the pure in heart . . . shall see God" (Matt. 5:8). His teachings were rooted in Judaism, but they were fresh, forceful, lively, true, and relevant to the people of His day. He taught using familiar forms and methods: parables, similes, antitheses, rabbinic argumentation, proverbs, blessings and woes. He used classic biblical images: the shepherd, the vineyard, the fig tree, weddings, banquets. He related His teachings to daily life: fishing, with its boats and nets; pastures with sheep and goats; farming with its sowing, reaping, and harvest; and housework, with its mending, grinding, sweeping, and measuring flour. He used examples of people in various walks of life and in a variety of relationships: kings and soldiers, merchants and householders, landlords and tenant farmers, scribes and day laborers, judges and litigants, fathers and children, masters and servants, tax collectors, bankers and borrowers. He used images of daily life because sanctification is possible by actively conforming ourselves to Christ in countless ways in our daily lives.

He called on us to study the Scriptures. "Search the Scriptures" (John 5:39), for they bear witness to Christ. He opened the minds of the apostles to understand the Scriptures (Luke 24:45). The Lord quoted and interpreted the Scriptures Himself, introducing them with the phrase, "Have you not read," or "It is written." "Have you not read what was said to you by God . . . ?" (Matt. 22:31). "Have you not read what David did, when he was hungry . . . ?" (Matt. 12:3). "Have you never read in the scriptures: 'The very stone which the build-ers rejected . . .'" (Matt. 21:42). Or He expressed His judgment in the form of a Scripture quotation: "Go and learn what this means, 'I desire mercy not sacrifice'" (Hos. 6:6/Matt. 9:13), or "Well did Isaiah prophesy of you when he said . . ." (Matt. 15:7, quoting Is. 29:13). The apostles received and preserved those interpretations and others, and the Orthodox Church in turn has pre-served that precious repository of faith that is expressed in our doctrines and daily lives.

The Lord rejected human interpretations and rationalizations that were designed to dilute the Scriptures and evade the will of God. He condemned the Pharisees for creating legal technicalities to circumvent oaths and avoid moral responsibilities (Matt. 23:16, 18). He did not employ rationalistic argu-ments but spoke of repentance, humility, prayer, fasting, mercy, alms, and forgiveness. Christ is our model because He did not conform to human or societal ideas but conveyed the truth from above. His message revealed that spiritual reality is not aligned with human perception and that God's princi-ples are not based on the values or mentality of this world. His teaching was replete with mystery and paradox: "Whoever would save his life will lose it; and whoever loses his life for my sake, he will save it" (Luke 9:24). His words contradicted and confounded human logic: "Whoever would be first among you must be slave of all" (Mark 10:44).

Jesus Christ is the ultimate paradigm of our Christian phronema. What we learn from Him is not limited to His words, either the content of His teaching or its application. Equally important are the purpose and spirit with which He spoke and acted. His words were pure, lacking guile, self-interest, or hypocrisy. The ministry of Christ often perturbed the powerful and influential of Jewish society. He had no desire to impress His hearers and made no effort to flat-ter anyone or gain social, professional, or political advantage by His words or actions. He did not present His own personal opinion or theorize about hypothetical matters. He was completely devoted to doing the will of the Father and taught with complete obedience to the Father (John 4:34; 5:30; 6:38–39).

Clearly, Christ's teaching was not based on human traditions, human wisdom, human authority, or the interpretations of the famous rabbis who had preceded Him. Jesus presented Himself as the source of authority. As God Himself, the Son of Man is Lord of the Sabbath, has authority over the Law of Moses, and even has authority to forgive sins. This was revolutionary, scandalizing, even blasphemous to the Jewish leaders who questioned His claims. "By what authority do you do these things?" they asked (Luke 20:2).

But His teaching thrilled and amazed the crowds, who marveled at the "gracious words which proceeded out of His mouth" (Luke 4:22). The Gospels frequently refer to the amazement of the crowds at His teaching (Mark 1:27). People "marveled at Him" (Luke 11:14), and the crowds were "astonished at His teaching, for his word was with authority" (Luke 4:32). The Lord even amazed His enemies, who were bewildered by His wisdom because they regarded Him as uneducated. "How is it that this man has learning, when He has never studied?" (John 7:15). His extraordinary and unexpected responses often left His opponents speechless: "Render therefore to Caesar the things that are Caesar's, and to God the things that are God's" (Matt. 22:21). When temple guards were sent to arrest Him, they returned to the Jewish leaders without Him. The authorities were frustrated and exasperated. "Why did you not arrest Him?!" The captain of the temple guards simply answered, "No one ever spoke like this man!" (John 7:46).

His statements were amazing but not a complete departure from Judaism; otherwise His teaching would not have been received by the crowds. His words resonated with the people, who recognized not only their truth, but a depth and power whose source could only be divine Wisdom. Likewise, when Orthodox Christians speak the truth faithfully according to our phronema, it is not uncommon for non-Orthodox to react with surprise and astonishment, because our explanation, statement, or interpretation can be strikingly different from the response offered by the secular world or Western Christianity.

In His many encounters and challenges by His antagonists, Jesus displayed His discernment and presented many wonderful examples for us to imitate in our daily lives. When Christ was asked a question, He responded, but He was not disputatious, nor did He initiate debates. He refused to answer a question if He knew the answer would not be received or the questioner had an ulterior motive (John 10:24–25; Luke 22:67). He recognized flattery and insincerity and rebuffed them. He would not become involved in worldly affairs; for example, He refused to settle a dispute over money (Luke 12:13–14).

Jesus never sought to prove or justify Himself, even when He was slandered, but sought only the spiritual benefit of His hearers. If He was not welcomed or received when traveling, He simply went elsewhere (Luke 8:37; 9:53–55), and He instructed His disciples to do the same (Matt. 10:14; Luke 9:5; 10:10–11). He did not seek His own glory but that of His Father. He said and did nothing out of self-interest. He considered the occasion and the audience. When He performed an action that He knew would not be understood at that moment, He gave the lesson by His example alone, without explanation: "What I am doing you do not know now, but afterward you will understand" (John 13:7). When the lesson required instruction with words that could not be received or understood at the moment, He did not speak at that time but waited until the proper time: "I have yet many things to say to you, but you cannot bear them now" (John 16:12).

The Lord adapted His lesson to His audience. He was gentle but also truthful. He spoke with genuine and divine love. He did not shrink from offending others when it was necessary for their salvation; He came "not to be served but to serve" (Mark 10:45). Everything He said and did was for the sake of the other, whether it was a mild explanation to the Pharisees about divorce ("For your hardness of heart Moses allowed you to divorce" [Matt. 19:8]), a correction to the Sadducees about the Resurrection ("You are wrong [because] you know neither the scriptures nor the power of God" [Mark 12:24]), a strong rebuke to a disciple ("Get behind me, Satan!" [Matt. 16:23]), or an outright condemnation ("Woe to you, scribes and Pharisees, hypocrites!" [Matt. 23:13–29]).

The phronema of the Lord was not appreciated or respected by the most important and influential Jewish leaders of His day. He had many followers among the Pharisees and elders, although often they kept their belief secret (John 12:42). Those who responded to Him openly and enthusiastically were usually the simple, the uneducated, the powerless, the lowly, children at heart who "had ears to hear," those who were willing to truly see and truly hear. The wise and learned often did not recognize the Messiah, but in their simplicity the ordinary folk realized the prophetic fulfillment taking place in their presence. This aspect of the Lord's phronema is yet another lesson for us: we should not expect the acceptance or admiration of most people, certainly not of those who are steeped in the values of this world. Rather, if we are being faithful, we should expect to suffer for Him; we should anticipate persecution, rejection, criticism, and slanders to be spoken against us falsely (Matt. 5:11).

Christ was not a revolutionary and did not set out to disrupt the established order of Roman society or of Judaism. When He healed a leper, He advised the leper to follow the proper procedure for being readmitted to society: "Go and show yourself to the priest" (Luke 5:14). He even advised His disciples to respect the teachings of His worst critics: "The scribes and the Pharisees sit on Moses' seat; so practice and observe whatever they tell you, but not what they do; for they preach, but do not practice" (Matt. 23:2–3). He made sure He paid the temple tax so as not to give offense, even though He believed He was not subject to the tax (Matt. 17:27).

What does this teach us about Christ's phronema and how we ought to behave? We should not instigate controversy and should beware of taking a stance against something as a matter of principle, convinced by our own self-righteousness. We should avoid becoming unnecessarily disruptive or championing a campaign simply because we do not personally agree with a practice, or we believe it is incorrect. At times action is required and a line must be drawn, but knowing when we ought to act requires discernment; we must never act from the wrong motives. Let us at least remember that Jesus was not a rabble-rouser nor motivated by ego.

He was, nonetheless, a sensation. People sought Him constantly, and He turned no one away, even when He was exhausted and needed to retreat from the large crowds to rest and pray. The evangelist Mark describes the massive crowds who came from all parts of the region, crowds so large that the Lord was often forced to sit in a boat offshore to preach in order to avoid being crushed (Mark 3:7–10). He healed all their sick, infirm, disabled, and demon possessed, and still the crowd would not leave Him. They hung on His every word and did not want to depart from His presence. He even provided them with food when they followed Him out into the wilderness (Matt. 14:13–21), and on at least one occasion the crowd followed Him for three days (Matt. 15:32). He could escape them only by sailing off in a boat or by going up into the hills to pray. Even then, they often waited for hours for Him to come down from the mountain (John 6:22).

Jesus was Love Incarnate. This aspect of His phronema jumps off the pages of the Gospels. He loved the people. They knew it, felt it, and responded to His love. He did not show His love by seeking to make them feel good about themselves. Rather, He challenged people to repent, not simply to return to their lives as they were before they met Him. "Go, and sin no more," He said (John 5:14; 8:11). He challenged His listeners to acquire true righteousness. "It was said to men of old, 'You shall not (commit adultery, kill, swear, take revenge), . . . but *I* say to you . . ." (Matt. 5:21–48). He encouraged the ordinary man and woman to realize that they were capable of a righteousness exceeding that of the Pharisees, who were widely considered the paradigms of Jewish virtue (Matt. 5:20).

Christ called all people to repentance and inspired them with the possibility of salvation, regardless of their circumstances—even if they were poor, uneducated, lowly, the worst sinners, Gentiles, or unable to fulfill all the technicalities of the Law of Moses. The Lord welcomed all to be His disciples—including women, something unheard of in Judaism—and even praised them for sitting and learning (Luke 10:42). Everyone who displayed faith and humility was commended as a good example, regardless of whether he or she was an anonymous Canaanite woman, a notorious tax collector, a Samaritan cured of leprosy, or a Roman centurion. Through the acquisition of virtues such as humility, faith, love, and mercy, everyone could have a seat at the banquet in the Kingdom of heaven (Matt. 8:11). How do we find a seat at that banquet? By acquiring the right phronema, acquiring virtue, and modeling our behavior after His.

The life of Jesus Christ was the most extraordinary example of a human life in the history of the world. But most amazing is that His humility was His chief characteristic. The humility of Christ, demonstrated especially on the cross, cannot be appreciated by those who do not understand its power and who reject the cross as weakness or failure. By rejecting humility, we fail to recognize the power or purpose of the cross. Saint Paul explained that the cross is a paradox and does not conform to the thinking of the world. In fact, the cross is a "scandal" or "foolishness" to those who do not believe (1 Cor. 1:23). "God chose the foolish things of the world to shame the wise" and "the weak things of this world to shame the strong" (1 Cor. 1:27 [NIV]). The cross is the power of God and the glory of God precisely because it contradicts the assumptions of our rational thought. Christ's accomplishment through the cross is contrary to human reasoning: life comes from death, victory comes from defeat, exaltation comes from humiliation. The cross is powerful because it confounds human wisdom. That is why the theology of the Church is not based on deductive human reasoning, as St. Paul explained, "lest the cross of Christ be emptied of its power" (1 Cor. 1:17).

The Lord gave us countless examples of His sublime humility and His phronema. From the moment of His conception, the pattern of humble service was in place. He "did not account equality with God a thing to be grasped, but emptied himself, taking the form of a servant" (Phil. 2:7). He accepted our human nature with all its challenges, difficulties, temptations, struggles, pain, and sorrows. He humbled Himself to accept baptism by the hand of His creature that He "might fulfil all righteousness" (Matt. 3:15). When tempted and challenged by Satan, "*If* you are the Son of God . . ." (Matt. 4:3, 6; Luke 4:3, 9), He responded but did not seek to prove Himself or make a display of His abilities. When challenged by the Pharisees to perform a "sign," a miracle, to prove His authority, He ignored their demand, replying that "an evil and adulterous generation seeks for a sign" (Matt. 12:38–39; 16:1–4). Even on the cross He was taunted to prove Himself: "Let Him come down now from the cross, and we will believe in Him" (Matt. 27:42), and yet He still exercised restraint.

Christ gave us the greatest example of true Christian phronema in His humility, His complete obedience to God, His refusal to make a display, to prove Himself or justify Himself, His tremendous restraint and discernment in His numerous encounters with various individuals, and in His wisdom, unselfishness, and love. We are called not simply to admire Him but to imitate Him to the fullest extent possible.

The Word became flesh to teach us who God is and what we are called to become. He is the One who established our phronema and taught it to His disciples, both by His words and by His behavior. Orthodox Christians are called not only to form a relationship with Christ the Logos, but to imitate Him. We are all called not only to hear the Word of God but to do it, not only to believe or intellectually assent to ideas but to act. "My mother and my brothers are those who hear the word of God and do it" (Luke 8:21). "Blessed rather are those who hear the word of God and keep it!" (Luke 11:28). The Church gives us countless tools—the discipline, prayers, services, Holy Mysteries—and wonderful examples and advice—the lives of the saints, the writings of the Fathers—on how to actualize the grace of the Holy Spirit in our lives and to conform ourselves to the image of God within us.

As we ponder the life of Christ and His example in all things, let us remember not merely the grace-filled, eloquent, and effective words of Jesus Christ but His entire demeanor and way of life. During the years He spent with the apostles, He formed them, shaped them, and guided them. He taught them not only what to believe but how to behave, primarily through His example. They observed Him constantly. They absorbed His phronema, and this is the basis of Tradition, that which became the foundation of the Church. This is what Orthodox Christianity preserved, and this is not only what we believe and think, but the way we live daily as expressed in our countless actions, great and small. Orthodox phronema is integrated into an entire way of life that both expresses and confirms our phronema. All religious systems have a way of life and a phronema. But only Orthodox Christianity has faithfully preserved the true phronema of the ancient Church, a visible and consistent way of life and manner of thought unbroken and unchanged from the time of the apostles.

May we all behave as theologians in the truest sense, speaking of God to others by both our words and our manner of life. Having "put on Christ" (Gal. 3:27), let us adopt the phronema of Christ and the apostles and authentically represent the Lord Jesus Christ through our way of life to all those whom we encounter.

To God be the glory.

355

Bibliography

Primary Sources

Athanasius the Great
"Letters to Serapion on the Holy Spirit." *The Letters of St. Athanasius Concerning the Holy Spirit*. Translated by C. R. B. Shapland. London: Epworth Press, 1951.

Life of Antony and Letter to Marcellinus. Translated by Robert Gregg. New York: Paulist Press, 1980.

Augustine of Hippo
Admonition and Grace. Saint Augustine: Christian Instruction, Admonition and Grace, . . . Vol. 2. Translated by John Courtney Murray. Fathers of the Church. New York: Fathers of the Church, 1947.

On the Holy Trinity, Doctrinal Treatises, Moral Treatises. Nicene and Post-Nicene Fathers of the Church, 1st series, vol. 3. Translated by Arthur West Hadden. Edited by Philip Schaff. Grand Rapids, MI: William B. Eerdmans, 1887.

Basil the Great
Basil: Letters and Select Works. Nicene and Post-Nicene Fathers, series 2, vol. 8. Translated by Blomfield Jackson. Edited by Philip Schaff and Henry Wace. Grand Rapids, MI: William B. Eerdmans, 1894.

On the Holy Spirit: St. Basil the Great. Popular Patristics, vol. 42. Translated by David Anderson. Crestwood, NY: St. Vladimir's Seminary Press, 1980.

St. Basil the Great: On Christian Doctrine and Practice. Popular Patristics, vol. 47. Translated by Mark DelCogliano. Crestwood, NY: St. Vladimir's Seminary Press, 2012.

Cyprian of Carthage
Hippolytus, Cyprian, Caius, Novatian, Appendix: Fathers of the Third Century. Ante-Nicene Fathers, vol. 5. Edited by Alexander Roberts and James Donaldson. Grand Rapids, MI: William B. Eerdmans, 1985.

Cyril of Alexandria
Commentary on John. 2 vols. Ancient Christian Texts. Translated by David Maxwell. Edited by Joel Elowsky. Downer's Grove, IL: IVP Academic, 2015.

Documents of the Christian Church
Documents of the Christian Church. Edited by Henry Bettenson and Chris Maunder. 4th ed. Oxford: Oxford University Press, 2011.

Eusebius of Caesarea
Eusebius: Church History, Life of Constantine, Oration in Praise of Constantine. Nicene and Post-Nicene Fathers, series 2, vol. 1. Translated by Arthur Cushman McGiffert. Edited by Philip Schaff and Henry Wace. Grand Rapids, MI: William B. Eerdmans, 1890.

Gregory Palamas
Saint Gregory Palamas: The Homilies. Translated, edited, and notes by Christopher Veniamin. Waymart, PA: Mt. Thabor Publishing, 2009.

Gregory the Theologian
Cyril of Jerusalem, Gregory Nazianzen. Nicene and Post-Nicene Fathers, 2nd series, vol. 7. Translated by Charles Gordon Browne and James Edward Swallow. Edited by Philip Schaff and Henry Wace. Grand Rapids, MI: William B. Eerdmans, 1893.

Faith Gives Fullness to Reasoning: The Five Theological Orations of Gregory Nazianzen. Translated by Lionel Wickham and Frederick Williams. Edited by Frederick Norris. Leiden, Netherlands: Brill, 1991.

Funeral Orations by St. Gregory Nazianzen and St. Ambrose. Fathers of the Church, vol. 22. Translated by Leo McCauley. Edited by Roy DeFerrari. Washington, DC: Catholic University of America Press, 1953.

On God and Christ: The Five Theological Orations and Two Letters to Cledonius. Popular Patristics, no. 23. Translated by Lionel Wickham and Frederick Williams. Crestwood, NY: St. Vladimir's Seminary Press, 2002.

Saint Gregory of Nazianzus: Festal Orations. Popular Patristics, vol. 36. Translated by Nonna Verna Harrison. Crestwood, NY: St. Vladimir's Seminary Press, 2008.

St. Gregory of Nazianzus: Select Orations. Fathers of the Church, vol. 107. Translated by Martha Vinson. Washington, DC: Catholic University of America Press, 2003.

Irenaeus of Lyons
The Apostolic Fathers: Justin Martyr, Irenaeus. Ante-Nicene Fathers, vol. 1. Edited by Alexander Roberts and James Donaldson. Grand Rapids, MI: William B. Eerdmans, 1885.

Jerome
Jerome: Letters and Selected Works. Nicene and Post-Nicene Fathers, 2nd series, vol. 6. Translated by W. H. Fremantle. Edited by Philip Schaff and Henry Wace. Grand Rapids, MI: William B. Eerdmans, 1892.

John Chrysostom

Commentary on St. John, the Apostle and Evangelist. 2 vols. Fathers of the Church, vols. 33 and 41. Translated by Sr. Thomas Aquinas Goggin. Washington, DC: Catholic University of America Press, 1957 and 1959.

St. Chrysostom: Homilies of the Acts of the Apostles and the Epistle to the Romans. Nicene and Post-Nicene Fathers, 1st series, vol. 11. Translated by J. Walker, J. Sheppard, and H. Brown. Edited by Philip Schaff. Grand Rapids, MI: William B. Eerdmans, 1889.

Saint Chrysostom: Homilies on the Epistles of Paul to the Corinthians. Nicene and Post-Nicene Fathers, 1st series, vol. 12. Translated by Talbot Chambers. Edited by Philip Schaff. Grand Rapids, MI: William B. Eerdmans, 1889.

St. Chrysostom: Homilies on Galatians, Ephesians, Philippians, . . . Nicene and Post-Nicene Fathers, 1st series, vol. 13. Translated by John Broadus. Edited by Philip Schaff. Grand Rapids, MI: William B. Eerdmans, 1889.

St. John Chrysostom: Homilies on Genesis. 3 vols. Fathers of the Church, vols. 74, 82, and 87. Translated by Robert Hill. Washington, DC: Catholic University of America Press, 1986, 1990, and 1992.

St. John Chrysostom: Homilies on Hannah, David and Saul. St. John Chrysostom Old Testament Homilies, vol. 1. Translated by Robert Hill. Brookline, MA: Holy Cross Greek Orthodox Press, 2003.

St. John Chrysostom: Homilies on Isaiah and Jeremiah. St. John Chrysostom Old Testament Homilies, vol. 2. Translated by Robert Hill. Brookline, MA: Holy Cross Greek Orthodox Press, 2003.

John of Kronstadt

Father John of Kronstadt. Spiritual Counsels: Select Passages from My Life in Christ. Edited by W. Jardine Grisbrooke. Crestwood, NY: St. Vladimir's Seminary Press, 1981. First published 1967 by James Clarke (Cambridge).

Maximos the Confessor

Four Hundred Chapters on Love. Maximus Confessor: Selected Writings. Classics of Western Spirituality. Translated by George C. Berthold. New York: Paulist Press, 1985.

On Difficulties in the Church Fathers: The Ambigua. 2 vols. Dumbarton Oaks Medieval Library, vols. 28 and 29. Edited and translated by Nicholas Constas. Cambridge, MA: Harvard University Press, 2014.

Nicodemus of the Holy Mountain

Unseen Warfare as Edited by Nicodemus of the Holy Mountain and Revised by Theophan the Recluse. Translated by E. Kadloubovsky and G.E.H. Palmer. Crestwood, NY: St. Vladimir's Seminary Press, 1978.

Paisios

Spiritual Counsels of Elder Paisios. Vol. 2, *Spiritual Awakening.* 5 vols. Translated by Peter
Chamberas. Edited by Anna Famelios. Thessalonika: Holy Monastery of the Evangelist John the Theologian, 2008.

The Philokalia

Philokalia: The Complete Text. 3 vols. Translated and edited by G.E.H. Palmer, Philip Sherrard, and Kallistos Ware. London: Faber and Faber, 1979.

The Rudder

The Rudder. Translated by D. Cummings. Chicago: Orthodox Christian Educational Society,
1957.

Symeon the New Theologian

St. Symeon the New Theologian: On the Mystical Life, The Ethical Discourses. 3 vols. Popular
Patristics. Translated by Alexander Golitzin. Crestwood, NY: St. Vladimir's Seminary
Press, 1995.

Symeon the New Theologian: The Discourses. Classics of Western Spirituality. Translated by C.
J. DeCatanzaro. New York: Paulist Press, 1980.

Secondary Sources

Aghiorgoussis, Maximos. *In the Image of God.* Brookline, MA: Holy Cross Orthodox Press,
1999.

Agourides, Savas. "The Social Character of Orthodoxy." In *The Orthodox Ethos.* Edited by
A. J. Philippou. Oxford: Holywell Press, 1964.

———. "Teaching Scriptures." Academic paper presented at the Second Consultation of
Orthodox Theological Schools, New York, 1982, 1–10.

Alfeyev, Metropolitan Hilarion. *Doctrine and Teaching of the Orthodox Church.* Vol. 2 of
Orthodox Christianity. 5 vols. Translated by Andrew Smith. Crestwood, NY: St. Vladimir's Seminary Press, 2012.

Bebis, George. "The Concept of Tradition in the Fathers of the Church." *Greek Orthodox
Theological Review* 15, no. 1 (Spring 1970): 22–55.

Beeley, Christopher. *Gregory of Nazianzus on the Trinity and Knowledge of God: In Your Light
We Shall See Light.* Oxford Studies in Historical Theology. Oxford: Oxford University
Press, 2008.

Bettenson, Henry, and Chris Maunder, eds. *Documents of the Christian Church.* 4th ed.
Oxford: Oxford University Press.

Bouteneff, Peter. *Sweeter Than Honey: Orthodox Thinking on Dogma and Truth*. Crestwood, NY: St. Vladimir's Seminary Press, 2006.

Bowyer, Archimandrite Sergius. *Acquiring the Mind of Christ: Embracing the Vision of the Orthodox Church*. Waymart, PA: St. Tikhon's Monastery Press, 2015.

Bratsiotis, Panagiotis. "The Fundamental Principles and Main Characteristics of the Orthodox Church." In *The Orthodox Ethos*, edited by A. J. Philippou. Oxford: Holywell Press, 1964.

Breck, John. *The Power of the Word: In the Worshiping Church*. Crestwood, NY: St. Vladimir's Seminary Press, 1986.

———. *Scripture in Tradition: The Bible and Its Interpretation in the Orthodox Church*. Crestwood, NY: St. Vladimir's Seminary Press, 2001.

Bush, William. *The Mystery of the Church*. Salisbury, MA: Regina Orthodox Press, 1999.

Casiday, Augustine. "Church Fathers and the Shaping of Orthodox Theology." In *The Cambridge Companion to Orthodox Christian Theology*, edited by Mary B. Cunningham and Elizabeth Theokritoff. Cambridge: Cambridge University Press, 2008.

———. *The Orthodox Christian World*. Routledge Worlds. Edited by Augustine Casiday. New York: Routledge, 2012.

Cassin, Barbara, Emily Apter, Jacques Lezra, and Michael Wood, eds. *Dictionary of Untranslatables: A Philosophical Lexicon*. Translated by Steven Rendall. Princeton: Princeton University Press, 2014.

Catechism of the Catholic Church. New York: Doubleday, 1994.

Cavarnos, Constantine. *Saint Cosmas Aitolos: Great Missionary, Awakener, Illuminator, and Holy Martyr of Greece*. Modern Orthodox Saints, vol. 1. Belmont, MA: Institute for Byzantine and Modern Greek Studies, 1985.

Chrestou, Panagiotis K. *Greek Orthodox Patrology*. Edited and Translated by George Dion Dragas. Rollinsford, NH: Orthodox Research Institute, 2005.

Chrysostomos, Archimandrite, Hieromonk Ambrosios, Alexey Young, and Vladimir Derugin. *Themes in Orthodox Patristic Psychology: Humility, Obedience, Repentance, and Love by Archbishop of Etna Chrysostomos*. Etna, CA: Center for Traditionalist Orthodox Studies, 1984.

Chryssavgis, John. *The Way of the Fathers: Exploring the Patristic Mind*. Minneapolis, MN: Light & Life, 2003.

Clendenin, Daniel B., ed. *Eastern Orthodox Theology: A Contemporary Reader*. Grand Rapids, MI: Baker Academic, 2003.

Daley, Brian. *Gregory of Nazianzus*. The Early Church Fathers. New York: Routledge, 2006.

Demacopoulos, George, and Aristotle Papanikolaou, eds. *Orthodox Constructions of the West*. Orthodox Christianity & Contemporary Thought. New York: Fordham University Press, 2013.

———. "Orthodox Naming of the Other: A Post-Colonial Approach." In *Orthodox Constructions of the West*. New York: Fordham University Press, 2013.

Dvornik, Francis. *The Photian Schism: History and Legend.* Cambridge: Cambridge University Press, 1948.

Efstathiou, Niko. "Islamic Educational Center Planned Next to Halki Seminary." *Ekathimerini,* September 24, 2018.

Every, George. *Misunderstandings Between East and West.* Richmond: John Knox Press, 1966.

Florensky, Pavel. *The Pillar and Ground of the Truth: An Essay in Orthodox Theodicy and Twelve Letters.* Translated by Jakim Boris. Princeton: Princeton University Press, 1997.

Florovsky, Georges. *Aspects of Church History.* Vol. 4 in *The Collected Works of Georges Florovsky.* Edited by Richard Haugh. Vaduz, Liechtenstein: Büchervertriebsanstalt, 1987.

———. "Basic Features of Theology in the Fourth Century." *Eastern Fathers of the Fourth Century.* Vol. 7 in *The Collected Works of Georges Florovsky.* Translated by Catherine Edmunds. Edited by Richard Haugh. Vaduz: Büchervertriebsanstalt, 1987.

———. *Bible, Church, and Tradition: An Eastern Orthodox View.* Vol. 1 in *The Collected Works of Georges Florovsky.* Edited by Richard Haugh. Vaduz, Liechtenstein: Büchervertriebsanstalt, 1987.

———. "The Function of Tradition in the Ancient Church." In *Eastern Orthodox Theology: A Contemporary Reader.* 2nd ed. Edited by Daniel Clendenin. Grand Rapids, MI: Baker Academic, 2003.

———. "Patristic Theology and the Ethos of the Orthodox Church." In *Aspects of Church History.* Vol. 4 in *The Collected Works of Georges Florovsky.* Edited by Richard Haugh. Vaduz, Liechtenstein: Büchervertriebsanstalt, 1987.

———. "Western Influences in Russian Theology." In *Aspects of Church History.* Vol. 4 in *The Collected Works of Georges Florovsky.* Edited by Richard Haugh. Vaduz, Liechtenstein: Büchervertriebsanstalt, 1987.

George, Timothy. "Delighted by Doctrine." *Christianity Today International: Christian History and Biography,* no. 91 (2006): 43–45.

Gibson, Lydialyle. "The Mirage of Knowledge." *Harvard Magazine,* March–April 2018, 32–35.

Guronian, Vigen. "The Secular Pilgrimage of Orthodoxy in America." In *Fundamentalism or Tradition: Christianity after Secularism.* Orthodox Christianity and Contemporary Thought. Edited by Aristotle Papanikolaou and George Demacopoulos. New York: Fordham University Press, 2020.

Hanson, R.P.C. *Tradition in the Early Church.* Library of History and Doctrine. Eugene, OR: Wipf and Stock, 1962.

Harakas, Stanley. *Health and Medicine in the Eastern Orthodox Tradition: Faith, Liturgy, and Wholeness.* New York: Crossroad Publishing, 1990.

———. "Tradition in Eastern Orthodox Thought." *Christian Scholar's Review* 22, no. 2 (December 1992): 144–165.

Harkianakis, Archbishop Stylianos. "The Theologian in Modern Society: Phronema and Behavior." *Voice of Orthodoxy* 19, no. 11 (November 1998): 121–124.

Hopko, Thomas. "Theological Education and Modernity." Academic paper presented at the Fifth International Consultation of Orthodox Theological Schools. Halki, Turkey, 1994, 1–9.

Human Rights Watch. *Denying Human Rights and Ethnic Identity: The Greeks of Turkey.* New York: Human Rights Watch, 1992.

Humphrey, Edith M. "Fundamentalism: Not Just a Cautionary Tale." *Fundamentalism or Tradition: Christianity after Secularism.* Orthodox Christianity and Contemporary Thought. Edited by Aristotle Papanikolaou and George Demacopoulos. New York: Fordham University Press, 2020.

———. *Scripture and Tradition: What the Bible Really Says.* Acadia Studies in Bible and Theology. Grand Rapids, MI: Baker Academic, 2013.

International Standard Bible Encyclopedia. 4 vols. Edited by Geoffrey Bromily. Grand Rapids, MI: William B. Eerdmans, 1979.

John Paul II. *Fides et Ratio: Encyclical of the Supreme Pontiff John Paul II to the Bishops of the Catholic Church on the Relationship Between Faith and Reason.* Publication 5-302, 79. Washington, DC: United States Catholic Conference, 1998.

Kaloghirou, John. "Sacred Tradition: Its Sources and Its Task in the Church." *Greek Orthodox Theological Review* 9, no. 1 (Summer 1965): 108–118.

Karavidopoulos, Ioannis. "The Interpretation of the New Testament in the Orthodox Church." *Jesus Christus ALS die Mitte der Schrift: Studien zur Hermeneutik des Evangeliums.* Berlin: Walter de Gruyter, 1997.

Kesich, Veselin. *The Gospel Image of Christ: The Church and Modern Criticism.* Crestwood, NY: St. Vladimir's Seminary Press, 1972.

Kishkovsky, Leonid. "Orthodoxy Today: Tradition or Traditionalism?" https://oca.org/holy-synod/statements/fr-kishkovsky/orthodoxy-today-tradition-or-traditionalism, 2005.

Kondothra, K. M. George. "Orthodox Theological Education: Some Historical Perspectives." Academic paper presented at the Fifth International Consultation of Orthodox Theological Schools, Halki, Turkey, 1994, 1–7.

Ladouceur, Paul. *Modern Orthodox Theology: Behold, I Make All Things New.* London: T & T Clark, 2019.

Lampe, G.W.H., ed. *A Patristic Greek Lexicon.* Oxford: Clarendon Press, 1991.

———. *The West from the Fathers to the Reformation.* Vol. 2 of *The Cambridge History of the Bible.* 3 vols. Cambridge: Cambridge University Press, 1969.

Lampert, Eugeny. "Theological Communication and the Certainties of Belief." In *The Orthodox Ethos.* Edited by A. J. Philippou. Oxford: Holywell Press, 1964.

Lewis, C. S. *A Mind Awake: An Anthology of C. S. Lewis.* Boston: Houghton Mifflin Harcourt, 2003.

Lossky, Vladimir. "Apophasis and Trinitarian Theology." *Eastern Orthodox Theology: A Contemporary Reader.* 2nd ed. Edited by Daniel Clendenin. Grand Rapids, MI: Baker Academic, 2003.

————. *In the Image and Likeness of God.* Edited by John Erickson and Thomas Bird. Crestwood, NY: St. Vladimir's Seminary Press, 1974.

————. *Orthodox Theology: An Introduction.* Crestwood, NY: St. Vladimir's Seminary Press, 1978.

————. "Tradition and Traditions." *Eastern Orthodox Theology: A Contemporary Reader.* 2nd ed. Edited by Daniel Clendenin. Grand Rapids, MI: Baker Academic, 2003.

Louth, Andrew. *Introducing Eastern Orthodox Theology.* Downer's Grove, IL: IVP Academic, 2013.

Mantzarides, Giorgios I. *Orthodox Spiritual Life.* Translated by Keith Schram. Brookline, MA: Holy Cross Orthodox Press, 1994.

Martinos, A., ed. *Thrēskeutikē kai Ethikē Egkyklopaideia.* 12 vols. Athens, 1962–68.

McBrien, Richard P. *Catholicism.* 2 vols. Minneapolis: Winston Press, 1980.

McGuckin, John Anthony. *The Orthodox Church: An Introduction to Its History, Doctrine, and Spiritual Culture.* Oxford: Blackwell Publishing, 2008.

————. "Orthodoxy and Culture." In *The Orthodox Christian World.* Routledge Worlds. Edited by Augustine Casiday. London: Routledge, 2012.

————. *St. Gregory of Nazianzus: An Intellectual Biography.* Crestwood, NY: St. Vladimir's Seminary Press, 2011.

McLees, Mother Nectaria. *Evlogeite! A Pilgrim's Guide to Greece.* Maysville, MO: St. Nicholas Press, 2002.

Meyendorff, John. "Doing Theology in an Eastern Orthodox Perspective." In *Eastern Orthodox Theology: A Contemporary Reader.* 2nd ed. Edited by Daniel Clendenin. Grand Rapids, MI: Baker Academic, 2003.

————. "Historical Relativism and Authority in Christian Dogma." In *The New Man: An Orthodox and Reformed Dialogue.* Edited by John Meyendorff and Joseph McLelland. New Brunswick, NJ: Agora Books, 1973.

Moore, Lazarus. *Sacred Tradition in the Orthodox Church.* Know Your Faith. Minneapolis, MN: Light & Life, 1984.

Newman, John Henry Cardinal. *An Essay on Development of Christian Doctrine.* Reprint. Westminster, MD: Christian Classics, 1968.

Nichols, Tom. *Death of Expertise: The Campaign against Established Knowledge and Why It Matters.* Oxford: Oxford University Press, 2017.

Nicozisin, George. *The Road to Orthodox Phronema.* Brookline, MA: Holy Cross Orthodox Press, 1977.

Nissiotis, Nikos. "The Importance of the Doctrine of the Trinity for Church Life and Theology." In *The Orthodox Ethos.* Edited by A. J. Philippou. Oxford: Holywell Press, 1964.

————. "Orthodox Theological Education: Reality and Perspectives." Academic paper presented at the Syndesmos Consultation on Orthodox Theological Education. Geneva: Orthodox Center of the Ecumenical Patriarchate, 1977, 1–18.

Oeldemann, Johannes. "Living Interpreters of the Treasure of Tradition." Fruits and Challenges of Theological and Spiritual Encounter Between Orthodox and Catholics in the Second Half of the 20th Century. *Conmmunio Viatorum* 57, no. 2 (2015): 144–155.

Papadopoulos, Gerasimos. "The Revelatory Character of the New Testament and Holy Tradition in the Orthodox Church." *Greek Orthodox Theological Review* 2, no. 1 (1956): 41–55.

Papanikolaou, Aristotle, and George Demacopoulos, eds. *Fundamentalism or Tradition: Christianity after Secularism.* New York: Fordham University Press, 2020.

Patsavos, Lewis. "The Methodology of Theology." Academic paper presented at the Second Consultation of Orthodox Theological Schools, New York, 1982, 1–4.

———. "Salvation and the Free Life of the Spirit in the Orthodox Canonical Tradition." *Road to Emmaus* 14, no. 4 (2013): 3–35.

———. *Spiritual Dimensions of the Holy Canons.* Brookline, MA: Holy Cross Greek Orthodox Press, 2003.

Pelikan, Jaroslav. *Credo.* New Haven: Yale University Press, 2003.

———. *The Emergence of the Catholic Tradition* and *The Spirit of Eastern Christendom.* Vols. 1 and 2 of *The Christian Tradition: A History of the Development of Doctrine.* 5 vols. Chicago: University of Chicago Press, 1971, 1974.

———. *The Melody of Theology: A Philosophical Dictionary.* Eugene, OR: Wipf and Stock, 1988.

———. *The Vindication of Tradition.* New Haven: Yale University Press, 1984.

Philippou, A. J., ed. *The Orthodox Ethos.* Oxford: Holywell Press, 1964.

———. *Orthodoxy: Life and Freedom.* Oxford: Studion Publications, 1973.

Plested, Marcus. "Tradition and Traditionalism." Academic paper presented at the Syndesmos Festival, Saint-Maurin, France, 2001.

Quasten, Johannes. *Patrology.* 4 vols. Westminster, MD: Christian Classics, 1986.

Rauch, Thomas. *Reconciling Faith and Reason: Apologists, Evangelists, and Theologians in a Divided Church.* Collegeville, MN: Liturgical Press, 2000.

Rodopoulos, Panteleimon. *An Overview of Orthodox Canon Law.* Rollinsford, NH: Orthodox Research Institute, 2007.

Romanides, John. *The Ancestral Sin.* Translated by George S. Gabriel. Ridgewood, NJ: Zephyr Publishing, 1998.

———. *Dogmatikē kai Symbolikē Theologia tēs Orthodoxēs Katholikēs Ekklēsias.* Vol. 1. Thessaloniki: Pournaras Press, 1973.

———. *Franks, Romans, Feudalism, and Doctrine: An Interplay between Theology and Society.* Patriarch Athenagoras Memorial Lectures. Brookline, MA: Holy Cross Orthodox Press, 1982.

Schmemann, Alexander. "Moment of Truth for Orthodoxy." *Eastern Orthodox Theology: A Contemporary Reader.* 2nd ed. Edited by Daniel Clendenin. Grand Rapids, MI: Baker Academic, 2003.

Schneider, Christoph, ed. *Theology and Philosophy in Eastern Orthodoxy: Essays on Orthodox Christianity and Contemporary Thought.* Eugene, OR: Pickwick Publications, 2019.

Siecienski, A. Edward. *The Filioque: History of a Doctrinal Controversy.* Oxford Studies in Historical Theology. Oxford: Oxford University Press, 2010.

Smalley, Beryl. *The Study of the Bible in the Middle Ages.* Notre Dame, IN: University of Notre Dame Press, 1989.

Stylianopoulos, Theodore. "Scripture and Tradition in the Church." In *The Cambridge Companion to Orthodox Christian Theology.* Edited by Mary B. Cunningham and Elizabeth Theokritoff. Cambridge: Cambridge University Press, 2008.

———. *Scripture, Tradition, Hermeneutics.* Vol. 1 of *The New Testament: An Orthodox Perspective.* Brookline, MA: Holy Cross Orthodox Press, 1997.

The Theological Dictionary of the New Testament. 10 vols. Edited by Gerhard Kittel, Gerhard Friedrich, and Geoffrey W. Bromiley. Grand Rapids, MI: William B. Eerdmans, 1988. First published in 1971.

Tsirpanlis, Constantine. *Introduction to Eastern Patristic Thought and Orthodox Theology.* Theology and Life, vol. 30. Collegeville, MN: Liturgical Press, 1991.

Vasileios, Archimandrite. *What Is Unique about Orthodox Culture?* Translated by Elizabeth Theokritoff. Montreal: Alexander Press, 2001.

Vatican Council II: The Conciliar and Postconciliar Documents. Translated by Austin Flannery. Collegeville, MN: Liturgical Press, 1975.

Veniamin, Christopher. *The Orthodox Understanding of Salvation.* Dalton, PA: Mount Thabor Publishing, 2013.

Vlachos, Met. Hierotheos. *The Mind of the Orthodox Church (Ekklēsia kai Ekklēsiastiko Phronēma).* Translated by Esther Williams. 2nd revised translated ed., 3rd ed. of the 1998 Greek original. Levadia, Greece: Birth of the Theotokos Monastery, 2017.

———. *The Person in Orthodox Tradition.* Translated by Effie Mavromichali. Levadia, Greece: Monastery of the Birth of the Theotokos, 1994.

Ware, Bishop Kallistos. "Theological Education in Scripture and the Fathers." Academic paper presented at the Fifth International Consultation of Orthodox Theological Schools, Halki School of Theology, Turkey, 1994.

Whiteford, John. *The Orthodox Mind.* Academic paper presented at the Southwest Missions Conference, Dallas, July 1995.

Yannaras, Christos. "Orthodoxy and the West." In *Orthodoxy: Life and Freedom.* Edited by A. J. Philippou. Oxford: Studion Publications, 1973.

Young, Alexey. "Obedience and the Layman." In *Obedience.* Brookline, MA: Holy Cross Orthodox Press, 1984.

Zalalas, Constantine, et. al. *The Church Fathers on Love in Truth.* Translated by Constantine Zalalas. Thessaloniki: Orthodoxos Kypseli, 2000.

Index

D R. EUGENIA CONSTANTINOU HOSTS THE popular podcast *Search the Scriptures Live!* on Ancient Faith Radio. She has been a professor and visiting lecturer on the Bible, patristic interpretation of Scripture, and early Christianity at Orthodox and non-Orthodox universities and schools of theology. She holds master's degrees in theology from the University of San Diego, Holy Cross Greek Orthodox School of Theology, and Harvard Divinity School; a juris doctorate from Pepperdine University School of Law; and a Ph.D. from Université Laval in Quebec City in the history of biblical interpretation. Dr. Jeannie is also the author of *The Crucifixion of the King of Glory: The Amazing History and Sublime Mystery of the Passion* (Ancient Faith Publishing, 2022). She is married to Fr. Costas, a Greek Orthodox priest.

Other Books of Interest

The Religion of the Apostles: Orthodox Christianity in the First Century
by Stephen De Young

Father Dr. Stephen De Young traces the lineage of Orthodox Christianity back to the faith and witness of the apostles, which was rooted in a first-century Jewish worldview. *The Religion of the Apostles* presents the Orthodox Christian Church of today as a continuation of the religious life of the apostles, which in turn was a continuation of the life of the people of God since the beginning of creation.

- Paperback, 320 pages, ISBN: 978-1-944967-55-0

Everywhere Present: Christianity in a One-Storey Universe
by Stephen Freeman

Have you ever referred to God as "the Man upstairs"? Most Christians living in a secular society have unwittingly relegated God and all things spiritual to the "second storey" of the universe: a realm we cannot reach except through death. The effect of this is to banish God, along with the saints and angels, from our everyday lives. *In Everywhere Present*, popular blogger and podcaster Fr. Stephen Freeman makes a compelling case for becoming aware of God's living and active presence in every moment of our lives here and now. Learning to practice your Christian faith in a one-storey universe will change your life—and make possible the living, intimate relationship with God you've always dreamed of.

- Paperback, 110 pages, ISBN: 978-1-936270-10-1

Orthodoxy & Heterodoxy:
Finding the Way to Christ in a Complicated Religious Landscape
by Andrew Stephen Damick

Are you an Orthodox Christian who wonders how to explain to your Baptist grandmother, your Buddhist neighbor, or the Jehovah's Witness at your door how your faith differs from theirs? Or are you a member of another faith who is curious what Orthodoxy is all about? Look no further. In *Orthodoxy &*

Heterodoxy, Fr. Andrew Stephen Damick covers the gamut of ancient heresies, modern Christian denominations, fringe groups, and major world religions, highlighting the main points of each faith. This book is an invaluable reference for anyone who wants to understand the faiths of those they come in contact with—as well as their own.

• Paperback, 416 pages, ISBN: 978-1-944967-17-8

The *Paradise & Utopia* series
by John Strickland
Volume 1—*The Age of Paradise:*
Christendom from Pentecost to the First Millennium
The Age of Paradise is the first of a projected four-volume history of Christendom, a civilization with a supporting culture that gave rise to what we now call the West. At a time of renewed interest in the future of Western culture, author John Strickland—an Orthodox scholar, professor, and priest—offers a vision rooted in the deep past of the first millennium. At the heart of his story is the early Church's "culture of paradise," an experience of the world in which the kingdom of heaven was tangible and familiar. Drawing not only on worship and theology but statecraft and the arts, the author reveals the remarkably affirmative character Western culture once had under the influence of Christianity—in particular, of Eastern Christendom, which served the West not only as a cradle but as a tutor and guardian as well.

• Paperback, 304 pages, ISBN: 978-1-944967-56-7

Volume 2—*The Age of Division:*
Christendom from the Great Schism to the Protestant Reformation
If you have ever wondered exactly how we got from the Christian society of the early centuries, united in its faithfulness to apostolic tradition, to the fragmented and secular state of the West today, *The Age of Division* will answer all your questions and more. In this second of a four-volume cultural history of Christendom, author John Strickland applies insights from the Orthodox Church to trace the decline and disintegration of both East and West after the momentous but often neglected Great Schism. For five centuries, a divided Christendom was led further and further from the culture of paradise that

defined its first millennium, resulting in the Protestant Reformation and the secularization that defines our society today.

- Paperback, 360 pages, ISBN: 978-1-944967-86-4

Volume 3—*The Age of Utopia:*
Christendom from the Renaissance to the Russian Revolution

Continuing the epic of Christendom told in earlier volumes, *The Age of Paradise* and *The Age of Division*, the author explains how, between the Italian Renaissance of the fourteenth century and the Russian Revolution of the twentieth, secular humanism displaced Christianity to become the source of modern culture. The result was some of the most illustrious music, science, philosophy, and literature ever produced. But the cultural reorientation from paradise to utopia—from an experience of the kingdom of heaven to one bound exclusively by this world—all but eradicated the traditional culture of the West, leaving it at the beginning of the twentieth century without roots in anything transcendent.

- Paperback, 416 pages, ISBN: 978-1-955890-05-2

For further information about these and other books, please visit our website: store.ancientfaith.com

We hope you have enjoyed and benefited from this book. Your financial support makes it possible to continue our nonprofit ministry both in print and online. Because the proceeds from our book sales only partially cover the costs of operating **Ancient Faith Publishing** and **Ancient Faith Radio**, we greatly appreciate the generosity of our readers and listeners. Donations are tax deductible and can be made at **www.ancientfaith.com.**

To view our other publications, please visit our website:
store.ancientfaith.com

ANCIENT FAITH RADIO

Bringing you Orthodox Christian music, readings, prayers, teaching, and podcasts 24 hours a day since 2004 at
www.ancientfaith.com